Joan of Kent

First Princess of Wales

PENNY LAWNE

AMBERLEY

For Pete, David and Richard

First published 2015

Amberley Publishing
The Hill, Stroud
Gloucestershire, GL5 4EP

www.amberley-books.com

British Library Cataloguing in Publication Data.
A catalogue record for this book is available from the British Library.

ISBN 978 1 4456 4465 3 (hardback)
ISBN 978 1 4456 4471 4 (ebook)

Typesetting and Origination by Amberley Publishing.
Printed in the UK.

Contents

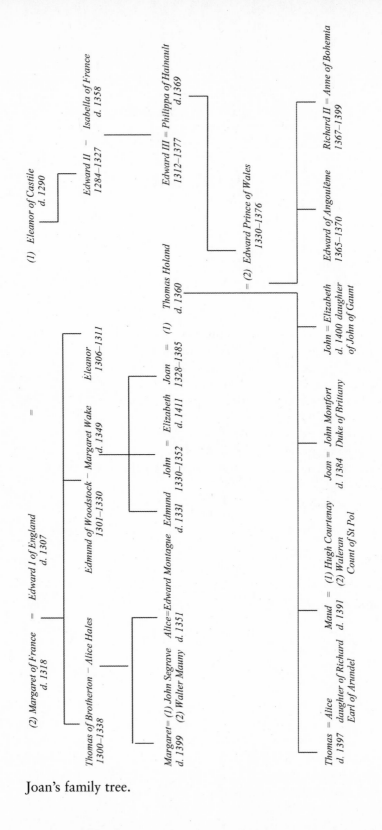

Joan's family tree.

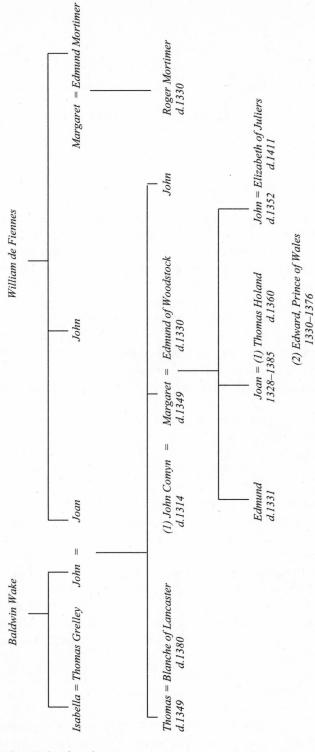

The Wake family tree.

Introduction

Jean Froissart, probably the most famous of the fourteenth-century chroniclers, described Joan as 'in her time the most beautiful woman in all the realm of England and the most loved' ('en son temps la plus belle dame de tout le roiaulme d'Engleterre et la plus amoureuse').[1] His description has proved remarkably enduring, and it is by her posthumously bestowed sobriquet of 'Fair Maid of Kent' that Joan is best known.[2] Successive chroniclers in the fifteenth and sixteenth centuries were fascinated by the legend of her beauty and desirability, and by the seventeenth century Joan had been identified as the blushing beauty rescued from embarrassment at the ball by Edward III in Vergil's account of the founding of the Order of the Garter.[3] Although historians have rejected the Garter story, it is the view of Joan that generally remains. Yet this description is misleading, and belies the significance of Joan's life. Joan was Princess of Wales for twenty-four years, and one of the most important and influential women of her age. A granddaughter of Edward I, in 1361 she married Edward III's eldest son, Prince Edward (after his death better known as the Black Prince), and became Princess of Wales, the first member of the English royal family to have that title.[4] Until the prince's death in 1376, Joan was expected to succeed her mother-in-law, Queen Philippa, as the next queen. For seven years she helped Prince Edward preside over the principality of Aquitaine, and bore him two sons. When Edward III died, a year after the prince's death, Joan's son Richard became king at the age of ten. As Richard's mother, Joan was in a position of considerable power and authority up to her death in 1385. Despite her distinction, there has been no full-length biography of her life, and her story remains largely untold. This book is an attempt to tell her story and examine the real woman behind the legend.

There are obvious difficulties in looking at Joan's life. There is no surviving collection of private correspondence by or to Joan, and there are no family or personal papers. None of the records kept for her, such as household accounts, administrative records, wardrobe accounts, livery rolls and estate accounts, have survived. Without such accounts, much that could be known about Joan is lost. The dearth of archive material relating to Joan is a serious handicap for a biographer, and partly explains why historical writing on her is lamentably limited. In addition, histories of the fourteenth century have traditionally been male dominated. The contemporary chroniclers and later historians concentrated their attention on war, politics and government, all areas from which women were largely excluded as they could not hold office, or go to war, and although they were allowed to own land they had no independent legal standing unless widowed. The law, reinforced by the Church's attitude, stressed the subordination of women. Inevitably the official records contain far more about the men in Joan's life (in particular the prince and Richard II) than they do about her, despite her rank and status. A biographer therefore also has to draw on the lives of those closest to Joan to help provide some of the missing details of her life.

Edward III's claim to the French throne initiated the start of the Hundred Years War, and the conduct of the war, the deliberate fostering of the chivalric culture by the king and the resulting upheavals in domestic politics, with the escalating tensions that culminated in the Peasants' Revolt in 1381, have fascinated writers for centuries. The fourteenth century is rich in tales of chivalry, expounded by contemporary writers such as Froissart and Jean le Bel. Men carry out brave deeds in accordance with a knightly code of conduct, often with the aim of winning the hearts of their fair ladies, as in Froissart's tale of the English knights at Valenciennes who vowed to wear eyepatches on one eye until they had performed feats worthy of their lady.[5] Edward III consciously promoted the chivalric ethos of his court, with his creation of the Order of the Garter as its most visible symbol, to foster unity among his nobility and to ensure support for his war with France.[6] His eldest son, Prince Edward, was considered by his contemporaries to be the exemplar of chivalric knighthood.[7] The Church assisted in the glamorisation of war, calling knights to the aid of fellow Christians on crusade. Tales of knight errantry and worthy deeds of arms were encouraged. Romantic literature with the tales of heroes like Arthur, Charlemagne, Roland and Oliver were popular reading among the aristocracy. Chivalry was an elitist culture, restricted to the nobility, in which women were portrayed as supportive adornments, and the dividing line between reality and fairy tale sometimes deliberately blurred, as in the depiction of Joan as one of the objects of gallantry at Valenciennes, and her representation by Chandos Herald as the perfect knight's lady.[8]

Much that is known about Joan derives from the accounts of the contemporary chroniclers, who present her as a popular figure in her lifetime. Although there are no contemporary portraits, her beauty was undoubtedly a real attribute, firmly established by Froissart, and her depiction by the prince's panegyrist, Chandos Herald, as beautiful, pleasant and wise ('que bele fu plesant et sage').[9] The *Chronique des quatre premiers Valois* described her as 'une des belle dames du monde et moult noble'.[10] Froissart and Chandos Herald had first-hand knowledge;

Froissart was a member of Queen Philippa's household at the time of
Joan's marriage to the prince and stayed at their home at Berkhamsted
after the marriage, and he was later a guest in their house in Aquitaine
when Joan gave birth to Richard in 1367, while Chandos Herald served
Sir John Chandos, one of the closest of Prince Edward's friends and
knights.[11] The prince's marriage is recorded by most of the chroniclers,
and these recite Joan's royal lineage and her marital history.[12] Joan's
desirability is evident from her colourful marital history; she was Thomas
Holand's widow when she married the prince, but was known to have
gone through a form of marriage with William Montague which had
been set aside. The births of her two sons by the prince are recorded,
and during Richard's reign there are more frequent references to Joan,
particularly of her intercessions on behalf of John of Gaunt during the
Peasants' Revolt, and her death in 1385 is attributed to her distress at her
failure to reconcile Richard with his half-brother John Holand.[13]

For historians, Joan's significance has traditionally attached to her role
as the prince's wife and Richard II's mother. In this spirit she was included
by the antiquarian Peck in his *Annals of Stamford* (Lincolnshire),
published in 1727, and two brief biographical sketches of her appeared
in articles in 1877 by Frederick Chambers, and in 1894 by Colonel
Babinet.[14] By the early twentieth century the definitive biographical
details of her life were contained in G. E. Cokayne's *Peerage* and the
Dictionary of National Biography, recently updated by Richard Barber
in the *Oxford Dictionary of National Biography*.[15] Despite the now
accepted importance of the role of women in medieval society, there has
been no more detailed study of her life. Indeed, while there have been
many individual studies on Edward III, the prince, John of Gaunt and
Richard II, apart from biographies of Katherine Swynford, there are no
major studies on their spouses: Queen Philippa; John of Gaunt's first
two wives, Blanche of Lancaster and Constance of Castile; and Richard
II's two queens, Anne of Bohemia and Isabella of France.[16] Instead, a
handful of articles have been written on Joan, each presenting a different
view of her. The best known is the 1948 article by Margaret Galway, a
Chaucerian scholar. Galway accepted Vergil's account of the founding
of the Order of the Garter, with Joan as its inspiration, and argued that
Joan was also the inspiration for Chaucer's Criseyde and Queen Alceste,
and his patroness for *The Legend of Good Women*.[17] Associating Joan
with various different imaginary and fanciful persona (the heroine in
the poem *The Vows of the Heron*; the Queen of England described by
Froissart defending England against the Scots in 1346 while the king was
in France; and the object of Edward III's passion in the stories of Froissart
and Jean le Bel), Galway presented Joan vividly as a beautiful woman
'more sinned against than sinning' who befriended the unfortunate,
relieved the poor, sheltered the unpopular and was tormented by anxiety
for those she loved, with a terror of insecurity enhancing rather than

diminishing her romantic credentials.[18] This interpretation was challenged in 1999 by Carolyn Collette, another Chaucerian scholar, who used Joan to contextualise Chaucer's depictions of noblewomen and in doing so presented a different Joan, noting that she was perceived as a woman of power and presence in her society, and considered Joan's life one of action, intervention and mediation, exemplifying the ideal noblewoman.[19] Collette's view in turn contrasts with Mark Ormrod's less favourable view of Joan when using her dramatic confrontation with the rebels in the Peasants' Revolt to discuss the possible interpretations of the chroniclers' contrasting reports.[20]

Joan's matrimonial history has also been used by scholars examining fourteenth-century attitudes towards marriage. The chivalric culture of Edward III's court, with its emphasis on the dominance of men and the subordinate position of their women, is recognised as a carefully constructed façade, but it was an important social framework expressing assumptions that set a premium on the knightly values and behaviour which bound the nobility together in loyalty to their king, subsuming their own ambitions.[21] Although it was a secular code, it was based on deeply Christian religious feelings. The attempt to blend the ideals of chivalry with the real world inevitably led to apparent contradictions and pragmatic compromises. This was particularly noticeable in the attitude towards marriage, where unorthodox relationships were not unknown among the higher nobility. Karl Wentersdorf examined this, using Joan's secret marriage to Thomas Holand, the later Montague match and the subsequent papal proceedings between Holand and Montague.[22] In 1996 Joanna Chamberlayne considered the values of chivalric society towards marriage, using Joan as an example, and rejected Galway's idealistic portrayal, arguing that Joan had manipulated the contemporary lack of respect for marriage to ensure her own choice of husband.[23]

Valuable though such articles are, each looks only at a particular aspect of her life to discuss an issue, and none focus on Joan herself. A study of Joan's life reveals much that is intriguing and fascinating and it is full of contradictions. Her close relationship to the king through her father was a significant feature of her life, resulting in her being brought up within the royal household and becoming an heiress of considerable wealth. Yet her marital history is particularly unusual for a girl of her birth. When she was barely more than a child she defied convention, her family and her royal guardian by secretly marrying a man of her choice, a humble household knight named Sir Thomas Holand. She was forced into a bigamous marriage with the Earl of Salisbury's son, William Montague, by her family, but withstood years of bullying and pressure to remain faithful to her chosen spouse. It took eight years and a decision of the Pope to restore Joan to Thomas Holand. As Thomas Holand's wife, Joan was almost the only noblewoman of her generation to accompany her husband as he fulfilled his military duties in France. When he died she put aside her grief and made a spectacular match in marrying the prince, and in doing so secured the future of her four Holand children. All of this suggests a woman of considerable independence, intelligence and courage. Yet, after Joan became Princess of Wales and the most powerful and influential woman at court after the queen, her influence is hard to discern. As the prince's wife, and Princess of Aquitaine, she jointly presided over their court, but the contemporary accounts detail the prince's actions and barely mention his wife. After the prince's death, Joan had charge of their son Richard and remained closely at his side after his accession to the throne up to her death. Unlike Edward III's mother, Queen Isabella, and Henry VII's mother, Lady Margaret Beaufort, Joan is not credited with exercising political influence during her son's reign. Nor is Joan renowned as a cultural or religious patron, like Edward IV's mother, Cecily Neville, Duchess of York, and Lady Margaret Beaufort. Yet she was not afraid to support John of Gaunt when he was at his most unpopular and fleeing for his life, and she showed that she was a natural conciliator and peacemaker, which makes her reticence curious. Did she deliberately refrain from exercising her influence? Although her posthumous sobriquet, the 'Fair Maid of Kent', suggests beauty and docility (or, perhaps, a more sensual and nuanced reputation due to her marital history), this is belied by the considerable independence she showed in her early life.[24] Was she a woman of modesty and intelligence who understood what was expected of her, and played her role admirably? Examining Joan's life and career reveals a more complex and interesting woman than a simple 'Fair Maid of Kent'.

1

A Royal Inheritance
1301–1330

Put not your trust in princes, nor in the son of man, in whom there is
no help.

Psalms, 146:3

Joan never knew her father, as he died when she was less than two
years of age. In early March 1330, Edmund, Earl of Kent, set off from
the family home at Arundel Castle to attend Parliament in Winchester,
leaving his pregnant young wife Margaret with their two infant children,
Edmund and Joan.[1] They never saw him again. On Wednesday 14 March,
shortly after his arrival in Winchester, Edmund was arrested by the king's
officers and charged with treason. Two days later his confession was read
out to the assembled Parliament. In the early morning of Monday 19
March he was escorted outside Winchester Castle to be executed, where
he was forced to wait until an executioner was found from among the
king's marshalsea, and then, later in the day, he was beheaded.[2] It was a
swift and brutal end. Edmund was twenty-nine years old.

Waiting at Arundel, Joan's mother Margaret may have been unaware
of her husband's fate until the arrival of two of the king's yeomen,
Nicholas Langford and John Payn, who had orders to escort her from
Arundel and transfer her into the custody of the sheriff of Wiltshire.[3]
Margaret's shock and distress can be imagined. As Langford and Payn's
orders were dated the day of Edmund's arrest, 14 March, they may have
arrived before his execution, but the news would have swiftly followed.
Margaret was told that only two of her female servants could accompany
her and her children; however, as she was so near to term, it was decided
that she would not be moved until after her delivery. In the meantime
she was kept confined in Arundel Castle, while most of her servants were
dismissed, and her jewellery and other goods were taken away.

Arundel, Joan's first home, and for a short time also her prison, was
a formidable castle, built originally by one of William the Conqueror's
henchmen, Roger de Montgomery, near the mouth of the River Arun,

and it dominated the surrounding Sussex countryside. Edmund had acquired it just three years before, in February 1327.[4] The castle had previously been the principal seat of Edmund Fitzalan, Earl of Arundel, and had been forfeited to the Crown with the remainder of Fitzalan's estates when he was executed in 1326 for supporting Edward II. As the largest and grandest of the properties acquired by Edmund in 1327 it would have been his principal seat, and it is possible that Joan was born there. Today, little of the original castle survives, other than the Norman motte, gatehouse, keep and curtain wall, as it was largely destroyed by Parliamentarian forces during the English Civil War and remained in ruins until the eighteenth century, when reconstruction of the castle started. In the late nineteenth century the main structure was almost completely rebuilt in the Gothic style. The present castle gives some indication of its fourteenth-century magnificence, as it is hugely imposing, with tall, grey stone buttresses and walls, and continues to dominate the town.

Joan's younger brother, John, was born at Arundel two and a half weeks after his father's execution, on 7 April 1330. John's birth, and baptism on the same day, was confirmed and noted in the records twenty-one years later when testimony was taken to prove his coming of age and his entitlement to his inheritance. With no central records of births or deaths it was customary to take evidence from witnesses who could attest to a person's birth and so prove their age. At Steyning in Sussex on 9 April 1351 a local Sussex resident, James Byne, affirmed that John had been born at Arundel and baptised the same day on Tuesday 7 April 1330 in the church of St Bartholomew in the priory adjoining the castle, and that Edmund, Joan and the prior, John de Grenstede, had lifted John from the sacred font, as his godparents.[5] Seven further witnesses confirmed the date. As Margaret and Edmund had married in the autumn of 1325 Joan and Edmund were very young children and can have been no older than eighteen months and three and a half years old. The poignant detail of Joan and Edmund's role in their brother's baptism is eloquent testimony of the family's dire fortunes in the weeks after their father's execution. Baptism was an important and indispensable rite of passage to bring children into the church, usually taking place within days of the birth, and it had become customary from the twelfth century for each child to have sponsors, or godparents, whose role included taking an interest in the child's future welfare.[6] By the fourteenth century noble families took great care to select suitably prestigious relatives or friends to act as godparents in anticipation that they would use their influence to help further their godchild's career later in life. Siblings would not normally be considered, and it was very rare to appoint small children. But Joan's mother had limited options. As a traitor, Edmund's title, lands and possessions were forfeit. Margaret was isolated and alone, under close guard, and had no family or friends with her at Arundel to console her. In her haste and anxiety to arrange John's baptism, Margaret had no choice but to appoint the only person of standing near to her, Prior John, and John's siblings, despite their youth. The baptism must have been a hurried and awkward affair, conducted by the prior with some trepidation and possibly reluctance in view of his patron's disgrace, while Joan and Edmund, who could have played little active part in the christening service, were probably bewildered and possibly frightened.

Edmund's arrest and execution was not just devastating for his family; it shocked and appalled his contemporaries, as it was intended to. Just four years before, in September 1326, Queen Isabella had swept her husband, Edward II, from power in a bloodless invasion, bringing to an end five years of tyrannical rule by the king and his favourites, the Despensers. In the January parliament of 1327 it was publicly announced that the captive Edward II had agreed to abdicate in favour of his fourteen-year-old son and heir, Prince Edward. The majority of the nobility were solidly behind the queen, and hoped the king's deposition would herald an era of political stability. At first the liberality of the new regime towards their supporters had contrasted favourably with the miserly and vindictive behaviour of Edward II and the Despensers. A council was set up to rule on behalf of the young Edward III which included his father's two half-brothers, Thomas Brotherton, Earl of Norfolk, and Joan's father, Edmund, Earl of Kent. However, it quickly became apparent that the council had little real authority, and that power remained with the queen, and her lover, Roger Mortimer, and it was not long before the nobility realised they had replaced Edward II with a different form of tyrant in Roger Mortimer. Retaining firm control, the queen and her lover issued orders in the king's name, ensuring that neither Edward III nor his council were able to act freely. By 1328 Mortimer, newly created Earl of March, was king in all but name. Inevitably, Isabella and Mortimer's exercise of power became resented, and their increasingly aggressive and acquisitive behaviour, reminiscent of the worst excesses of the Despenser rule, successively alienated most of the nobility, while Edward III's dislike of Mortimer grew and he chafed at his lack of independence. By the autumn of 1328 opposition had united under the most powerful of the earls, Henry of Lancaster, the king's second cousin. But when Lancaster's forces gathered outside London in December 1328, it was Mortimer who took the initiative and launched an attack in the king's name, and his quick thinking and decisive action induced Lancaster and his followers to withdraw. However, the encounter was not conclusive, as the opposition remained intact and entrenched in resistance, and throughout 1329 there was an uneasy peace. Isabella and Mortimer knew they could not hope to rely on securing their position through her son for much longer. Their agenda in calling the Winchester parliament in March 1330 was to reinforce their hold on power by giving the gathering of lords, prelates and knights a demonstration of the extent of their authority. They planned to do this by targeting someone with rank and status, close to the throne, but who lacked support among the nobility and who could be safely attacked with little fear of reprisal. Lancaster was too strong to openly challenge. They found a perfect victim instead in Joan's father.

Joan's Father, Edmund, Earl of Kent

Edmund, Earl of Kent, was the youngest son of Edward I and his second wife, Margaret of France.[7] Edward I was sixty-two when his youngest son was born, and at the height of his powers. A powerful and authoritative ruler, Edward I was regarded with awe and respect by both his subjects and his enemies, and he remained vigorous and forceful despite his advancing years. Having enjoyed a long and happy marriage with Eleanor of Castile, their contentment together reflected by their numerous progeny (they had at least fourteen children, although only five survived to adulthood), nine years after Eleanor's death Edward put aside his grief and entered into a second marriage with Margaret of France in 1299 as part of a diplomatic rapprochement to foster better relations with France.[8] Despite the difference in their ages (Margaret was seventeen when she married Edward I, over forty years younger than her husband), their marriage was also reputedly a happy one, and soon blessed in 1300 with the birth of a son, Thomas, born at Brotherton in Yorkshire as Margaret journeyed north to join her indefatigable husband as he engaged in yet another campaign against his unruly Scottish neighbours. Within a year Margaret bore him a second son, this time in the more comfortable surroundings of the royal palace at Woodstock, and the king named his youngest son Edmund, a family name shared by the king's brother, Edmund of Lancaster, who had died in 1296, and his cousin Edmund, Earl of Cornwall, who had also just died. Five years later, Margaret gave birth to a girl, Eleanor, their last child.

With only one surviving son by Eleanor, Edward of Carnarvon, it is probable that Edward I welcomed the birth of his two younger sons, Thomas and Edmund. Although Thomas was born while Margaret was travelling to meet Edward, no expense was spared, with his cradle provided with fine Lincoln scarlet, dark-blue cloth, sheets of Rheims linen and fur coverlets and decorated with heraldic arms.[9] Born in a secure and comfortable palace, Edmund would have been cosseted and spoiled. Delighted with his youngest son's arrival, Edward I rewarded the messenger John Prade handsomely for bringing news of Edmund's birth.[10] Although little is known of the young princes' childhood years, it can be assumed that they were well cared for and enjoyed the normal accoutrements of noble childhood; they did, for example, have a toy drum which was so well used it needed repair, and an iron bird cage given to them by their mother.[11] The boys were kept together, and when their sister was born in 1306 she joined their nursery, the royal siblings all within the same household.[12] Their shared childhood forged a bond between Thomas and Edmund which they retained in adulthood. However, they had very different personalities. Edmund appears to have been easy-going and peaceable, a likeable young man but lacking in the leadership and drive which characterised his father, whereas Thomas was an altogether more difficult man, prone to outbursts of temper. Contemporary chroniclers present a generally favourable impression of Edmund, with Jean le Bel describing him as a man who was most honourable and courteous ('qui estoit moult proeudomme et debonnaire'), and Jean Froissart as 'wise, affable and much beloved', whereas Thomas had a 'wild and disagreeable temper'.[13] There are no portraits or descriptions of them physically. Their mother, Margaret, was described in complimentary terms in her youth; her brother Philip, who became King of France, was known as Philip the Fair for his handsomeness, and chroniclers considered their cousin Isabella, Philip's daughter, with her long, blond hair, to be lovely.[14]

Edward I died in July 1307 when Thomas was seven years old and Edmund a year younger. Given the king's advanced age at their birth it was hardly surprising that the princes lost their father while they were so young. Initially his loss would have made little difference to their lives, and their education would have continued as before under the supervision of their mother. The now dowager Queen Margaret was no longer required to preside over the court and therefore probably spent more time with her children as a widow than she would otherwise have done. Sadly, their sister Eleanor did not long survive her father, but despite this tragedy, and the loss of their father, there is no reason to suppose that Edmund and Thomas had anything other than a happy childhood. It was customary for the royal nursery to remain reasonably static, while the court in contrast travelled from place to place following the king, and it is therefore unlikely that the children spent much time with their much older half-siblings, Edward of Carnarvon and his sisters. There is no evidence that Edward II took an active part in his brothers' upbringing, and he probably saw them infrequently, but he was likely to have been fond of them as he had a good relationship with his stepmother, and may have had some sympathy for them as he too had experienced the loss of a parent at an early age (his mother, Queen Eleanor, had died when he was six). They quickly acquired a sister-in-law when Edward II married Isabella of France in January 1308. The new queen was their twelve-year-old cousin, daughter of their mother's brother, Philip IV of France. The princes attended their brother's coronation at Westminster Abbey in February 1308.[15]

Edmund's relationship with his older half-brother, and his involvement in his affairs, would dominate his career. It is likely that, young as they were, the princes quickly became aware that their brother was having a difficult time. Edward I's legacy to his heir of the campaigns in Wales and Scotland, resulting in more or less empty coffers, with the ongoing requirement for vigilance and possible military enforcement, together with the uneasy peace with France, would have challenged a more able and politically astute man than Edward II. As it was, Edward II managed to exacerbate his own problems and create an immediate crisis at the very beginning of his reign by antagonising the majority of the nobility over his friendship with Piers Gaveston and in ennobling and enriching him within a month of the old king's death. Gaveston was the son of a French baron and had entered royal service, being placed in the then Prince Edward's household as a squire. The two young men had quickly developed a very close friendship, the nature of which has been much debated by historians but was probably fraternal rather than homosexual. Edward II's coronation, which should have been a splendid and festive occasion, was marred by the barons' anger at the prominence given to Gaveston during the ceremony, and by Gaveston's behaviour at the banquet afterwards.[16] It is notable that the author of the *Vita Edwardi Secundi* interpreted Gaveston's elevation to the earldom of Cornwall in 1307 as a direct insult to Thomas and Edmund.[17] They were far too young to feel personally aggrieved, but the chronicler's observation was acute. Edward II's action was to be symptomatic of his attitude towards providing for his younger brothers, creating a problem he never satisfactorily addressed.

As royal princes Thomas and Edmund could reasonably expect to become, as adults, among the most powerful and influential at the king's court, but this could not be sustained on birth alone. Traditionally princes were given an earldom (the highest noble rank) which brought with it attendant lands and income to support their status. However, earldoms were scarce, with limited opportunities for obtaining one through death and forfeiture. The option of creating new titles was impractical without ensuring the availability of estates which could be attached. The business of ensuring adequate financial provision for royal siblings had vexed successive English kings who had struggled to find suitable endowments for their progeny. Henry II, for example, despite the huge Angevin empire he created, had notably failed to satisfy his sons. Edward I was more prudent than many of his predecessors, and took considerable care to provide for Thomas and Edmund. He was obliged under the terms of the marriage settlement with Margaret to assign to any male children of their marriage land to the value of 10,000 marks a year, and in 1306 he set out his plans for their children. In the charter dated 31 August 1306, Edward I promised that Thomas should be endowed with land with an annual income of 10,000 marks (a mark was worth 13*s* 4*d*), that Edmund would receive land with an annual income of 7,000 marks (in May 1307 the king increased this to 8,000 marks), and that Eleanor would have a dowry of 10,000 marks with 5,000 marks for her trousseau.[18] The charter was a formal promise, intended to be binding, and a copy of the charter was made for each child, sealed and sent to the wardrobe under the chancellor's seal for safekeeping. Very few of the nobility would have incomes greater than those the king promised his sons, and it is clear that Edward I was being intentionally generous; he wanted and expected his sons to become powerful and influential noblemen.

Edward I had planned his charter meticulously. The basic endowments for Thomas and Edmund were the two vacant earldoms of Cornwall and Norfolk which, with their attendant lands and incomes, the king already had within his gift. He had inherited the earldom of Cornwall on the death of his cousin Edmund in 1300, and in 1302 Edward I persuaded the childless Earl of Norfolk, Roger Bigod, to entail his title and lands to the Crown. When the earl died in 1306, the king secured the earldom. Edward I's intentions were simple; Edmund, naturally, would have the Cornwall earldom after his namesake, while Thomas, as the charter made clear, would receive the earldom of Norfolk. The respective incomes attached to each earldom would provide the majority of their promised income, and he would make up the shortfall, probably anticipating arranging a suitable marriage for them to an heiress, or possibly by making separate grants at a later stage. The king's confidence in his plans was apparent in his promised timescale, which envisaged each of his children being endowed by the age of seven or eight; Thomas could receive his immediately, Edmund within two years and Eleanor within seven.

When Edward I died in July 1307, less than a year after creating the charter, he had not had a chance to implement its provisions, but he had foreseen this possibility and had known that he might have to rely on his heir to carry it out. It was unfortunate that the king had fallen out with his eldest son, first in a spectacular row in 1305 over the treasurer Walter Langton, which resulted in a four-month estrangement, and then a further unpleasant row in January 1306 over Prince Edward's close friendship with Piers Gaveston.[19] Edward I was particularly incensed by his heir's demand that Gaveston be granted a title, and by the further suggestion that this might be the earldom of Cornwall, which the king had specifically earmarked for his youngest son. Queen Margaret, at her stepson's request, acted as peacemaker and intervened on his behalf in an attempt to patch things up with his father, persuading her short-tempered husband to forgive his son, and after Prince Edward had reluctantly agreed to Gaveston leaving his household and going into exile an uneasy peace between father and son was restored. When it came to making the charter in August 1306, Edward I took the precaution of making his son a party to it, clearly intending to bind his heir by the public promise to honour the charter.[20] It was hardly surprising that his son did not see the fulfilment of the charter as a priority after Edward I's death, but no one anticipated what was to happen next. Within a month of his father's death Edward II had given the earldom of Cornwall to Gaveston, newly returned to his household and high in his favour, thus upsetting his father's carefully laid plans. In effect, he had given away Edmund's inheritance.

The author of the *Vita Edwardi Secundi* noted this as an insult to the young princes, fuelling the general hostility and uproar generated by Edward II's ill-considered action and adding to the resentment and hatred of Gaveston.[21] Although Edmund and Thomas were far too young to have seen it as a personal affront, their mother may well have done, and she, and probably others close to the princes, would have made sure they became aware of it.

Edward II was nevertheless morally, if not legally, bound to carry out his father's intentions, and it is unlikely that the new king forgot his father's charter, or intended to ignore it. However, he made no immediate attempt to make any award to his brothers. The indications are that Edward II initially failed to appreciate the limitations on the Crown's resources, and having squandered the Cornwall earldom on his favourite he subsequently found it difficult to find a suitable replacement. Edward II ignored or avoided the issue of providing for his brothers, as, beset on all sides, he struggled with his father's inheritance. Within months of his marriage to Isabella, the French king was complaining that his daughter had not received the promised dower. While his marriage to Isabella temporarily satisfied the French, Edward II found the continuing problems with neighbouring Scotland, Wales and Ireland almost intractable, lacking Edward I's military competence and implacable will, but worst of all was his continued inability to reach an accord with his most powerful subjects. Having antagonised the nobility so early in his reign over his marked favouritism towards Gaveston, Edward II paid no heed to their protests, and his fondness for his friend increased rather than diminished as time passed. Under the leadership of his cousin Thomas, Earl of Lancaster, the opposition of the nobility grew. Civil war seemed increasingly inevitable, initially averted when Edward II bowed to pressure and sent Gaveston to Ireland and reached an accommodation with the earls by submitting to ordinances restricting his powers. Matters came to a head when Gaveston, having returned from Ireland early in 1312 and surrendered himself to the Earl of Pembroke, was forcibly removed by the Earl of Warwick in June 1312 and taken to Warwick Castle, and then, on the orders of the Earl of Lancaster, executed. Shocked and grief-stricken, Edward II was distraught; but he was also angry, and intent on revenge. Plotting and planning what he would do, preoccupied with arranging his friend's funeral, the king had no time to spare for his brothers.

Within six months of Gaveston's murder, Queen Isabella gave birth to a son and heir on 12 November 1312. This could have been a turning point in Edward II's relationship with the nobility, as the event was heralded with national joy and brought with it a wave of loyalty. The new baby, Prince Edward, was created Earl of Chester and granted the counties of Chester and Flint within a few days of his birth.[22] However, Edward II failed to take full advantage of the goodwill engendered by his heir's birth, and his lack of forethought was abundantly apparent in his treatment of his brothers. Probably recognising that the grants to his son made his brothers' lack of endowment blatantly obvious, a month later, on 16 December, Edward II created his twelve-year-old brother Thomas Earl of Norfolk. As the earldom brought with it an annual income from its estates of 6,000 marks a year, this substantially fulfilled Edward I's charter promise to Thomas.[23] Yet the king failed to make similar provision for Edmund. This was curious, as Gaveston's execution, with no male heir, had left the earldom of Cornwall providentially vacant. It is possible that Edward II intended awarding the earldom to Edmund, just as their father had intended, but he did not. Since Gaveston's murder he had been conspicuously preoccupied with planning and spending lavishly on the funeral and future interment, and had granted Margaret de Clare, Gaveston's widow, lands with an annual income of 2,000 marks.[24] The problem was that months, and then years, passed, and the king continued to do nothing for Edmund. It is hard to excuse his delay. It may be that Edward II's deep affection for Gaveston left him with a sentimental attachment to the Cornwall earldom, but not even his friend's eventual interment at his favourite manor of King's Langley in January 1315 prompted him to grant the title to Edmund. Although in practical terms it may not have seemed important (as Thomas and Edmund were barely teenagers and remained together in the same household), it was a potentially damaging and provocative omission which could have alienated the young Edmund from the king. It was certainly unfair, and when, in October 1315, Edward II at last made a grant to Edmund, it amounted to no more than a small income of less than £450 a year, hardly an adequate provision for the brother of the king.[25] It is difficult to understand why he was not more generous or to discern a convincing reason why Edward II failed to make better provision for Edmund. When he created Thomas Earl Marshal in February 1316, and provided no equivalent honour for Edmund, his younger brother must have wondered if he had offended the king in some way.[26]

The king's attention was undoubtedly elsewhere. The acrimony of many of the nobility towards him had hardly abated after Gaveston's execution, and Edward II continued to struggle for support. Affairs went disastrously in Scotland, with the English army under the king's personal command suffering complete humiliation in a crushing defeat at Bannockburn in 1314. Desperate to exert his authority, Edward II slowly flouted the restrictions imposed on him by the ordinances and tried to build up support to counter the opposition towards him. He found an able and sympathetic friend in Hugh Despenser the Younger, who gradually replaced Gaveston in the king's affections. It was perhaps inevitable that it was only when they were of an age to provide him with support that Edward II showed a more direct interest in his brothers. He summoned Thomas to serve in a new Scottish campaign in 1317, nominating him as joint commander with his older and more experienced cousin Thomas, Earl of Lancaster.[27]

When Queen Margaret died in February 1318, appointing her sons as her executors and beneficiaries (Edmund received two manors), Edward II appears to have realised that Edmund was now also of an age to be useful to him, and almost immediately he took advantage of this to appoint him custodian of the strategically important Gloucester Castle and later Knaresborough Castle, both part of the disputed Gloucester inheritance.[28] These were nominal appointments intended as interim measures, as Edward II did not seriously contemplate his seventeen-year-old brother having sole command, but Edmund's promotion marked his emergence into his brother's world. When the series of negotiations intended to mend the serious rift between the king and the Earl of Lancaster culminated in an agreement which forced Edward II to agree to give up his closest counsellors and accept an advisory council of nobles and churchmen, Edmund was a signatory to the treaty confirming this, signed at Leake on 9 August 1318. Now clearly identified as his supporter, Edward II enhanced Edmund's status by making grants to him in November 1319 which would bring his annual income to nearly £2,000.[29] But although this was a significant award, it was limited, being restricted to Edmund's lifetime, and considerably less than that envisaged by their father, with no accompanying title to boost Edmund's prestige. In March 1320 Edward II boosted his brother's career by sending him on a diplomatic mission to Paris, in advance of Edward II's planned visit to their cousin Charles IV, with Bartholomew Badlesmere, an experienced diplomat, and Edmund also accompanied Badlesmere on a further visit to the Pope in Avignon.[30] On his return in August 1320, Edmund was summoned to Parliament for the first time, styled Edmund of Woodstock.[31]

At this stage there is no evidence that Edmund was unduly concerned about his lack of title or the considerable financial distinction which remained between him and Thomas. He was young, and eager to prove his worth to his brother. He also had other things on his mind, and arranged to see his brother at King's Langley in Hertfordshire to discuss his marriage.[32] It is not known who initiated the meeting but it is a reasonable supposition that it was at Edmund's behest, as he needed the king's permission to marry, and he had found his bride. Joan's mother, Margaret Wake, was from a family of northern gentry. The Wakes held land in Lincolnshire, Yorkshire, Westmorland and Cumberland, and had a tradition of royal service; Margaret's ancestor Baldwin Wake had been held hostage for payment of Richard I's ransom, while Hugh Wake died on crusade in the Holy Land, although Margaret's grandfather, Baldwin Wake, had supported Simon de Montfort against Henry III.[33] Margaret's father, John, served with Edward I in Gascony and Scotland, and was created 1st Baron Wake. He fought for Edward I, and died in 1300, leaving his widow Joan with three small children, Thomas, Margaret and John.[34] Joan Wake could claim kinship with Eleanor of Castile through her father, Sir William de Fiennes, a connection recognised by Edward I, who described Lady Wake as his cousin and kinswoman.[35] Joan was one of Queen Isabella's newly established household when Isabella first came to England in February 1308, but had died by 1310, leaving Margaret and her two brothers orphans.[36] They became royal wards and Edward II granted the Wake lands, and Thomas' marriage, to Piers Gaveston, and after Gaveston's death to Queen Isabella.[37] After their mother's death, Margaret presumably remained in Isabella's household, while Thomas appears to have been taken into the household of Henry of Lancaster.[38] Thomas Wake married Henry's daughter Blanche in October 1316, when they were both under age and without the king's permission. Henry was evidently fond of Thomas, as he persuaded the king to allow Thomas to inherit his family title and lands before he came of age, in June 1317.[39] A marriage was arranged for Margaret with John Comyn of Badenoch but his death at Bannockburn in 1314 left Margaret a childless widow (they may never have lived together as a couple), and it is likely that she stayed in the queen's household.[40] Margaret had a small dowry as Comyn's widow but was otherwise without expectations. As marriage to Margaret could not be considered an advantageous match for a man of his birth, Edmund's choice seems to have been a matter of personal inclination; he had presumably fallen in love with her. The fact that their betrothal was not announced and that they did not marry until 1325 suggests that Edward II may have expressed some doubts and did not immediately give his brother permission.

Dissatisfaction with Edward II's increasing subservience to his new favourite Hugh Despenser, and Despenser's father, erupted into violence in May 1321 when the Marcher lords attacked lands held by the Despensers in Wales. This open attack swiftly precipitated a crisis. With the Earl of Lancaster still hostile towards him and sympathetic to the Marcher lords, Edward II needed all the assistance he could muster, and his young brothers were an obvious source of support. Edmund was an immediate beneficiary of the king's changed attitude, being successively appointed constable of Dover Castle, warden of the Cinque ports, and constable of Tonbridge Castle.[41] His loyalty, and competence, brought him the reward of the long-awaited title when Edward II created him Earl of Kent on 29 July 1321.[42] Meanwhile the rebel Marcher barons advanced on the king in London to present their demands in Parliament, forcing Edward II to concede to their ultimatum to get rid of his favourites, and the Despensers fled into exile in August 1321. The king then sent his steward, Bartholomew Badlesmere, to mediate with the Marcher barons on his behalf, but instead of doing so he unexpectedly joined then. Like many others he had no doubt been alienated by the Despensers, and possibly too he was offended that the earldom he had hoped for had been given to Edmund. Enraged by Badlesmere's treachery, deserted by most of his supporters and bereft of his favourites, Edward II took stock. With the rebels' sphere of influence being in the north and west, the king decided to launch a counter attack in the south, and determined on targeting Badlesmere's lands, as they were in Kent and therefore vulnerable. According to the *Vita Edwardi Secundi*, only six earls responded to the king's request for aid, making Edmund and Thomas foremost among his supporters, as the *Anonimalle Chronicle* also noted.[43] For a few months Edmund and Thomas became their brother's chief advisers, and they revelled in their newfound importance, playing a prominent part in the successful attack on Badlesmere's stronghold in Kent at Leeds Castle, which helped to re-establish the king's authority.

Edmund may well have felt considerable satisfaction with his enhanced position in the autumn of 1321. Now an earl, with sufficient income to support the title, publicly recognised and associated with his brother as a principal supporter of the Crown, he could justifiably have felt that his future was assured. However, Edward II had behaved less than generously towards him. Having decided to grant Edmund an earldom, the obvious choice would have been the still vacant earldom of Cornwall. Instead, the king chose an empty title. The last Earl of Kent, Hubert de Burgh, had died in 1243 without an heir, and the estates and income had long since been sequestered elsewhere.[44] Earls were expected to maintain a certain lifestyle and it had long been accepted that this required a minimal annual income of around £1,000. While the grants made to Edmund in 1315 and 1319 already ensured him an income of nearly twice this, the collection of manors and rentals which provided it were spread over a number of geographically diverse counties. There was no region of the country where Edmund was the main landowner, and although he was now Earl of Kent he had nothing apart from some rental income to connect him to the county, a deficiency which his appointment as constable of Tonbridge Castle did not disguise.[45] Without a concentration of landholding in any specific area, Edmund's authority as a landowner would be limited. More significantly, Edward II had made the 1315 and 1319 grants lifetime awards only and he had not chosen to change this. So apart from the title, Edmund had only the estates inherited from his mother which he could pass on to his heirs. These disadvantages placed Edmund in a much weaker position than most of his peers, and continued to differentiate him from Thomas of Brotherton, whose earldom of Norfolk, with its concentration of land and estates in Suffolk and Norfolk, brought him extensive local influence and financial independence from the Crown. Edward I had not intended such a distinction between his two youngest sons. Edward II was no fool, and his treatment of Edmund was quite deliberate. He chose not to award the earldom of Cornwall, with its attendant estates and income, to Edmund, while he significantly failed to convert the grants he had already made from being limited to Edmund's lifetime.[46] Although he increased Edmund's income slightly in 1321, he specifically instructed his brother to repay part of this to the exchequer on the grounds that the income exceeded what the king 'deemed fit to grant at present'.[47] This was less than generous treatment, and it is an indication of Edmund's devotion and loyalty that he does not appear to have objected.

Edward II continued to rely increasingly on his brothers. In January 1322 Edmund and Thomas led the negotiations which resulted in two Welsh barons, Roger Mortimer of Chirk, and his nephew, also called Roger Mortimer, surrendering to the king. Their success did little to enhance their reputations among their peers. The *Anonimalle* chronicler was dubious about the tactics used by Edmund and Thomas, describing them as 'false brokers' who 'did so much by their cunning and conspiring'.[48] The Mortimers were locked up in the Tower and sentenced to life imprisonment; Roger Mortimer of Chirk died there, but his nephew made his plans and achieved a spectacular escape in 1323. Roger Mortimer did not forget the part Edmund had played in his uncle's death and his own downfall, and he would later take his revenge on Edmund. In March Edmund and Thomas joined the king as he waged war on his most implacable enemy, Thomas, Earl of Lancaster. The earl was captured after a convincing defeat at Boroughbridge. Triumphant, and intent on revenge, the king ruled that the earl be tried for treason. No one was in any doubt of the outcome the king wanted. Testing Edmund's loyalty, Edward II appointed Edmund to be one of the judges, ensuring that his young brother was irretrievably associated with his revenge.[49] Lancaster was duly convicted, and executed. His followers, and in particular his heir, his brother Henry, would not forget Edmund's part in the earl's downfall.

With the removal of his most powerful enemy, Edward II was able to secure the return of his favourites from exile, and the Despensers were reinstated at the York parliament in May 1322. The king immediately found the means to give them generous financial rewards and he restored the strategically important geographical power bases on the Welsh borders to them, while making the elder Despenser Earl of Winchester.[50] In comparison, Edmund's rewards of the sheriffdom of Rutland and the town of Oakham were meagre.[51] Both Despensers now enjoyed significantly larger incomes than Edmund (the younger Despenser's annual income by 1326 has been assessed as being over £7,000, more than three times greater than Edmund's). The return of the Despensers also relegated Thomas and Edmund to the sidelines. It would have been extraordinary if this blatant favouritism had not strained the brothers' relationship with the king, while Edmund remained at a disadvantage compared to Thomas. Edmund could reasonably have expected better treatment from the king, but if he felt any resentment it was not apparent. In the face of Edward II's grudging attitude towards him he continued to show remarkable devotion. Edmund accompanied him on a renewed Scottish campaign in the autumn, and was with the king when he was forced to flee ignominiously to Bridlington after being routed at Byland

Abbey. Subsequently he worked willingly with the Despensers, even going to the aid of the Earl of Winchester in January 1323 when the latter was attacked and forced to take refuge in Windsor Castle, and then joining with him in recapturing Wallingford Castle from the rebels.

Despite Lancaster's defeat at Boroughbridge there remained persistent political opposition to the king. Edmund's unwavering loyalty was an unusual quality among the disaffected nobility, and a virtue that the king was forced to rely on. Edmund's consistent reliability earned him successive military appointments, in February 1323 as lieutenant in the marches of Scotland and then commander, and in March as chief commissioner of array in Cumberland, Westmoreland, Lancashire and Craven, and lieutenant north of the Trent.[52] Although the king showed no abatement in his preference for the Despensers, throughout the rest of that year Edmund's increased attendance on the king suggests a growing attachment.[53] On a personal level Edward II appears to have found Edmund the more congenial of his brothers, and it was easy to use Edmund's abilities and rely on his dependability. Yet, despite the improved relationship the king did not take the opportunity to improve Edmund's financial situation, nor did Edmund obtain permission to marry Margaret during this period of relative political calm. Edward II's attitude towards his brother appears ungracious and he seems to have taken his goodwill for granted. It was almost certainly Edmund's dependable allegiance which led the king to appoint his brother, rather than a nobleman with more experience, to undertake a delicate diplomatic embassy to France in 1324. On 30 March 1324 Edmund was appointed by Edward II to go to France with instructions to inquire into affairs in Gascony, reform its status and regime, and negotiate a marriage for Prince Edward.[54] He was to be accompanied by two experienced diplomats, the Archbishop of Dublin and William Weston.

Gascony belonged to the English Crown, the last remaining vestige of Henry II's great Angevin empire. Successive English kings had balked at the insistence of the French Crown on overlord suzerainty, and Edward II shared his father and grandfather's reluctance to pay annual homage, doing everything he could to delay doing so. The French king did whatever he could to exert French authority in the region, and the local Gascon nobility used the dispute to their own advantage. In October 1323 the issue of sovereignty became critical when the French parlement held that the Benedictine priory in the village of Saint Sardos in the Agenais was exempt from English jurisdiction. The French sergeant sent to display the royal French arms was murdered, and on the initiative of the local Gascon lord, Raymond-Bernard de Montpezat, the village was burned. Delighted to have a legitimate excuse for reasserting French influence, Charles IV summoned local officials including Ralph Basset, the English seneschal in the region, to Paris to give an account of their actions. When they failed to respond Charles IV ordered the local French seneschals to take possession of de Montpezat's castle. The questionable legality of his actions went to the heart of the sovereignty issue and Edward II could not ignore this open challenge to his authority. He ordered de Montpezat to defend the castle, and in March 1324 advised Charles IV that he was sending his 'dear' brother Edmund.[55] Edmund probably set off for France with high hopes, as it was a prestigious appointment in keeping with his special status as the king's brother, and he no doubt anticipated that a successful outcome would prompt his brother to be more generous in honouring the terms of their father's charter. Although he was still unmarried, he would have felt it worth deferring his personal affairs until he returned.

Unfortunately, Edmund's embassy was doomed to failure. Charles IV had no incentive to reach an agreement, as the crisis had given him a legitimate excuse to reassert French influence in the region. Arriving in Paris, Charles IV reputedly received Edmund's deputation coldly, and it seems unlikely that the ambassadors could ever have suggested a solution which would satisfy all parties. The talks dragged on for three months, with obvious vacillations on the part of Edmund and the other English delegates. Charles IV had no intention of allowing the impasse to continue and by early July it was clear that he had determined on military action. When in desperation Edmund and his fellow ambassadors conceded some of the French demands, Edward II reacted with public anger and appointed replacement ambassadors. Privately, the king was finding his brother extremely useful. Edmund's failed diplomatic overture had gained valuable time, and now invasion by the French was imminent he had a further use for him. On 20 July 1324 Edward II appointed Edmund to be his royal lieutenant in Gascony.[56] This was, for the king, an expedient appointment. Edmund had obvious status as his brother; he was on the spot, loyal and known to have competence as a commander. If, as seemed likely, he failed to prevent a French invasion, then he was also a convenient scapegoat, enabling the king to distance himself from personal responsibility for any debacle. Unhappily for Edmund, this is exactly what happened. Within six weeks of his arrival in Gascony the French invading force had swept aside everything in their path. While there were many good reasons for the overwhelming French victory – the English garrison was small and poorly equipped, promised support from England never materialised, local support evaporated in the face of French numerical superiority – for Edmund it was a mortifying personal failure to add to his unsuccessful diplomatic overture. The prospect of returning to England with his reputation in tatters was not appealing. When Edward II asked Edmund to stay on as royal lieutenant in Gascony after signing the truce, he was probably relieved and thankful, and may have interpreted it as a sign of implied trust, helping to salve his bruised confidence. However, any comfort he derived may not have lasted for long. Once Edmund was established in Bordeaux, Edward II insisted that his reports and requests were channelled through Hugh Despenser.

This was humiliating, and made worse by Hugh Despenser rebuffing Edmund's friendly overtures towards him and undermining his position by conducting his own correspondence with Edmund's officers.[57]

Isolated in Gascony and distanced from the English court, with the opprobrium of defeat, Edmund's confidence in his brother was shaken and this was not helped by the news from England. The situation in Gascony dominated foreign affairs in England. In September Edward II used the defeat in the Agenais and the resulting fear of a French mainland invasion as an excuse to deprive his wife of her lands and her French servants, and to reduce her allowance. It was even rumoured he might try to obtain a divorce. These actions prompted angry reactions from many of the nobility, and considerable sympathy for Isabella. Throughout the autumn there were rumours Edward II would go in person to settle matters with Charles IV, but by February 1325 he had been persuaded by the Despensers that his wife would be a suitable emissary to her brother. Isabella departed on 9 March 1325 – joyfully, according to the *Vita* chronicler. With the deepening crisis at home and his supporters starting to desert him, Edward II belatedly felt concern about Edmund, and wrote to his 'dear brother' personally on 23 February 1325, ostensibly about his duties but in reality to ensure his loyalty.[58] But although Edmund seems to have served his brother faithfully in the duchy, he was wary and no longer unhesitatingly compliant. The first indication of Edmund's newfound independence came in April when Edmund refused to comply with the king's order to send his chancellor, John Ellerker, back to England.[59] Edward II was undoubtedly taken aback, and angry, as his order in June reveals, demanding that Edmund 'at once lay aside all excuse' because he was 'putting forward certain excuses which the King deems insufficient'.[60] The king sensed that it was time to bring his brother home, and when an expedition, headed by the earls of Surrey and Atholl, was dispatched to bring the long-awaited reinforcements and money to Gascony in May 1325, he recalled Edmund.[61]

It is not clear when Edmund left Gascony, but it is likely to have been in the autumn. The king evidently envisaged that it would take him some time to comply with his orders to complete his business before leaving, as he was paid as lieutenant until January 1326, but having received his recall Edmund turned his attention to his own personal affairs. Edmund had not forgotten Margaret, whom he knew was in Paris with the queen, and when her brother Thomas Wake arrived in Gascony with the expeditionary party, it gave him the opportunity to finalise arrangements for their marriage. Whether Edward II approved or not, Edmund was now determined to marry Margaret at the earliest opportunity, and had no intention of returning to England and leaving her in France. Knowing he would need a papal dispensation for their marriage (he and Margaret shared a common ancestor and so were related within the Church's prohibited degrees of consanguinity), he lost no time in applying to the Pope. The necessary papal dispensation was granted on 2 October 1325, and by December Edmund had journeyed to Paris and married Margaret.[62] Edward II does not seem to have objected to Edmund's marriage, but he must have been appalled when he realised his brother was now in the enemy camp. When Edmund arrived in Paris, he found that Isabella was now surrounded by a sizeable body of supporters, all in opposition to the king. Isabella's position had been strengthened by Prince Edward's arrival in Paris in September to pay homage to Charles IV in his father's place, and she had defiantly told her husband that she would not return to England until the Despensers were removed.[63] Belatedly realising his mistake, Edward II made repeated demands for her to return, but to no avail. Having thoroughly alienated his wife, she ignored him, and an increasing number of disaffected nobles left England to join the queen in Paris.[64]

Edmund may not have appreciated the seriousness of his brother's position in his enthusiasm and determination to complete his own personal affairs, but once he had arrived in Paris he could have been in no doubt of the antagonism and hostility felt towards Edward II, or the strength of support for the queen. Edmund's loyalty and allegiance towards his brother, already weakened by his Gascon experience, was further weakened by his marriage. Margaret's brother Thomas Wake was a favoured intimate of Henry of Lancaster, who headed the Lancastrian opposition to the king. Her own loyalties naturally lay with the queen, and her cousin, Roger Mortimer, was quickly becoming the queen's champion. Isabella was also Edmund's cousin, and he may well have felt sympathy for her complaints, while being conscious that he had a duty towards her, and his nephew. Once in Paris, he dithered. Margaret, as her later career indicated, was a forceful woman, and her influence on him would have been decisive.[65] Throughout the autumn and winter of 1325 Edward II wrote to Isabella requesting her return; by March 1326 he was begging Prince Edward, and Edmund, to return.[66] Edmund's deep devotion and loyalty to his brother resurfaced, and he resolved to return, but, unsure of his welcome, he wrote to the king requesting permission.[67] Unfortunately, it was by then too late. Having ignored so many of his orders, Edward II had lost patience with Edmund, and on 4 April ordered Edmund's lands, goods and chattels to be sequestrated.[68] Edmund now dared not return, and found he was committed to the queen's cause.

Nevertheless, Edmund's newfound allegiance to the queen was lukewarm. The driving force in her party was Roger Mortimer, who had not forgotten Edmund's part in persuading him to surrender to Edward II in 1322. However, the recruitment of the king's brother was a propaganda victory for Isabella, and Edmund was soon publicly associated with her. As the rift between king and queen widened Charles IV became uncomfortable with his sister's presence and requested Isabella to leave his court, and to take her followers with her. Not yet ready to return to England, the queen travelled instead to Hainault, with the excuse of trying to arrange a match for Prince Edward. Edmund and Margaret accompanied her. Making no attempt to consult with her husband, Isabella negotiated with the Count of Hainault and agreed that Prince Edward would marry one of his three daughters in return for his promise of military support. Edmund was called on to undertake to see that the marriage took place.[69] Armed with this assurance, and with a considerable body of support around her, Isabella planned her return to England. Her stated aim remained the removal of the Despensers. Meanwhile, realising that his wife was not going to return on his terms, Edward II prepared for the worst, assuming an invasion was imminent. He amassed an army, putting the Earl of Surrey in command, and appointed his remaining supporters to take command of the country's defences, deputing Thomas of Brotherton to take charge of defences in Essex, Hertfordshire and East Anglia. However, when Isabella and her supporters, including Edmund and Margaret, sailed for England in September 1326 they chose to land on Thomas' Suffolk estates. There they were greeted in safety by sympathisers, including Thomas, whose change of allegiance was almost certainly due to Edmund's influence.[70] Edward II had not anticipated that his brothers would betray him and could barely credit it, being at pains to exclude Edmund from the warrant issued for the arrest of Roger Mortimer and the other rebels on 27 September.[71] But by October he could be in no doubt of Edmund's changed allegiance after a joint proclamation issued in the name of Isabella, Prince Edward and Edmund called on him to be rid of the Despensers.[72]

Isabella's actual intentions on returning to England, and whether or not she and Mortimer had planned all along to depose Edward II, have been much debated by historians. Whatever their real aims, they were careful to keep them secret. There was no reason for Edmund not to believe Isabella's publicly stated objective of removing the Despensers, and he probably anticipated that an accommodation would be reached with Edward II, such as had been imposed in 1311 and 1321. No one predicted the complete and total collapse of support for the king, or the enthusiasm and approval with which the queen was greeted as she slowly made her way to London. The defeat of the king, without a single battle being fought, was overwhelming. The Earl of Winchester, the elder Despenser, was captured at Bristol, and his son at Hereford. Both were tried and executed, with Edmund and Thomas judges at their trials, showing that Edmund had long since lost any goodwill he may once have felt towards them.[73] Abandoned by almost all of his supporters, Edward II was captured and imprisoned at Henry of Lancaster's castle at Kenilworth. In January 1327 Isabella called an assembly of leading nobles to decide the king's fate, at which the call was made for Edward II to step aside in favour of his son, Thomas Wake being one of the most vociferous of those calling for the king's abdication. A deputation was sent to persuade the king to abdicate in favour of Prince Edward, and Edward II was forced, reluctantly, to agree. To unanimous acclaim, Prince Edward was crowned king on 29 January 1327, and shortly afterwards a council of four prelates, four earls and six barons was appointed to assist him in governing, on the grounds that at fourteen he was too young to do so himself.

Events had moved quickly and Edmund's part in them is hard to discern. Although he had been closely involved in the Despensers' fate, he does not seem to have been a party to his brother's capture, or included in the deputation persuading him to abdicate, yet he was, with Thomas, on the newly formed governing council. The absence of both brothers from the removal of the king suggests that neither was comfortable with the forced abdication, but neither appear to have raised a dissenting voice. Perhaps any qualms Edmund felt were allayed by Isabella's assurance that the king would be permitted to live out his life in comfortable seclusion. But the truth is that they had both, in effect, been bought by Isabella. Knowing how Edmund had been treated by Edward II, Isabella astutely offered to fulfil the terms of Edward I's charter in full as the price for his acquiescence in his brother's deposition. Naturally Margaret would have urged him to accept, and with an heir to consider (Edmund and Margaret's first child, Edmund, was probably born in the late autumn of 1326 or early in 1327), self-interest played its part.[74] Edmund was anxious that his gain would not be seen as a reward for his change of allegiance, and he tried to distance himself from his sister-in-law by formally petitioning Parliament for completion of the charter terms, making it clear that he was asking for the fulfilment of a long-standing, legitimate claim. On 10 January 1327, just days before Edward II's abdication, the exchequer was ordered to work out what property should be granted to Edmund to provide him with sufficient further rents to ensure he enjoyed an annual income of 8,000 marks a year, as promised by Edward I.[75] Thomas followed Edmund's lead and similarly submitted his own petition, stating that he had only received 6,000 of the 10,000 marks promised.[76] On 27 February 1327, in addition to a substantial grant of former Despenser and Arundel holdings, including Arundel Castle, Edmund had the satisfaction of having Edward II's 1315 and 1319 grants to him confirmed and extended to his heirs.[77] Thomas also received grants to fulfil his charter terms. At long last they both had what their father had promised them so long ago, but they would have to live with the fact that the price they had paid to achieve this was their silence in the face of Edward II's abdication.

With Edward II's abdication, Edmund's position was publicly at its height and he appeared to enjoy considerable authority. He was the new king's favourite uncle and he was on the council. Froissart described him as one of the young king's main advisers, with Isabella and Mortimer.[78] However, Edmund was not as powerful as his new position suggested. His reputation and standing had not been enhanced by his career in France, and nor had his cause been improved by the modest part he had played in Edward II's deposition. With charisma, drive and force of personality Edmund could have made himself a dominant figure in the new regime, but he was not ambitious, and once he had obtained what he felt was his due as Edward I's son he was content to follow the lead of others. Although he was a member of the council of twelve appointed to assist his young nephew, with Thomas Brotherton and Thomas Wake, it was headed by Henry of Lancaster and there is no evidence that Edmund enjoyed greater influence than the other council members. He was not intimate with Isabella and Mortimer, despite Froissart's remark, and he made no attempt to become more closely associated with them. Even his achievement in obtaining the fulfilment of the charter terms indicates a crucial weakness on his part. Aware of Edmund's ambivalence towards her cause, Isabella had been careful to ensure that (with the exception of Arundel Castle) Edmund received few key strategic properties, and that his lands were scattered (they were spread over twenty-six counties) so that he remained without a natural power base.[79] Edmund must have realised this, but he does not seem to have objected, and he made no attempt to challenge Isabella and Mortimer's dominance. In the summer of 1327 Edmund was appointed with Thomas of Brotherton, and Henry of Lancaster, to command the Scottish campaign, but it was not a successful partnership and the campaign ended badly, with Isabella and Mortimer forcing them to agree an unpopular truce. From the start of the new regime, the council had proved ineffective in taking control of affairs away from them, and Isabella and Mortimer's acquisitive behaviour and firm grip on power started to arouse hostility. When opposition to Isabella and Mortimer started to grow in earnest, the disillusioned and unhappy nobility looked for leadership and found it in Henry of Lancaster, rather than in Edmund.

In July and August, while Edmund was in Scotland, there were attempts to free Edward II. Edmund had not made any attempt to visit his brother, and it is impossible to know how he felt about the king's incarceration. When it was announced at the end of September 1327 that Edward II had died at Berkeley Castle, barely eight months after his abdication, Edmund, like everyone else, appears to have accepted this calmly, even though it was unexpected, and obviously convenient for Isabella and Mortimer.[80] He went to the funeral in Gloucester in December 1327, and afterwards he continued with his official duties, attending his nephew's wedding to Philippa of Hainault in York at the end of January 1328.[81] However, within a few months Edmund became convinced that Edward II had not died and was being held in Corfe Castle. Having passively acquiesced in his brother's removal from power, accepted his imprisonment and the announcement of his death, the intelligence that Edward II remained alive shook Edmund and appears to have resurrected all of his old loyalty towards his brother. Edmund would have realised that the only people who could have engineered the news of the king's death, and the funeral, while concealing his survival, were Isabella and Mortimer, and that any attempt on his part to act on the information would threaten their position. There is frustratingly little in the way of evidence to explain why Edmund came to believe that Edward II was still alive, and even less to understand his reaction or intentions. At his own trial in October 1330 Roger Mortimer confessed that he had planted the information which led Edmund to believe Edward II was still alive in order to engineer Edmund's downfall. Edmund was not stupid or credulous. Self-interest alone dictated that he ignore such information; he was in a very comfortable position, with the title and estates he had wanted, a wife and family (Joan was born during 1328) and a prominent position at court. Edmund had nothing to gain from Edward II returning, and a great deal to lose. But however the information came to him, Edmund believed it and determined to do something to support his brother.

While Edmund was working out what to do, opposition to Isabella and Mortimer was becoming more pronounced under Henry of Lancaster's leadership, and in the autumn of 1328 matters came to a head with a direct armed confrontation between the parties. It is possible that Edmund had already approached Henry of Lancaster, as any plan he might have to help Edward II would obviously be to Isabella and Mortimer's detriment. In November the Earl of Lancaster had written to the mayor and citizens of London saying that he had news from Edmund which he dared not put in writing.[82] However, if he was referring to Edward II's survival, it was soon evident that Henry had no intention of doing anything himself, perhaps not surprisingly given Lancaster's earlier implacable hostility towards the king. Edmund and Henry were not natural allies either, as Henry would not have forgotten Edmund's involvement in the defeat and execution of his brother Thomas in 1322. Edmund would have confided in his own brother, but it is clear that Thomas Brotherton was not prepared to take the lead on this. In the crisis the brothers were careful to appear neutral, and acted in a mediatory capacity, issuing a joint letter, probably sent to all the bishops, summoning them to a meeting in London on 19 December, and in January they accompanied the archbishop and the Bishop of London to the king as intermediaries to negotiate peace.[83] Before they could start to discuss a settlement, Mortimer seized the initiative, advancing on Lancaster, and by mid-January 1329 he had gained the advantage and Lancaster had conceded defeat. In the aftermath Lancaster and his followers were fined and many, including Thomas Wake, fled abroad. The neutral stance Edmund and Thomas had taken ensured they suffered no repercussions, but they won few admirers, with one chronicler blaming Lancaster's defeat on their failure to support him.

Almost immediately after Lancaster's defeat, Edmund made preparations to go abroad, appointing attorneys in April 1329, and he crossed to France in June with Margaret.[84] His ostensible purpose was to carry out official duties in Gascony, probably initially accompanying Edward III to Amiens to pay homage to the new French king, Philip VI. However, it appears that he had made up his mind to find and free Edward II, and had decided that he needed to find support. It is probable that Margaret and Edmund visited her exiled brother, with Edmund hoping for sympathy and assistance from Thomas Wake which, as a previous opponent of Edward II, he was unlikely to have given. While in Paris Edmund had discussions with exiled supporters of the king, Sir Henry Beaumont and Sir Thomas Rosslyn, and he also visited the Pope in Avignon to take his advice, later claiming that the Pope had commanded him to do what he could to secure Edward II's release.[85] Appealing for support in this way was risky, and Edmund received news from England warning him that there was a plot against him. He had planned to undertake a pilgrimage to Santiago in Spain with Margaret to fulfil a vow his mother had made, but once he heard of the plot he abandoned the trip and returned to England in the late autumn.[86] On their return to England Edmund and Margaret outwardly resumed normal court and family life, yet, despite the obvious danger, he continued with his plans in secret, buoyed by the support he now had, which included the Archbishop of York and the Bishop of London. With Thomas of Brotherton also in his confidence, Edmund had no hesitation in involving his wife, and Margaret, perhaps surprisingly given her experience of Edward II, was supportive. In February 1330 Edmund and Thomas escorted Queen Philippa to Westminster Abbey for her coronation, and it is probable that Edmund took the opportunity at such a gathering to discuss his plans with others. By now Edmund was fairly certain that Edward II was being held at Corfe Castle, and after he had returned to Arundel to join Margaret and their children she assisted him in writing to John Deveril, the castle commander at Corfe Castle, to ascertain if it was indeed his brother's prison.[87]

Unfortunately, Edmund did not keep his intentions sufficiently secret, and he unwittingly played right into Mortimer's hands. When he attended Parliament at Winchester, Mortimer sprung the trap he had set. On 14 March 1330, shortly after Edmund arrived at the Winchester parliament, Isabella and Mortimer arranged for his arrest, and accused him of plotting to rescue Edward II and restore him to the throne.[88] On 16 March, to the consternation of the gathered assembly, Edmund's confession was read out. He admitted that he had indeed planned to rescue Edward II. This, Mortimer claimed, was treason – and the penalty for treason was death. Edmund's confession was recorded and has survived.[89] A curious mixture of fact and fiction, it was probably altered for effect by Mortimer. Nevertheless, in essence Edmund admitted that he believed his brother was being kept captive in Corfe Castle, that he had been ordered by the Pope to obtain support and rescue the imprisoned king, and that he had been planning to do so. Edmund appears to have wanted to protect, as far as he could, the others involved, and in particular his sources, and he did so by undermining his own credibility with a bizarre story that a friar had conjured up the devil and revealed to him that Edward II was still alive, a patent nonsense described as 'fantastic and false' by at least one chronicler.[90] Although he named some of his supporters, including the Archbishop of York and the Bishop of London, it was a short and far from comprehensive list, and Mortimer later admitted that he had already known about those Edmund did name. Most of those named in his confession had been loyal to Edward II. The most striking thing about Edmund's confession is that his stated aim was simply and solely to rescue Edward II and help him escape abroad. There appears to have been no serious intention of restoring Edward II to the throne or of threatening Edward III's position, and the only evidence of Edmund's rescue plan, apart from his confession, was the letters he and Margaret had written to the garrison of Corfe Castle.[91]

Nevertheless, appalled and paralysed, no one, not even Edward III, dared speak in Edmund's defence. It is notable that Thomas Brotherton, who might reasonably have been expected to defend Edmund, made no attempt to help him. Isolated and deserted, Edmund realised the danger he was in and tried to save himself. He begged his nephew for forgiveness, and offered to abase himself by going barefoot wherever the king wanted, with a rope around his neck. The *Brut Chronicle* records that Edmund wept as he knelt before his nephew.[92] Edward III either could not, or dared not, help him, and sentenced his uncle to death. In the early morning of the 19 March Edmund was escorted outside the walls of Winchester castle to be beheaded. The *Anonimalle Chronicle* records that, out of pity, no one wanted to behead him, and that Edmund was forced to wait all day until vespers around three o'clock in the afternoon, until at last a menial retainer of the king's marshalsea was persuaded to act as executioner.[93] It is doubtful if the reluctant recruit was skilful with the axe.

Edmund's execution greatly shocked his contemporaries. When Edward II was deposed the revolution had been largely bloodless, other than the trials and executions of the king's favourites, the Despensers, whose deaths were widely considered to be well deserved. But Edmund's death was different. The chroniclers unanimously condemned the dubious legality of the proceedings, suggesting that even if Edmund's confession was true, the punishment was too severe.[94] Nothing like this had happened since Edward II wreaked vengeance on his enemies at Boroughbridge in 1322 and had executed his cousin, Thomas, Earl of Lancaster. Edmund's judicial murder showed breathtaking ruthlessness by Mortimer and Isabella. Edward III was known to be fond of his uncle (evidenced by his affectionate address to Edmund in letters in contrast to his neutral greetings to his other uncle, Thomas Brotherton). Aside from his close relationship to the king, Edmund was Isabella's cousin as well as her brother-in-law, and his wife Margaret was Roger Mortimer's first cousin as well as having been one of Isabella's attendants.[95] But there was a rational purpose behind Mortimer and Isabella's action. However incredible his belief that Edward II was still alive, Edmund's actions in seeking support for his rescue plan jeopardised Isabella and Mortimer's position. By his own admission Edmund had obtained a respectable body of support, and Isabella and Mortimer treated his plan as a serious threat. Edmund's fate was an intentional act of terror designed to quash opposition, and he proved an easy target. Edmund may have been liked, and even regarded with respect because of his birth, but he was not a forceful, charismatic personality and Isabella and Mortimer gambled – correctly – that none of the nobility would be prepared to risk their own careers in defending him.

Isabella and Mortimer were swift to capitalise on Edmund's execution. Between 18 and 22 March orders were issued in the king's name to arrest forty-one named associates of Edmund, with a number of more minor implicated figures in the following months, and Edmund's friends and associates fled, some abroad.[96] Thomas Wake was condemned to death in the Winchester parliament for sedition; he also managed to leave the country.[97] Thomas Brotherton surprisingly escaped any reprisal, probably because his son Edward had married Mortimer's daughter Beatrice the previous year, but in April he took the precaution of absenting himself on official business in Gascony.[98] The Pope disassociated himself from Edmund and several months later expressed surprise to Isabella that anyone could assert that he would have believed Edmund's 'incredible' story.[99] For the time being, at least, Isabella and Mortimer had succeeded in their plans.

Edmund's Bereaved Family

Edmund's execution had dire consequences for his family. Margaret had every reason to fear for her own future and that of her children. She was complicit in her husband's offence, and could have no confidence she would be shown mercy. The queen and Mortimer were insecure in their hold on power, and in their weakness sought to impose their will by terrifying the aristocracy. In the civil war of 1321, nine years earlier, Edward II had shown little mercy to the families of his defeated opponents, and the wives and children of most of the Contrariants were subjected to long periods of detention. Roger Mortimer's own wife, Joan Mortimer, had been imprisoned in the Tower and their children placed in different priories scattered around the country. Lady Badlesmere and her children had suffered similar treatment after the execution of her husband in November 1321, and even the Earl of Lancaster's elderly mother-in-law, the Countess of Lincoln, had been imprisoned.[100] There was no one to whom Margaret could turn for help. Her husband's family had already shown their incapacity to aid Edmund, and Margaret's closest relative, her brother, Thomas Wake, had fled abroad as soon as the orders for the arrest of Edmund's confederates had been issued.[101]

Margaret did not have long to wait. The king's yeomen, Nicholas Langeford and John Payn, arrived within days of Edmund's arrest with orders to escort Margaret and her children from Arundel Castle into the custody of the sheriff of Wiltshire at Salisbury Castle.[102] Her advanced pregnancy gave Margaret temporary respite, but she was immediately placed under house arrest, deprived of all but two of her women and restricted to an allowance of 13s 4d for her daily expenses, while her jewels and other goods were to be taken away and delivered to the king's clerk, William Holyns, and Arundel Castle was placed in the hands of the king's yeoman Roger Ashe.[103] Edmund's title, estates and moveable property were all forfeit. By an order dated 5 April Edmund's goods and possessions were to be sold without delay and the proceeds sent to the Treasury.[104] Margaret lost her own dower property from her first marriage, and within days of Edmund's execution her stepson by her first husband, John Comyn, demanded her dower lands as his right on the grounds that it had exceeded her entitlement and he should have it because he had been awarded custody of his father-in-law's estate.[105]

Under house arrest, deprived of her servants and all contact with the outside world, Margaret was completely on her own, with no female companions other than the two attendants left to her, and her only male companions other than her guards was the Prior and his community. Margaret's loss of her husband, her position, the family's wealth and possessions and the uncertainty of her own future were compounded by a deep sense of personal betrayal. Edmund's fate had been engineered by Queen Isabella, whom she had served for many years, and by her own cousin, Roger Mortimer.[106] Margaret's own fate, and that of her children, was now at the whim of the queen and her lover, and she was helpless to prevent the disposal of her husband's estates, goods and chattels; her children's inheritance. Isabella and Mortimer could not resist the opportunity to enrich themselves from Edmund's estates, and because there were so many, they took care to reward their own supporters as well. Isabella took Edmund's houses in Westminster, the rental income from the towns of Gloucester and Cirencester, and Barnsley manor in Gloucestershire.[107] Mortimer's son Geoffrey was awarded a handsome share: Castle Donington in Leicestershire, two manors in Gloucestershire, the manor of Woking in Surrey, two manors in Derbyshire and one each in Nottinghamshire, Rutland and Wiltshire.[108] Isabella and Mortimer divided the remainder of Edmund's sixty manors, fourteen farms and assorted income sources between their supporters.[109] The indecent haste with which they parcelled out Edmund's property was such that it had not been possible for the king's officers to complete the assessment and valuation usually done of forfeited estates, and less than eight weeks after

Edmund's death Isabella and Mortimer found it necessary to appoint commissioners to ascertain exactly what Edmund had owned, and who now had that property.[110]

It is not clear what Isabella and Mortimer planned to do with Margaret and her children, but incarceration for Margaret and the placing of her children into religious establishments was an obvious possibility. Although Edmund's family hardly represented a threat to the queen and her lover, they may well have wished to make an example of his widow and children, and the orders to move them to detention at Salisbury Castle were merely an interim measure before transferring them to the Tower. John's birth had given Margaret breathing space, as she would have been allowed to remain at Arundel Castle for at least six weeks afterwards until she was churched. This proved fortuitous, as with no record of Margaret being moved into the custody of the sheriff of Wiltshire at Salisbury Castle it appears that Isabella and Mortimer were content to leave the family at Arundel indefinitely. Probably they had not yet decided what to do with her. Luckily for Margaret, Isabella and Mortimer never got the chance to do so.

2

The Changing Fortunes of the Kent Family 1330

The wheel is come full circle.

King Lear

Within seven months of Edmund's execution, the fortunes of Margaret and her children changed radically when the seventeen-year-old Edward III seized power in a dramatic coup in October 1330. With the aid of a small group of friends led by William Montague, and the cooperation of the castle constable, the young king arrested Mortimer in Nottingham Castle and took his mother into custody. The events that led to this are obscure and the chroniclers have little to say about it. Secrecy was obviously vital as the ruthlessness Mortimer had displayed with such compelling force over Edmund would have made it extremely dangerous for any hint of such plans to become known. It is probable that very few people knew of the king's plans or of the details. The king's motivation in taking such drastic action is easier to interpret. Mortimer and Isabella had known that it was only a matter of time before Edward III asserted himself, and their attempts to quash his independence merely exacerbated the personal humiliation they inflicted on him by denying him any say in government, and keeping him on such a restricted income that he was personally embarrassed for money. The birth of his son and heir, Edward of Woodstock, on 6 June 1330, is generally considered to be the impetus which impelled Edward III to act, but Edmund's murder was also a significant factor. Within weeks of the coup, Margaret and her children had been taken into the royal household.[1] Margaret can only have been relieved at this reprieve after six months at the mercy of Isabella and Mortimer.

Many years later the chronicler Froissart credited the transformation of their lives to the young Queen Philippa, recounting how she had taken pity on Joan, adopted her as a member of her household and taken responsibility for her upbringing.[2] Froissart was in a good position to have discovered this kind act, as he spent much of the 1350s and 1360s at court as a member of Queen Philippa's household. Writing more than twenty years later, Froissart omitted all mention of Margaret, Edmund and John, and cites Joan's age incorrectly as seven; but as Joan's mother and brothers had all died by this time, these oversights are understandable. However, if Philippa initiated the invitation to Margaret and her children, it was with her husband's encouragement and support. Edward was motivated by more than a sense of family responsibility. Now that power lay firmly with him, he needed to reassure the nobility that in asserting his own authority he brought stability and peace, and in the process re-establish respect for himself and for the Crown, damaged by the long, divisive years of his father's reign and by the greed and aggression of Mortimer and Isabella's two-year rule. Edmund's execution was widely regarded as judicial murder and, as it had been carried out in Edward III's name, remained a damaging and potentially divisive issue. To obtain, and retain, the confidence of his nobility, it was vital that the king disassociated himself from responsibility for his uncle's death. The most public statement he could make was to take Margaret and her children into his household, so distancing himself from the actions of his mother and Mortimer, and, even more importantly, demonstrating that he was now willing and able to protect his own family. It was in the king's interest to arrange for his aunt and his three cousins to be escorted from Arundel Castle to join him and the queen as soon as he could arrange it. As a public statement of his new persona, he gathered his family around him at Windsor for Christmas, pointedly including his mother as a symbol of domestic harmony (although Queen Isabella was given little choice, as the king sent an escort, including Joan's uncle, Thomas Wake, to accompany his mother from Berkhamsted Castle).[3]

Suddenly released from their isolation at Arundel and transported to join the bustling, privileged circle around the king and queen, Joan and Edmund must have found the change bewildering (John was only six months old). They were taken into the queen's household, and Philippa took responsibility for them. The young queen had a kind heart and generous nature, and had known Edmund well (he and Thomas Brotherton had attended on her at her coronation). Some months younger than her husband, and still barely more than a teenager herself, she had been overshadowed by her forceful mother-in-law. Now independent, Philippa lost no time in demonstrating her good nature in her concern for others. Apart from the Kent family, she also showed generosity towards others, such as the Mautravers family. John Mautravers was a Mortimer supporter, and had been closely involved with Edward II's death and Mortimer's conspiracy to trap Edmund in March 1330. Shortly after seizing power in October Edward III ordered a warrant to be issued for Mautravers' arrest, and forfeited his possessions. Mautravers fled, leaving his wife and children behind, without means. When Philippa heard of Agnes Mautravers' plight, she intervened with her husband to ensure that Agnes secured at least her dower from her first husband.[4] Philippa's kindness to Agnes, the wife of her husband's enemy, would hardly have exceeded her concern for Margaret and her children, a family so much more closely related to her own and deserving of her help. Her natural sympathies as a new mother would have been drawn to Margaret, also with a new baby, and her fatherless family. Offering the family a home within the royal household would have been an instinctive act of compassion and practical support while the family's affairs were sorted out, as well as suiting her husband's purposes.

Edward embarked on a general programme of vigorous reconciliation, showing mercy and generosity to his enemies. However, Mortimer's fate was inevitable. He could not be allowed to survive. At his trial Edmund's judicial murder was cited as one of the principal charges against Mortimer, and he admitted he had tricked Edmund, and staged the charade of his trial. Mortimer was executed, suffering the full penalty for treason of being hanged, drawn and quartered. Edward III took great care to immediately disassociate himself from his mother and Mortimer's regime. He ordered that the county sheriffs publish a proclamation in all public places which stated that 'the king's affairs and the affairs of his realm have been directed until now to the damage and dishonour of him and his realm'.[5] He restored to favour all of Edmund's associates, and encouraged those who had fled abroad to return.[6] A warrant for the protection of Margaret's brother, Thomas Wake, was issued on 25 November, and in December he was formally pardoned and his lands, goods and offices restored.[7] On 8 December Edward III ordered that all of Edmund's lands should be taken back into the Crown's hands.[8] This, together with Mortimer's admission that he had tricked Edmund, was an indication to Margaret that the way was now clear for her to secure the restoration of her husband's title and estates, and look to her own, and her children's, future.

The circumstances of Edmund's death and their close blood relationship ensured that both Edward III and Philippa took a considerable interest in the young Kent family. The king and queen were themselves very new parents and they are known to have been fond parents, having a strong and affectionate relationship with all their children throughout their lives.[9] Although Prince Edward was awarded revenue from the earldom of Chester to maintain his own household from the age of three months, he remained in his mother's care, with Philippa managing his revenues.[10] Initially, Edmund, Joan and John would have been in the care of the queen's household, joining the baby Prince Edward (John was the same age as the prince). Unfortunately, Edmund did not long survive his adoption into the royal household and he died within the year, in late September or early October of 1331.[11] Meanwhile the royal nursery expanded. In April 1332 Philippa gave birth to a daughter, Isabella, and a year later to a second daughter, Joan. Princess Joan was probably named after her aunt Joan, Edward III's younger sister, married to David Bruce, the Scottish king, but the choice of name may also have been prompted by the presence within the household of the four-year-old Joan. The princesses shared the household with their older brother Prince Edward.[12] By 1334 Princess Isabella and Princess Joan had a household of their own in the Tower of London, which Joan probably shared with them, while her brother John remained with Prince Edward.[13]

The admission of Joan and her brothers to the royal household may initially have been intended as a temporary measure, but it soon became permanent, a change which can only have been effected with their mother's agreement. Having secured her children's safety, Margaret threw her energies into restoring the family name and estates. Edmund had appointed her co-executor of his will with Adam Lyndburgh, the rector of Algarkirk (Lincs) and a canon of Lincoln Cathedral, and left the choice of his final resting place to her.[14] Edmund had been buried in the Grey Friars church at Winchester, and Margaret decided that he should be given a more appropriate burial place in Westminster Abbey, where his father, Edward I, and others of his royal forebears were buried. She petitioned the Pope requesting the reburial, and in April 1331 Pope John XXII granted her request, ordering the bishops of Winchester, Coventry, Lichfield and London to cause Edmund's body to be exhumed and reburied at Westminster.[15] There is, however, no evidence that the order was ever carried out.[16] There is no record of a monument or chantry chapel being founded for him at Westminster Abbey, which is unusual in the circumstances (one would have thought that his wife or later on his son and heir would do so), and it is curious that his son John later chose to be buried in the Grey Friars church at Winchester, when his only connection to it was his father's burial there.[17] There is no obvious reason why Margaret should have changed her mind, but she may well have done so, and certainly throughout 1331 her priorities became increasingly focussed on dealing with her family's inheritance.

On 18 December 1330 Edward III reversed and annulled his mother and Mortimer's cavalier distribution of Edmund's lands by ordering that they should all be taken into the king's hands.[18] Margaret might reasonably have expected her royal nephew to order full restoration of her husband's title and estates to his heir, her oldest son, Edmund. Mortimer's confession should have made this a priority, especially as this would be an obvious way for Edward III to disassociate himself from any complicity in his uncle's execution, clearing the way for full restoration. But Edward III did not do so, for a very good reason. To restore stability to the political order he needed not just to placate his aunt, but to win over all those members of the nobility who had been alienated by his mother and her lover. As the bulk of Edmund's estates comprised property which his mother and Mortimer had confiscated in 1327 from his father's favourites, the Despensers, and the Earl of Arundel, Edward III wanted to take careful stock of the conflicting interests of their heirs and that of his young cousin before attempting full restoration. An additional and not insignificant complication was the sheer practical difficulty of identifying all the Kent estates. Isabella and Mortimer had parcelled out Edmund's estates so rapidly between themselves and their supporters that it was difficult to determine who had been given what, resulting in inevitable confusion of ownership, and the inquisition post mortem itemising Edmund's estates was not completed until January 1331.[19]

Edward III's understandably cautious approach did not suit Margaret, and her numerous petitions from December 1330 are evidence of her persistence and tenacity in appealing to her nephew. Her first concern was the family name. In early December 1330 Margaret wrote personally on behalf of the young Edmund to her nephew, as well as formally petitioning the king and Parliament, and she also wrote again separately for herself and her younger children, requesting a re-examination of Edmund's trial on the basis of Mortimer's confession, praying that 'right might be done'.[20] She then turned her attention to property, astutely starting with her own rights as a widow. Edward III found he could not ignore his aunt's pleas, and in December 1330 he reluctantly granted her petition for her dower entitlement from Edmund's estates, pointing out that this was a special concession as 'he might have deferred the assignment by reason of certain claims, especially as the extent of the lands have not yet been returned to chancery according to custom'.[21] Margaret was on firmer ground in pressing for the return of her Comyn dower, as this had been wrongfully taken from her in March 1330 and had become the subject of dispute between her stepson Richard Talbot and Talbot's nephew David, who had become entitled to his share of the Comyn estates on coming of age in August 1330.[22] In January 1331, Edward III conceded and ordered that the Comyn dower be returned to his aunt as 'she has besought him to cause them to be restored to her'.[23] Margaret's appeal for her husband's honours to be restored to her son closely followed, and was similarly successful. On 12 January 1331 an order was made that Edmund's heir should be admitted to his inheritance, and 'the possessions and blood of Edmund, Earl of Kent' were formally restored to his heir on 8 February.[24] On 14 February Margaret and her co-executor obtained the right to recover all the possessions Edmund had at the time of his arrest on 14 March 1330, notwithstanding the judgement passed on him.[25] Writs were issued for the payment of rent to her.[26] Her request that all goods and chattels from the Castle Donington estate and manors in Rutland, Surrey, Gloucester, Hampshire and Somerset should be appraised in her presence was granted on 1 March 1331 because 'the king wishes to do what is just'.[27] Edmund's posthumous rehabilitation was completed when the judgement against him was annulled on 8 March 1331, a year after his death.[28]

However, despite Margaret's determination, and Edward III's evident desire to assuage his aunt, she was not able to persuade her nephew to restore all of Edmund's estates. The order of 12 January 1331 restoring Edmund's lands to his heir specifically excluded those which had formerly been held by Thomas Fitzalan, Earl of Arundel, prior to his execution in 1327 for supporting Edward II.[29] Edward III was determined to rehabilitate the earl's heir, Richard Fitzalan, and he restored the Arundel estates in full to Richard, including those which had been granted to Edmund.[30] To mollify his aunt Edward III granted her alternate rental income to compensate for the loss of her dower share from the Arundel estates, but he refused to award substitute property for his cousin.[31] This was a heavy loss for the Kent inheritance, as the Arundel land had an annual rental income of around £700, and included Arundel Castle, the family's home prior to Edmund's arrest.[32] Nevertheless, even without the Arundel property, the Kent earldom remained a significantly valuable one, comprising forty-three manors with the right to thirty advowsons as well as extensive annual rents and knight's fees, with the most important individual property now being the extensive Castle Donington estate in Leicestershire. Edmund's heir would still become one of the largest and wealthiest landholders in the country.

Having restored his uncle's name and his cousin's inheritance, Edward III might well have kept management of the valuable Kent inheritance during his cousin's minority in his own hands. He would then have had the advantage of being able to award stewardship of some or all of the estates to his supporters as rewards. However, Margaret was resolved to remain actively involved, and she lobbied her nephew to give her control of them as well. The experience of watching Edmund's estates being dispersed among Isabella and Mortimer's followers may have made Margaret more determined than otherwise to ensure that there was no repeat, albeit under the more paternal aegis of her nephew. Margaret was obviously extremely persuasive, as on 21 March 1331 she was awarded wardship of all her son's inheritance during his minority, subject to an annual payment to the exchequer, and in May the king confirmed she would also receive the estates he had held and committed elsewhere.[33] This was a significant victory for Margaret.

Management of the estates would not have been an easy matter. There was the simple practical difficulty that Margaret was unlikely to have extensive or detailed knowledge of them. Despite the loss of the Arundel estates, the remaining Kent lands were spread over seventeen counties, with income due from fees payable in a further six counties. The bulk of Edmund's holdings had only been granted to him in February 1327, and the sheer number of manors, with their disparate geographical locations, coupled with Edmund's absence on military and diplomatic duties (including the six months he and Margaret spent abroad in 1329) made it unlikely that either of them had fully familiarised themselves with the estates by the time of his death in March 1330. The estates then changed hands three times in a year, forfeited from Edmund, dispersed by Isabella and Mortimer, taken back by the Crown in December 1330 and then restored to Edmund's heir in March 1331. There was inevitable confusion among tenants regarding lordship rights, and some tenants took advantage of the situation to withhold payment of rent. Margaret had no hesitation in requesting her nephew's assistance when she had difficulties. In February 1331 Edward III issued orders that rents due from Alton, Andover (Hants) and Droitwich (Worcs) in addition to the Stratford and Ramsey abbey rentals should be paid to his aunt.[34] In March, he issued similar orders for the payment for rents due from Ormesby (Norfolk), Chichester (Sussex), Cheddar, Congresbury, Bath and Brampton (Somerset), Grimsby (Lincs) Cirencester and Gloucester (Gloucs).[35] In August 1331 a writ was issued directing payment of the fee farm of £60 from the town of Aylesbury (Bucks) to Margaret, acknowledging that it had formed part of Edmund's estates.[36] Despite these orders, Margaret's problems persisted, and in October Edward III confirmed that the issues from all the Kent estates from 21 March 1330 should be delivered to Margaret.[37] The ecclesiastical tenants of the abbeys of Kirkstall (Yorkshire), Stratford (Essex) and Ramsey (Huntingdonshire) were particularly troublesome and had still not paid when young Edmund died. On 5 October 1331 the king reiterated his original order that the respective abbots pay their due rents to his aunt.[38] Margaret also experienced problems with her own dower property; in December 1332 she was forced to obtain an order for the sheriff of Lincoln to assist her in recovering fealty and services due to her from her dower manor at Greetham in Lincolnshire.[39] There were also Edmund's debts to pay, and little available cash to hand. The London merchant John Pulteney, for example, was owed more than £400, and for repayment he was granted custody of one of the Kent estates with an annual rental income of £30, for the duration of Edmund's minority.[40]

Margaret had been in charge of her son's affairs for barely six months when young Edmund died in the autumn of 1331, leaving John as the heir with the prospect of an even longer minority. Unfortunately for Margaret, on Edmund's death her authority ceased and the Kent estates were returned to the Crown.[41] The tragedy gave Edward III the opportunity to reappraise his approach, and by this time he was less susceptible to accommodating his aunt. Instead of giving her complete authority over John's inheritance, Edward III gave his aunt a carefully selected number of estates to manage, and retained the rest himself. On 16 October Margaret was granted wardship during John's minority of the largest and most valuable of the estates, Castle Donington in Leicestershire, and a further eight manors: Ollerton in Nottinghamshire; Ryhall in Rutland; Miserden in Gloucestershire; Lifton, Shebbear and Chettiscombe in Devon; Bagshot and Tolworth in Surrey; and rental from the town of Caistor in Lincolnshire.[42]

Edward III required his aunt to pay £180 a year for custody of the estates, and imposed on her an obligation to keep them in good order at her own cost, while reserving the rest of the estates to the Crown together with a substantial part of the cash income due. This came largely from knight's fees (originally knights were obliged to provide their lord with one mounted soldier for combat; this was translated into an annual payment of 20s instead) and advowsons (rights of presentation to a church benefice).[43] Undaunted by her nephew's refusal to grant her outright wardship of her son's inheritance, Margaret tried to take control where she could of the estates which remained in crown hands. In November she persuaded the king to grant her custody of the houses in Westminster to use and stay in at her will.[44] She continued to remind the king of the injustice endured by her family and had some success in requesting compensation for the goods taken from Edmund's estates after his death. On 12 August 1332 Edward III granted Margaret's petition to be given an allowance of half the sum due for her wardship to the exchequer in recompense.[45] Margaret continued to chip away at her nephew, and on 1 July 1333 persuaded the king to grant her the hundred of Barstable (Essex).[46]

Edward III took the time-honoured traditional royal approach towards the estates held in trust, successively parcelling them out as rewards for service. In November 1331, for example, the king rewarded his brother and sisters' nurses, Matilda de Pirye and Joan de Boys, with the rent from the farm of Chichester.[47] Other beneficiaries included men close to the king: William and Edward Bohun, William Montague, Edmund Bacon and Thomas Bradeston.[48] Edward III also used grants as a means of settling his own debts.[49] Inevitably there was confusion in the handling of some of the Kent estates by the Crown, such as when the original grantees died and their grants were reallocated, resulting in some estates having a succession of temporary owners.[50] Where mistakes by the Crown impinged on Margaret's area of influence she was quick to defend her rights. When John Warenne, Earl of Surrey, was ordered to hand over Swanscombe manor to Margaret as part of her dower entitlement, he pleaded that he should retain it until after the harvest, as he had caused a great part of the manor to be tilled and wanted the corn and other issues during his ownership of it. Margaret refused to agree and the king was forced to intervene, formally requesting his aunt in March 1331 to agree to Warenne retaining the manor until September.[51] In February 1331 Edward III granted the rentals from Ramsey and Stratford abbeys and rental due from Ormesby (Norfolk) to his friend Edward Bohun, in effect restoring them to Bohun as they had originally been granted to him by Mortimer and Isabella after Edmund's execution.[52] Margaret immediately appealed, arguing that these valuable rentals should be granted to her, and forced her nephew to confirm the grant to her and give Bohun a substitute.[53] Margaret also tried to extend her influence, and in May 1331 her nephew had to order her not to meddle with the three Gloucestershire manors he had given to Thomas Bradeston, and in June to reiterate his order that the Gloucester rent farm was due to Bradeston and not to Margaret.[54]

Margaret's perseverance paid off. Within a year of Edmund's death her efforts had secured the reversal of the judgement against him, and restored his title, and the majority of his land and estates to his heir. By March 1333 the estates were in sufficient order for Margaret and her co-executor to be able to comply with the Treasury's requirement for an audit of their affairs to check the debts still owed to the Crown.[55] Subsequently, Margaret's active involvement seems to have continued unabated. In May 1335, in her capacity as executrix, Margaret successfully prosecuted the parson William Kirkeby for stealing a bull, twelve oxen worth £20, £15 cash and other goods from her Woking manor (Surrey).[56] A commission of oyer and terminer was set up on her complaint in April 1336 to look into a trespass and theft of deer at the park at Torpel manor (Northants).[57] To settle an outstanding debt of £287 14s 4d due from Edmund to Raymund Seguyn, Margaret agreed to lease Seguyn the yearly rental from the town of Andover (Hants) for three years, and this was confirmed by the king on 2 March 1338.[58] Her constant vigilance was evident. On 29 June 1338 Margaret wrote personally to request Edward III's intervention, and in July a warrant was issued to arrest John Musard and others for breaking into and occupying Miserden manor (Gloucs), assaulting Margaret's servants and stealing her goods.[59] Margaret's dogged persistence was well founded, as it is doubtful if Edward III would have been as assiduous in maintaining the interests of the Kent estates. It was not, for example, until 10 June 1339 that the king was persuaded to supersede the order for Margaret to pay for corn, animals and other goods confiscated on the day of her husband's arrest on 14 March 1330.[60] Margaret continued to keep a watchful eye on her son's interests, and as late as April 1347 ensured that the king would excuse the customary payment of knight's fees due to the Crown on the occasion of knighting the king's eldest son.[61]

Margaret never remarried. This was almost certainly her personal choice, as she was in her early thirties when Edmund died, and a widow of her status and circumstances would have been an attractive matrimonial proposition. There can have been no lack of opportunity to meet suitors at Edward III's court. Perhaps Margaret never met anyone she wanted to marry, but it is also possible that it suited her not to do so. Her interest and active participation in obtaining and managing the Kent estates, even where they remained under the control of the Crown, shows how anxious she was to remain in charge. The shock of Edmund's execution and the threat to herself and her children immediately afterwards may well have made Margaret more than usually anxious to protect her and her children's position. Despite the October coup Edward III was an unknown quantity for Margaret, and she would not have forgotten his failure to help Edmund. Trust and a belief in a stable future would take time. As a widow, Margaret had control over her own land and affairs and could be appointed to act for her son, so making her own decisions. In addition, her widowed state ensured there was no reason for her children to be removed from the protection afforded to them by being in the royal household. Margaret's success in restoring the family's estates amply justified the trust Edmund had indicated in his wife when he appointed her co-executor in his will. Undeterred by her successive bereavements, Margaret was assiduous in protecting her children's interests, and her actions demonstrate fortitude and determination. She was clearly a woman with considerable strength of character.

It is impossible to know how much Joan and John saw of their mother. Although Margaret could rely on the knowledge, expertise and loyalty of the various stewards who had responsibility for the day to day management of the estates it is likely that she embarked on a succession of visits to see for herself what she had to deal with, and to establish personal contact with the stewards. Initially, Margaret probably left Joan and John behind, secure in the knowledge that her children were well protected and cared for within the royal household, and so would have been away from her children for extended periods of time. It would have been natural for Margaret to want to discuss family affairs with her children and make them aware how this affected their future. Joan would have been included, as she was John's heir, and their elder brother's early death was a reminder that there was no certainty John would survive to inherit at the age of twenty-one. Margaret would have wanted John and Joan to become familiar with the Kent estates and as they grew older would have ensured they accompanied her occasionally. From an early age Joan would have been made aware of the responsibilities that accompanied her heritage. Although there is no record of which, if any, of the estates John and Joan might have visited as children, it is reasonable to suppose that Margaret took them to the largest and most important one at least. Now that Arundel Castle no longer formed part of the inheritance, the largest holding and only castle in the Kent estates was Castle Donington in Leicestershire, situated in a commanding position beside the River Trent. The moated castle had a chequered ownership history. It had been part of the Lincoln earldom, and when this earldom passed by marriage to the Earl of Lancaster the castle became part of the vast Lancastrian estates. Forfeited by Thomas of Lancaster when he was executed in 1322, Castle Donington was then granted by Edward II to Hugh Despenser, but quickly reverted to the Crown when Despenser was executed in 1326, before being granted to Edmund in 1327.[62] It was not in an ideal location, as flooding was a habitual problem. The inquisitors taking stock after Edmund's death had noted that twenty-two acres of land in tillage had not been sown because they were under water, while faggots and hurdles from the woods were regularly made and used to preserve the meadows from flooding.[63]

As Margaret remained unmarried there were two male relatives other than the king who might have been expected to show an interest in John and Joan's welfare. These were Edmund's brother, Thomas Brotherton, Earl of Norfolk, and Margaret's brother, Sir Thomas Wake. Edmund had been very close to his brother Thomas during his life, but after his death the Earl of Norfolk appears to have had very little to do with his sister-in-law and her children. When Edmund was arrested in March 1330, Mortimer had issued a warrant very quickly for the arrest of a number of named associates, including Thomas Wake. Thomas Brotherton had not been on that list, almost certainly because his son Edward had married Mortimer's daughter Beatrice the previous year. The Earl of Norfolk's secure position meant that he had been in a position to assist his sister-in-law when his brother was executed, and might reasonably have been expected to do so. However, instead of interceding on Margaret's behalf, he had taken fright and gone abroad almost immediately, using the excuse of an overseas mission for the king to go to Gascony a few weeks after Edmund's death.[64] The earl seems to have been a man of uncertain temper and preoccupied with his own interests. According to Froissart, Thomas Brotherton had a 'wild and disagreeable temper'.[65] Edward III showed no sign of affection towards this uncle, in contrast to Edmund. After Mortimer's downfall the earl's estates were also in a state of flux in the general rearrangement. Like Margaret, he too in early 1331 was petitioning the king for the restoration of his estates, anxious to retain what he had obtained from Isabella and Mortimer, but with considerably less success than Margaret.[66] It took him until 1 March 1334 to obtain formal confirmation from the king of the grants made to him in 1327 and, although he persuaded his nephew to make him a substantial additional grant of £800 a year, Edward III limited this to a life interest.[67] The Earl of Norfolk was also preoccupied with his own family. His son died at an early age, leaving his two daughters, Margaret and Alice, as his heirs. They were similar in age to Joan and John, but the distancing between their respective parents makes it unlikely that they saw much of one another in the early years. The earl arranged Margaret's marriage to his ward, John, Lord Segrave, and in 1333 reached agreement with Edward III's close friend William Montague (Montague led the small group of supporters with Edward in the coup at Nottingham Castle) for Alice to marry Montague's son William. For some reason this marriage never took place; possibly on Montague's initiative, Alice married Montague's brother Edward instead. Thomas Brotherton's health also deteriorated dramatically and he died in 1338 at the comparatively early age of thirty-eight. A possible sign that he had been ill for some time was his consent to the appointment in March 1337 of Sir Constantine Mortimer, one of his retainers, to survey his household after complaints had been made of their unruly behaviour.[68]

In contrast, Thomas Wake, Margaret's brother, was much more involved with Joan and John. Thomas was an able commander and staunchly loyal to the Earl of Lancaster, in whose household he had spent his formative years. He had an impetuous streak, having married Blanche of Lancaster, the earl's niece, after a whirlwind romance in 1316 or 1317, without royal approval and when he was underage (he would have been about eighteen). Thomas had taken a considerable risk in doing so; fortunately for him, he appears to have been held in high regard by his father-in-law, Henry of Lancaster, and although Edward II imposed a stiff fine, at Henry's request the king allowed Thomas to take possession of his inheritance even though he was not yet twenty-one.[69] Loyalty to Henry kept Thomas at the earl's side throughout the conflict with Edward II, and then later with Isabella and Mortimer in 1329 (after Henry's defeat in January 1329 he was compelled to give a £10,000 recognisance), but Edward III recognised and valued his qualities and treated him with noticeable favour after Mortimer's fall. Thomas Wake's estates were restored in December 1330, and he was granted an immediate pardon for the recognisance.[70] The king showed his considerable trust in Wake by entrusting him with bringing Queen Isabella to join the royal family at Windsor for Christmas in 1330.[71] In January 1331 Thomas Wake was one of the commissioners appointed to look into complaints made in Yorkshire against the actions of the last regime's officials, and he was appointed keeper of the Channel Islands from 18 October 1331.[72] By 1330 he had been married for fourteen years and it must have seemed unlikely to him and Blanche that their union would be blessed with children, which probably caused them some sadness. As his only sibling, Margaret was his heiress, and as time went on it would have become apparent that one of Margaret's children would eventually inherit the Wake estates. It would have been natural for Thomas and Blanche to have wanted to spend some time with Joan and John, and Margaret may also have visited them when she went to her own dower manor in Lincolnshire. Thomas continued to be held in high regard by Edward III, and held a succession of royal appointments up to his death in 1349, while Blanche was Edward III's cousin and was on good terms with the king throughout her life. Thomas and Blanche were in a position to offer Margaret and her children considerable support, and to assist her in arranging her children's future.

3

Growing up in the Royal Household
1330–1338

Train up a child in the way he should go; and when he is old, he will
not depart from it.

Proverbs, 22:6

Family support aside, while Joan and John were under the king's
protection and in the queen's household, the major influences on their
lives, and their future, were the king and queen. Edward III celebrated
his eighteenth birthday in November 1330, an extremely young man
just entering into the full responsibilities of kingship, and having to
cope with the legacy left by his father's deposition and the two years
of political domination by his mother, Isabella, and Mortimer. He was
still developing his kingly style, and his young queen, Philippa, had had
little time to adjust to her new independence. What was life like for Joan
and John in the royal household, away from their mother's watchful eye
while she was preoccupied with family affairs? Childhood, even of a royal
child, was not particularly well recorded in the fourteenth century, and
there are no records referring to Joan during her early years. However,
it is possible to speculate on aspects of her childhood from some of the
known background.

The king and queen had their own separate household, although they
spent much time together, and the royal children and their companions
came under the aegis of the queen. Naturally the queen's household was
extremely large and made up of many different parts, so that day-to-day
supervision and care of the children was delegated and separately
regulated. Prince Edward had a nurse, Joan of Oxford, and a nursemaid,
Matilda Plumpton, appointed to attend his cradle. Matilda seems to have
nursed Edward's younger brother, Edmund of Langley, twelve years later.
Both were later given generous pensions, and as an adult Prince Edward
remembered his nursemaid Matilda, sending her a tun of wine in June
1357.[1] These ladies may both have assisted in the care of Joan's baby
brother, so similar in age to the young prince. Prince Edward was given

his own household, and a steward, Sir William Saint Omer, appointed to take charge of it for him. In 1332 Sir William's wife, Lady Elizabeth, took charge of the prince himself. Her role expanded as the royal nursery did, and by 1334 she is described as mistress to the king's other children.[2] The Saint Omers were in charge of all aspects of the household and day-to-day lives of the royal children, including their early education, and the Saint Omers would have been expected to look after Joan and John as well as their royal charges. In April 1336 William and Elizabeth Saint Omer received a grant of £25 a year for their service to the king in looking after Prince Edward and the princesses, and Elizabeth received a further reward of £12 a year specifically for her service to the prince in December 1337.[3]

When Prince Edward reached the age of seven in 1337 he was given a completely independent household, and taken out of what would have been a largely female environment. His education was amended to one more suitable for his age and rank, acquiring a tutor, possibly the scholarly philosopher William Burley, Queen Philippa's almoner, and by 1338 he was receiving military training, possessing a quantity of armour and accoutrements.[4] The princesses remained together, mostly with their mother. It is probable that Joan and her brother were similarly separated, Joan remaining with the princesses and John with the prince. Traditionally other children were placed with the royal children to give them the company of others their own age; both Edward I and Edward II had their childhood households expanded in this way. Joan and John were merely the first to join their cousins. An early recruit into the prince's household was almost certainly William Montague, eldest son of the king's best friend. The Montagues were among the entourage closest to the king. In January 1331 Edward III appointed Montague keeper of the royal manor at Woodstock, and his wife Catherine Montague brought the king the news of Princess Isabella's birth in June 1332.[5] It has been thought that they may have become Joan's governor and governess, but there is no evidence to substantiate this.[6] The young William Montague was the same age as Joan, and two years older than Prince Edward. Joan's later relationships with Prince Edward and the Montague family were based on the familiarity acquired during these early childhood days. An indication of that childhood familiarity is the use of the diminutive 'Jeanette' by Prince Edward in a gift to Joan made in 1348 many years before their marriage.[7]

As was usual at that time, the first language of the nobility and royal family was French, and English was used to communicate with less privileged members of the household. Joan would have spoken both, and been taught to read, and write, in French at least. Her parents were literate; Edmund's conviction was based partly on the letters that he and Margaret had written to the guards at Corfe Castle. A limited amount of correspondence to and from Joan survives which implies literacy, the most well known being the letter written in French by Prince Edward to his wife from Spain after the Battle of Nájera in 1367.[8] She would have had some knowledge of Latin, though this may have been limited to the religious services. English was little used by the higher nobility as a written language at that time, and she may not have learnt to read in it. The usual accomplishments for girls of Joan's background included dancing, singing, the ability to play a musical instrument and embroidery. She would also have learned to ride, and probably falconry, a sport in which women participated fully and which was extremely popular with the royal family. Her brother John would in addition have received military training and enjoyed hunting and hawking, activities favoured by Edward I, Edward II and Edward III and enjoyed by Prince Edward.

Religion was a fundamental and important part of Joan's life. Like her brother John, Joan would have been christened shortly after her birth, and her godparents expected to play an important part in her life, providing her with a spiritual family. There is unfortunately no indication as to the identity of Joan's godparents, and although it was common for the chief godparent's name to be given to a child, this does not seem to have been the case for Joan and her brothers. Her elder brother Edmund was clearly named after his father, and her younger brother John was probably named after Margaret's father, John Wake. It seems likely that Joan was named after her maternal grandmother, Joan Wake. Living in the royal household meant that Joan and John had access to chapels, with chaplains and regular services. Initially they were too young to attend services, but as they grew older a daily routine of worship would have become part of their lives, such as saying matins (the hours of the Virgin) just after they got up. It had become so much an accepted part of a noble child's day that in the 1370s the French knight Geoffrey de la Tour Landry instructed his daughters to begin their day in this way before they had breakfast.[9] The calendar was punctuated by feast days of saints and religious holidays and celebrations, and it was on those days that Joan was most likely to have attended the royal chapels, which would have been richly furnished and brightly decorated with pictures of religious scenes. Aids to worship, such as statues, crosses and books, were also lavishly decorated. Queen Isabella is known to have had chapel furnishings that included an alabaster statue of the Virgin and one of St Stephen, a number of embroideries and wall hangings.[10] Joan was no doubt given her own reader, probably a book of hours as this was the most popular devotional item and a traditional gift for a young girl learning to read. As Latin was not normally taught to women, even in the royal household, this would probably have been in French. Many ecclesiastics encouraged learning among women and religious texts might be combined with other material, such as the psalter given by Lord de Lisle to his daughters in 1339 which contained a number of scholarly schematic diagrams including the Tower of Theology of Master John of Metz.[11]

Attitudes towards religious observances varied widely. The Church regarded charity and almsgiving as an essential part of religious practice and Joan would have learned that noblewomen were expected to give food and money to the poor. There were some great ladies of the court who were renowned for their piety, such as Elizabeth de Burgh (an older half-cousin of Joan's through her father) and Marie de St Pol, Countess of Pembroke. Both ladies were wealthy widows when Joan was a child, and gave generously to religious foundations, each also founding a college at Cambridge. Some noblewomen showed a devotion to a particular saint and there were many shrines devoted to different saints in England, such as the site to Our Lady at Walsingham, which were visited on pilgrimage. However, those closest to Joan did not show any marked inclination towards piety. Her mother, Margaret, does not seem to have been deeply interested. Not only did she not make a chantry foundation for her husband, but there is no indication that she ever went on pilgrimage or made any significant donation to one of the many religious foundations, in contrast to her brother Thomas Wake. Edward III and his queen were naturally important religious patrons but appear to have been conventional and conformist in their religious practices, and although there has been a suggestion that Philippa shared her eldest son's later interest in the Trinity she does not seem to have made any major benefactions.[12]

Apart from religious works, such as the lives of saints, what sort of books would Joan have read? This is indicated from the literature popular among the aristocracy at the time. Courtly and historical romances were widely circulated, with the most popular subject matter being the tales of King Arthur and his knights of the Round Table, Charlemagne and his paladins, the classical histories of ancient Greece and Rome, the tales of Troy and Thebes, Alexander and Caesar. All of these tales were among the collection of books Queen Isabella is known to have had. In romantic stories the heroes were given the qualities associated with good knighthood: prowess in arms, bravery, loyalty, generosity and courtesy. There was a direct link between Christian belief and chivalry, with knights upholding justice, defending the Church, protecting the weak and the poor. It was an honour to aid and defend women, with love portrayed as an emotion which rewarded while sharpening and refining the knight's honourable ambitions. The values expounded in these chivalrous tales were reflected in the life around Joan, with tournaments as an obvious visual display. Tournaments acted as social gatherings for the elite as well as training grounds for young knights, and bestowed prestige and prizes on the successful contenders. In the tournaments women supplied the support, the appreciative audience, the decoration – and possibly the prize, as wearing a token of an admiring lady was a usual and popular practice.

Joan grew up in an environment that encouraged and endorsed chivalry as well as the majesty of the Crown. As Edward III gained in confidence he gathered the nobility around him and set the style for his court. He started to behave in such a way as to reflect his ideas for the splendour and grandeur of monarchy. Although dress was not extravagant in the first years of Edward III's reign, the king's enjoyment of fine clothing was apparent early on.[13] He gave Philippa several robes to wear for her churching after Prince Edward's birth in July 1330: one of violet velvet embroidered with gold squirrels, one of cloth of gold faced with miniver fur and a robe of silk and gold to wear in evening.[14] The reading of chivalric romances such as the Arthurian legend, common among the nobility, was reflected in the plentiful royal library.[15] Edward III fostered this, deliberately encouraging a chivalric ethos in his court to help to unite the nobility and create camaraderie among them. Chivalric ideas permeated his court from 1330 onwards. In 1333, for example, Philippa gave Edward III a silver and enamelled cup decorated with figures from Charlemagne and the court of King Arthur stories as a New Year gift.[16] Tournaments, watched by the court, such as the Cheapside tournament held in 1331, increased in number. In the 1340s Edward III was to give his ideas their apotheosis with his creation first of a round table for up to three hundred knights at Windsor in 1344, then in 1348 by setting up the Order of the Garter. All the noble, and royal, children were exposed to this atmosphere, with the boys expected to acquire knightly attributes, and the girls to provide a suitable supporting role, and their role models were the king and queen. It is no coincidence that all of Joan's male playmates were to become renowned knights.

Queen Philippa was devoted to Edward III and followed him whenever she could, taking her children with her.[17] It is therefore probable that in joining the royal nursery Joan experienced an itinerant lifestyle as a child, staying with the queen's household when it accompanied the king on his journeys. In the early 1330s the king remained mainly in and around London, staying in different royal residences: the palace at Westminster, the royal apartments in the Tower, Windsor, Havering, Eltham and Sheen. In September 1331 the household was based at Westminster, while the king and queen attended the jousts held at Smithfield arranged by Montague. By April 1332 the queen was at Woodstock, one of her favourite palaces (Havering was another), some distance outside London but within easy reach should she need to return. Woodstock had particular associations for Joan as it was her father's birthplace, was comfortable without being elaborately grand and had a park built by Henry I surrounded by a stone wall, turned into a menagerie for the amusement of the royal family which was being maintained for wild animals in 1334.[18] In 1334 the prince is recorded as staying in the Tower (where Princess Joan had been born a year earlier) with his sisters and Elizabeth Saint Omer, receiving gifts from the City of London, and in July 1335 they were at Peterborough Abbey and then at Nottingham Castle.[19] Joan and John probably accompanied their royal cousins on each of these trips, and may have been with the queen at Hatfield in Yorkshire in 1336 when she gave birth to another son, William. Given complete protection in a stable and secure environment, those early years may have been happy ones for Joan and John.

4

A Clandestine Marriage
1338–1340

The most secret love is the most joyful, lasting and loyal.

Geoffrey de Charny

In the spring of 1340, when Joan was twelve, she married a household knight, Sir Thomas Holand. This was an extraordinary match, not so much because of the difference in rank between Joan and Thomas but because she married him in secret without the knowledge or consent of her family or her guardians. How did this clandestine marriage come about? Joan would have known at an early age that she would be expected to marry, and that her marriage would be arranged for her. It was customary for children of noble families to enter into marital alliances carefully planned by their parents. Negotiations for marriages often started when the children were very young (although betrothals were not considered binding by the Church until the age of puberty, which for girls was twelve and for boys fourteen). Marital proposals were invariably for political or financial reasons rather than based on personal inclination. Joan's uncle, the Earl of Norfolk, for example, had secured a political affiliation when he agreed to his son and heir marrying Roger Mortimer's daughter in 1329, while marrying his daughter Margaret to his ward John Segrave was for purely financial reasons. In the case of royal children it was taken for granted that their marriages represented a diplomatic opportunity to foster alliances. Edward III's matrimonial plans for his own children had started almost as soon as Prince Edward was a year old. The king considered Joan and John's marriages to be his responsibility and felt that as they had royal blood they should make suitably prestigious matches. In March 1334 the Archbishop of Canterbury, Sir William Clinton, Geoffrey Scrope and John Shoreditch were ordered to treat for a marriage for John with the daughter of 'some French noble', while negotiating a match between Edward III's younger brother John, Earl of Cornwall, with Mary, daughter of the Count of Blois.[1] Although this particular proposal for Joan's brother did not come to fruition, John did later make an equivalent match, and Joan could expect to be similarly provided for. Yet instead, Joan made her own personal choice, and married without the king's consent.

In July 1338, when Joan was ten years old, she left England for Antwerp, with Princesses Isabella and Joan, in the company of the king and queen. The royal entourage set sail from Orwell in Sussex. Going on board ship, sailing with the fleet, with the colourful flags displaying the royal arms and those of the king's favourite saints (St George, St Edward and St Edmund) must have been an exciting adventure for the princesses and their cousin.[2] Joan was parted from her mother and brother, who remained in England, with Margaret looking after the family estates, while John stayed with Prince Edward. The eight-year-old prince was appointed guardian of the realm in his father's absence and was assisted in his duties by members of his council, the earls of Huntingdon, Arundel and Ralph Neville.[3] The purpose of the trip was Edward III's need to secure allies as part of his plan to launch his campaign against France to settle the long running dispute over sovereignty in Aquitaine. The obvious place to look for allies was in the Low Countries. The count of Hainault was his father-in-law, and the export of English wool had built up close trading links with a number of important cloth weaving towns in Flanders. Edward had already tried to obtain support by sending an embassy to the Low Countries a year earlier, in May 1337, promising economic benefits such as trading concessions, but when this was unsuccessful he decided he needed to go in person. Philippa's presence would remind her Hainault relations of their dynastic connection to the English throne, while those of his daughters and Joan would suggest the potential for securing alliances by marriage.

Edward III had another object in mind: his claim to the French throne. When Charles IV of France died in 1328 the succession to the French throne was in dispute. Edward's mother, Queen Isabella, was Charles IV's only sister, making him the closest surviving male relation. However, the French preferred the claim of Philip of Valois, Charles IV's uncle. When Edward seized power from his mother in 1330, he had initially tried to use his grandfather's example of marriage alliances to resolve Anglo-French relations, rather than pursue his claim. However, his negotiations for Prince Edward to marry Philip VI's daughter, and for Princess Joan to marry the French king's son, came to nothing, while Philip took advantage of Edward's war with Scotland to strengthen the French position in Aquitaine, declaring the duchy confiscate to the French crown in May 1337.[4] Edward's response was to assert his own claim to the French crown. Once in Antwerp Edward left the queen and her household, and travelled down the Rhine to drum up support among his allies, returning in November 1338 to join Philippa when she gave birth to their second son, Lionel. Campaigning against the French started in the autumn of 1339, and in January 1340 Edward formally assumed the title of King of

France. In February 1340 he returned to England, to persuade Parliament to give him financial support, but he was forced to leave Philippa behind in Antwerp, with his friend William Montague (created Earl of Salisbury in 1337), and the Earl of Derby, as pledges for payments of his debts. The queen was pregnant again, and in March 1340 gave birth to a third son, John, in Ghent, possibly at the abbey of St Bavo.[5]

By March 1340 Joan had been away from England for nearly two years, and she had probably not seen her mother or her brother in all that time. Lady Saint Omer had presumably accompanied the princesses, and it is likely that Catherine Montague had accompanied her husband William with the royal party. Philippa would have relied on both women to take charge of her daughters and Joan. Edward III had not forgotten Joan's presence, with her value as a potential matrimonial bargaining counter. Anxious to secure the loyalty and support of his subjects in the duchy, and preoccupied with the necessity to raise money to pay his allies, a marriage alliance was an obvious means at his disposal, and Joan a suitably attractive prospect, with her royal kinship. Bernard, Lord of Albret, the head of a leading and powerful Gascon family, had been persuaded to support the English cause in the autumn of 1339, having formerly been an ally of the French Crown. He brought much-needed cash and many friends and allies, and it clearly behoved Edward to offer him inducements to keep him on his side.[6] In April 1340 the king authorised Oliver Ingham, his seneschal in Gascony, to negotiate a marriage between Joan and Armand d'Albret, Bernard's eldest son.[7] The clerk recording the details muddled the names and cited Joan as 'Margaretam filiam, clarae memoriae, Edmundi Comitis Kantiae', clearly confusing Joan's name with that of her mother. However, the negotiations were never concluded (although the hoped for alliance with the d'Albrets remained high on the king's agenda, as he considered it of sufficient importance to propose his eldest daughter Isabella as a bride for the d'Albret heir in 1351).[8]

Joan had other ideas about her own future. She was now twelve, and the arrangements for her supervision were probably considerably laxer than they would have been in England. There was an atmosphere of impermanence, as it was unclear from the start how long the queen would remain abroad. The comings and goings of the king and his retinue, with the constant round of diplomatic initiatives with one after another potential ally, and the talk of war with France, created an element of insecurity. The age gap between Joan and the princesses (Joan was three years older than Princess Isabella, and five years older than Princess Joan) was more noticeable now that Joan was entering her teens, and she may have spent less time with them. Although Joan would not have been consulted, it is possible that she was aware of the discussions regarding her own future, and realised that if she married d'Albret it was likely that she would stay in France and might never see her mother or her brother again. At twelve she would have been showing signs of the great beauty for which she would become renowned. This was a family characteristic, and one certainly inherited from her father's side of the family; her grandfather, Edward I, was considered a handsome man, and her uncle, Edward II, was described as tall, strong, golden-haired and good-looking. The same striking good looks and height were attributes shared by Edward III (Joan's cousin) and his sons.[9] Alone, vulnerable and pretty, it is not remarkable that Joan attracted the attention of an admirer.

Joan's admirer was one of the king's household knights, Sir Thomas Holand, the second son of a Lancastrian knight, a young man in his early twenties. Surprisingly, no one among the royal household appears to have noticed his attentions to the young Joan. Thomas' wooing was ardent, and Joan fell headlong in love. In March or April 1340 Thomas persuaded her to marry him in secret, without the knowledge of any of her family or anyone in the royal household.[10] According to Thomas Holand's later testimony, he and Joan exchanged marriage vows in the presence of witnesses, and consummated the marriage.[11] Accomplishing this necessarily meant that Joan would have been absent from the royal household for a period of time, but her absence can only have been very brief – a matter of hours rather than days – as it was not remarked on when she returned to the household afterwards and resumed her place. Joan does not appear to have confided in anyone, either before or after the marriage. The fact that Joan placed her trust in a young man she hardly knew, rather than turn to any of those closest to her (it is hard to believe that a girl of her age would have been able to resist telling someone very close to her) suggests that Thomas was an extremely charming and plausible young man, who was able to completely captivate Joan and persuade her to enter into a clandestine marriage which she knew would be frowned on by her guardians. Perhaps for Joan theirs was a truly romantic love affair, resembling some of the stories she would have read.

Proof of the marriage comes from the proceedings taken eight years later by Thomas Holand in the papal courts when he needed to establish its legality beyond doubt. The papal court considered the evidence for the marriage, examining the witnesses and taking statements from both Thomas Holand and Joan herself. The outcome of their deliberations was a pronouncement by Pope Clement VI in November 1349 confirming the validity of the marriage.[12] Although no exact date for the marriage is given in the transcript of the proceedings, on 3 May 1348 the Pope wrote to the Archbishop of Canterbury and the bishops of London and Norwich about Thomas Holand's petition and in his letter made reference to the marriage having taken place 'upwards of eight years ago', indicating the spring of 1340.[13] The date can be confidently narrowed to March or April by Thomas Holand's duties. He was on the king's payroll between July 1338 and November 1339, returning to the royal household in Ghent with the other household knights, and then resumed active duties in the early summer of 1340, taking part in the naval engagement at Sluys on

24 June 1340, after which he remained with the army, going to France and taking part in the Siege of Tournai.[14] His marriage to Joan would have taken place in the spring of 1340, in Edward III's absence (the king returned to England on 21 February 1340) and around the time the queen was confined, giving birth to John of Gaunt in March 1340.

Joan's secret marriage to Thomas Holand was extraordinary, and poses many questions. How could a girl of her age, presumably still closely supervised, mainly in the company of the princesses and Lady Saint Omer, if not the Countess of Salisbury as well, manage to escape the attention of all these people, form a relationship of such strength and then marry without the knowledge, let alone the permission, of any of those closest to her? Why did Joan agree to it? At twelve years old, Joan would have understood the importance and significance of entering into marriage, and been well aware of what was expected of her by her family and her guardians. Why the secrecy? There is no obvious explanation for this. Thomas Holand could, and should, have wooed her openly, presented his suit and obtained her guardians' permission. Joan's birth made her a very attractive matrimonial prize, and if her nine-year-old brother John predeceased her – not an entirely unlikely possibility – then she would become an extremely wealthy heiress as well. Admittedly, Thomas Holand would not have been regarded as a good match for Joan, but he was not ineligible. He was the second son of a Lancastrian knight and born into the ranks of the gentry. It was not unknown for men and women of rank to marry a social inferior, even those of royal blood. There were precedents in Joan's own family. Both her father and her uncle, Thomas Brotherton, had married women of considerably lower social status than themselves, while her uncle Thomas Wake had done the opposite when he married Blanche of Lancaster. Blanche was the king's cousin, and had married Thomas when they were both underage, without Edward II's approval.[15] But they had not done so in secret. The clandestine nature of Joan's marriage made it extremely unusual.

As to how Joan could have escaped the notice of her elders and formed the relationship in the first place, there can be no doubt that she was unquestionably inadequately chaperoned while she was in Ghent, despite being with the queen's household. Quite simply, it should not have been possible for Thomas Holand to have been able to spirit Joan away and marry her in secret. His attentions should have been noted, and remarked on, his intentions questioned and either discouraged or formally acknowledged. At twelve, Joan was far too young to have had any part in making the arrangements for her marriage to Thomas Holand; the initiative was clearly his. The possibility that Joan was abducted cannot be discounted. This was a rare but not unknown occurrence among the nobility, when the attraction of an heiress could outweigh the risks involved. Joan's older cousin, Elizabeth de Burgh, had been abducted by Theobald de Verdun in 1326, and Margaret Audeley, another well-born young lady, by Ralph Stafford in 1334.[16] Both were heiresses, and married their abductors, having their marriages subsequently recognised by the king and the rest of noble society. However, if Thomas Holand did abduct Joan, he managed the affair extremely well. Not only was her absence unnoticed, but he was able to secure Joan's full co-operation, with her consent to their marriage, as witnesses later testified, and when she returned to the royal household she was sufficiently persuaded by her husband to keep their secret.[17]

Joan was obviously greatly attracted to Thomas Holand, and quite literally, perhaps, swept off her feet. He was more than ten years her senior, and although his career was still in its infancy he was already starting to gain a reputation as a brave and talented knight. The chroniclers all describe him with approval, Froissart and Jean le Bel as 'un gentil chevalier', the chronicle of Meaux Abbey as a 'miles strenuus' and Chandos Herald as 'le bon Thomas de Holand qui en huy eust proesce grand'.[18] He may have been good-looking but it is impossible to know. By 1346 he had lost an eye, presumably an injury sustained while on campaign, and it seems likely that this occurred sometime after he met Joan.[19] Nevertheless, however attractive he may have been, Joan was well aware that she was not free to decide her own future and that her marriage was an important matter which would be decided for her by her guardians or her family. However, she was also very young and vulnerable, and Thomas' confidence and authority perhaps offered her a security she lacked. It is an indication of the strength of Thomas Holand's attractiveness and persuasiveness that he was able to overcome her scruples and induced her to agree to a course of action of which she knew her family would disapprove.

From Thomas Holand's point of view, marrying a girl of Joan's birth and age in secret was a hugely risky enterprise. He was, after all, employed by the king. Marrying the king's cousin, without Edward III's knowledge or permission, while Joan was under his protection, seems foolhardy. Thomas risked the king's disapproval, and possible dismissal from his service. It was hardly a well-judged career move. Then there was the question of the validity of the marriage. Clandestine marriages were discouraged by the Church, and extremely unusual for a girl of Joan's background. Canonical law was complex on these matters, especially where a child was involved. In theory, a marriage could be contracted in secrecy without witnesses and any formalities whatsoever, provided both parties had capacity and consented, either expressed in the present tense at the marriage ceremony (consent 'de praesenti'), or through the exchange of words of future consent ratified through subsequent sexual intercourse.[20] The Church considered that the age at which a couple had capacity and could give such consent was the age of puberty, i.e. twelve for a girl and fourteen for a boy. Although the Church allowed marriages for children from the age of seven, they could be dissolved if the marriage had not been consummated by the age of twelve. The danger in a clandestine marriage was that one of the parties could change their mind, or parents could intervene. In 1349, on the basis of testimony from Thomas Holand and Joan that they had voluntarily exchanged marriage vows in the presence of witnesses and consummated the marriage, the papal court recognised their marriage as a 'de praesenti' contract, but it was by no means a straightforward argument and the outcome had not been certain.[21] Thomas Holand is unlikely to have had any great understanding of Church law when he arranged his marriage in 1340, but he must have realised that it was quite likely that it would be challenged by Joan's family. If a challenge was mounted, even with witnesses testifying to Joan's consent, much would depend on Joan. Why did Thomas Holand take such a gamble, rather than present his suit openly and secure a legitimate match with Joan? He can only have done so because he knew that Joan's family would not accept him as a suitor, and the reason for this lay with his father.

Thomas Holand's father, Sir Robert Holand, had been a particular favourite of Thomas, Earl of Lancaster, and the earl's generosity and patronage had enabled him to dramatically improve his status. Robert inherited two or three manors and modest means; the earl's influence secured for him a wealthy bride, Maud la Zouche, and considerable other material advantages. He was able to build a castle at Melbourne in Derbyshire, with his friend and patron contributing the vast sum of £1,202 towards the building costs, and in 1311 he obtained permission to crenellate the castle, while the earl also built another house for him at Lancaster.[22] When Maud's father died in 1314 his estates were divided between his two daughters, with the largest share of the inheritance going to Maud. By 1321 Robert Holand possessed around twenty-five manors, and he was the most valued and trusted of Thomas of Lancaster's retinue. It would be difficult to exaggerate the extent of the material wealth Robert Holand had obtained through the earl's favour, or the depth of trust and friendship shown by the earl towards him. Robert Holand's loyalty to the earl seemed beyond question, and yet it was at this point that their relationship fell apart. In 1321 a fresh civil war erupted, provoked by Edward II's favouritism of the Despensers, with the opposition headed by Thomas of Lancaster. Matters came to a head with a confrontation between the king and the Lancastrian-led forces at Boroughbridge in 1322. The earl confidently summoned his close friend Robert Holand to bring additional support. At the last moment, and with no warning or explanation, Robert Holand failed to do so. His default precipitated Thomas of Lancaster's flight and his subsequent surrender to Edward II, followed by his execution.[23] Even in a period of civil war most of the nobility were shocked by the enormity of Robert Holand's betrayal of his friend and patron.

Robert Holand's betrayal of the Earl of Lancaster has never been explained. The author of the *Vita* suggests that loss of support for the earl led directly to Robert's desertion.[24] One historian has suggested that Robert Holand was persuaded to support the king because Edward II held one of his children hostage, but this is unsupported by evidence.[25] Certainly Robert Holand did not benefit from deserting his friend. After his victory at Boroughbridge, Edward II, far from rewarding Robert Holand, imprisoned him for five years and confiscated his lands. Robert was not released until after Edward II was deposed, and his estates were then restored to him in December 1327 by Isabella and Mortimer, despite the protests of Henry of Lancaster, Thomas' brother and heir.[26] The Lancastrians did not forget or forgive Robert Holand for his treachery at Boroughbridge, and in October 1328, when he was probably on his way to visit Queen Isabella, Robert Holand was murdered by Lancastrian supporters at Borehamwood in Hertfordshire. However, Robert Holand's death barely assuaged the strong feelings his betrayal had aroused, and even eighteen years later Henry of Lancaster sought to protect John Tebbe, one of the men who had been responsible for Robert Holand's murder.[27] Whatever the cause of Robert Holand's desertion of Thomas of Lancaster, there is no doubt of the extreme Lancastrian antipathy towards him as a result and this almost certainly extended towards his family.

Robert and Maud had seven children: Robert (born in 1314), Thomas, Alan, Otto, Isabella, Matilda and Margaret.[28] Their second son, Thomas, was in all likelihood born in 1316 and probably named in honour of Thomas of Lancaster. It is likely that the earl stood as his godfather, as Robert Holand's friendship with the earl was then at its height. For the first few years of Thomas Holand's life the family basked in the favour shown to their father by Thomas of Lancaster. All this changed after Boroughbridge. Maud's own inheritance was confiscated along with her husband's estates, leaving her in considerable difficulties. By March 1327 Edward II belatedly recognised her problems and agreed to give her a small annuity of £60 'for the support of herself and her children until other provision be made for them'.[29] Maud Holand was left to fight her own battles. She was her husband's executor, and like Joan's mother, Margaret, showed a similar determination and ability in restoring the family fortunes after Robert's death, although she was forced to borrow heavily to do so. Maud Holand was also successful in obtaining an annuity for Thomas of £26 in December 1329.[30]

Somehow Maud Holand arranged for her sons to receive training as knights, as all four are known to have been knighted and fought for Edward III on campaign in France. This was quite an achievement, as the vilification of Robert Holand after Boroughbridge meant few would have welcomed a young man bearing the Holand name as a protégé, with the attendant affront this would cause to Henry of Lancaster.[31] According to the *Brut* chronicler Robert Holand was favoured by Queen Isabella and Mortimer, and the likelihood is that Maud appealed to Isabella after

Robert's murder, resulting in the four Holand boys being taken into the young king's household to train as knights. This would have been in 1328 or 1329, when Thomas would have been around twelve or thirteen. Their sister Isabella chose her own route, and by 1331 was living openly as the mistress of John Warenne, Earl of Surrey, but there is no evidence that her brothers benefited from this liaison.[32] In the early 1330s the successive campaigns in Scotland gave Thomas Holand a chance to prove his worth, and by the time he was twenty-one he had been knighted, presumably by Edward III, and probably while serving in Scotland. In 1337 he is mentioned by Froissart as one of a group of knights accompanying Robert d'Artois' expeditionary force which sailed from Southampton to Bordeaux, and in February 1338 he received a grant and a New Year bounty of £10 from the Crown for 'good service in Scotland and elsewhere'.[33]

It is impossible to know when Thomas Holand first met Joan. As a member of the king's retinue he may well have been aware of her existence from the time that she entered the queen's household in 1330, but it is obviously unlikely that he would have had anything to do with her while she was a small child. When Edward III sailed for Flanders on 16 July 1338 Thomas and his brother Otto were among his retinue. Thomas was paid for serving in Flanders for 483 days from 22 July 1338 to 16 November 1339 and received 4 marks for sets of robes in winter and summer.[34] Edward III was satisfied with his services and in February 1339 made him the handsome gift of granting him permission to lade forty sacks of wool in the port of London without paying customs duty.[35] In September 1339 Thomas was in Brabant fighting alongside William Montague, Earl of Salisbury, Sir Walter Mauny and Sir John Chandos, and was part of the embassy to the Count of Hainault at Valenciennes, where he witnessed a grant by Sir Walter Mauny with the earls of Salisbury and Northampton on 14 September.[36] By January 1340 Thomas was back in Ghent with the royal household. On 21 February Edward III returned to England to raise money and support, leaving the queen and his daughters behind. The king took only a handful of his household knights with him, and Thomas Holand was one of those left behind in Ghent. It seems probable that it was then that Thomas Holand first really noticed Joan.

In January 1340 Thomas Holand was about twenty-four years old. Whereas his older brother Robert had inherited the family estates their mother had carefully regained, as a second son Thomas' career choice of becoming a household knight had been forced upon him. Apart from a small annuity of £26 which his mother had secured for him in December 1329 he was dependant on what he could earn.[37] As a knight he was paid, but he had to pay for his own horses and equipment, and these were expensive. To take part in a campaign a knight needed several horses, and a considerable quantity of clothing: a quilted tunic or gambeson;

a short-sleeved hauberk or mail tunic, and over this a habergeon of soft material; a tight, short surcoat bearing his arms (a jupon); a metal breastplate, with plate on his arms, shoulders and legs; a sword belt; a heavy plate helmet with a visor, for battle; perhaps a fluted bascinet; and at least one page to look after and carry all this equipment. Acquiring all of this was costly. In 1338 his mother and older brother Robert had borrowed £368 13s from Prince Edward, probably to cover the cost of Thomas and Otto's campaign equipment.[38] It has been suggested that to support himself a knight needed an annual income in the region of £40, and as a commander would be expected to recruit sufficient soldiers of an adequate standard to form a retinue.[39] In wartime on campaign the king paid an earl a daily rate of 6s 4d, and a banneret 4s a day; knights such as Thomas and Otto Holand could only expect a daily wage of 2s.[40] Luckily for Thomas he proved naturally able militarily, and the lifestyle suited him. As one of the king's knights he could expect to continue in that employment and in wartime he could reasonably expect to gain promotion through merit, and to benefit financially from the profits of ransom and booty in times of war, but in 1340 he had no means of knowing how many opportunities might come his way in the future. Mixing with men like the Earl of Salisbury in the course of his duties, Thomas was acutely aware of the considerable gulf between them and there is no doubt that he was an extremely ambitious young man. His father's reputation was a handicap which might slow his advancement despite his abilities. The fact that he was not already married suggests that he had found it difficult to secure a legitimate advantageous marriage, and the stigma of the Holand name may well have been the bar. His younger brother Otto, similarly placed, never married.

So Thomas probably had an eye for any chance that came his way, and Joan must have seemed like a heaven-sent opportunity. She was young, susceptible, attractive and available, but most importantly of all she had royal blood, and marriage to her would secure a connection to the king and queen that would immeasurably improve his standing, and that of his family. It is possible that Thomas was genuinely attracted to her, and it may even have started as an innocent dalliance. There could be no advantage to Thomas in his romance with Joan unless he was able to marry her with formal approval and support, and he knew that his suit would not be looked on with favour by Joan's mother and aunt and uncle. Thomas and Blanche Wake were firm Lancastrians, and extremely unlikely to approve of an alliance between their niece (who might one day inherit the Wake lands) and the son of the man who had deserted Blanche's uncle, Thomas of Lancaster. Thomas Holand needed the king's support.

Timing was the crucial element which determined Thomas Holand on his fateful course of action in arranging the clandestine marriage. With Edward III absent in England, Thomas had to await his return in order to present his suit. He could hardly approach the queen, as Philippa was in an advanced state of pregnancy and gave birth to John of Gaunt in March 1340. Probably Thomas discovered the plans for Joan's betrothal to d'Albret. A different sort of man would at that point have given up on the scheme to marry Joan, deterred by the combination of circumstances which effectively put her out of his reach. But this was not Thomas Holand's character. He was not only ambitious, but bold and forceful, with confidence and initiative, qualities that would later serve him well in his military career. In the spring of 1340 they induced him to take an audacious gamble. The stakes were high and to him the risk was worth taking. Acting quickly, Thomas persuaded Joan to marry him in secret, made the necessary arrangements, and carried them out. He was prepared to face the possible disapproval of the king, confident that he would be able to obtain Edward III's retrospective consent and support, anticipating that the king would excuse his unorthodox behaviour and approve the marriage, even in the face of opposition from Joan's family. Thomas appreciated that this might take time, and so persuaded Joan to keep their relationship a secret, no doubt assuring her that he would sort it all out.

Thomas was not foolish in gambling that he would be able to persuade Edward III to support him. Unorthodox marriages were not unknown and certainly not unacceptable. Edward III's attitude towards marriage among the nobility showed a touch of ambivalence. After all, he had effectively rewarded Ralph Stafford's effrontery in carrying Margaret Audeley off in 1334 by recognising the marriage thus enabling Stafford to obtain her inheritance of a third of the Gloucester estates, worth an annual income of over £2,000 (and in 1351 Edward III went even further by granting Ralph an earldom). Thomas Holand might not have been an ideal husband for Joan, but if the king could be persuaded to accept their marriage, royal support would ensure that her family would recognise it. Edward III was known to applaud and reward initiative on the part of his knights and he needed and wanted knights with ambition, enterprise and resourcefulness. Men like Sir Walter Mauny and Sir John Chandos were being advanced rapidly in the king's service for displaying just such qualities, and Edward III's closest entourage comprised men such as William Montague whose boldness and daring had secured his freedom from the rule of Roger Mortimer. The contemporary taste in literature reflected a willingness to accept unconventional matches, as exemplified in the tale of *Tristan and Isolde*, and the abduction of Helen by Paris. Writers such as Ghillebert de Lannoy had advised that knights could acquire riches in three honourable ways: by service at court, in war, and by making a good marriage. Thomas Holand might even have taken encouragement from the advice of an older French contemporary, Geoffrey de Charny, who wrote in his book, *Le Livre de chevalrie*, that 'the most secret love is the most joyful, lasting and loyal'.[41] Spiriting Joan away and marrying her in secret was daring and chancy, but given the right opportunity and a mellow mood on the part of the king he would probably have succeeded.

Unfortunately for Thomas' plans circumstances prevented him from presenting his case to the king and obtaining that vital approval. Having returned Joan to the royal household, asking her to keep their secret, Thomas waited for his chance to get the king's ear. But when he returned from England Edward III was completely preoccupied with preparations for his campaign against France, and the mood at court was tense and nervous. Thomas hesitated, perhaps fearing that he might annoy the king, and failed to present his case, fatally losing his opportunity. Instead, he was swept up in the new venture, and resumed active military service, taking part in the naval battle held off the coast at Sluys on the mouth of the River Zwyn on 24 June 1340. Afterwards he stayed with the army as it invaded France, and took part in the siege at Tournai. When the siege ended unsuccessfully in September, Thomas was released from his military duties. This, surely, was the moment for him to seek his audience with Edward III, present his suit and secure royal approval for his marriage to Joan. But it was not a propitious time for an impecunious suitor to present himself to the king. The failed campaign had left Edward III greatly in debt and in considerable embarrassment, and he was probably in a bitter mood. The king was not even able to pay his daily living expenses in Ghent and found it difficult to get credit.[42] Thomas would not have known the extent of the king's difficulties, but he would have had no difficulty in deciding that the king's mood was not right for his approach. Thomas reasoned that he could afford to delay, and determined that he needed to distinguish himself further before declaring himself. Although the hostilities with France had temporarily ceased, another opportunity offered. In August 1340 Pope Benedict XII had proclaimed a Crusade against the Tartars, who had invaded from Asia and threatened the Teutonic knights. From France and England many ambitious and adventurous young knights responded to the Pope's call and set off for Prussia on crusade. In the autumn of 1340 Thomas obtained the king's warrant to travel abroad and embarked, getting his permission extended for a further six months in January 1341.[43] Probably he saw Joan before he left and explained his intentions, reassuring her that he would claim her on his return, but nevertheless, after his whirlwind courtship and clandestine marriage, abandoning his young bride to embark on crusade seems extraordinarily callous behaviour even for such an ambitious and bold young man. Joan was left on her own in the queen's household, harbouring her secret.

5

A Bigamous Marriage
1341–1349

The most beautiful lady in all the kingdom of England and the most loved.

Froissart

In agreeing to marry Thomas without the knowledge or consent of the king and queen or her family, Joan had effectively disobeyed them. The king had already made it clear that he considered her marriage to be within his gift as her guardian, as the d'Albret proposal showed. When this proposal was abandoned, another match would be arranged for her, if not by the king as a means of securing a diplomatic alliance, then certainly a match to advantage her family. For Joan the crucial question was therefore whether her guardians, and her mother and uncle, Thomas Wake, would accept her marriage when they were told about it. They would not be happy with her choice, but if the king approved it then her family would also. Did Joan understand the vulnerability of her marriage with Thomas? The clandestine nature of the marriage was not a bar to its validity, nor the fact that she did not have the consent of her family. Although the Church preferred and encouraged marriages to be public, the Fourth Lateran Council in 1215 having laid down specific procedures to be followed for marriages, nevertheless the only requirement in canon law for a valid marriage was that it was made with free consent by both parties who were of an age to fully understand what they were doing, and could consummate the union.[1] However, the secrecy, Joan's age and the issue of consent made it vulnerable, and open to challenge. If Joan's family did not approve of her choice, and she was persuaded that she had not given her consent, they could apply to the ecclesiastical courts for an annulment on the grounds that she was coerced. Unfortunately for Joan, not only did her family not approve her marriage but they did not even recognise it. Within a few months of her return to England, in January or February 1341, Joan was forced into an arranged marriage with William Montague, the son of the Earl of Salisbury.[2] Now married secretly to Thomas Holand and openly to William Montague, inevitably, Joan's bigamous status became a problem. Remarkably, this was not resolved until the pronouncement of the papal court in favour of Thomas in November 1349. This was a completely unsatisfactory state of affairs for all concerned, and left Joan's marital status effectively in limbo for eight years. How did this debacle come about?

After Thomas Holand left Joan in the early summer of 1340 she had no means of knowing when she would see him again. It is evident that Joan did not tell anyone about the marriage at this stage. She must have known that the king and queen and her family would disapprove of her marriage, and she was probably fearful of the consequences when they were told. Several of the king's knights had gone on the Prussian Crusade and reports of the expedition and their exploits would be sent to the king and circulated among his household. For Joan this was presumably the only means of getting news of Thomas. With no means of contacting her husband or of joining him, the only option open to her was to remain with the royal family in Ghent. On 25 September 1340 Edward III reluctantly agreed a truce with Philip VI at Espléchin, near Tournai. Rejoining Philippa in Ghent at the end of September, Edward III nevertheless kept up appearances, and a tournament was held to celebrate his return, attended by the princes of the coalition. The campaign over, in November 1340 the royal party returned to England.

Once back in England Joan was reunited with her mother and brother. They had been apart for two and a half years, and had much to catch up on. Joan was burdened with the secret of her marriage, and may have welcomed the prospect of a sympathetic ear. Thomas was many miles away, and Joan did not know when she would see him again. But it was not destined to be a happy homecoming for Joan. Almost immediately she was told by her mother that a marriage had been agreed for her with her erstwhile playmate William Montague, the son and heir of the Earl of Salisbury. Joan's reaction can only be imagined. Her first instinct would have been to contact Thomas, but this was impossible because of the distance between them. Joan had no alternative but to tell her mother about her marriage. Margaret, delighted to have agreed such a promising match for her daughter, could only have been horrified. Unfortunately, she was also quite unsympathetic. Either she did not believe her daughter, perhaps wondering if Joan was fabricating an implausible excuse to prevent an unwanted match, or she doubted the validity of the marriage itself. Margaret hurriedly consulted her brother, Thomas Wake, and they decided that the marriage to William Montague should go ahead regardless, and on 21 January 1341 they concluded the arrangements with the Earl of Salisbury, agreeing a dowry sum of £3,000.[3] Joan protested, but she was helpless. It does not appear that anyone had any sympathy for Joan in her dilemma, and it is understandable that she was unable to withstand the pressure upon her. Possibly her family persuaded her that her marriage to Thomas Holand was invalid, but whatever arguments were used, in the end she capitulated.[4] Sometime towards the end of January or early February 1341 Joan and William were married.

The match between Joan and William Montague was exactly the sort of marriage that Joan might have expected to make had circumstances been different. Unlike her match with Thomas Holand, the wedding to William was publicly celebrated, and had the full approval of the king. On 10 February the Earl of Salisbury was given permission by the king to grant the castle, manor and lordship of Mold in North Wales to his son William and 'his wife Joan', together with the reversion of the manor of Marshwood in Dorset.[5] On 10 March the Earl of Salisbury proudly confirmed the grant to his son in front of his brother Edward Montague, Joan's uncle Thomas Wake, the Bishop of Ely and the earls of Arundel, Devon and Huntingdon.[6] The initiative for the marriage had come from the Earl of Salisbury rather than from Joan's mother or uncle. William Montague, Earl of Salisbury, was a close friend of Edward III. His loyalty and support for the king had brought him the earldom in 1337, as well as considerable wealth. The earl had a modest background. His grandfather had been the first knight in the family, and his father had been steward of the royal household under Edward II. Salisbury himself had started as a yeoman, before being knighted in 1325.[7] After leading the Nottingham Castle coup in 1330 his career had soared, and he used his position to his family's advantage. In 1337, within days of being created earl, Salisbury's brother Simon became Bishop of Ely through Edward III's influence, and by 1338 Salisbury's youngest brother, Edward, had married Joan's cousin, Alice Brotherton, daughter and co-heiress of the Earl of Norfolk.[8] Salisbury's efforts to secure advantageous marriages for his own children were similarly impressive. In 1335 he had reached agreement for the marriage of his daughter Agnes to John, heir to Lord Grey of Ruthin, and in 1336 he purchased the wardship and marriage of Roger Mortimer, Earl of March, so securing a husband for his daughter Philippa.[9] In March 1340, high in the king's esteem, Salisbury was granted the manor of Merton in Somerset, given permission to found Bisham Priory and obtained endorsement for his negotiations for the marriage of his daughter Elizabeth to Hugh Despenser, a union which would end a family feud (although it required a papal dispensation in 1341 to secure it).[10] During the winter of 1340, while negotiating with the Countess of Kent and Thomas Wake to obtain Joan as a bride for his eldest son William, Salisbury was also securing the marriage of his younger son, John, to an heiress, Margaret, daughter of Thomas of Monthermer.[11]

Unlike most of the other brides secured by Salisbury for his family, Joan was not an heiress. Her attraction lay in her royal blood. Salisbury would have preferred wealth and lineage, and had originally set his sights on Joan's cousin Alice for his heir. In February 1333, when his son William was barely five years old, and four years before Salisbury received his earldom, he had agreed a marriage contract with Joan's uncle Thomas Brotherton, Earl of Norfolk. Edward III gave his approval. Norfolk and Salisbury agreed a dowry of £1,300, and Norfolk was to assign estates in Ireland and Berkshire to Salisbury which would revert to young William and Alice if Salisbury died within fifteen years.[12] When Norfolk's son died, leaving Alice and her sister Margaret as joint heiresses, Salisbury appears to have had second thoughts about the arrangement. He had plenty of time to find another bride for his son, and meanwhile he had an opportunity to provide his younger brother Edward with an heiress. Salisbury persuaded Norfolk to agree to Alice marrying Edward instead. When Norfolk died in 1338 Edward Montague became a wealthy man through Alice's inheritance. For Salisbury, the lure of linking himself to the royal family by marriage remained strong, and when the king's plans for Joan with d'Albret came to nothing, it must have seemed too good an opportunity to miss. His son William was the same age as Joan and they had spent time together as children. Salisbury would have known Margaret fairly well from his regular contact with the royal household, and his duties at Woodstock Palace. His approach to the Countess of Kent and Thomas Wake on returning to England was swift, and an agreement easily arranged. They welcomed the proposal. Salisbury was powerful at court, with money, power and influence, and a marriage to his heir would secure Joan's future and benefit the rest of her family.

Yet the fact remains that Joan's marriage to William Montague in 1341 was bigamous, and the intriguing question is the extent to which the families concerned were aware of the Holand marriage and complicit in ignoring it. It can of course only be speculative to suggest that the Earl of Salisbury was made aware of the Holand marriage, but it is a reasonable conjecture in the circumstances. It is entirely credible that Margaret and Thomas Wake had doubts about the validity of Joan's marriage to Thomas Holand. As it had been conducted in secret no one else knew about it, and with Thomas abroad they only had Joan's version of what had happened. But they could not afford to ignore what Joan told them, and they would have wanted to check what had actually taken place. Immediately that presented a problem, as no one in the royal household knew anything about it, and Holand was not available to question. Assuming the marriage was valid, it could be set aside on the grounds that Joan had not consented to it. However, this would take time as it would require an application to the ecclesiastical courts, and success could not be guaranteed, as the crucial factor would be Joan's willingness to repudiate it. Another possibility that would not have been overlooked was the very real chance that Thomas Holand might not return. He had gone to fight, and he would not be the first young knight to die on crusade. Nevertheless, it is most unlikely that Margaret and Thomas Wake deliberately deceived the Earl of Salisbury. Apart from anything else, Joan's resistance to the marriage indicates that she would have been prepared to have made the Montagues aware of it. Margaret and her brother would not have wanted to take the risk of proceeding with Joan's marriage to William Montague without first warning and discussing the matter with the Earl of Salisbury.

The logical solution to the problem would have been to delay the proposed marriage to William and to wait for Thomas Holand's return so that the validity or otherwise of his marriage to Joan could be established, and it is curious that this did not happen. An agreement could still have been made in principle, and a delay would hardly have mattered as Joan and William were only thirteen years old. It is very unlikely that their families expected or wanted the marriage consummated at this stage. Although the Church regarded the age of puberty for a girl as twelve, it was generally recognised that marital intimacy should be deferred until the girl was at least fifteen, because of the dangers intercourse and pregnancy could pose for someone of that age.[13] The Earl of Salisbury's part in the matter may have been decisive in propelling the parties forward. He had only just been released after several months of captivity in France, having been captured by the French while on an expedition outside Lille in April 1340.[14] He was an important prisoner and a high value had been placed on his ransom. Fortunately Edward III had been anxious to secure his release and had raised the ransom sum by securing a levy of wool in October 1340 and agreeing to release one of his Scottish captives, the Earl of Moray, in exchange.[15] Salisbury was probably released around the time of the truce at Espléchin in September, returning to England in November or December 1340, and had yet to complete the terms agreed for his release. As Edward III's most trusted friend he was privy to the king's plans and knew that it was only a matter of time before campaigning in France resumed. He was ambitious for his son and doubtless anxious to settle his affairs before he returned to France, so was prepared to take a risk in order to secure the king's cousin as a bride for William. He also had an advantage over Margaret and Thomas Wake in that he knew Thomas Holand well. They had served together several times over the years, probably first in Scotland in 1335 and 1337, when Thomas was just starting his military career, and then latterly in France. In more recent years Thomas' military abilities had brought him to the attention of the leading commanders. He had fought alongside the earl with Sir Walter Mauny and Sir John Chandos at Brabant in September 1339, and witnessed a grant by Sir Walter Mauny at Valenciennes on 14 September 1339, with Salisbury and the Earl of Northampton.[16] The earl's personal knowledge may well have determined his approach to the problem. Salisbury knew Thomas was ambitious but impecunious, and was well aware of his background and the Lancastrian aversion to the Holand family. He probably believed that Thomas' clandestine marriage had been a calculated gamble, and assumed that Thomas could be bought off. In many respects they were similar; both were ambitious, bold, had drive and energy, and shared a willingness to take risks. Salisbury was doubtless confident that he could offer sufficient inducement to persuade Holand to agree to his marriage being set aside, and convinced Margaret and Thomas Wake that they could leave this to him.

No record of the details of what was agreed between Salisbury, Margaret and Thomas Wake survives, but there would have been a detailed marriage contract, and some idea of the likely terms can be surmised from the detailed agreement reached between Salisbury and Lord Ruthin in June 1335 for Agnes' marriage to John Grey. Like Joan and William, Agnes and John were still children so had no say in the arrangements. Their parents agreed that a dowry of £1,000 was to be paid by Salisbury (then plain Sir William Montague) to Ruthin in instalments over a five-year period, during which time Agnes would remain living with her parents, and as additional insurance, a penalty was payable of £2,000 if either party defaulted.[17] The terms agreed for Joan would have been similar, and it was probably anticipated that she would either remain living in the royal household, or with her mother, until the parties felt the young couple were old enough to live together and consummate their marriage. However, the peculiar complication of the Holand marriage warranted the inclusion of some safeguards. The sum of £3,000 agreed for Joan was a much larger marriage portion than usual, and considerably more than the £1,300 agreed for Alice in 1333, or the £1,000 agreed for Agnes.[18] The explanation for this may simply be that Salisbury was a shrewd negotiator, and that in contrast to the Earl of Norfolk Margaret was not in a position to grant the earl any land. But a possible interpretation is that the price was deliberately high to compensate for the risk, and that a large proportion of it would be forfeit if the match failed. Another safeguard was to ensure that the marriage was not consummated until it was certain that the situation over the Holand marriage had been resolved. Non-consummation was a common term in marriage settlements where the principals were very young, as Joan and William were, and it would have been a reasonable provision to include. Salisbury had the additional advantage that William was only thirteen, and under canonical law he could reject the arranged marriage provided he did so before he was fourteen (the recognised age of puberty for boys).

The other intriguing aspect of the affair is what role, if any, the king and queen played in it. Joan had been living under their protection, and arguably the whole Holand marriage debacle was the result of their failure to provide her with sufficient chaperonage and protection. Margaret may well have felt strongly that Edward III had once again let her family down. It is difficult to believe that Edward III and Philippa were not made aware of the whole sorry story once it came out, if not by Margaret and Thomas Wake then by the Earl of Salisbury. Salisbury was the king's closest friend, and at the time he was arranging his son's marriage to Joan he was also acting for the king in a matter of considerable importance. When Edward III returned from France in November 1340 he had been furious with the council which he had left to handle affairs in his absence, blaming them for the lack of funds which had caused his allies to withdraw their support, and he had summarily dismissed the council members, including Thomas Wake. The head of the council, Archbishop Stratford, who enjoyed powerful support in the City of London, refused to be intimidated, and launched a sustained attack on the king. Edward III found himself without support and faced by a constitutional crisis which paralysed the government. As before, when in trouble, the king turned to his friends for help. He asked Salisbury to be his intermediary and negotiate with Stratford along with the Earl of Northampton.[19] Their successful intervention in April 1341 restored the equilibrium and enabled domestic harmony to be restored. The relationship between the king and Salisbury was one of great trust as well as friendship, and it would be natural for the earl to discuss the problem over his son's marriage with Edward III. As the king was overwhelmed by the distractions of the political crisis he was more than happy to leave his friend to sort out the problem. His agreement to Salisbury's grant of land to William and Joan was a clear endorsement of his friend's actions.

It is hard not to feel considerable sympathy for Joan, still no more than a child. She had first been flattered and cajoled by an attractive and strong man into agreeing to a secret marriage, then bullied and persuaded by her family to enter into a bigamous marriage. Thomas' behaviour towards Joan can hardly be regarded as chivalrous, as he took advantage of her youth and her lack of protection to rush her ruthlessly into a clandestine marriage without the approval or knowledge of her family. Yet it is striking that when the Montague marriage was proposed and Joan's secret marriage was revealed, she received no support or assistance from anyone. She might at least have expected sympathy from her mother, but Margaret forced her to enter into the marriage with William despite her objections, suggesting a lack of empathy between mother and daughter. Perhaps the separation in early childhood with Joan living in the royal household and Margaret attending to family affairs meant they had never enjoyed a close or particularly affectionate relationship. Certainly their separation while Joan was in Ghent had not helped. Joan might also have looked to the queen for support, as she had, after all, been under her protection, and it is indeed curious that Philippa, so notable for her willingness to intervene on behalf of others, did not become involved. The most obvious explanation is that, however sympathetic Philippa was towards Joan, the queen felt obliged to support the stance taken by her husband, albeit against her own wishes. It is difficult to see how Joan, on her own, could have withstood the pressure on her to marry William, and with no one apparently on her side it is remarkable that she still tried so hard to convince her family that she was not free to marry. The attitude taken by all concerned showed both a lack of concern for Joan as an individual, and ambivalence towards the institution of marriage. Joan was treated simply as a rich matrimonial prize, and her secret marriage to Thomas Holand perceived as a surmountable hurdle. Had he been killed in Prussia it is doubtful that their marriage would ever have become known. However, he survived.

It is not clear when Thomas returned from Prussia to England, but it was probably sometime between the summer of 1341, when the campaign ended, and the spring of 1342. Certainly by May 1342 he was back in the king's service and, according to Froissart, guarding the border at Bayonne in France with John Darvel.[20] On his return to England he was immediately faced with a situation he had not anticipated. Instead of being able to present his case to the king and obtain royal approval, he was confronted with Joan's marriage to William Montague as a fait accompli. He may not even have been able to see Joan, as it is not known if she was staying with her mother or had remained with princesses Isabella and Joan in the royal household. Undaunted, Thomas presented himself to Margaret and asserted his claim to Joan. However unwelcome his declaration, it did not come as a surprise to Margaret and Thomas Wake as his return had been envisaged as a possibility. On the other hand, they had assumed that the Earl of Salisbury would be on hand to deal with Thomas, and unfortunately he was not. The earl had returned to France to complete the arrangements for the payment of his ransom, a process which dragged on for some months. One of the conditions was that he would promise not to bear arms against the French king, a not unusual requirement but one for which the earl needed the king's permission and this was granted in May 1342.[21] Salisbury's absence, albeit unavoidable, was regrettable. Had the earl been present when Thomas made his declaration it is likely that an agreement could have been reached to satisfy all concerned (except perhaps Joan, but her views had not been considered important by anyone anyway), probably resulting in Thomas' withdrawal in exchange for a cash payment and promise of advancement.

In the earl's absence, Margaret, Thomas Wake and William Montague stalled for time, refusing to admit that Thomas had any right to Joan. It is clear that Joan continued to refuse to repudiate her marriage to Thomas. Had she been persuaded to do so, then Margaret and Thomas Wake would have been able to initiate the requisite proceedings for Joan to secure an annulment, and clear the way to validate the Montague marriage. But this was not an option while Joan remained steadfast in her support of Thomas. William was far too young to be able to make any decisions without his father's guidance. Having agreed on a course of action with the earl, Margaret and Thomas Wake no doubt hoped that the matter could be shelved until the earl returned, and that he would then be able to persuade Thomas to drop his claim. Faced with their opposition, there was little that Thomas could do without irrefutable proof of his marriage, and this he did not have. He could have appealed directly to Edward III, and requested his involvement, but as it was apparent that the Montague match had been arranged with the king's blessing the chances of finding the king sympathetic to his situation were slim. Thomas probably preferred the prospect of dealing with the earl, realising that this would be to his advantage. What none of them were prepared to do was to relinquish their respective claims to Joan, and so they were effectively in stalemate, waiting for the earl. But Thomas could not afford to wait indefinitely as he was under the command of the king. His military duties took priority and by May 1342 he had left England again. It is doubtful if Margaret would have given him the opportunity to see her daughter, depriving Joan of any comfort she may have derived from seeing Thomas again.

Joan's continuing loyalty to Thomas is notable. William Montague was not a stranger to her; they had shared childhood experiences and probably many happy memories. Their marriage could have been a most successful and contented one, had Thomas Holand never noticed Joan. But he had, and Joan had fallen in love and married him, and now she was prepared to oppose her family's wishes, and wait for him. In the meantime, as her family and the Montagues hoped to resolve her marital status with Thomas Holand, it was in no one's interest for the problem to be made generally known. Very few people would have been aware of Thomas Holand's claim. Joan's marriage to William Montague was a very public affair, and to all intents and purposes Joan would have been treated afterwards as if she was William Montague's wife. Although the grant to William and Joan of Mold manor in North Wales in February 1341 might suggest an intention for them to live together, this is unlikely. William was thirteen in 1341 and training for knighthood in Prince Edward's household. There was no reason for his marriage to change this, especially as their families did not anticipate the marriage being consummated until they were older, after the complication of the Holand marriage had been resolved. William's and Joan's ages made it perfectly natural and normal that they did not live together. Margaret could hardly have been happy with the situation, and relations between mother and daughter were probably strained. It seems likely that Joan remained with the royal household. There she would have the company of the princesses, now under the supervision of Isabella de la Mote. This would have the advantage for all concerned that it was suitable for Joan to remain under royal protection where she would continue to be educated.

The campaign on which Thomas had embarked this time was in Brittany. The Duke of Brittany, John Montfort, had succeeded his half-brother in April 1341 with Edward III's support, but had been defeated and imprisoned by Philip VI in September 1341, in favour of his nephew, Charles of Blois. Brittany, with its maritime outlets, was strategically far too important for either king to want to see it in the hands of a duke favourable to the other. Two separate expeditions, the first commanded by Sir Walter Mauny, and the second and larger by the Earl of Northampton and Robert of Artois, were being sent in response to the plea made by John Montfort's wife for aid. At the beginning of May 1342 Thomas and his brothers Otto and Alan were placed under the command of the Earl of Northampton, who assembled his troops at Southampton and Portsmouth. The late arrival of the ships and adverse winds delayed departure, and the army did not set sail for Brittany until August 1342.[22] Northampton landed at Brest, which was being besieged by the French, and then advanced with the objective of securing a harbour further north. By September they were besieging the French-held harbour of Morlaix, and in early October Edward III reached Brittany. The main objective of the campaign became the recapture of Vannes. In November the main Anglo-Breton army settled down to besiege Vannes, while Northampton attacked Nantes in December. By this time Thomas had been promoted and had become one of the commanders.[23] The Earl of Salisbury was also on the Brittany expedition (paid for service between 8 September 1342 and 7 February 1343), and in December commanded a raiding party in the north-east corner of Brittany.[24] It is possible that Thomas encountered Salisbury while in Brittany, but neither would have wished to discuss domestic affairs in such an environment.

By January 1343, with no significant engagement between the English and French armies, a truce was concluded at Malestroit, and the army was disbanded. Thomas' pay ended on 15 February, and he probably returned to England with the king in February or March 1343. Joan would have heard the news that the army was returning, and must have hoped that surely now her future would be resolved. Thomas and the Earl of Salisbury should have had the opportunity once back in England to sit down together and reach agreement over Joan. But curiously they did not. Instead, they both departed almost immediately on crusade – the second time for Thomas. In March 1343 a military expedition, headed by the Earl of Derby accompanied by the Earl of Salisbury, left for Granada on a crusade against the Moors.[25] Thomas appointed attorneys in March and in May appointed John Holand and Henry Fitz Roger to act until the following Easter.[26] It is not known if he saw Joan, or made any attempt to contact her. He left England shortly after Easter with Sir John Hardeshull's small force of 200 men-at-arms and 300 archers.[27] For Thomas, participation in the crusade in Granada undoubtedly furthered his career, enhancing his military reputation. Although it is possible that the earl and Thomas were not in England at the same time before leaving for Spain and so did not encounter one another, it is nevertheless extraordinary that both should have been willing to allow the crusade to take priority over sorting out the issue of Joan's marital status.

Joan was forced to wait another six months until the autumn of 1343 when the campaign in Spain ended and the crusading knights returned to England. The earl did not immediately return to England as he was sent by the king to treat with Alfonso of Castile with Henry, Earl of Derby.[28] However, once this had been accomplished and the ambassadors returned to England, Thomas and the earl would at last have both been in England and in a position to meet with one another and discuss Joan. It was now more than two years since Thomas had returned to find Joan married to William Montague and almost certainly the first time that all the interested parties had been together with no immediate military expeditions planned. Despite the delays and Thomas' absence, it is evident that Joan had still not been persuaded by her family to withdraw her support for Thomas. This again ruled out the obvious route of getting a decision from the ecclesiastical courts. So, as Thomas had not withdrawn his claim, some accommodation would have to be reached, though the fact that he had not pressed it either indicates he was amenable to a settlement. With the king available to arbitrate if necessary, everyone involved had every incentive to resolve the matter once and for all. The earl's seniority and wealth, coupled with his familiarity with Thomas and their shared experiences, probably ensured that their meeting was fairly amicable. Providing Thomas would accept a price which the earl and Joan's family were prepared to pay a mutually satisfactory solution could confidently be expected. Margaret and Thomas Wake had been happy to leave matters in the earl's hands, expecting the earl to inform them of the outcome. Joan's views were not considered of importance and she would not have been consulted. As Joan's position remained unaltered it seems probable that the earl offered sufficiently attractive terms for Thomas to agree to release his claim. Unfortunately for all concerned, at the beginning of 1344 the earl unexpectedly died after being wounded in a tournament held at Windsor, ending any chance of completing the agreement he had reached with Thomas.

The week-long tournament held at Windsor in January 1344 had been planned by Edward III for some months and was deliberately intended to be a colourful, lavish and entertaining spectacle. In January the king sent heralds to France, Brabant, Flanders, Burgundy, Hainault and Scotland offering safe conduct to the elite of Europe's knights to attend. From 1330 Edward III had used tournaments to foster the idea of chivalry and to encourage a sense of camaraderie among the nobility which would draw them together in supporting him. His undoubted success in doing so was reflected in their increasingly favourable response to his call on them to support him in the successive campaigns in Scotland and France. The Windsor tournament was to be the culmination in a series of tournaments with the object of recruiting as many knights as possible to assist him, and the occasion at which, pursuing his Arthurian theme, Edward III announced his plan to found his own round table with a select group of knights. To this end the king embarked in February on a massive building project at Windsor with the construction of a circular building of around

200 feet in diameter, larger than the Pantheon in Rome.[29] The intention was for this building to house a round table which would seat 300 knights and act as the headquarters and a meeting place.

Everyone assembled at Windsor for the tournament and it must have been a truly impressive and dazzling display of knights and their entourage, engaged in a succession of exciting and impressive challenges. Everyone who could be there was there. Among the onlookers were the queen and her mother-in-law Queen Isabella, the princesses, nine countesses, including Margaret, Countess of Kent, as well as Prince Edward and among his escorts Joan's brother John and William Montague. Joan was well chaperoned with both her mother and William's mother, Catherine, Countess of Salisbury, present. Thomas Holand was doubtless one of the many young knights entering the lists, and the Earl of Salisbury was also among those participating. The earl, as Marshal of England, and Henry, Earl of Derby, as Seneschal of England, played a prominent role in the proceedings. Unfortunately the Earl of Salisbury was wounded in one of the engagements and had to withdraw from the field. His wounds were severe, and he died shortly afterwards.[30] This was a personal misfortune for the king as well as the earl's family, as the earl had been Edward III's closest friend and mentor since the coup of 1330. Poignantly, the earl remembered his friend in his will, providing that all debts unpaid by the Crown at his death should be cancelled – as these amounted at the time to over £6,000, this was effectively a substantial gift.[31] Although the earl's death was not marked by a lavish funeral, it is tempting to wonder whether Edward III's grief manifested itself in a different way. No one knows why the king never completed his round building, but it would not be surprising if the tragedy of his friend's untimely death was a contributory factor.[32] It was also another four years before the king set up his knightly order.

The Earl of Salisbury's demise was a catastrophe for Joan, and she was destined to spend another five years trapped between her two marriages. In 1344 William Montague was only sixteen and too young to inherit his father's dignities or estates. He therefore had no power to fulfil whatever promises his father had made to Thomas Holand. Margaret and Thomas Wake may have had second thoughts about the terms Salisbury had agreed, and probably looked to the king to resolve the situation. Edward III was now drawn directly into the affair as William became his ward.[33] This should have been decisive. Joan was his cousin, and Thomas Holand his household knight. The king had earlier abrogated his responsibility towards Joan when he left the Earl of Salisbury to resolve the matter with Thomas but he now had the opportunity to remedy the situation. Edward III was better placed than anyone else to effect a settlement, and if necessary he could invoke the Pope's intervention, as he did a year later in February 1345 when he asked the Pope to confirm the dissolution of the Earl of Arundel's marriage to Hugh Despenser's daughter to enable Arundel to marry the Earl of Lancaster's daughter, Eleanor.[34] Yet the king appears to have made no attempt to resolve his cousin's marital dilemma. Instead, he appointed one of the earl's executors, Sir John Wingfield, to be William Montague's guardian, and granted William some of his father's estates in Somerset which brought him an annual income of around £300.[35] This was not enough to enable William to offer Thomas a sufficiently generous inducement to relinquish Joan. While his relinquishment of the guardianship of his best friend's heir could be interpreted as the king's wish not to be seen to be taking sides, it is hard to explain or understand Edward III's failure to take any further action. Maybe he had a sneaking sympathy for Thomas and Joan but did not want to offend the Montagues or his aunt and Thomas Wake by supporting them, but whatever his reasons, his lack of action meant that he was effectively washing his hands of the matter.

It was some time before Margaret and Thomas Wake realised that the king was not going to settle the affair. Joan would again have been subjected to pressure to withdraw her support for Thomas, which would have enabled them to get the Holand marriage annulled. But Joan remained steadfast. There remained the possibility of reaching terms with Thomas for him to withdrawn his claim. Although they had hoped the earl would resolve the matter, and assumed the king would, they were both more than capable of taking decisive action themselves. In dealing with the family estates Margaret had proved she could be formidable in pursuing her objectives, and Thomas Wake had many years of experience in command. They knew they had the support of the Montague family. William was not given the opportunity to withdraw. It was now too late for him to reject his marriage under canonical law on the grounds of his age and lack of consummation, and he was too young to institute ecclesiastical proceedings himself unless his guardian undertook them on his behalf. The fact that no deal was reached suggests that Margaret and Thomas Wake were prepared to take a hard line with Thomas Holand, and hoped that if they simply refused to acknowledge his marriage and denied him access to Joan he would have no alternative but to drop his claim eventually. Nevertheless, the impasse was clearly unsatisfactory. Thomas might have been more effectively deterred from persisting in his claim if William and Joan had consummated their marriage, and had children. As they were now both sixteen there was no obvious bar to them doing so, but the fact that Joan did not become pregnant makes it evident they did not (both would later have several children). This was probably due to William. Maybe he hoped that her feelings for Thomas would lessen with time and she would become reconciled to their marriage.

Offered no inducement to relinquish his claim to Joan, and faced with the combined opposition of Joan's family and the Montagues, Thomas' choices were limited. It was evident he could not appeal to the king for support, but he could request an ecclesiastical investigation to validate his marriage. This is what Sir John Grey had done in 1333 when his wife Eleanor had been abducted and then married by William la Zouche. Grey first brought proceedings before the Bishop of Lincoln, requesting Eleanor's return. When the bishop refused to make a ruling despite being ordered to do so by the Archbishop of Canterbury, Grey was forced to appeal. His success, however, was short-lived, as the Pope then ordered the Bishop of Coventry and Lichfield to reconsider the whole affair. The problem for Thomas was that he lacked the funds to mount what would probably be lengthy and expensive proceedings, and he may well have feared that he would not get a fair hearing. As his marriage had taken place abroad it might have been difficult for him to gather the evidence to support it. The alternative was for him to preserve his position by leaving matters as they were, and hope that a future change in either his or William Montague's circumstances would provide a solution. He probably discussed it with his mother, always someone who had his best interests at heart. In September 1344 he was with her in Sussex, acting as godfather to Thomas FitzRoger, attending his christening at St Bartholomew's church, Merston.[36] In the event, it appears that Thomas decided to do nothing, and turned his attention back to his career.

Thomas rejoined the Earl of Northampton's forces as a fresh campaign was planned in France. In the autumn of 1344 Pope Clement VI had attempted to reconcile the French and English sides but he failed to do so. Edward III had already secured the support of Parliament to mount an expedition, and early in 1345 the king and his closest advisers drew up the first detailed plans for a fresh campaign, with an initial proposal to send two armies in the summer, one led by the king and the other by Henry of Lancaster, Earl of Derby.[37] The plans expanded in the spring of 1345 when Edward III secured the allegiance of John Montfort of Brittany and some other noble Frenchmen, and with their support a third army was planned. The exact details of the planned campaign were kept secret. In June 1345 Edward III renounced the truce with France and the first of his armies, commanded by the Earl of Northampton, left Portsmouth in June 1345, landing in Brittany. Thomas and his brothers, having previously served with Northampton, were almost certainly among this first advance party. In July 1345 Northampton's army laid siege to Quimper in Brittany, and in September and October Henry of Lancaster successfully engaged the French in battle at Bergerac and Auberoche south of Limoges in Périgueux. Meanwhile, the king, who had initially diverted to Sluys to deal with a sudden crisis in Flanders which threatened the Anglo-Flemish alliance, was delayed in England. On his return from Sluys, storms had scattered the fleet, and the ships were forced to make their way back individually to England, each disembarking on finding a safe haven. This made the original intention to re-embark and join Northampton and Henry of Lancaster's armies in France impractical, and the king dispersed his army. It was clear to Edward III and his council that with the end of the campaigning season in sight the king would not be joining them and that the initiative could not be sustained. The expedition was cancelled, with Northampton and Derby wintering in France before dispersing in the spring of 1346 and Thomas among those who now returned to England.

Joan's whereabouts between January 1344 and the spring of 1346 are not known. We do not know where Joan was living and with whom during this period. While it is probable that she remained with the queen's household, she may have accompanied Margaret when she visited the family estates. Joan was still her brother's heir, and Margaret would have wanted her daughter to have some familiarity with the Kent estates. In addition, publicly at least, Joan was William's wife and the Montagues would naturally have expected Joan to show an interest in William's affairs and visit the Montague estates. Unfortunately there is no evidence to confirm or support this. The respite in the hostilities against France did little to change Joan's position, and it is doubtful if she even saw Thomas Holand when he returned from Brittany. Edward III had been planning a renewed campaign for 1346, which would this time rely primarily on English troops rather than foreign allies. It was a huge expedition, with the army, once assembled, probably numbering between 7,000 and 10,000 men.[38] The organisation required to gather such a large army was a complicated and lengthy business which kept those involved occupied for weeks, sometimes stretching into months, even before the start of a campaign. Within days of his return from Brittany in the spring of 1346 Thomas was immediately engaged in supervising arrays in Leicestershire and Warwickshire, under the command of the Earl of Warwick, leaving him little time to spare for Joan. Thomas was paid war wages from 4 June, but money was still a problem for him, for in the same month his mother Maud obtained permission to give him the manors of Halse, Brackley and King's Sutton in Northamptonshire, boosting his income.[39]

The new expedition affected Joan even more directly than the previous campaigns, as this time both William Montague and her brother John were involved. On 11 July the fleet of over 600 ships left Portsmouth and set sail for France.[40] All four Holand brothers were aboard; Thomas' older brother Robert served with him, while his younger brothers, Otto and Alan, were in the king's retinue with Robert's son.[41] Also with the king was the sixteen-year-old Prince Edward, accompanied by William Montague (now aged eighteen) and Joan's brother, John. The fleet's destination had been kept a close secret; according to the royal clerk Adam Murimuth, 'no one could know for certain where he [Edward III] intended to sail, or in what place overseas he meant to land'.[42] In fact, the destination was Normandy, territory not previously campaigned on, and, as Jean le Bel and Froissart noted, a country ill-equipped to deal with the invading English.[43] When Edward III landed at La Hogue his first action was to knight Prince Edward, and several young noblemen, including William Montague and John.[44] The army was divided into three divisions which were to march separately and come together at night; the vanguard or advance force was commanded by Prince Edward with the earls of Northampton (the constable) and Warwick (the Earl Marshal) to assist him, the rearguard by the Bishop of Durham, Thomas Hatfield, with the main body under the king's direct control.

The first notable success of the campaign came within weeks at the end of July with the successful siege of Caen, the largest walled town west of Rouen, where the French had planned to halt the English army.[45] One significant incident in the capture of the town would change Joan's fortunes completely. Caen's defences were commanded by the constable of Paris, the Count of Eu, and the chamberlain, the Count of Tancarville. On realising their hopeless position, and in fear of being killed by the attacking English soldiers, the two commanders surrendered themselves individually to two English knights known to them. The Count of Tancarville surrendered to Sir Thomas Daniels, a retainer of Prince Edward, while the Count of Eu surrendered to Thomas Holand, recognising him from the Crusades in Prussia and Granada.[46] According to Froissart, Thomas was easily recognisable because he wore an eyepatch, shielding his lost eye.[47] The Count of Eu's surrender was a significant stroke of fortune for Thomas, as he could expect to be handsomely rewarded by the king for his captive. Such funds would give him the wherewithal to take William Montague to the ecclesiastical courts and reclaim Joan. On Edward III's orders, the two counts were removed from the field and were taken to England in August by the Earl of Huntingdon, with instructions for them to be kept in captivity until the king had made more progress with his campaign before they were released against ransoms raised by their families or the French king.[48] After the town surrendered Thomas lived up to his chivalrous reputation, securing the town with his companions and restraining the English troops from raping the women and girls and killing the townsfolk.[49]

Being in the king's army was not without personal risk for Thomas; he had already lost an eye. Shortly after leaving Caen, Thomas and a steward of the king's household called Sir Richard Talbot were wounded attacking one of several castles which guarded the various crossings of the Seine.[50] The wound was not serious and Thomas remained in service. Outmanoeuvring the French, the army crossed the river at Poissy and advanced to within ten miles of Paris, continuing to lay waste to the countryside and burning and pillaging towns. Failing to make contact with the French army, Edward III then turned north and headed towards Calais, hoping to engage Philip VI at a site of his choosing.[51] On 26 August the two armies faced each other at Crécy. Philip VI, commanding an army superior in size and well equipped, was confident of success, but the English won an overwhelming victory, with the French king barely escaping from the battlefield. The French losses were enormous, and included most of the flower of the French nobility as well as King John of Bohemia and the King of Majorca. Thomas fought in Prince Edward's division in his newly promoted position as a joint commander of the vanguard with the earls of Warwick and Northampton, on an equal footing with Sir John Chandos. The prince's division was the front line and bore the brunt of the fighting in the battle; at one point it was feared the prince might be captured. William Montague and Joan's brother John also took part in the battle, John serving with the prince. Many knights apart from Thomas distinguished themselves on the battlefield, none more so than Prince Edward, whose courage and chivalric conduct won him general admiration.

Waiting in England, Joan was aware of the tremendous success of the victory, but there is no evidence that Thomas informed her of the change in his circumstances. Thomas and William Montague, remained in France. With the French in disarray after their crushing defeat at Crécy, the English army advanced to the outskirts of Calais. According to Edward III, Calais was chosen for its location and in order to be within reach of reinforcements and supplies from England, needed because of the long and continuous marches.[52] However, Calais was well defended and the king made no attempt to assault the town and instead had organised his army to besiege the town. The siege started in September 1346 and did not conclude until August 1347. The defenders were able to obtain fresh supplies which were brought in by sea, and proved equal to withstanding the immense resources thrown at them by the English army. The siege turned into a vast and costly exercise involving around 32,000 English troops, all housed in a purpose-built and fortified camp named Villeneuve-le-Hardi (Bold New Town) by Edward III.[53] Eventually, by April 1347 Edward III had been able to ensure Calais was surrounded on all sides and blockaded from the sea so that supplies were no longer able to reach the town. The inhabitants and the garrison began to starve. Philip VI dithered, hoping initially to draw Edward III away from the town by sending an army into Flanders and encouraging the Scots to invade England (where they suffered a devastating defeat at Neville's Cross). In July 1347 Philip VI finally arrived with his army, hoping to relieve the Calais defenders, but soon abandoned the idea when he realised the strength of the English defences. He departed, having failed to achieve anything. The citizens of Calais, deserted by their king, came to terms with Edward III and on 4 August 1347 the king took possession of the town. The siege had lasted eleven months.

Thomas Holand served with distinction in the Crécy campaign and his outstanding performance dramatically enhanced his reputation and prospects. But, more significantly for Joan, his capture of the Count of Eu at Caen proved incredibly lucrative. It was usual for all the more important prisoners to be purchased from their captors by the king, who then negotiated their release. In April 1347 Edward III formally agreed to pay Thomas the sum of 80,000 florins (£13,333 6s 8d) for the Count of Eu, to be paid in instalments over three years: 12,000 florins (£2,000) in 1347, 41,000 florins (£6,633 13s 4d) in 1348 and the final 27,000 florins (£4,500) in 1349, and as the hide and wool subsidy was being used to provide the cash, each yearly instalment was to be paid in two equal payments at Michaelmas and Easter.[54] At a stroke, Thomas was promised riches beyond his dreams. It was also a huge and unprecedented sum for the king to pay, and there is no record of any captive, other than crowned heads of state, for whom Edward III was prepared to pay as much.[55] Thomas Daniels, for example, to whom the Count of Tancarville had surrendered at the same time as the Count of Eu had surrendered to Thomas Holand, received £666 and an annual pension of £26 13s 4d.[56] Some months later, when Sir Thomas Dagworth captured Charles of Blois, the claimant for the duchy of Brittany supported by the French, he was promised the sum of £4,900.[57] Ten years later, after the Battle of Poitiers in 1356, the Earl of Warwick received £8,000 for the Archbishop of Sens, and Sir Bartholomew Burghersh secured £6,666 13s 4d for the Count of Ventadour.[58] The sum Edward III agreed to pay Thomas Holand is disproportionately high in relation to the count's importance as a political prisoner, and indicates clearly the value he placed on Holand as a military commander and his desire to reward him. Perhaps it also indicated something further.

Edward III would have been well aware that the sum he had agreed to pay for the Count of Eu would enable Thomas to pursue his claim to Joan, and there can be little doubt that Thomas' courage and exceptional performance had secured him the king's tacit support. Although the king was still not prepared to intervene in person to resolve Joan's marital dilemma, he was effectively communicating his message by giving Thomas ample means to take the necessary legal steps required to regain her. It is likely that Edward III was also well aware of his young cousin's desire to be reunited with Holand. The queen, accompanied by princesses Isabella and Joan, had joined the king outside Calais to celebrate Christmas in 1346, and remained with him until the siege ended. Joan, now eighteen years old, was among their party.[59] The queen's sympathies must have been drawn to Joan's awkward situation, and her continued determined support for Thomas in the face of her family's opposition. Joan's presence in Calais also gave Thomas an opportunity to see her again after many months of enforced separation. This was a decisive moment for the couple. Having secured the promise of such a rich reward from the king, Thomas no longer had any reason to surrender his right to Joan in exchange for cash and now had the financial wherewithal to challenge William Montague.

With the king's approval, Thomas took the opportunity during the long-drawn-out siege of Calais to return to England to attend to his personal affairs. Maud Holand must have been extremely relieved to see Thomas, delighted with her son's newly won royal favour and hopeful that he would restore the family fortunes. Apart from his own marital situation, there were other pressing matters to claim his attention. First, there was his sister Isabella. She was living with the Earl of Surrey, a relationship which the king did not view with favour. The earl had obtained Edward III's permission to leave property to Isabel, but in December 1346 revoked this at the request of the Earl of Arundel. Then, Thomas' older brother Robert had incurred the king's wrath. Edward III had appointed his second son, Lionel, to be keeper of the realm in his absence with Prince Edward. While Prince Lionel and some of the other royal children had been staying at Sir Gerard Lisle's manor, at Beams in Berkshire, Robert Holand had forced an entry, threatened Sir Gerard and abducted and raped Lisle's wife, Margery, 'to the terror of the said keeper [Lionel] and the rest of the king's children then with him there'.[60] Thomas also had to decide what to do about Joan. He probably discussed his marriage with his mother and in March 1347 he and Maud obtained permission from the Pope to have portable altars, a sure sign that they envisaged taking a journey together.[61] They may have returned to Ghent to gather the evidence of his marriage, or travelled to the papal court at Avignon to seek advice on how he could resolve the situation. It was probably during this time that Thomas made the decision to pursue his claim to Joan and determined how he would set about doing so. He had no time to do anything further, as in May he was ordered to rejoin the king at Calais, and when the town finally surrendered in August he was one of the English commanders involved in the negotiations.[62]

After the fall of Calais a large part of the army was released from service, including some of Edward III's own household retinue and those of Prince Edward. The king and the remainder of the army returned to England in October 1347, and to celebrate the English successes the king embarked on a round of tournaments, held at Bury, Eltham and Windsor, with jousts held at Canterbury, Lichfield and Lincoln, culminating in a tournament at Windsor in June 1348. Thomas lost no time in putting his plan to regain Joan into action. The first payment from the king for the Count of Eu was due in September, and shortly afterwards, instead of applying to an English ecclesiastical court, Thomas submitted a petition to the Pope, requesting that Joan's marriage to William Montague be annulled on the grounds of his own prior marriage.[63] There was to be no more waiting, no more tentative negotiation. His action was clear and unequivocal; he wanted his wife back and could not be bought off, and he was not taking the risk that an English curial court might favour William, as an English peer. It provoked a furious reaction from William Montague. Up to this point, both parties had kept Joan's marriage to Thomas secret, and few outside their immediate families (and the king and queen) were aware that there was any question of Joan not being legally married to William. She was publicly regarded, and treated, as the Countess of Salisbury. As the news of Thomas' proceedings circulated, William was humiliated, but although he knew that Joan supported

Thomas he was determined not to give her up. He was still under age and did not yet have access to his income, so he fought back in the only way he could, and took the drastic action of seizing Joan, and keeping her prisoner, preventing her from any contact with Thomas.[64]

William's action was outrageous, but he was neither rebuked nor punished for it by the king. Instead, in November 1347 Edward III sent his old friend Elizabeth Montague, William's grandmother, to Avignon, probably to ascertain Thomas' chances of success, and in December, shortly after her return, he granted William a substantial part of his inheritance.[65] The king could have chosen to grant William the whole of his inheritance outright, and it is odd that he did not do so. The effect of his action was to ensure that publicly, the king stayed aloof, but he had levelled the playing field by granting William sufficient funds to counter the papal proceedings Thomas had initiated, which William duly did. It is sad to note that none of Joan's family, not her mother Margaret, her uncle Thomas Wake, or her brother John, made any attempt to intervene and indeed Margaret went out of her way to support William. Joan was probably taken to the Montague family seat of Donyatt in Somerset, perhaps accompanied by Margaret, and probably chaperoned by William's mother, Catherine, and grandmother Elizabeth. Joan was given no opportunity to speak for herself.

Froissart's later description of Joan as 'the most beautiful lady in all the kingdom of England and the most loved' could never have been more apt than at this time. In the series of tournaments held from October 1347 to June 1348 Thomas and William fought on opposite sides (Thomas for the prince and William for the king), and at the same time they were fighting for Joan's hand through the papal courts. As their rivalry was at its height, Edward III inaugurated his chivalric order, the Order of the Garter, and Thomas and William were both among the founder members. Edward III had been considering an elite fraternity of knights for some time, based on the Arthurian ideal, and had announced his intention at the Windsor tournament in 1344, starting work shortly afterwards on the round tower which he planned would become the headquarters of his foundation. Flushed with the triumph of his victories in France in 1346 and 1347, the king finalised his plans when he returned to England, and put them into effect. The result was the Order of the Garter, which Edward III intended would reflect his ideals of chivalry and link him closely with his greatest knights.

The exact date the order was founded is unknown, but it is generally considered to have been first instituted at the Windsor tournament in June 1348, a fitting finale to the round of celebratory tournaments started on the king's return from France in October 1347. The first formal meeting of the Knights of the Garter appears to have been held at the chapel of St George at Windsor on St George's Day, 23 April 1349. The established pattern for the meeting became a Mass followed by a feast.

For the ceremony members were expected to wear special robes: a white garter tunic trimmed with ermine and embroidered in blue, with a blue sash garter on which the motto was embroidered in silk and gold letters, worn diagonally across the body from shoulder to waist, a Garter mantle and cap. The king provided garters and robes from his wardrobe for certain favoured knights and in December 1348 Prince Edward paid for twenty-four garters for the knights of the companionship of the Garter.[66] The early records of the order are incomplete and the derivation of the order's symbol of the blue garter, and its motto, 'honi soit qui mal y pense', remain unclear. The Order of the Garter was deliberately elite and exclusive, comprising only twenty-six knights, including Edward III himself and his eldest son, Prince Edward. Each was allocated a stall in St George's chapel, identified by a plate displaying their shield. Election as a member was a signal honour bestowed only on the king's most trusted companions in arms. Apart from Edward III and the prince, the identity of the other twenty-four members suggests they were chosen for their military prowess rather than their status, as along with the king's great war captains Henry, Earl of Lancaster, and Thomas Beauchamp, Earl of Warwick, were ordinary knights such as Sir John Chandos, Sir Nigel Loring and Sir James Audley, all of whom fought with Prince Edward at Crécy. Also among the chosen elite were William Montague, Thomas Holand and his brother Otto Holand.

There has been considerable speculation about how and why the order was founded. The most popular and enduring story explaining its origins derives from Polydore Vergil's *History of England*, which was written in the late sixteenth century. According to Vergil, Edward III held a ball at Calais to celebrate the fall of the town during which his young and beautiful dance partner, the Countess of Salisbury, dropped her garter. The king gallantly rescued her from embarrassment by picking it up and rebuked the titters of onlookers with the words 'honi soit qui mal y pense'.[67] The king then swore to honour the garter, and so set up the Order of the Garter. For most scholars this romantic tale is apocryphal as there is no contemporary evidence to substantiate it, and no subsequent research has been able to verify it; nevertheless it remains an appealing story. There are confused accounts by the chroniclers Jean le Bel and Froissart regarding the king and a love affair with a Countess of Salisbury, but these appear to amount to no more than rumour, with no clear identification of the woman concerned. Joan has become inextricably associated with the story simply because she was, at the time of the siege of Calais, the Countess of Salisbury (as William's wife), and she was young and beautiful. If there was a ball, it is possible that Edward III danced with her, but it is extremely unlikely that she was wearing a garter, as this was not a usual item of clothing worn by women at that time. On the basis that Joan was his partner, the suggestion that the king was in love with, or desired, his beautiful partner, can be safely discounted. Edward III would never have seriously entertained any such thought in relation to Joan.

Thomas' initiation of proceedings in the papal courts in October 1347 were the start of a long legal wrangle which dragged on for more than two years, with the court alternately sitting, adjourning and reconvening before two successive cardinals and involving more than five lawyers specialising in canon and civil law. At the start of the proceedings the Pope, Clement VI, appointed his nephew, Cardinal Adhemar Robert, to hear the case. Thomas' lawyer, Magister Robert Siglesthorne Beverley, who acted for him throughout, had been in service with the queen and had previous experience acting for English litigants before the papal court at Avignon.[68] Thomas' argument was reasonably straightforward. He gave the date, place and names of those who had witnessed his marriage to Joan, argued that the contract had been made 'per verba de praesenti' (a spousal in front of witnesses), followed by physical consummation.[69] Under medieval ecclesiastical law this was sufficient to create a valid marriage, even though it had been held in secrecy.[70] The papal courts in Avignon were notoriously slow, and the requirements for each side to present their case and for witnesses to be heard involved inevitable delays. Cardinal Adhemar, having heard from Thomas, decided he needed to hear from William and Joan, either in person or via their attorney. He considered, but decided against, calling Margaret. William was desperate, and did everything he could to delay the proceedings, hoping against hope that Thomas would give up. He raised more cash by granting a licence to grant Sir John Wingfield and three other knights the reversion of four of his manors in Somerset.[71] Keeping Joan in seclusion could only be a temporary strategy, as Thomas submitted a second petition to the Pope, appealing for papal intervention to free her. In May 1348 the Pope ordered the Archbishop of Canterbury and the bishops of London and Norwich to secure Joan's release so that she could appoint her own proctor to provide her evidence.[72] Freed from imprisonment, but isolated from her family by her support of Thomas, Christmas that year with the royal family at Otford must have been a difficult occasion for Joan, perhaps lightened by the gift she received of a silver beaker from Prince Edward, addressed to her using her childhood diminutive of 'Jeanette'. [73]

Joan's evidence was crucial to the proceedings, for without her confirmation of consent the court could not make a determination. Extraordinarily, even when she was freed to appoint her own attorney and present her evidence, she was unable to do so. Her first attorney, Magister Nicholas Heath, was in the queen's service, but proved a poor choice as an order was issued for his arrest by Edward III in February 1349 on unrelated charges.[74] His replacement, Magister David Martyn, inexplicably failed to submit anything on Joan's behalf to the papal court on two successive occasions. Perhaps he had been persuaded or bribed not to do so, although there is no evidence to support this. The result was to stall the proceedings indefinitely, at which point the Pope intervened again, appointing another cardinal, Bernard d'Albi, to take over from Cardinal Adhemar. A new attorney was secured for Joan, Magister John Vyse, sub-dean of the diocese of Salisbury. On Joan's instructions, Vyse confirmed that she had voluntarily married Thomas and consummated their marriage. In citing Joan's evidence, he explained the great pressure Joan had been subjected to by her family to marry William, and that she had submitted out of fear of the consequences. William knew that it was just a matter of time before he lost Joan, but he continued to delay matters by ensuring his lawyer failed to appear at the next sitting of the papal court. Possibly he had lost faith in his representative, as a new attorney, Magister Reginald Bugwell, represented him at the court's last sitting and heard the final pronouncement. Cardinal d'Albi judged that the marriage between William and Joan was null and void, found the marriage of Thomas and Joan to be valid, and indicated that Joan should be restored to Thomas and their union publicly solemnised.[75] On 13 November 1349 the Pope confirmed d'Albi's judgment, and ordered the papal nuncio in England and the bishops of Norwich and London to see that the finding of the papal court was carried out.[76]

As Thomas and William battled through their lawyers for Joan in Avignon a plague epidemic reached England, probably brought aboard two ships sailing from Gascony which arrived in Dorset in the early summer of 1348. The Black Death had already ravaged most of Europe, and its effects in England were devastating. It spread throughout the entire country within twelve months, with an alarmingly high mortality rate. The numbers of people who died are impossible to verify but it is generally accepted that probably between a third and a half of the population of England died. The economic effects of the plague were catastrophic, with whole villages abandoned and an acute shortage of labour which left crops uncollected and fields untilled. The human cost was appalling, with so many dying in some places that there was no one left to bury the dead. No family was immune, although the better housing and living conditions of the better off might explain why there was a lower level of mortality among the aristocracy. The court was plunged into mourning in the late summer of 1348 when it was learnt that Joan's childhood companion, Princess Joan, had died en route for her marriage to the heir of King Alfonso of Castile, but she was the only member of the royal family to succumb. Thomas, William and Joan all lost relatives to the plague. In the spring of 1349 William's mother, Catherine, died.[77] Joan's uncle Thomas Wake died on 31 May, and he was buried at the priory whose foundation he had financed at Haltemprice in Yorkshire.[78] By June Thomas had lost his mother, Maud, as well as his sister, Margaret (who had married Sir John de la Warr) and in September Joan's mother, Margaret, died.[79] The tragic consequences of the spread of the plague meant that William had lost all his supporters, and with them his appetite for the battle to keep Joan. Indeed, he had accepted that he would lose Joan some months before Cardinal d'Albi made his final decision, and sensibly made alternative plans. As soon as the annulment of his marriage to Joan was publicly pronounced by Pope Clement VI he married Elizabeth, daughter and co-heiress of John, Lord Mohun of Dunster.[80]

It is to be hoped that Joan was reconciled to her mother before she died, for relations between them must have been strained to the utmost during the course of the papal proceedings. They do not seem to have ever had a warm or close relationship, and it is sad to reflect that Joan never had her mother's blessing for her marriage to Thomas. Margaret's natural desire to see her daughter safely and securely established as the Countess of Salisbury cannot excuse her forcing Joan into a bigamous marriage and her failure to provide her daughter with moral and emotional support at such a crucial time. The fear and insecurity Margaret endured when Edmund was executed may explain her insistence on the Montague match, with the protection it offered her daughter, but it seems unlikely that Joan ever understood or accepted her mother's views on her future. Similarly Joan may have had little cause to mourn the death of her uncle Thomas Wake whom she had probably seen very seldom in the last years of his life. Joan's relationship with her brother John would have been much closer, as they had much in common, having spent their childhood together in the royal household. Being two years younger than Joan, John was hardly in a position to impose his views on his mother or uncle and so could do little to support his sister in her troubles initially. He became free to do so once he obtained independence from his mother, which he achieved in August 1347 when Edward III agreed to grant John his inheritance during his minority.[81] There was no obvious reason for the king to permit his cousin to take his inheritance early, but it may reflect Edward III's growing lack of patience with his aunt and her intransigence over Joan, at a time when his own sympathies lay with Thomas Holand. Edward III also arranged John's marriage and in April 1348 papal dispensation was granted for John to marry Elizabeth, daughter of William, Marquess of Juliers, and Queen Philippa's niece (her mother Joanna was Philippa's younger sister).[82] The terms of the dispensation indicated that one aim behind the marriage proposal was an intention to end the strife between Juliers and the Duke of Guelders. The marquess, subsidised by the English Crown, was one of Edward III's chief allies in Flanders, supplying 1,000 men-at-arms towards the war, and the marriage between John and Elizabeth created a personal connection between the marquess and the king which would cement the alliance.[83]

The death toll and dreadful effects of the plague had disrupted all normal activities throughout 1349 but it must nevertheless have been a relief to everyone concerned when the papal court made its final determination on Joan's marital status. Although the outcome had been expected for some months, it was an incredibly important moment for Joan. She had married Thomas when she was twelve and now she was a young woman of twenty. It is striking that throughout the eight-year period Joan had consistently supported Thomas, against all the odds. She had stood virtually alone in her refusal to deny their marriage. While the outcome of the papal proceedings was undoubtedly a victory for Thomas, it was surely a triumph for Joan, a vindication of her unswerving support for a man who had swept her off her feet when she was a child and yet left her unprotected and isolated with the burden of their secret marriage. Joan had hardly known Thomas when they married, and subsequently her meetings with him had been brief and fraught with the difficulties of their situation. She could never have been sure that she would be able to live as Thomas' wife. He had consistently given his career priority over his duty towards his young wife, and Joan can hardly have been unaware of his ambivalent attitude towards their marriage and of his probable willingness to abandon her if the right price had been offered him by the Earl of Salisbury. In contrast, she knew William very well and he had made it abundantly clear that he cared for her and wanted to keep her as his wife. William, his family and Joan's family had done everything they could to deter her from supporting Thomas, and it would have been so easy, and so convincing, for Joan to have told the court that she had not really understood what she was doing in the spring of 1340. In acknowledging her marriage to Thomas, and standing by him, she had turned away from her family – and from the life she could have had. The suggestion has been made that Joan was ambitious and chose Thomas because he was a rising star, but although Thomas had indeed gained fame and fortune by 1346, the fact remained that William was far wealthier and as an earl considerably outranked him in status.[84] Joan's motives in supporting Thomas over such a long period of time had little to do with ambition and more to do with her own attitude towards the commitment she had made when she exchanged marriage vows with Thomas in the spring of 1340.

Vergil's story of the founding of the Order of the Garter is a powerful and attractive tale which gave Joan iconic status many years after her death, and in some ways it is fitting given the background of the papal proceedings over her marital status, and her close relationship to four of the order's founding members. Yet it is also ironic that Joan should have this close association with Edward III's great symbol of chivalry, for there was nothing chivalrous about the way Joan was treated. The chivalric ideals were of courage, courtesy and respect, and generosity towards the weak and the poor. Women were regarded as deserving special treatment, with knights having a duty to honour and defend them; treatises on knighthood suggested that love for a woman should be an ennobling and inspirational force. However, it is evident from Thomas and William's behaviour that it was Joan's value as a matrimonial prize, rather than her beauty and desirability, which was at stake for them. In their legal wrangling for recognition as her husband, they treated her as a means to an end, and in the process gave little thought to her feelings. Consideration for Joan's general welfare was similarly lacking in two other renowned knights, her uncle Thomas Wake and William Montague, Earl of Salisbury, William's father. Edward III's own conduct throughout the marital debacle is hardly edifying, as he allowed his young cousin to be treated shamefully by his household knight, by her family, by his best friend and his best friend's son and heir. Yet historically it was Joan's reputation which suffered, enabling the chronicler Adam of Usk in 1399 to suggest that Joan had been guilty of 'slippery ways' in her marital affairs, while no hint of disapproval or blame has been attached to the conduct of the male protagonists in the affair.[85]

6

Lady Holand: A Wife at Last
1350–1352

Wives should be wise and sound administrators and manage their affairs
well.

Christine de Pizan

More than eight years had passed since Joan married Thomas Holand in
the spring of 1341, and they had never lived, or spent much time, together.
What would married life hold for Joan, and how would she be treated
now she was Lady Holand, and no longer the Countess of Salisbury? In
the papal bull dated 13 November 1349 Pope Clement VI required the
bishops of London and Norwich, and the Bishop of Comacchio, the papal
nuncio, to publicly solemnise Thomas and Joan's marriage. No one was to
be left in any doubt that Joan was properly married to Thomas, and that
she was not married to William. The service confirming their marriage
would have taken place in England shortly after the date of the Pope's
injunction, and would have been conducted by one of these bishops. It
would have been fitting for the king and queen to have attended or at
least to have been represented if they were not actually present. Edward
III was possibly absent, as he and Prince Edward left secretly for France
with a handful of knights shortly before Christmas, having learned of
a plan by the French commander Geoffrey de Charny to retake Calais
by stealth. By Christmas 1349 Joan was at last formally recognised as
Thomas' wife, and able to take her place at his side. Any celebrations
for Joan were muted by the effect of the plague's relentless course, but it
would have been unthinkable for the king and queen not to acknowledge
the new Lady Holand and Joan probably celebrated her first Christmas
with Thomas with the royal family before she embarked on her new life.
Although Edward III and Philippa must have been relieved that the matter
was finally settled, the occasion was not noted by the granting of any
individual favours to either Joan or Thomas. It is difficult not to imagine
that Joan's emotions were mixed, with her happiness perhaps tinged with
apprehension, as leaving the court meant parting from all those who had

been close to her over the years to start a life with a man she barely knew, despite all that they had gone through together.

In material terms Joan's circumstances also changed considerably. Edward III's court was an affluent, colourful and busy place thronged with people, the large royal family surrounded by members of the nobility, served and supported by armies of servants. Joan had spent most of her life living at court, and for the last eight years she had enjoyed a publicly prestigious status among her peers as Countess of Salisbury. William Montague was also extremely wealthy, with substantial lands and estates. Joan was exchanging this for a very different lifestyle as the wife of a member of the lower gentry. Thomas was still a knight of very modest means. As a household knight Thomas was probably paid about £12 a year, and this was increased on campaign to a daily contractual payment of 2s a day, whereas an earl like William Montague was paid three times as much for his service.[1] Thomas' mother had done her best to help him, and he did have two small annuities, and during Maud's lifetime the income from three Northamptonshire manors. When she died she left him a lifetime interest in two manors, Yoxall in Staffordshire and Broughton in Buckinghamshire, which did at least mean that he had somewhere to live with Joan, but a great deal less than he might have hoped to achieve. His success in the Crécy campaign should have warranted his promotion to the rank of banneret, but the fact that this had not happened suggests that he lacked the £200 annual income needed to support the status.[2] He was by no means alone in being in this position; his fellow companion in arms Sir John Chandos, for example, despite a similarly excellent record, did not become a banneret until 1360, when he received estates which enabled him to support the rank.

Yet by the end of 1349 Thomas should have received in full the three instalments he had been promised by Edward III for the Count of Eu, and had he done so he would have been a very rich man, and could have purchased estates to provide the requisite income and augment his status. Thomas had evidently received some, if not all, of the first instalment at least, as it had been this which had given him the ability to take the papal proceedings, but it appears that he did not receive the second or third instalments. The suggestion has been made that Thomas had not completed the transfer of the count to the king in the approved manner and therefore Edward III had good reason to refrain from making full payment.[3] The king had placed the Count of Eu in the custody of Otto Holand (Thomas' brother), and Otto had disobeyed his orders by taking the count out of England, for which he was punished with imprisonment in July 1350.[4] However, Otto was not Thomas' responsibility, and the king is unlikely to have used Otto's failing as a justification for reneging on his agreement to pay Thomas. It is more probable that as the count's ransom was still being negotiated in France the king had yet to receive any money, and Edward III was short of cash.[5] In November 1350 the count was released on parole and returned to France in order to raise the money for his ransom, and had he been able to do so Thomas would probably have been paid.[6] Unfortunately the count was arrested shortly after his arrival in Paris, accused of treason and summarily executed; thereafter the French had little incentive to pay the count's ransom. This would explain why the exchequer made no further payments to Thomas, although it is hardly a justifiable excuse as the wording of the grant to Thomas by the king had been unambiguously unconditional. Whatever the real reason, the failure to make full payment was a blow for Thomas, and left him dependant on his career and any prospects he might now acquire as Joan's husband.

It was probably in January 1350 that Thomas took his bride to her new residence, taking leave from a triumphant Edward III. The king had achieved an exhilarating success in Calais by a daring ambush which had prevented Geoffrey de Charny from retaking the town. Thomas had not had time since Maud's death to be at either of his manors, and taking Joan to them was his first opportunity to become more familiar with them himself. Broughton, with its closer proximity to the court, was probably his preferred choice as a residence. The universally catastrophic depredations of the Black Death would have left both manors short of workers, and in a poor state of repair. Thomas' first priority would have been to re-establish the arable crops and livestock to bring in food and income. Inheriting his mother's manor staff, he would have relied on their knowledge and expertise to overcome the effects of the plague. This was also Joan's first experience of running her own household. As Countess of Salisbury, she should have been the head of a large household with many servants and attendants, helping to run William's estates with his council in his absences abroad, but the peculiar circumstances of their marriage had denied her this position. As William's wife she had been kept closely cocooned, first within the royal household and then as William's captive, with William's mother and forceful grandmother filling her role. The most obvious impact of her new status must have been the freedom she now enjoyed. Even if her role in the day-to-day affairs of running the two manors was fairly limited, she now enjoyed an independence she had previously lacked.

This was also the first opportunity Thomas and Joan had to be alone together as a couple and to get to know one another properly. Almost immediately Joan conceived (their first child was born in 1350), indicating that her marriage to William had indeed been celibate.[7] Joan did not enjoy her solitude with her husband for long. In March 1350 Thomas was ordered to report for duty, and rejoined the rest of the army, which was gathering at Sandwich. This time the intended target was the Castilian navy. After Princess Joan's death, the alliance made with Castile had foundered, and Philip of France had bribed Alfonso of Castile to allow him the use of the Castilian navy. These ships engaged in piratical acts along the shipping lanes, and posed an invasion threat. Edward III could not allow this, and planned to remove the danger by attacking the Castilian fleet. In August the king set sail with his force from Sandwich, and engaged the Castilians off the English coast at Winchelsea in Sussex. The Castilians were defeated, their ships sunk, captured or fled. The battle took place so close to the shore that the queen, who had travelled to be with her husband, was able to watch from the cliff tops, with her household. Joan may well have been invited to join the royal party, and would doubtless have been welcomed by the queen, who would have been able to give her some practical advice on her pregnancy. After the king's triumph, the army was once again disbanded, allowing Thomas to take his wife back to their manors.

Thomas no doubt hoped that the recognition of his marriage to Joan would result in a new relationship with the king which would be reflected in his career. Initially there is no indication that his hopes were realised, as after the engagement at Winchelsea there was an uneasy truce between England and France, with a suspension of military activities which limited the opportunities for advancement. With no military engagements Thomas was forced to spend many months away from active service, giving him time with Joan that she must have valued highly. There was little to occupy Thomas in the management of two manors, and he would have looked elsewhere for an outlet for his energies. He was not a man to sit and wait without occupation. His opportunistic marriage to Joan indicated that he fully realised the importance of making connections with people of rank, and it is inconceivable that he would neglect the opportunity afforded by his enforced idleness to capitalise on strengthening his newly won ties with Joan's influential relations. His choice of godfather for his firstborn son is significant. By the end of 1350 Joan had borne Thomas their first child, a boy named Thomas, after his father.[8] Prince Edward stood as godfather, attending the christening, which was probably held at Broughton church. As Thomas had been under his command the prince was perhaps a natural choice for godfather, and the prince was also known to be fond of his cousin, but there is no doubt that he was also an extremely valuable and influential patron for the young Thomas. The prince did not neglect his godchild in his first few years either, as the prince's household accounts record that in April 1353 he presented his godson with a handsome gift of two silver basins, enamelled at the bottom, worth more than £10, suggesting that he probably gave him regular annual gifts.[9]

The affection between Joan and her brother would have made a visit to the young Earl of Kent and his wife Elizabeth natural. The vicissitudes of the last few years had seen great changes in John's life as well. John had taken part in the Crécy campaign, probably under the aegis of Henry of Lancaster (as he appears among Henry's retinue for 1346–7), but unlike Thomas Holand and William Montague, and in contrast to his cousin Prince Edward, he does not seem to have shown any military prowess and may not even have been present at the battle.[10] Nevertheless, Edward III had granted him his full inheritance in 1347 when he was only seventeen, giving John independence from his mother. John had become a very wealthy young man, with estates in seventeen counties, comprising forty-three manors, with the right to thirty advowsons as well as extensive income from annual rents and knight's fees, the latter extending over a further six counties. At a conservative estimate these brought in a collective annual income of just under £6,000, nearly six times the income considered necessary to support the style of an earl.[11] When John had married Elizabeth in the spring of 1348, Joan may not have been able to attend their wedding, as it was around this time that the Pope was issuing instructions for Joan to be freed from confinement by William. When Margaret died in 1349 John inherited his mother's dower properties and the Wake estates which she had inherited from her brother, Thomas Wake. These were granted to John in February 1350, and a year later, on 10 April 1351, Edward III confirmed his inheritance.[12] Until John and Elizabeth had children, Joan was John's heir, a fact of which Thomas would have been keenly aware, while John may well have been in awe of his formidable brother-in-law, whose achievements on campaign had been matched by his determined pursuit of his sister. Possibly Thomas and Joan stayed with them at Castle Donington in Leicestershire, and if so then they may have extended their trip to pay their respects to Blanche Wake, Thomas Wake's widow, at Bourne Castle in Lincolnshire. As Henry of Lancaster's sister, Blanche had doubtless supported her husband's views on Joan's marriage to Thomas and it seems unlikely that she ever developed warm feelings for her niece's husband. Blanche, however, knew what was due to family, and Joan was probably able to repair her own relationship with her aunt, although there is no evidence that they ever became close.

Apart from her brother, Joan's two closest blood relatives were her cousins, Margaret and Alice, the daughters of her father's brother, Thomas Brotherton, Earl of Norfolk. Margaret was the elder and about eight years older than Joan. In her earliest years at court Joan would have seen little of her cousins, and it would certainly not have been a connection encouraged by her mother, who would not have forgotten or forgiven Thomas Brotherton for his failure to help her when Edmund was executed. The Earl of Norfolk died in 1338, and after Joan 'married' William Montague in 1341 it is likely that she became more familiar with her cousin Alice, who was married to William's uncle Edward Montague. The youngest of Edward and Alice's five children was called Joan, quite possibly named after Joan and with her acting as godmother.[13] Unfortunately Alice died in January 1352, preventing a closer relationship between the cousins.[14] Margaret was a more forceful and determined personality, and seems to have taken encouragement from Joan's matrimonial tangles. Margaret had been married as a child by her father to his ward, John Segrave, and by 1338 had borne him two children.[15] The marriage did not, however, please Margaret, and in October 1350 she went in person to Rome to secure a divorce from her husband, claiming that she had agreed to marry before she was of a marriageable age and had never agreed to cohabit with him.[16] She was unsuccessful, and had to wait for her freedom until 1353, when Segrave died, whereupon she immediately married Sir Walter Mauny, one of the queen's favourite knights.[17] In doing so Margaret incurred the king's disapproval as she had failed to get his permission first, as well as having crossed the Channel in contravention of the king's orders, and a year later she found herself imprisoned for a short time when the council took proceedings against her.[18] It was many months before the king pardoned her. There is nothing to suggest that Margaret and Joan ever became close, and this may partly be due to Margaret's matrimonial affairs. While Thomas Holand might have had some sympathy with Margaret, recognising in her determination and willingness to take risks a kindred spirit, he might have felt it prudent to maintain a distance between them until the king's wrath had abated.

There is unfortunately no evidence to indicate what kind of relationship Joan enjoyed with the royal princesses. Joan had been brought up with princesses Isabella and Joan, and of all her contemporaries these were her most obvious bosom companions. Although Princess Joan had died, Princess Isabella remained unmarried and at court, and was a favourite with her parents. Joan was about four years older than Isabella, and it would have been natural for her to have become close to Isabella as they grew up, and to maintain any attachment in adulthood. Joan had been living with Isabella when she married Thomas Holand in 1340, and had remained with the princess for most of the subsequent nine-year period, with Isabella witnessing at close hand the effects on her cousin of her anomalous situation. The eventual triumph for Joan in being united with the man of her choice and surviving her family's opposition was a lesson Isabella might well have taken to heart. In 1351 Isabella was nineteen, and Edward III announced his consent to the marriage of 'our very dear daughter whom we have loved with special affection' to Bernard, heir to Bernard d'Albret – almost the same match which had been agreed for Joan eleven years previously in 1340.[19] The importance of the alliance for the king in diplomatic terms was obvious but it seems a surprising match to impose on a daughter of whom he was unashamedly fond if she was unwilling, and it is therefore intriguing to note that Isabella refused to board the ship that had been ordered to take her to Gascony, and the match was subsequently called off. Isabella's spirited defiance and independence enabled her to avoid matrimony until July 1365, when at the age of thirty-three she married Enguerrand de Coucy, a French knight being held hostage in England at the time; quite clearly a personal choice.

In February 1352 Thomas resumed his military career. He was appointed captain of Calais Castle, responsible for the castle garrison, with his brother Otto as his deputy.[20] This was just the sort of important command for which he had hoped. Calais had been won by Edward III after an extremely costly siege, and had strategic military importance as it provided a haven for English shipping and a safe bridgehead for entrance into France. Its trading role was just as significant, and Edward III intended to repopulate the town with Englishmen.[21] The French were anxious to retake the town if they could, and its vulnerability had been demonstrated at Christmas 1349 by Geoffrey de Charny's raid. The town was almost totally dependent on England for its food, munitions and other supplies, and had a large garrison.[22] The king needed to place the defence of the town in the hands of an able, loyal, resourceful and courageous commander, and Thomas' experience ideally suited him for the post. The appointment was to be until Christmas, and Thomas appointed attorneys to act for him in his absence and to aid Joan in managing his affairs while he was abroad.[23] Joan was pregnant with their second child, and when the baby was born he was named John, after her brother, a sign of their affectionate relationship. It is likely that Joan asked her brother to be godfather to the baby John Holand.[24] The expenses of Thomas' new command and the additional family responsibilities stretched his resources and in August 1352 he petitioned the king for financial assistance, reminding Edward III of his relationship with Joan.[25] It is possible that Thomas also reminded the king that he had not received the full amount he had been promised for the Count of Eu; if he did there is no written record. Edward III granted Thomas' request but his response was not particularly generous. The king grudgingly agreed a grant of only 100 marks a year limited to Joan's lifetime 'in aid of her sustenance', stating that the annuity would cease immediately if Joan's brother John died, and Joan inherited his lands; as John was only twenty-two, this must have seemed most unlikely. The fact that Thomas felt the need to ask for financial assistance, and the king's reaction, is a clear indication that the king's attitude remained equivocal towards him. He valued Thomas for his military abilities but this was a separate matter from their personal relationship. Although Edward III had indirectly helped Thomas to achieve the formal recognition of his marriage to Joan, the king was making it plain to Thomas that he did not intend to reward him for this, and did not welcome him with open arms as a new relation.

On 23 December 1352 John was conducting business as usual at his favourite manor of Woking in Surrey, granting his manor of Ryhall in Rutland to Bartholomew de Burghersh, when he was taken ill, and died a few days later on 27 December.[26] He was twenty-two years old. His sudden death was a tremendous shock for his widow, Elizabeth, and no doubt for Joan too, as he was her only surviving close relation. Their early shared childhood, their dependence on one another, the unusual difficulties endured by Joan as John was growing up and their more recent closeness meant that his death left a huge gap in her life. John was buried in the Grey Friars church in Winchester. The only known connection John had with the church is the fact that his father was buried there after his execution in 1330. The choice of John's resting place suggests that despite Margaret's plans Edmund's body had never been moved to Westminster, and that John's widow, Elizabeth, felt it appropriate to bury her husband with his father.[27] Elizabeth had evidently loved her husband very much. Shortly after John's death she took the veil and became a nun, entering Waverley Abbey in Surrey.[28] Although Elizabeth later returned to the outside world, her feelings for John remained strong, and more than fifty years later she left instructions in her will that she was to be buried with him.[29]

Joan's grief at her brother's death was overshadowed by the immense implications for her of his death. As John and Elizabeth had no children, Joan was her brother's heir, and her unexpected inheritance transformed her into one of the greatest and wealthiest landowners in England. When John died the inquisitions post mortem compiled after his death show that he had interests in twenty-three different counties, a mix of landed estates (manors) and a right to income in the form of fee farms (a fixed sum of money due annually), knight's fees (an annual cash payment made by a knight to lieu of military service) and advowsons (the right to present a clergyman for appointment to a living).[30] Forty-three manors are listed: Chesterfield and Ashford in Derbyshire; Kenton, Lifton, Shebbear and Chettiscombe in Devon; Northweald and Lamarsh in Essex, Lechlade, Barnsley, Siddington and Miserden in Gloucestershire; Bedhampton and Alton in Hampshire; Bushey in Hertfordshire; Caldecot in Huntingdonshire; Wickham in Kent; Castle Donington and its manor in Leicestershire; Greetham, Bretby and Beesby in Lincolnshire; Torpel, Upton and Easton in Northamptonshire; Ollerton in Nottinghamshire; Whissendine and Ryhall in Rutland; Somerton, Kingsbury and Queen's Camel in Somerset; Leyham and Kersey in Suffolk; Woking, Pirbright and Tolworth in Surrey; and Cottingham, Weighton, Buttercrambe, Kirkbymoorside, Cropton, Middleton, Ayton and Hemlington in Yorkshire.[31] In many of these counties there was further income from fee farms and knight's fees as well as advowsons, and in addition an entitlement to rental income in a further six counties: Buckinghamshire, Norfolk, Sussex, Warwick, Wiltshire and Worcestershire.[32] By any standard of measurement this was a major inheritance.

Elizabeth, as John's widow, was entitled to a third share of John's estates as her dower; on her death these would revert to Joan or her heirs. Although the valuations given in John's inquisitions post mortem are incomplete, a calculation of the income to which Joan became entitled on his death can be estimated from the dower grant to Elizabeth, which carefully lists the properties and annual income she received.[33] Elizabeth's

dower income comes to nearly £1,800 a year, and so the remaining
two-thirds inherited by Joan can be estimated conservatively as nearly
£3,500 a year. This was a huge income at a time when £1,000 a year
was considered necessary to support the style of an earl, and with the
exception of the Earl of Lancaster it is difficult to find any other noble
who enjoyed such an income. As a point of comparison, contemporaries
considered Joan's cousin Margaret Brotherton extremely wealthy with
an estimated income of £3,000 a year, likewise an older cousin of Joan's,
Elizabeth de Burgh, who enjoyed between £2,000 to £2,500 a year.
Thomas and Joan's income previously had been under £200 a year.
Thomas had probably never thought that his gamble in marrying Joan
would pay off in such a lucrative fashion.

Thomas was still in France when news of John's death reached him, and
he immediately returned to England. As Joan's husband he would take
responsibility for, and have control over, all of the estates and income to
which she would be entitled. This was not a matter which could be dealt
with by his attorneys. The first business which needed to be agreed was
to sort out Elizabeth's dower. John had left a will and his executors were
Elizabeth, Gerard Braybrooke – a knight and justice of the peace in Kent,
Bedfordshire and Buckinghamshire and a distant relative and long-standing
family friend who had known Edmund and acted for Margaret over many
years – and James Beaufort, a clerk and another long-time family friend.[34]
Elizabeth's dower was quickly agreed with Thomas and Joan in January
1353 and on 15 February the dower estates were formally vested in
Elizabeth, while on 22 February the escheators were ordered to deliver the
remaining estates, and the tenants ordered to pay their rents, to Thomas
and Joan.[35] The ease and speed with which Elizabeth's dower was agreed
would undoubtedly have been helped by Joan's knowledge of the family
estates, enabling Thomas to recognise the immense practicality of the split
which was suggested, probably by the executors. Elizabeth was given a
geographically composite group of holdings; all of the holdings in the
south-west in Devon and Gloucestershire, and those in the south-east in
Hampshire and Surrey. Joan took possession of the remaining twenty-
seven manors, which were spread over twelve counties.

An inheritance of this magnitude completely changed Thomas' status.
He took immediate advantage of his newfound wealth to ease his penurious
position, and on 23 February 1353 he acknowledged a debt of 200 marks
to Richard, Earl of Arundel, and on 12 March a debt of 400 marks to Sir
Ralph Neville.[36] He repaid these debts quickly but cash flow remained a
problem for a while as a year later, in February 1354, he was granted a
six-month respite from his obligation to pay debts and produce accounts to
the exchequer.[37] Naturally, now the king would not be paying the promised
annuity to Joan. Official recognition of Thomas' new status came swiftly
with a summons to Parliament. However, as Joan's husband, Thomas was
not entitled to become Earl of Kent until the king granted him the title,

and Edward III made no move to do so.[38] While this was not necessarily an unusual delay on the king's part, it is possible that Edward III continued to have reservations about rewarding Thomas for having won Joan, despite his acceptance and endorsement of their marriage. Nevertheless Thomas had every anticipation that the king would grant him the earldom in time, and by 1354 his seal included a flowering tree with his shield of arms suspended by a strap, closely resembling part of John's seal, while on the left-hand or sinister side he had a helmet out of a ducal coronet (a feature shared by Otto Holand in his shield of arms) and a plume of ostrich feathers (the ostrich feathers were adopted by Prince Edward after Crécy).[39]

The most important individual estate now owned by Thomas and Joan was Castle Donington in Leicestershire, and they would quickly have moved themselves, with their two boys, into residence.[40] The castle occupied a strong position to the west of the town itself, above the Trent, dominating the river crossing and overlooking a wide stretch of low-lying land, with its own chapel, park, fishery and ferry to cross the river, and it was surrounded by its own woodland, meadows and pasture land on which cattle grazed. The original castle was Norman, but it had been dismantled on the orders of the king in 1216 during the First Barons' War and then rebuilt later that century, probably by the Earl of Lincoln and using some of the materials from the earlier castle.[41] The castle had its own chapel, and at the nearby church of St George in Stamford, Thomas' relation, John Holand, had been the vicar since 1349.[42] Castle Donington was reasonably centrally located in relation to the other estates, and within easy travelling distance of Blanche Wake at Bourne Castle in Lincolnshire and Robert Holand at Thorpe Waterville in Northamptonshire.

Apart from his newfound status and wealth, Joan's inheritance had also made Thomas a major landowner, and their son Thomas was now heir to the Kent earldom and all its assets. This meant not simply a change of lifestyle for Thomas, but the potential for a completely different career. Previously Thomas had shown little interest in land, and with only a lifetime interest in the Broughton and Yoxall manors he had done no more than ensure he received their income on a regular basis. Now he controlled his wife's enormous inheritance, and had an incentive to take an active interest in the estates, assess their condition, plan their future, looking at improving and consolidating them, with the aim of preserving and enhancing his son's inheritance. It is difficult to know what condition the estates were in when John died, but many would still have been suffering from the devastating effects of the plague. When Margaret died in 1349 the escheator noted that the value of her dower manors at Torpel, Upton and Easton in Northamptonshire, and the extensive Wake manors in Yorkshire, were 'showing great decreases in value because of the pestilence'.[43] John's escheators give a grim description of the deprivations wrought on other parts of the estates. In Derbyshire, the water mill, fulling mill and lead mine at Ashford manor, formerly worth £20 a year, were valued at 100s, as they had been 'stopped for want of workers', while the town of Ollerton in Nottinghamshire is described as 'remain[ing] mostly without inhabitants and the dwelling houses broken down and empty, and none will hire them'.[44] The general picture is of land left untended, properties empty and in poor repair, a lack of labour and tenants, resulting in rents at risk. This of course was a national problem, but recovery on the Kent estates may have been hindered by a lack of effective management. Edmund's death and John's long minority had meant that many of the estates had been managed for twenty years by Margaret and various nominees of the Crown. This did not apply to the Wake estates, which Thomas Wake had enjoyed from 1317 up to his death in 1349, but much of his land was held in border areas and had suffered considerably from the Scots' frequent incursions. John was swift to grant the reversion of the Cumberland barony to Edward III (who then granted it to John of Gaunt in 1357) but it was hardly a loss as it was described by the inquest jury as 'worth nothing ... because it is totally laid waste ... by the Scots'.[45]

If Thomas and Joan were not to spend all their time in estate management they would need to place more than usual reliance on the people whom they entrusted to run the estates on their behalf. The management of the many estates comprised in the Kent earldom required a complex and hierarchical structure.[46] Overall supervision would have been placed in the hands of a council, comprising the lord himself, advisers chosen from among his entourage (usually his leading knights) and the officials who had charge of the day-to-day management of the manors; his receivers, stewards and auditors. The administrative centre for the council would have been at Castle Donington, and the chief officials probably resided there with Thomas and Joan. The council's job was to act as a central advisory body, making decisions and giving advice, hearing petitions and giving judgment on them. As the Kent earldom consisted of estates spread over so many counties, it would have been necessary to geographically divide the manors into convenient groups for administrative purposes, each with their own steward or bailiff and accounting to the same receiver who was in turn responsible to the council. The individual steward's duties extended to presiding over the manorial and hundred courts – each manor had its own court and each hundred (administrative districts within a shire) its own judicial court. Beneath the stewards were the officials representing the lord on each individual manor, including the reeve, whose duties covered collecting the rents due and accounting for them as well as speaking for the interests of the tenants. Reeves were exempt from labour services but the duality of the role meant it was not an easy one to discharge well and was often an unpopular duty imposed rather than sought after. The rents received were collected up and delivered to the lord's receiver, who in turn distributed the money to each part of the household. Beneath the reeve were the tenant farmers, the people who actually cultivated the land and tended the livestock.

It is unfortunate that the extensive records which Thomas and Joan's council would have kept for each individual manor, detailing its extent and its value, every tenancy, the rents received and payments made, have not survived.[47] The lack of these papers means that reliance has to be placed on incomplete information, much of it gleaned from the inquisitions post mortem completed after John's death and then after that of Thomas Holand, and Joan herself. Management of large estates was inevitably complicated but Joan's inheritance, notably so because of certain fairly unique features. It was, firstly, unusual to have two dowager interests. Naturally Thomas and Joan would have considered it important to be on good terms with Blanche Wake and Joan's sister-in-law Elizabeth, especially as one day their dower interests would fall back into the Kent estates. In 1352 none of them could have foreseen that both dowagers would live for as long as they did; Blanche Wake died in July 1380, while Elizabeth outlived Joan by more than twenty years, and died in 1411.[48] Secondly, in contrast to most large landowners, the Kent estates had no obvious geographical concentration. The Earl of Lancaster's estates, for example, were located largely in the north and the Midlands, the Earl of Salisbury's (William Montague) in the West Country. Thomas Brotherton's estates, inherited by Joan's cousin Margaret, were mainly in Norfolk and Suffolk. In contrast, the Kent estates were spread widely over different counties, with very few holdings in the county of Kent, and had Thomas and Joan wished to visit every estate they now owned it would have taken them weeks to do so.

Many of the Kent manors were rented out rather than managed directly, an example being the manor of Ryhall in Rutland which was leased to Sir Bartholomew Burghersh.[49] There were obvious advantages for a landlord in leasing and receiving annual rent rather than being directly involved in cultivation, harvesting and selling the produce, increasingly so after the Black Death had decimated the labour market. Renting was an attractive and obvious option for Thomas Holand, with his lack of experience and knowledge of estate management, and he had no incentive to alter any such arrangements that John had already made. Nevertheless, careful and extensive management was needed in order to realise the wealth of Joan's inheritance. Rents had still to be collected and accounted for, and when these were not forthcoming it was necessary to pursue those in dispute or arrears. When tenants died, new tenants had to be found. Margaret's experience had shown that some tenants, especially the ecclesiastical tenants, were prompt to find excuses not to pay and tardy in making payment when ordered to do so.

Thomas and Joan initially inherited John's council, and they would not necessarily have made any immediate changes. Continuity was obviously important and replacements may have been in short supply. Some of these knights and clerks can be identified. When John signed the lease renewal shortly before he died his witnesses were Gerard Braybrooke,

Thomas Aspale, Henry Loxley (all knights), Thomas Brembre and James Beaufort (both clerks).[50] Gerard Braybrooke and James Beaufort were also his executors.[51] These men were almost certainly on John's council. Gerard Braybrooke, a justice of the peace in Kent, Bedfordshire and Buckinghamshire, was particularly close to Joan's family, a distant relation (through Margaret's grandmother Lora Wake, who married Gerard's ancestor Gerard Braybrooke) who had originally served Edmund with his brother Henry and then continued to act for Margaret, before serving John.[52] Thomas Aspale's family similarly had a long association with Joan's family, Robert and John Aspale having both served Edmund (John had been in France with Edmund in 1329), while Thomas and John had acted for Margaret; John, like Gerard Braybrooke, was a justice of the peace (in Norfolk and Suffolk).[53] Thomas already knew Thomas Aspale as they had served together in 1346.[54] Thomas Brembre had probably also served the family for a long time, as in November 1349 he had been presented to the church at Cottingham (one of the Yorkshire estates John inherited on his mother's death), presumably as a reward for his services.[55] Brembre also acted as a clerk for the king and by 1351 Brembre held prebendaries at Chichester, Southwell and Westminster; in 1352 he was presented to the church in Iver in Buckinghamshire.[56] These men had considerable experience with a history of loyalty to the family, and they would have been well aware of the troubles Joan had experienced in her marriage to Thomas. James Beaufort may have known more than most, as he had been one of the Earl of Salisbury's executors when he died in 1344.[57] It would have been natural for these men to be happy to serve Joan, and Thomas would have had little reason to replace them. However, their age meant that in time replacements would need to be found. Thomas Aspale died within a year of John's death, and a year after Thomas appointed Gerard Braybrooke as one of his attorneys Gerard's son John was murdered and Gerard seems to have stepped back from affairs; possibly he was simply too old to manage any more.[58]

Given Thomas' willingness to take risks in his career it is perhaps surprising that he proved to be conservative in his approach towards the estates. The huge geographical diversity of the many manors made the inheritance unwieldy to manage, and the sheer inconvenience of this coupled with the disadvantage of the lack of concentration in any one area, made a rationalisation of the estates an obvious and logical ambition. Neither Joan's father nor her brother had enjoyed control for sufficient time to attempt this. Thomas had the opportunity, but he gave no indication that he had any inclination to do so, unlike some of his contemporaries. William Bohun, whom Thomas served with in France, became Earl of Northampton and bought considerable amounts of land in the 1350s to increase his Bohun inheritance.[59] Thomas could have reduced the geographical spread of Joan's inheritance and achieved a more concentrated mass of estates by actively pursuing a policy of buying and selling or even exchanging land. But he did not do so, and instead simply chose to preserve what Joan inherited, no doubt with his son in mind. Just as John had benefitted from his mother's careful stewardship of the estates, so Thomas did, as there do not seem to have been any major disputes over any of the manors, while minor disputes appear to have resolved largely without resort to the courts. The official records reveal only two individual instances: in June 1355 Thomas and Joan agreed to pay Sir Thomas Dale 300 marks to release his claim to Leyham manor in Suffolk, and in February 1360 Thomas and Joan petitioned Edward III to recognise Joan's claim to property in Cottingham in Yorkshire which Thomas Wake had given to Robert and Alice Cottingham.[60]

Apart from the actual management of the lands, Thomas now headed a huge household. In addition to the receivers, stewards and other officials such as lawyers required to run the estates, there were a host of other retainers; Thomas had his own retinue of knights, squires and heralds, clerks to handle his papers and records, a chaplain, confessor and almoner, grooms and valets for his horses, domestic servants to staff his residences, minstrels to entertain. It is difficult to estimate how many people now comprised Thomas and Joan's household, as their household records have not survived, but an idea of the numbers can be surmised from their contemporaries. In 1343, with a smaller income and fewer estates, Joan's widowed cousin Elizabeth de Burgh (Elizabeth was the daughter of Edmund's half-sister Joan of Acre) maintained a household of around 250, including fifteen knights, ninety-three esquires, thirty-nine clerks and four goldsmiths to take care of her jewellery and plate, seven ladies of her chamber each with their own maidservant plus a laundress and chambermaids.[61] Elizabeth was famously hospitable, enjoying her visitors and notably generous in dispensing alms; her accounts show that in one five-month period 5,090 people received alms from her.[62] In 1384 the Earl of Devon is known to have had a similar number in his household. Thomas and Joan may have inherited a more modest household due to the depredations of the plague, but they would have added to it with Thomas' knights and esquires. This meant a significant change of lifestyle for Joan, as she was now head of an extremely large household and was expected to take an interest in their affairs.

Thomas and Joan were now in a position to reward members of their entourage, and to exercise patronage in accordance with their taste and wishes. Some of their contemporaries, like Elizabeth de Burgh and her friend Marie, Countess of Pembroke, were notably generous benefactors, while Joan's uncle Thomas Wake had been a keen patron of religious orders and founded a house of Augustinian canons near Cottingham at Haltemprice and supported the Augustinian priory of Bourne. However, there is little evidence to suggest that Thomas and Joan followed their example. In March 1354 they were described as patrons of a religious house at Wothorpe in Lincolnshire, a very small house of nuns who requested their aid in order to unite with the larger Benedictine priory of St Michael at Stamford, having lost most of their incumbents to the plague in 1349.[63] This was no more than might be expected from people in their position, just as they obtained permission for the weekly market at Buttercrambe manor in Yorkshire with the annual fair on St Botolph's Day.[64] The only records of any notable gifts made by Thomas were to his brother and nephew. In July 1355 Thomas and Joan granted Otto the Derbyshire manors of Ashford and Chesterfield with the advowson of the hospital of St Leonard, and subsequently they also granted Otto the manors of Tolworth in Surrey and Kersey in Suffolk.[65] Thomas also passed his Yoxall manor to Otto.[66] In November 1360 they granted Thomas' nephew John Holand the manors of Northweald in Essex and Whissendine in Rutland.[67] Even these gifts were lifetime interests only, reverting to Joan or her heir on their respective deaths.

The great landed wealth Thomas now enjoyed gave him an independent importance in national politics which he had not previously had. To put it simply, the king needed his support, because of the resources in terms of money and men which he now commanded. This gave Thomas the potential for power and influence, and he could now expect to find the king courting him, rather than having to sue for favours himself. Thomas had amply demonstrated his ambition in engineering his secret marriage to Joan and in his subsequent behaviour, and his newfound status gave him a position he could never have dreamed of attaining. His marriage had also proved to be a considerable success on a personal level, with Joan comfortably adapting to her new roles as his wife and mother to their children, and assisting in the management of their newfound wealth. With her experience of the court, Joan would also be a valuable ally to Thomas in pursuing any political ambitions he cherished.

7

A Soldier's Wife
1352–1360

Un gentil chevalier …

Froissart

In spite of their newfound wealth and responsibilities as a result of John's death, it was not long before Joan discovered that Thomas' energy and enthusiasm remained focussed on his military career. He showed no interest in politics, and there is no record of him even attending Parliament on a single occasion, although he was summoned there in his new capacity. Far from showing ambitions at home, for the next eight years, from 1352 up to his death in 1360, Thomas spent long periods of time away from England on military duties in France. He was by no means the only committed career soldier among the nobility, and, like other similarly placed noblewomen, Joan's place in her husband's absence should have been to run the estates with the assistance of their council. She could have used their increased wealth, and Thomas' absences, to extend her personal influence, exert her own control over her family estates and enhance their status by re-establishing her position within the royal circle. Instead, the records show that Joan accompanied Thomas to France on at least four occasions between 1354 and 1359, each for months at a time. The war in France would set the agenda for the remainder of Joan's marriage to Thomas. Away from England for extended periods, she could have had little involvement in court circles, or local affairs. Joan was extremely unusual among her peers in choosing to accompany her husband, and it is not clear why she did so. To gain some insight into what happened to her during these years it is necessary to examine Thomas' career in more detail.

Edward III was a shrewd judge of character and realised that despite his changed circumstances Thomas' priorities remained his military career. He did not even make Thomas a justice of the peace, a quite extraordinary omission for a man of his position. It was the king, rather than Thomas, who took advantage of his change of circumstances. With the continuing conflict with France there would be ample opportunity to pursue military ambitions. On 18 March 1354 Edward III formally appointed Thomas as his royal lieutenant in Brittany and Poitou. This was a significant career advancement for Thomas, now aged about thirty-eight, and the command put him in charge of an entire region rather than a single castle garrison, and gave him administrative as well as military duties. He was to be paid by the exchequer for the first quarter and thereafter to receive all the profits and rents from Brittany from Easter 1354.[1] The intention was that he would be financially independent from the English Treasury, relying on Brittany to fund his costs, and he would be expected to make up any shortfall from his own money. The king would not have contemplated Thomas for this appointment before John's death, for the simple reason that Thomas had lacked the private wealth to support the position. This promotion meant that Thomas was back serving in Brittany within a few months; once again he would be leaving Joan behind.[2]

Thomas' new appointment was important because of the significance of Brittany for Edward III. Since the fall of Calais in 1347 there had been an uneasy peace between England and France, broken by intermittent skirmishes, raids and sieges in northern and north-eastern France, with the only major engagement being the sea battle off Winchelsea in 1350. The devastating effect of the Black Death in both countries was to a large extent responsible for the inability and unwillingness of both sides to engage in active campaigning, but the basic elements of the conflict remained unresolved. In August 1350, just weeks after Winchelsea, Philip VI died and was succeeded by his son, John. Faced with English supremacy in the field and the unreliability of some of his more senior nobles, such as his son-in-law, Charles of Navarre, the new King of France, John II (known as John the Good), showed more willingness than his father to reach an agreement with Edward III in order to end the war. Renewed negotiations resulted in a draft treaty concluded at Guines in April 1354, although as it was not due to be made public until October the provisions were kept secret for several months. The terms of the draft treaty were distinctly favourable to Edward III. In exchange for giving up his claim to the French throne, he was to be given full sovereignty of the duchy of Aquitaine, with significant territorial concessions, including Calais and its environs. Until the treaty was ratified and published there was to be a truce suspending hostile activities.

With the alluring prospect of achieving his ambitions in France within his grasp, Edward III naturally ordered his supporters to observe the truce. However, this did not prove to be a simple matter. There were many soldiers still in France, including several of the king's captains and other commanders, and not all of them were prepared to obey. Some saw it as their right to take advantage of the weakness of France and seize goods and lands for profit. The duchy of Brittany was an area of particular difficulty. Succession to the dukedom had been in dispute since Duke

John III died in 1341, and although Edward III had both claimants in his hands (Charles of Blois, who was supported by France, had been his captive since 1347, and he was guardian to Charles' rival, Duke John's heir), exercising control in the duchy proved difficult. With support from France, Charles of Blois' wife Jeanne retained control of large parts of the duchy including the towns of Rennes and Nantes, despite the valiant efforts made by the Countess of Montfort on her son's behalf. Edward III's influence in the duchy depended on a loose alliance of local lords and English captains in command of individual garrisons whose tendency to look after their own interests blurred their allegiance to the English Crown. As the peace negotiations advanced throughout 1353 Edward III was increasingly conscious that his lieutenant in Brittany, Sir John Avenel, was failing to keep control of the duchy. By November 1353 the king had decided he needed to replace Avenel, and chose Thomas as his replacement.

Now that Thomas had become sufficiently wealthy to support the position, he was a logical choice. He was one of the king's more senior captains, and had a proven track record as a strong and forceful commander. He had previous experience of service in Brittany, having served in the 1343 summer expedition to the duchy led by the Earl of Northampton with Robert d'Artois. At Calais Thomas had been an outstanding captain, proving that in addition to his worth as a fighting knight and his leadership abilities on campaign he was also capable of using his abilities to secure long-term strategic aims. During his command Calais' defences had been consolidated, and the surrounding regions secured, with the nearby local forts strengthened and an efficient supply line secured, thus preparing the port for its use as a long-term base.[3] Thomas' new position would put him in overall command of one of the main theatres of the conflict with France. Although the appointment in Brittany was not formalised until the spring, Thomas immediately threw his energies into planning for his new command, and by December 1353 had assembled a small force at Plymouth of 160 men – 60 men-at-arms and 100 archers – including Otto as his lieutenant, his brother Robert, and his nephews John Holand and his sister Margaret's son, John de la Warr.[4] Adverse sailing conditions delayed their departure until March 1354, incurring expenses for Thomas of £200, a sum which only two years earlier would have equated to the whole of his income from his estates.

In Thomas' absence, the obvious role for Joan was to manage their affairs at home and to be involved in running the great estates they now owned. Shortly before he departed Thomas appointed attorneys to act on his behalf in his absence. Conscious of his newly enhanced status, he chose carefully: Roger Mortimer, Earl of March; the knights Sir Richard Pembridge, Sir Edward Bereford, Sir John Wingfield and Sir Henry Green; and clerks Gervase Wilford, John Winwick, David Wollore, Randolf

Saleby and John Raynford.[5] Most of these were men he had either served
with or knew because of his royal service. Roger Mortimer, like Thomas,
had distinguished himself during the Crécy campaign, and had only
recently been granted his grandfather's title. Sir Richard Pembridge was
a fellow household knight whom Thomas had known for many years,
having served together under Robert d'Artois in 1338.[6] Sir Henry Green
was a member of Prince Edward's council and Sir John Wingfield was one
of the prince's household knights, Thomas would have known both men
well from their joint military service under the prince's command during
the Crécy campaign. Sir John Wingfield had also been a close friend of the
Earl of Salisbury and served as one of the earl's executors; subsequently
he became William Montague's guardian and in 1351 had been William's
attorney.[7] It is remarkable that Thomas chose Wingfield given the latter's
close ties to the Montagues. Gervase Wilford, John Winwick and David
Wollore were all senior royal clerks, Wollore the keeper of the chancery
rolls, Winwick the keeper of the privy seal and Wilford having acted
as Queen Philippa's attorney but also bearing a family connection as
he had acted for Thomas' mother, Maud, in 1335.[8] Although Thomas
had appointed ten attorneys, the only ones who would actually have
been expected to have much to do with the day-to-day running of the
estates were his own clerks. Randolf Saleby and John Raynford were
almost certainly members of Thomas and Joan's household. In July
1353 John Raynford had become parson of Tinwell church in Rutland
on an exchange of benefices from St Clement's church in Hastings, an
arrangement made by Edward III presumably at Thomas and Joan's
behest.[9] Otto Holand also appointed John Raynford as his attorney.[10]

It is curious that Thomas did not choose to appoint Joan as one
of his attorneys. He could easily have done so, as it was certainly not
uncommon for women in her position to be appointed by their husbands.
Indeed, bearing in mind that the estates were Joan's, it would have been
natural to do so. He was leaving her in charge of their great household
and the supervision of their children's care. Even though Joan was not his
attorney, she would still be involved in overseeing their estates. Her role
in running them would be important, as she would be consulted regularly
by the stewards about their management and would assist in important
decisions. Possibly Thomas expected Joan to further their interests by
strengthening her relationships with her aunt Blanche, and her sister-
in-law Elizabeth (with their dower interests), and re-establish her place
within the royal circle. Yet it seems that Thomas was uneasy about
leaving Joan behind. Pope Clement VI, who had issued the papal bull
confirming their marriage, had died in December 1352. Shortly before
his departure in the spring of 1354 Thomas petitioned the new pope,
Innocent VI, requesting confirmation of Clement VI's 1349 papal bull.[11]
In July 1354 Thomas received his reassurance when Innocent VI duly
reaffirmed the 1349 judgment. Although there is no evidence to suggest

that William Montague ever considered doing so, Thomas was evidently alert to the possibility that his erstwhile rival, now Earl of Salisbury, might take advantage of his absence and press the Pope to review the decision confirming the validity of their marriage. His brother-in-law's death had made Joan a more desirable prize than ever before. Thomas may have been prudent to do so, as it was not unknown for a new pope to revoke his predecessor's decision.

Thomas was initially away for several months. His orders in Brittany were to secure all the captured towns, execute grants of Breton castles by Edward III to English nominees and, most importantly, ensure the truce was observed. Shortly before his arrival in late April 1354, Hugh Calverley, the English commander of the garrison at Becherel, was defeated and captured in a fight with the French marshal, d'Audrehem. This threatened the English position in the north-east of the duchy. Thomas' first act on arriving was to join his own force with that of local allies and to launch a counter-attack, sweeping through north-eastern Brittany and into Lower Normandy. By June Thomas was satisfied that he had restored English authority in the area and drew his campaign to a close.[12] Edward III must have viewed his activities with a mixture of irritation and satisfaction. Thomas' aggressive actions had flouted the truce, but he had swiftly and successfully protected the English position. Having exerted his authority decisively Thomas returned to England, possibly for further reinforcements and supplies but probably in response to orders from the king. Pleased that English dominance in the duchy had been reasserted, in November Edward III entrusted Thomas with the custody of the young heir to the duchy, John Montfort, now aged about fifteen. The boy had reached an age where it was more appropriate for him to return to his own land rather than remain with the royal household, and the king now had a competent lieutenant on whom he could rely to keep the boy safe.

Thomas returned to England in the early autumn of 1354, but he was only in England for a matter of weeks. When he returned to Brittany at the end of November Joan sailed with him. They evidently anticipated that Joan's sojourn in the duchy would be commensurate with her husband's, as they appointed Randolf Saleby and John Raynford jointly to act as their attorneys in their absence.[13] Joan was unusual among her contemporaries in accompanying her husband to his military command in Brittany. In this she followed the example set by Queen Philippa, who notably escorted her husband on campaign whenever she could, but few noblewomen did so. The majority stayed in England tending to their family and their estates, and they were not encouraged to do otherwise. It would hardly have been practical if all of the English nobility participating in the French campaigns had taken their wives with them. It was possibly unwise, and certainly rare, for a noblewoman of Joan's standing to accompany her husband, even to a securely held command.

Although hostilities between France and England were theoretically in abeyance, and Thomas had successfully established military superiority in the duchy, the situation could change at any time. Thomas was a hard-headed soldier and it is most unlikely that he brought Joan because he could not bear to be parted from her. The king may have encouraged Thomas to take his wife, as Joan's presence added to the care which would be provided to John Montfort. However, there is no evidence that Edward III made this a requirement of placing the boy in Thomas' custody. Why, therefore, did Thomas take her, and why did Joan agree? The likelihood is that this was a further precautionary step in safeguarding his marriage. Joan's inheritance from her brother had made her an even more desirable match than when Thomas had married her in 1341. The legal validity of their marriage remained questionable. While Joan was with him, Thomas was confident of being able to deal with any renewed threat. Leaving her behind when he took up the Brittany command was unavoidable, but he had done what he could to secure his position by applying to the Pope for ratification of the papal bull confirming the validity of their marriage. Nevertheless, the threat remained. Once he had secured his position in the duchy, it probably seemed to Thomas that it was safer for Joan to accompany him rather than stay in England.

Thomas was also well aware that despite Edward III's tacit support in helping him to legitimise his marriage the king did not regard it with unqualified approval. Since John's death the king had given Joan due recognition of their relationship, by referring to her in official records as 'the king's kinswoman', but there was a lack of warmth.[14] Although there was no set pattern for the transference of a title through the female line, Thomas could reasonably have expected the earldom of Kent to be conferred on him when John died, and Edward III had signally failed to do so. The king clearly felt that he had done enough to support Thomas. The marriage debacle had not reflected well on Edward III, and he was not yet prepared to give Thomas the public endorsement which elevating him to the earldom would have given. Ambitious for his sons as well as himself, Thomas naturally hoped to change the king's mind. Taking Joan with him to Brittany gave a public demonstration of the consolidation of their marriage, and Thomas no doubt hoped that in the process Edward III would fully restore him to favour; this, for him, far outweighed any advantage that might have been gained by Joan remaining in England.

However, Thomas and Joan would not have taken their two sons with them to Brittany. They were no more than four and two years old, and far too young to have provided companionship for John Montfort. In their absence it is probable that they were placed with a relative rather than left in the care of family servants. Thomas was notably close to his own family, with his brother Otto as his invariable lieutenant, while his brothers Robert and Alan and his nephews John Holand and John de la Warr all served with him, but there was a marked lack of suitable female members to take on the role of caring for his sons. Among his brothers the only suitable candidate was Robert's wife, at Thorpe Waterville in Northamptonshire. But there were other, arguably more appropriate, alternatives. As Joan's inheritance secured his sons' future it would be natural for Thomas to look to his wife's side of the family, and although his sister-in-law Elizabeth, John's widow, had entered a convent and taken the veil shortly after John's death, his formidable and immensely capable aunt-in-law Lady Blanche Wake was available to assist. Blanche Wake was the widow of Joan's uncle Thomas Wake, sister to the Duke of Lancaster, and the king's cousin. Her main residence was at Bourne Castle in Lincolnshire. She had no children of her own, and the substantial estates she enjoyed were all Wake properties which would pass to Joan on her death. Although Blanche may have had no great liking for Thomas Holand, Joan's children were her family and this was extremely important. Blanche was resolute in her determination to protect her family's interests, and had no hesitation in using her Lancastrian influence to do so. She demonstrated this in July 1354 when her dower manor at Colne in Huntingdonshire was burned down by the Bishop of Lisle's officials. Undaunted by the identity of her antagonist, Blanche embarked on a spirited two-year legal battle, demanding Edward III's support by invoking their familial relationship. The bishop was comprehensively defeated despite appealing for the Pope's intervention.[15] None of the family could doubt Blanche's tremendous energy and abilities, and when her brother Henry, Duke of Lancaster, made his will in March 1360 he had no hesitation in appointing his 'very dear sister Lady Wake' as his principal executor.[16] Blanche would have relished the opportunity to school the young Thomas, as he would eventually inherit the Wake estates. Even in old age she showed a willingness to look after the children of her relatives, caring for John of Gaunt's young family in the early 1370s after the death of his wife, Blanche, while John was abroad. An indication of the ties forged between Blanche, Joan and Thomas Holand is their common interest in Stamford and its Franciscan Grey Friars church, where they all chose to be buried. Joan's eldest son, and her heir, Thomas, also developed a special affection for Bourne, as he chose to be buried there rather than in any of the other resting places on his estates, ignoring Stamford, where his parents were buried.[17] The other possible guardian for their two sons was Lady Elizabeth de Burgh, who, although now elderly, was notably sociable. Elizabeth's household accounts record a visit by the Countess of Kent in October 1355; this could have been Joan returning from Brittany and collecting her sons from her cousin's care.[18]

Joan left England in November 1354 and sailed to Brittany with Thomas. She had not been to the duchy before, and there is no record of where she stayed. The main centres of English administration in Brittany were the town of Vannes, in the south, and the port of Brest, on the north-west coast. Vannes had been in English hands since 1343 and Thomas' predecessors as lieutenant had sited their council and administrative headquarters in the town, with the mint. Edward III had a high regard for Vannes, describing it as the best town after Nantes, which remained under the influence of the French king.[19] In all probability Thomas also chose to be based in Vannes, and occupied the same buildings as the previous king's lieutenants. What was life like for Joan in Brittany? As there are no records or accounts of her stay there it is only possible to speculate. As a child in the queen's household she had spent many months abroad, in Ghent where she had married Thomas and then outside Calais while it was besieged. As the wife of the king's lieutenant in Brittany, her position was quite different. Although it is unlikely she enjoyed many luxuries, Joan would have brought several servants with her, and quite possibly a few of the wives of her husband's knights to keep her company. It was usual for a commander to regularly spend time with his leading knights, especially over meals, and as Thomas' wife Joan may have presided over dinners. Apart from his own relatives, Thomas' retinue consisted of knights with a gentry background, all of whom were serving soldiers looking for advancement in their chosen profession. They were largely separated from their families, and Joan would have been one of very few women with whom they had contact overseas, as well as being in a position of seniority because of her husband's position and her royal birth. It is also likely that Thomas and Joan had occasion to entertain the local nobility who supported the English cause. Joan's responsibilities would also have included caring for John Montfort; quite possibly she had a hand in ensuring his continuing education while he was with them.

Accompanying Thomas to Brittany inevitably brought Joan into much closer contact with the war, even if he was careful to keep her well away from any actual fighting. With the progress of the war as an everyday topic of conversation, she would have at least become familiar with aspects of it. The war in France was an everyday fact of life for Joan, brought up in the English court, but her experience hitherto had been limited. Now she was seeing a different side of war, more able to appreciate the grim purpose and necessity of the skills and practice gained by knights participating in the colourful jousting tournaments she had watched and enjoyed. Living in a war-torn land, Joan cannot have been entirely sheltered from the harsh truths of conflict, and when travelling within the duchy she may have seen at first hand the effect on the local population. Joan's experiences with Thomas gave her a more intimate knowledge and greater understanding of the realities of warfare than most of her peers would have had, and probably made her more at ease with the men around her, while they may have come to hold her in greater respect for being a part of their working lives.

It is likely that Joan was occasionally left in Vannes when Thomas needed to travel. Although he had exerted his authority in his first few months in Brittany, there remained a number of individual fortresses held by different commanders who were refusing to acknowledge the authority of the English Crown. Thomas' personal presence was probably required to extend his control and fulfil his orders, necessitating leaving Joan behind. Whatever sympathies Thomas might have had for the defiant captains, he achieved considerable success in bringing them into line and also proved remarkably adept at exerting financial control in the duchy, appointing officials to collect the local taxes in a methodical way.[20] Edward III was obviously satisfied with his lieutenant, as he renewed Thomas' appointment in February 1355 to run for another year, once again with the revenues from the duchy being assigned to him in June 1355.[21] Thomas returned to England with Joan in July 1355 to get reinforcements, and they sailed back to Brittany almost immediately, in August.[22] By July Joan had been away from England for eight months, a long time to have been separated from her two boys, and she may not have had the opportunity to see them in her short stay. Joan was nevertheless willing to accompany Thomas back to Brittany, although she must have known that she might not be able to see her sons for several more months. However, in September, within weeks of arriving back in Brittany, Thomas received news that he was to be replaced as lieutenant in Brittany by Henry, Duke of Lancaster. This would mean that Joan would be returning to England much sooner than she had anticipated.

Henry of Grosmont, Duke of Lancaster, had succeeded to his father's dignities in 1345, and he had been Edward III's principal adviser and his leading commander for some years. Henry was also the king's cousin. His appointment heralded a change of policy in the conduct of the war with France rather than any royal dissatisfaction with Thomas. Shortly before Christmas 1354 the king had sent an embassy, led by Lancaster and the Earl of Arundel, to Avignon, to formally sign the draft treaty of Guines. In the Pope's presence Lancaster had duly pronounced the terms of the peace, and confirmed Edward III's willingness to sign the treaty, but to his consternation the French ambassadors had refused to do likewise, saying they could not consent to it.[23] Considering how favourable the proposals were to Edward III, the French refusal to honour the terms of the agreement was not entirely surprising. Nevertheless their action does not seem to have been anticipated and Edward III reacted angrily when he heard the news. According to Froissart he declared that since peace could not be made at Avignon he would wage war more strongly in France than ever before. In the early months of 1355 the king conferred with his council and his leading commanders, devising a new strategy. The decision was made to launch a fresh attack in France, this time in the form of two major expeditions which would commence when the truce expired in June 1355. Edward III, with Lancaster at his side, was to lead the main expedition into Normandy, relying on the support of Charles of Navarre, the Count of Evreux, who controlled the Cotentin and parts of Normandy. Navarre was John II's son-in- law, and had fallen out with the

French king. The second expedition was to be into Gascony, in response
to a plea for help from the Gascons, who had suffered repeated French
raids which had weakened English control of the duchy. At Westminster in
April 1355 the council agreed that Prince Edward would lead the Gascon
expedition, supported by the earls of Warwick, Suffolk and Oxford – and
William Montague, Earl of Salisbury.[24] Both expeditions were to be large-
scale mounted raids intended to devastate the countryside, so emphasising
the weakness of the French king and his inability to protect his subjects in
the hope that John II might be enticed into battle.

Edward III had planned to leave England in August, but was delayed
at Portsmouth by bad weather. When he received news from spies that
Charles of Navarre had made peace with John II, and that French troops
were being sent to the ports in Normandy to ambush him when he arrived,
he called the expedition off on 12 September. In the meantime, Prince
Edward had already embarked from Plymouth for Bordeaux. A change of
plan was needed, and the king decided the Duke of Lancaster should take
command of the Anglo-Navarrese army and launch a new attack from
Brittany. It was therefore appropriate to appoint Lancaster lieutenant in
Brittany, replacing Thomas Holand.[25] But almost immediately the king and
his advisers had second thoughts, and the Brittany project was deferred
in favour of an expedition from Calais, making use of the originally
mobilised army and arrangements. In late October Edward III and his
reassembled army sailed to Calais with Lancaster at his side, and on
landing they were joined by troops from Flanders, Brabant and Germany.
Their resulting campaign through Picardy was closely shadowed by the
French king and his much larger army, while in Gascony the prince led his
small force on a devastating eight-week *chevauchée* to the Mediterranean
and back. Sir John Wingfield, one of the prince's knights, and a member
of his council, reported that the countryside and towns which were
destroyed in the prince's raid produced more revenue for the King of
France than half his kingdom.[26] Edward III's efforts were less obviously
successful, as he was unable to engage John II in battle, despite giving the
French king ample provocation and several opportunities to attack him,
even sending him a personal challenge for single armed combat. After a
campaign of only three weeks Edward III realised that he was not going
to draw John II into battle, discharged his foreign support and returned
to England in November 1355.

Thomas' whereabouts during these two campaigns is not known. His
absence from the record of the list of commanders in each campaign is
distinctly curious, considering his reputation and loyal service. Conducting
two major offensives against France, Edward III had need of every
able-bodied knight and there is no obvious reason why he would not have
made use of the talents of one of his best commanders. As Lancaster's
commitments with the king delayed his departure for Brittany, Thomas
would not have immediately relinquished his command in September,

thus ensuring that he would have been unable to join the prince in time to take part in the Gascony campaign.[27] This might also explain why he was not given a senior command in the king's campaign. His charge, John Montfort, is known to have been with Edward III during the Picardy campaign, in the company of the king's two younger sons, and it seems likely that the king ordered Thomas to bring the boy in person rather than delegate this duty. Once back in England Edward III was almost immediately engaged in a fresh campaign against the Scots, who had taken advantage of his absence to seize Berwick, but again there is no record that Thomas was part of his army.

Back in England for Christmas, Thomas and Joan were reunited with their two young sons, and it is probable that she was pregnant with their third child, whom they named Maud, after Thomas' mother. It was an opportunity for Joan and Thomas to catch up on their own affairs on their many estates, although Thomas was not likely to be satisfied with that for long. He would have been very conscious of the fact that for the first time in his career he was not a part of an ongoing major campaign. Ironically, his promotion to Brittany had precluded him from being part of the prince's company, and denied him the opportunity of being a part of that campaign. After the conclusion of his highly successful and destructive *chevauchée*, the prince remained in Gascony and spent the winter of 1355 and early spring of 1356 generally reasserting English control in the duchy. Many of Thomas' old comrades in arms were with the prince, including his cousin Roger de la Warr. William Montague, Earl of Salisbury, was also with the prince, in joint command of his rearguard, with the Earl of Suffolk. On 2 April 1356 Thomas was appointed keeper of the Channel Islands, a post once held by Joan's uncle Thomas Wake.[28] This was hardly a promotion but there does not seem to have been any real intention on the king's part that Thomas should fulfil the duties in person. Thomas immediately delegated his command to Otto, as he was engaged elsewhere on the king's orders, and in June 1356 Otto was authorised to act as his deputy, and duly rewarded by Thomas with the gift, for his lifetime, of the manors of Ashford and Chesterfield in Derbyshire.[29] Although there is no evidence of Thomas' whereabouts over the next few months, it is a reasonable supposition that he had been ordered by the king to join in the fresh campaign planned for the summer of 1356. Building on the twin *chevauchées* of 1355, Edward III and his commanders planned an attack in France to start in the summer of 1356. Prince Edward was to progress from Bordeaux up into north central France, Henry, Duke of Lancaster, was to start with his army in Brittany, and the king would himself lead a third army from Calais.

However, once again a campaign planned for Brittany was changed at the last moment. In May Navarrese envoys approached Edward III and implored his support. Charles of Navarre had been arrested and imprisoned by John II in a surprise attack in April, and his brother Philip of Navarre was desperately holding out. Edward III reacted swiftly to support his ally, and immediately ordered Henry of Lancaster to deploy his force to Normandy instead. On 18 June 1356 Lancaster set sail with his army for St Vaast la Hogue, taking with him the earls of March and Pembroke and John Montfort. Once in Normandy Lancaster was joined by Philip of Navarre and Sir Robert Knolles, who had brought a force from the garrisons of Brittany. The combined forces then advanced through Normandy, capturing fortresses, plundering the countryside, moving towards the beleaguered Navarrese strongholds at Pont Audemer, Breteuil and Verneuil. While Lancaster progressed through Normandy and then on into Brittany, Prince Edward mustered his forces at Bordeaux and in August started his campaign, taking a northerly route. With the prince were the earls of Warwick, Suffolk, Oxford and Salisbury. On 19 September the prince met the French king, John II, and his army at Poitiers. In the battle the earls of Warwick and Oxford commanded the vanguard, the prince the second division, and the earls of Salisbury and Suffolk commanded the rearguard.[30] Despite having a much larger army, the French were comprehensively and overwhelming defeated, the final humiliation being the capture of John II, along with his young son Philip and most of his nobles. The prince's Poitiers campaign had ended with a stunning and unexpected victory.

Although Thomas' whereabouts during this period are not known, it seems probable that in April 1356 he had been ordered to join the Duke of Lancaster. The intention at that time was for the duke to take his force to Brittany, and so Thomas would be on hand to supply his recent knowledge and experience of the duchy. When the duke was ordered to Normandy instead, Thomas would have remained with him. It is inconceivable that such an experienced and able commander would not have been part of one of the major campaigns, although it is curious that Thomas' name is not mentioned among the duke's entourage. The two men knew each other, as they had served together before (they were on crusade in Prussia in 1343), but it is possible that Henry had inherited his father's antipathy towards the Holand family, reluctantly accepting Thomas' presence but failing to accord him a prominent role among his retinue. By the winter of 1356/57 Lancaster's forces had left Brittany and moved into Lower Normandy, bringing successive areas back under English control and establishing English commanders in some of the strategically important garrisons.[31] Here his campaign stalled, and he spent six months trying to take the town of Rennes. It was not until July 1357 that the siege was resolved and Lancaster left Normandy. Thomas had had no opportunity in over twelve months to carry out his duties as keeper of the Channel Islands, leaving Otto to do so on his behalf. Recognising this, in June 1357 Edward III appointed Otto Holand to succeed Thomas as keeper.[32]

During this period it is likely that Joan remained in England. Certainly, on the basis that Thomas was with Lancaster, the nature of the campaign would have precluded her accompanying him this time. Ostensibly there would be no reason for Thomas not to appoint Joan as his attorney, but there is no evidence to confirm this. While Joan was in England she had the opportunity to renew her friendship with Princess Isabella and other members of the royal family. In May 1357 Prince Edward arrived back in England with the French king, and made a triumphal entry into London where John II was temporarily installed in the Duke of Lancaster's Savoy Palace. An outline of the peace treaty had been agreed as early as March, and in June papal envoys arrived to assist in the negotiations to agree terms for a lasting peace. In the meantime the court celebrated the prince's victory jubilantly. Joan would have been among the ladies of the court attending the banquets, jousting and general festivities, congratulating her cousin on his achievement and updating him on his godson's progress. The cousins would not have seen each other for some years, and it seems reasonable to suggest that it was during this period that the prince fell in love with his cousin, although he could only admire her from afar while she was married to Thomas.

Once back in England it was not long before Thomas was given another command. A truce had been agreed between the two sides until Easter of 1359 to give time for the peace negotiations to be concluded, but in the meantime Edward III wanted to safeguard his gains in France. He needed men like Thomas, and on 18 November 1357 entrusted him with the custodianship of the strategically placed Cruyk Castle in Normandy.[33] In a further demonstration of his faith in Thomas' military capabilities, in December he appointed Thomas to assist Philip of Navarre, whom he had made lieutenant in Normandy in October 1356.[34] There is no record of Thomas taking up his appointment immediately, and in April 1358 he would have attended the annual Garter celebrations at Windsor with his fellow Garter knights. The Garter celebrations were particularly splendid that year, as the guests of honour included the captive King of France. Champions had been invited from all over England, Germany and the Low Countries and hundreds of knights, including the prince and his four brothers, competed in the lists. Shortly afterwards Thomas visited the Channel Islands in May to negotiate the ransom for one of the captured French nobles, the Viscount of Rohan.[35] Thomas did not leave for Normandy until October, and by this time he had additional responsibilities. Godfrey of Harcourt, a Norman lord with substantial lands in the Cotentin, including the thirteenth-century fortress at Saint-Sauveur-le-Vicomte, had willed these to Edward III before he died and despite the claim of his ally Philip of Navarre the king had taken possession of the castle by appointing one of his lieutenants and installing a garrison there. On 10 October 1358 the king appointed Thomas warden of the castle of Saint-Sauveur-le-Vicomte.[36] The major fortress was at the heart of the Harcourt inheritance, and Thomas would have the delicate task of maintaining English control against the Navarrese claim while at the same time working with local

Navarrese forces against the French. With occasional raids and intermittent fighting, his command was by no means purely administrative.

Thomas appointed attorneys – Roger Mortimer, John Oulton, Robert Thorpe (another on the prince's council), David Wollore, John Winwick, Randolf Saleby and Gervase Wilford – and returned to Normandy with Otto, his nephews John de la Warr and John Holand, their clerk John Raynford and, this time, with his wife as well.[37] Thomas and Joan had spent much of the last two years apart, with Joan in England and Thomas abroad. This would be Joan's first trip to Normandy. They now had three children (Thomas, John and Maud), and it is possible that Joan had just given birth to their last child, another girl, whom they named Joan.[38] It was not unusual to name children after their parents, but it is sad to note that while Thomas and Joan saw fit to name their elder daughter after Thomas' mother, they did not honour the memory of Joan's mother, Margaret, in this way. But although Margaret had been responsible for restoring most of the Kent estates, Joan and her mother had not had a close or easy relationship. We do not know if the children accompanied their parents to France. As they would have been an additional responsibility for Joan and required an increased household for support, Thomas and Joan may have decided to leave their young children behind in safety and called on the services of Joan's relations again. Thomas' appointment was a success, and four months later, in February 1359, his commission was renewed. Then, in May, Otto Holand was badly wounded on a raid, dying four months later.[39] This was a devastating loss for Thomas, as Otto had been at his side throughout his career and had faithfully acted as his deputy on so many occasions. Otto's incapacity may explain why Thomas and Joan remained in Normandy, missing John of Gaunt's marriage to Blanche of Lancaster in May. Although they would have been invited (especially as Joan was the groom's cousin, and related by marriage to the bride through her aunt Blanche Wake), they are not listed as having given a gift, which suggests they did not attend. Held in Reading, the wedding was a magnificent display, the guests including the captive kings of France and Scotland, and was followed by two weeks of festivities and jousting, with a tournament in London in which Edward III and princes Edward, Lionel, John and Edmund participated, disguised as aldermen of London.

Thomas' command in Normandy as one of the most senior English officers ensured he was closely involved in the next phase of the king's campaign in France. By June 1359 it was apparent that Edward III would not obtain the settlement in France for which he had hoped. Despite English military dominance, and the captivity of John II, securing a lasting treaty of peace with the dauphin and the estates general in France was proving increasingly difficult. The king and his council determined on a major new campaign in France, with the principal objective of capturing the city of Rheims. Preparations for the invasion, planned to commence in August, began straight away. Then, in August, Charles of Navarre made his peace with the dauphin at Pontoise, turning his back on his alliance with Edward III. The Navarrese were torn between Charles and his brother, Philip, who remained loyal to Edward III. It was imperative to reinforce English support for Philip of Navarre, and the king had no hesitation in promoting Thomas to bolster English authority. In October Thomas was ordered to secure Barfleur, and he was appointed joint lieutenant of Normandy with Philip of Navarre.[40] Following his orders, Thomas reacted swiftly and occupied the harbour at Barfleur in the north-east of the Cotentin peninsula to secure it for his king.[41] This renewed military activity brought with it a need for reinforcements, and this necessitated a return to England. Although Joan accompanied Thomas back to England, where she would have the opportunity to see their children, her stay was brief; she returned to Normandy with her husband the same month, appointing Randolf Saleby and Gervase Wilford as their attorneys.[42] This was the fourth occasion on which Joan is known to have accompanied Thomas to France, and, as it is unlikely that Thomas had any continuing concern about the status of their marriage, indicates that it was her personal choice, and preference, to do so.

At the end of October Edward III and his invasion force of around 10,000 men left England and landed at Calais. The army was divided in three, with the king in personal command of the main body, and Prince Edward and the Duke of Lancaster commanding the other two sections. At the beginning of December the army arrived outside the walls of Rheims. Hopes were riding high, but the English found the French resistance more efficient than they had hoped, and their own supply trains, efficient though they were, were less adequate than they had anticipated. Barely four weeks later, in January 1360, the king was forced to abandon the siege, having failed to take the city by assault and diminished the supplies of food necessary to sustain his army. There followed four months of desultory campaigning in northern France, without any major engagement. The dauphin withdrew his forces in front of the English army, and successfully attacked the English supply lines. With inadequate supplies, dogged by poor weather, and unable to engage in a decisive action, and urged by the Duke of Lancaster and Prince Edward, at length Edward III agreed to settle terms.[43] By May 1360 the peace negotiators had reached an agreement. Although the Rheims campaign appeared to be a miserable failure after the previous stunning successes, the terms of the Treaty of Brétigny were immensely favourable to Edward III. In return for abandoning his claim to the French throne, Edward III received full sovereignty over the whole of the old Angevin duchy of Aquitaine (Gascony, Poitou, Saintonge, Angoumois, Perigord, Limousin, Quercy and Rouergue), based on the new boundaries defined by the successful English campaigns, with further territory in the north and west near the Pyrenees including Calais and the surrounding area and the county of Ponthieu, a landmass amounting to nearly a quarter of France.[44] Arrangements were agreed for the release of John II, including a ransom of 3 million écus to be paid in instalments over six years. On 19 May Edward III and his sons sailed for England from Honfleur while the rest of the army followed shortly afterwards from Calais.[45]

Thomas served on the Rheims campaign, although it is not known in what capacity. As he left to join the army, perhaps arriving after the siege of the city had ended, Joan presumably returned to England. Her stay in Normandy had been short. Thomas returned to England in May 1360, relinquishing his command of Saint-Sauveur-le-Vicomte to Sir John Chandos.[46] Joan might reasonably have expected and hoped that their stay in England would be extended now that peace had been agreed. That autumn held a surprise in store for Joan. Her sister-in-law, Elizabeth, Countess of Kent, left Waverley Abbey and on 29 September broke her vow of chastity by marrying the Hainaulter knight Sir Eustace d'Aubrichecourt at Wingham church in Kent.[47] How Elizabeth met d'Aubrichecourt is unknown but it is a reasonable supposition that it was through her brother-in-law Thomas. Eustace d'Aubrichecourt was, like Thomas, a founder member of the Order of the Garter, and within that close-knit elite fraternity the members all knew each other well.[48] Eustace was also a professional soldier of considerable ability and had served with Prince Edward in Gascony and on the Poitiers campaign. Subsequently he had chosen to loosen his ties with the prince and operate independently in France with his company of Hainaulters, becoming another of the many bands of soldiers plundering the French countryside for their own advantage. After being captured by the French in 1359, he purchased his freedom in time to join the English army on the Rheims campaign in January 1360, serving in the Duke of Lancaster's division.[49] Presumably he came to England in May with the remaining troops, as in August 1360 he was granted an annuity of 40 marks for his good service to the king.[50] He evidently became acquainted with Elizabeth during that summer and it seems likely that Elizabeth may have been visiting Joan when d'Aubrichecourt was Thomas' guest. An ambitious and unscrupulous soldier, he lost no time in pressing his suit. Marrying the widowed Countess of Kent substantially augmented his social status, enabling him to enjoy Elizabeth's dower and establishing a bond with Thomas, one of the king's favoured captains.

Joan's time back in England with Thomas was short-lived. Six months after he had returned, on 30 September 1360, Thomas was indented to serve as captain and lieutenant in Normandy and France for a quarter of a year with a retinue of sixty men-at-arms, including a banneret and ten knights, and 120 mounted archers.[51] He immediately prepared to return to France, with ten ships commissioned for his passage, and on 24 October was instructed to publish the peace and to supervise handover of English fortresses as agreed at the Treaty of Brétigny.[52] This new promotion was the highest point in Thomas' career, and he was at last made Earl of Kent by the king, in due recognition of his services.[53]

Thomas' newfound confidence found expression in an unusually generous gesture on his part towards his nephew John Holand, granting him the manors of Northweald in Essex and Whissendine in Rutland for life.[54] Unfortunately Thomas did not live to enjoy the fruits of his labours. In December he was taken ill at Rouen, and he died on 28 December 1360.[55]

Joan does not seem to have accompanied Thomas on this last trip, and she must have been devastated when news of his death reached her. As a career soldier, Thomas had survived many arduous and dangerous campaigns, and his death now, in his early forties, was unexpected. For twenty years his strong, dominant personality had been the centre of Joan's life. There can be no doubt of her love for him. She had agreed to marry him when she was still a child, and had stoutly maintained her support for their marriage despite their separation for eight years and the opposition of her family. Their ten years of married life together had been fruitful and varied; Thomas had risen from humble household knight to being one of the king's most trusted commanders, a respected and valued companion of the military elite as a knight of the Garter. When they married, Thomas had no more than £26 a year to his name; he died Earl of Kent with vast landed estates. Joan had been at his side throughout; unlike most of her peers she had accompanied Thomas on three tours of duties in France, her wifely devotion amply demonstrated by this and their four children. Initially Thomas was buried at the church of the Friars Minor in Rouen, but Joan arranged for his body to be brought back to England and for him to be reburied in the Franciscan church of which they had been patrons at Stamford in Lincolnshire.[56] Thomas' body was laid to rest in the chapel adjoining the church. Mourning her loss, Joan gave instructions to her constable at Castle Donington for a chaplain to regularly sing for Thomas' soul.[57]

8

A Royal Bride
1361–1363

The gentle prince married ... a lady of great renown, who enkindled love in him, in that she was beauteous, charming and discreet.

Chandos Herald

Joan was now a widow. Left bereft with four young children (Thomas was the eldest, aged ten), she was still comparatively young at thirty-two. On 20 February 1361 Edward III confirmed Joan in possession of her inheritance.[1] As an extremely wealthy and beautiful widow she would attract many suitors, despite the drawback of her unfortunate marital history and her four children, but she was also free to choose her own lifestyle and she did not have to marry again. Several of her contemporaries in similar circumstances had chosen to remain single, such as her cousins Elizabeth de Burgh and Margaret Brotherton, and enjoyed the freedom which their new position brought. Joan's own experience of marriage had been attended by considerable difficulties and she might have relished the lack of constraint conferred by widowhood. She had genuinely loved Thomas and grieved his loss. She could, like her mother, devote her life to her children and her estates, and she need never again leave England. As Countess of Kent she could take her place as one of the ladies of the court, strengthen her ties with the king and queen, build up her contacts, become a patron of note, enriching her own and her family's reputation. But the freedom widowhood brought Joan had to be balanced against the possible disadvantages. Whatever her own personal inclinations, she had the future of her children to consider. Although her royal connections might help to further her children's interests, as a widow Joan would have limited influence in securing their future, and she had few close relations who would have an interest in helping her do this. The possibility of a challenge to the validity of her marriage to Thomas, while unlikely, could not be discounted, and this would jeopardise her children's' position. In contrast, marriage to the right man could bring protection, security and influence, which would benefit her children. What would Joan choose to do?

In the event, Joan made her decision very quickly. Wooed almost immediately by Prince Edward, after a whirlwind courtship they were secretly espoused in the spring of 1361 and they were married in October 1361, just ten months after Thomas' death. The prince was deeply in love and Joan appears to have been swept off her feet, just as she had been with Thomas Holand. Once again, Joan made a completely unexpected and surprising marriage; once again she entered into a secret espousal. This time, though, it was Joan who was the surprising choice. The prince was thirty-one years old, and the most eligible bachelor in Europe. A widow of dubious marital history, with four children and no obvious diplomatic, political or economic attractions, was not the bride anyone would have suggested as suitable for the heir to the throne. It is hardly surprising that many subsequent commentators assumed that the secret espousal meant the marriage was conducted without Edward III's consent, and that the king and queen disapproved of the marriage. But, as a closer examination of the circumstances surrounding their marriage reveals, this was not the case.

Created Prince of Wales when he was thirteen in 1343, the prince was also Earl of Chester and Earl of Cornwall, and he owned extensive estates in Wales, Chester and Cornwall. An idea of his physical appearance can be obtained from the surviving contemporary representations of him: the effigy on his tomb at Canterbury Cathedral, and the image of him kneeling before his father to receive the principality of Aquitaine.[2] These are conventional representations and depict the prince as tall, lean, and good-looking, with his father's long face, high forehead and straight nose, and as was common at the time he is shown with a moustache and beard. As a formidable fighter he would also have been physically strong and muscular, and there was no doubting his bravery. He was fond of hunting and gambling, he was an excellent jouster and a gifted military commander, and he was also intelligent and well educated.[3] He also had a more than conventional interest in religion. Born on 15 June 1330, the prince had a lifelong devotion to the Trinity, celebrating the festival every year in his household. His favoured pilgrimage was to Canterbury Cathedral, a church dedicated to the Trinity, where he would worship at the site of Thomas à Becket. The prince has come to be known as the Black Prince, but this description was never used during his lifetime and did not come into common usage until the sixteenth century, when it was used by Holinshed in his *Chronicles*, and by Leland in his *Itinerary*.[4] It is not known how or why the epithet was bestowed, and there is no evidence that his armour was black, as has been alleged, or that the French gave him this name for his deeds during the Hundred Years War. During his lifetime he was known as Prince Edward, or occasionally referred to as Edward of Woodstock (his birthplace), and later as Edward IV, in anticipation of succeeding his father (used, for example, by the *Anonimalle* chronicler).

At the age of sixteen Prince Edward had fought at Crécy, and his crucial role in the battle together with his great personal bravery had established his reputation as a soldier. His badge of a white ostrich feather (later to become three feathers) and the motto 'Ich dene' appears to have come into use around this time, and according to John Arderne, writing at the time of the prince's death, the feather was obtained from the King of Bohemia, killed at Crécy.[5] The prince is known to have signed letters 'Houmont ich dene'.[6] When his father founded the Order of the Garter the king and the prince were the two leading members. The prince had become a commander of distinction, showing a real gift for leadership and a flair for tactical and strategic planning, with the success of his *chevauchée* through Brittany in 1355 culminating in his dramatic (and unexpected) victory at Poitiers, confirming his military genius. He came to share overall command of the military operations against France with his father and the Duke of Lancaster, discussing and planning operations including the most recent Rheims campaign, and he was a leading participant in the peace negotiations, individually ratifying the Treaty of Brétigny before he left France in May 1360.

The prince also acquired a reputation for chivalry, based on his behaviour on the battlefield, his courteous treatment of his prisoners and his care for his men. Probably the most famous tale regarding his chivalry relates to his actions after the Battle of Poitiers in which he captured the French king, John II. Froissart recorded that after the battle the king was invited to dine with the prince, and that Edward insisted on serving John personally rather than leave it to a servant, while the chronicler Geoffrey Baker wrote that when the prince received word that Sir James Audley had been brought to his tent seriously wounded, he left the table to attend to his friend.[7] Although these stories are somewhat contradictory they reflect the contemporary favourable view of the prince as a man who was courteous and considerate to his enemies and cared for his friends. By 1361 he was renowned throughout Europe as the exemplar of the chivalric knight. The *Chronique des quatre premiers Valois* described him as 'one of the greatest knights on earth, having renown above all men', while Froissart dubbed him 'the flower of chivalry of all the world'.[8] His panegyrist, the herald of his close friend Sir John Chandos, described him as a 'noble prince … [with] no thought but loyalty, nobleness, valour, and goodness, and was endued with prowess'.[9] However idealised a portrait these fulsome tributes painted there is no doubt that the prince, like his father, was genuinely popular. He was gifted with the ability to mix easily with his peers and had many close friends among the nobility while enjoying an excellent relationship with his father and mother. By 1355 his entourage included most of the more renowned military nobles, many of them close personal friends, including the earls of Salisbury (William Montague), Suffolk, Warwick, Oxford, Sir Reginald Cobham, Sir John Chandos, Sir John Wingfield (who headed his council), Sir Bartholomew

Burghersh (on his council), Sir Nigel Loring (his chamberlain), Sir James Audley and Sir James Lisle. All apart from the Earl of Oxford were fellow members of the Order of the Garter, while William Montague and John Chandos had been friends from his earliest boyhood. Conscious of his status as heir to the throne, in peacetime the prince copied his father and lived in a fashion intended to impress, entertaining lavishly, and spending large sums of money on jewels and finery. He was also extremely generous to his friends and his retinue, with his household records testifying to the numerous thoughtful gifts he gave year after year to those in his service.

When Thomas Holand died the prince was still a bachelor, with at least one known illegitimate son, Roger Clarendon.[10] His unmarried state was almost accidental. Plans for his marriage had first been mooted when he was barely a year old. As Edward III's eldest son, and his heir, naturally the prince's marriage was of national importance and presented a diplomatic and political opportunity. His father, grandfather and great-grandfather had all married foreign princesses in just such a pursuit, and the prince had grown up with the expectation that he would do likewise. When he was no more than a year old, in 1331, his proposed bride was Jeanne, daughter of Philip VI of France, a match which, had it been achieved, might conceivably have averted the outbreak of war. Later, with the advent of the war with France, Edward III entertained various possible brides for his son with the emphasis on their diplomatic potential. In 1339, October 1340 and again in April 1345 a match with Margaret of Brabant was proposed to secure the alliance of Brabant, then in 1347 with Princess Leonora of Portugal, and as late as 1360 the widowed Margaret of Burgundy was being considered.[11] Political factors rather than any unwillingness on the prince's part had prevented their fruition. The most obdurate obstacle was the papacy, as on each occasion the Pope effectively blocked the proposed alliance by refusing the requisite dispensation. Since the Fourth Lateran Council the Church had forbidden marriage within four degrees of relationship, including kindred relationships, marital kin and godparents.[12] Relationships between members of different royal families (and indeed between members of the nobility) frequently came within these degrees and in order to facilitate the desired union the accepted way around it was to obtain a papal dispensation. This gave the papacy potential political leverage when it came to marriages between the royalty of different countries. To complicate matters further, since 1308 the Pope had been exiled from Rome and had taken up residence in a palace on the Rhone in Avignon. Geographical location within the French king's sphere of influence had an inevitable effect on papal politics. From the outset of the war with France the papacy had tacitly, and at times overtly, supported the French king; withholding permission when Edward III applied for a dispensation, and so frustrating his matrimonial plans for his heir, was just part of the running battle between the English Crown and the Pope.[13] In December

1344, for example, the Pope had openly stated that he would not grant the dispensation to facilitate the prince's marriage to Margaret of Brabant because he hoped this would instead promote a match between Brabant and either the French Crown or the Duke of Normandy.[14] Nonetheless, had Edward III been particularly determined on any of these matches, it is hard to imagine that his resourcefulness would not have found a way to persuade the Pope. Edward III does not seem to have been determined on forging a diplomatic alliance by means of a marriage or to have been unduly concerned about his son's continuing bachelor status, and showed no inclination to secure an alternative bride for his son after the proposed match with Margaret of Burgundy foundered.

It may seem surprising that the king appeared content for his heir to remain single, but Edward III was of course in the then enviable position of having several sons, and so no lack of heirs. His attitude towards his children's nuptials appears to have combined a concern for their financial well-being with a willingness to take their preferences into account. Foreign alliances were often considered, but rarely achieved, and with his sons the prime consideration appears to have been financial. It is hardly coincidental that of Edward III's five sons who reached adulthood (princes Edward, Lionel, John, Edmund and Thomas) only one did not marry an heiress.[15] By 1360 both Lionel and John were married, Lionel in 1341 to Elizabeth de Burgh and John to Blanche of Lancaster in 1359.[16] Both brides were considerable heiresses, and their fortunes secured a financial independence for their respective husbands which released their royal father-in-law from any obligation to find estates with which to endow his sons. Edward III failed to secure a similar match for Edmund, whose later marriage to Isabella of Castile was arranged in conjunction with John of Gaunt's second marriage to her sister. Thomas of Woodstock, the baby of the family, in due course also married another heiress, Eleanor de Bohun. Edward III's dynastic and political ambitions for his children were never overbearing, and his genuine care and affection for them is particularly evident in his attitude towards his eldest daughter, Princess Isabella. As with Prince Edward, various matches were proposed for her with foreign nobles, each of which foundered, including Pedro of Castile and Louis de Male, son of the Count of Flanders, in 1347 and Charles IV of Bohemia in February 1348.[17] Princess Joan was substituted for her sister for the Castilian match, but when she died in 1348 en route to her wedding, Edward III made no attempt to rearrange the match for Isabella. In May 1351 the king arranged a match between Isabella, his 'very dear eldest daughter whom we have love with special affection' and the d'Albret heir, resurrecting the prospect of an alliance contemplated some ten years previously (when Joan had been the intended bride).[18] But when Isabella refused to embark for Gascony to marry Bernard d'Albret in November Edward III did not attempt to force her.[19] He was then apparently content to leave her unmarried until she chose her own groom, which was not until 1365, when she was thirty-three years old. Her choice of husband was unexpected, and arguably unsuitable, as she chose to marry Enguerrand de Coucy, a French knight held hostage and captive in England at the time. In fact, Edward III only completed one foreign match among his sons or daughters, with the marriage of Princess Mary to John of Brittany in 1361; even his youngest daughter, Margaret, married an English nobleman: John Hastings, Earl of Pembroke. Later three of his sons married foreign brides (Lionel wed Violanta of Milan, and John and Edmund married the Castilian princesses Constance and Isabella) but these were arranged by his sons, and were second marriages for Lionel and John, albeit with their father's blessing. Joan was as well born as any of the heiresses chosen for the prince's brothers, and she was in fact considerably wealthier than either Elizabeth de Burgh or Eleanor de Bohun. Therefore, although Joan was a surprising choice for the prince, on the grounds of birth and wealth she could have been considered eligible.

Thus, when Joan became a widow in December 1360, Prince Edward was a bachelor and free to follow his personal inclinations. The couple knew each other well; Joan had grown up with the prince's sisters, and the prince had remained affectionate towards his cousin throughout her marriage to Thomas Holand. However, according to the French author of the *Chronique des quatre premiers Valois*, the prince and Joan's love affair owed much to Joan's feminine wiles. The chronicler recorded the death of Thomas Holand and described his widow as one of the most beautiful women in the world and the most noble ('Thomas de Hollande avoit espousée une des plus belles dames du monde et moult noble').[20] According to the chronicler, after Thomas' death many of the knights who had served the king and his son in their wars came to the prince with a request that he speak on their behalf to the beautiful widow, and one in particular, Sir Bernard Brocas (one of the prince's own knights), asked the prince to approach his cousin for him and convey his feelings. When the prince did so, addressing Joan as 'my beautiful cousin', she became distressed, and maintained she would not marry again. The chronicle continues:

> Thereupon the prince became greatly enamoured of the countess. And the countess commenced to weep like a subtle and far-seeing woman. And then the prince began to comfort her and kiss her passionately, grievously distressed at her tears, and said to her, 'I have spoken to you on behalf of one of the most chivalrous knights of England and one of the most honourable of men.' Madame the countess replied in tears to the prince, 'Ah, Sir, before God do not talk to me thus. For I have given myself to the most chivalrous knight under heaven, and for love of him it is, that before God I will never marry again as long as I live. For it is impossible that I should have him to be my husband, and my love for

him parts me from all men; it is my intention never to marry.' On being pressed by the prince to say whom she meant Joan conceded, 'My dear and indomitable lord it is you, and for love of you that I will never have any other knight by my side.' The prince's feelings apparently then overwhelmed him and he embraced his cousin, insisting that he would marry her and 'I also vow to God that as long as you live never will I have any other woman save you to be my wife'.[21]

This highly romantic story is unsupported by any evidence, and it is notable that the source is French and uncorroborated by any of the English chroniclers. The tale was probably a propaganda exercise, with the chronicler mixing fact and fiction in an attempt to discredit the prince, as the story subtly undermines the prince's reputation by presenting Joan as a clever and scheming woman who was able to entrap the most renowned knight of the day by her beauty and guile. In reality it was the other way round. The quick and businesslike way in which the prince wooed and won his cousin indicates that he was the driving force in their love affair from start to finish. Prince Edward had only returned to England from the Rheims campaign in France in November 1360, just a few weeks before Thomas Holand died at the end of December, and yet by the spring of 1361, barely three months later, the prince had not only persuaded Joan to marry him but had also secured his father's approval for their marriage. There is no doubt that the prince's affections were deeply engaged. Froissart and Chandos Herald, both contemporaries who knew the prince and Joan personally, record the prince's great love for Joan, the latter succinctly stating that 'he loved her greatly'.[22] His fondness for his cousin was long-standing, as is evident from the gift noted in his accounts in 1348 where she is described in affectionate terms as 'Jeanette', and the strength of his love is evident from the letter he wrote to her in 1367 after six years of marriage, addressing her as 'my dearest and truest sweetheart and well beloved companion'.[23]

It is much more difficult to determine Joan's feelings for the prince. Her love for Thomas Holand was apparent throughout their relationship from her steadfast loyalty and commitment to him, and his early death was a real tragedy for Joan. It is hard to imagine that she felt as strongly about the prince within a few weeks of Thomas' death. It is far more likely that she was genuinely fond of her cousin, even loved him, but was not in love with him. Joan did not have to marry the prince. Her independent wealth and her widowed status gave her a choice in deciding her own future in a way she had not had before, and the prince could not have coerced her into agreement. The long wrangle over her marriage to Thomas Holand had shown that she was not ambitious and there is no evidence that she became either forceful or calculating during their marriage. However, it seems probable that as a widow she was concerned for the future of her four children now that they were left fatherless.

She had lost her father at an early age and the subsequent problems she had endured over her marriage, combined with her knowledge of the challenges Thomas Holand had experienced due to his father's disgrace, followed by her husband's early demise, would have made her acutely aware of the potential difficulties her own children might now face. The prince, like Thomas Holand, was a strong and forceful person, and with the combined attractions of his undoubted genuine ardour for her and his status, her agreement to wed him was both sensible and intelligent. As his wife she would not only be brought back within the fold of the royal circle, she would enjoy a prestigious and protected position as Princess of Wales and she could be sure that her children's futures would be secure. Nevertheless, the picture painted by the French chronicler of Joan as a scheming temptress does not fit with her personality. When the prince made his feelings known, it is clear that Joan agreed willingly; her affection for him together with the undeniable material advantages that marriage to him would bring made his proposal more than welcome, but this was a personal choice, rather than being planned and calculated.

Many historians consider the marriage surprising, and have concluded not only that Joan was an unsuitable bride for the prince but also that he married her in defiance of his parents' wishes, after harbouring a secret love for his cousin for years, having confided his hopeless passion to his friend Lady Elizabeth de Burgh, in the twenty-three visits he made to Elizabeth between December 1357 and August 1359 (Elizabeth died a month before Thomas Holand).[24] Froissart must be held partly responsible for this view, as he claimed that the marriage was made without the king's knowledge ('sans le sceu dou roy son pere').[25] This is simply incorrect. Prince Edward may have been in love, but he was still heir to the throne and well aware of what was expected of him. He was every inch his father's son. He was also, unlike his father and grandfather, fortunate in having a close and genuinely fond relationship with his father. Contrary to the idea that Edward III did not approve of the match, he not only endorsed his son's choice but was involved right from the beginning in the arrangements which were needed to ensure the marriage could take place. In fact, it was the plans for the prince's future which necessitated a speedy courtship and wedding rather than the strength of the prince's ardour.

The peace treaty with France, signed at Brétigny on 24 October 1360, had given Edward III territory which greatly expanded the Gascony of his father's day to include the land more recently conquered and occupied by the English forces, to be held in full sovereignty from the French Crown. This new, politically constructed landmass was described as the duchy of Aquitaine and closely resembled the old Angevin duchy. As soon as the treaty was signed the king and his council debated the issue of how to manage Aquitaine and almost immediately the idea of it being an independent principality with the prince at its head was put forward. This suggestion had two immensely practical points in its favour. It gave the adult prince a job and a focus for his energies in the peace, and it solved the dilemma for Edward III of having to rule what was in effect a separate kingdom at a distance via a succession of paid deputies. The prince was eminently suitable. He was the perfect deputy, having already been appointed his father's lieutenant in Gascony in 1355; he had the military credentials to ensure the principality was protected from any resurgent French encroachments; he was respected by his enemies as well as his friends; and he had his father's complete and unequivocal trust. By the spring of 1361 the idea of appointing the prince as ruler in Aquitaine had taken root with the council in serious discussion about its implementation, and by July several of the prince's closest companions and officers had been appointed to positions in Aquitaine to secure the annexation of the new territories and to set up the administration for the new principality.[26]

One of the many considerations in planning for the prince's future in Aquitaine was his financial position. Between 1348 and 1360 more than half the expenditure in Gascony had been financed by the English exchequer, the troops and administration costing between £1,500 and £3,750 a year.[27] This was a huge drain on the Crown's resources and could not continue. The king and the council were determined that the much larger Aquitaine should be self-financing. The prince would be expected to raise money within the duchy and use this income to support his government; this meant that initially he would need to rely on his own resources. As the king's eldest son the prince had been well provided for financially. As Prince of Wales, Earl of Cornwall and Earl of Chester his estates in Wales, Cornwall and Chester brought in an annual income of probably around £8,000, and he was the principal beneficiary of his grandmother, Queen Isabella, when she died in 1358.[28] The prince probably enjoyed almost the largest income of any of his father's subjects (although his younger brother John of Gaunt would later enjoy considerably greater wealth, when his wife Blanche of Lancaster became sole heiress to the entire Lancastrian inheritance with its income of around £12,000 a year). However, the prince had huge demands on his wealth. As his father's principal lieutenant in the war he was expected to have the largest retinue after the king and the cost of financing this was exorbitant.[29] His estates and household institutions were directed for him by his council, which worked hard to provide him with sufficient funds. The records of his accounts provide evidence of the strain on the prince's resources. As early as 1352 the council was finding it difficult to meet the demands made on them, and resorted to measures designed to maximise income, such as ordering that wardships and marriages granted to the prince should be sold for as much as possible, noting that if any were concealed this would be to the prince's 'great damage'.[30] The Poitiers campaign was a particularly large drain on the prince's resources. Despite his victory and the capture of John II, the prince derived little net benefit from this in financial terms, with the added cost of maintaining the French king, whom he hosted for many months after his capture at vast expense. By November 1356 the prince was having difficulty meeting his commitments and ordered his council to use any money available to pay his debts to local traders, as 'the people [of Cornwall] are making a great clamour on account of the failure to pay', in this instance at the expense of his own friend and comrade in arms, William Montague, Earl of Salisbury, who three years later in 1359 complained to the prince's council that the arrears of his Cornwall annuity remained outstanding.[31]

Prince Edward's exceptional generosity exacerbated his financial difficulties. His accounts are full of lists of gifts to his knights and servants, mainly cash for the latter but often valuable items such as silver gilt and enamelled cups and ewers for his knights. Generosity was highly regarded and jewels and plate were welcome presents. The prince was frequently short of ready cash and forced to borrow, which he seems to have done indiscriminately, including from friends. For example, his household accounts show that in 1355 he owed money to Henry Picard, John Wesenham, Sir Guy Brian, the Bishop of Durham, Sir Walter Mauny, the earls of Huntingdon, Stafford and Arundel, Sir Edmund Bereford, John Wode, Sir James Beaufort, Sir James Audley, Ralph Copey, Sir Frank Hale, the king and even a yeoman of the queen's buttery called Richard, while in July 1359 he borrowed the enormous sum of £2,000 from the Earl of Arundel, which enabled him to repay a surely small but outstanding debt of 4 marks he owed to Alice Slappele, an attendant of his mother, who had written to him praying that he would remember the loan she had made to him while he was staying with the queen at Chertsey.[32] In view of the financial difficulties the prince was experiencing, his father's determination that he should manage Aquitaine without support from the English Treasury was a daunting prospect.

Once the decision had been made regarding Aquitaine, Edward III and the prince had much to discuss, and they would have discussed his marriage. Although the king had previously displayed no urgency over the marriage of his heir, Aquitaine changed this. The prince was expected to succeed his father (he was even occasionally referred to as Edward IV during his father's lifetime), and it was important for him to beget an heir.[33] The prince's younger brothers Lionel and John were already married, and in March 1361 John's father-in-law, Henry of Lancaster, died, leaving John heir to the richest patrimony in the country. This reinforced the desirability of the prince's marriage, while marrying an heiress would help resolve the prince's financial situation. From a practical aspect, it would greatly facilitate the prince's appointment if he married before he travelled to Aquitaine, giving him a consort with whom he could set up his own establishment in the duchy and hold court. Joan's sudden availability, and the prince's own attraction to her, presented an unexpected opportunity. But however ardently the prince desired Joan, he was no fool. As heir to the throne, he knew he had been expected to make a match which would benefit the Crown. For many years different possible foreign matches had been mooted, and although none had come to fruition this did not mean that the king had abandoned all hope of negotiating one. Joan was not an ideal bride and would be an unusual choice. The prince would have discussed his desire to marry Joan at the earliest opportunity with his father. He wanted and needed his father's approval, as well as his father's assistance to facilitate the marriage. Perhaps surprisingly, despite the fact that the marriage would not bring any apparent advantages to the king, Edward III appears to have had no reservations about his son's choice, and to have given him every encouragement. The prince's personal inclinations were allowed to be decisive, although in Joan's favour was the fact that she did at least have royal blood, and having been part of the royal household Joan was well versed in royal protocol; happily, and importantly, she was also extremely wealthy. Joan's inheritance was a vital factor. The marriage would significantly augment the prince's income, swelling it by at least another £3,000 a year, an increase of about 40 per cent.[34] Evidence of the benefit this gave the prince can be seen from the fact that by 1369 he was able to give £1,537 in annuities to his staff and friends, a sum which represented more than 60 per cent of his own income from Cheshire and which would surely have been beyond his means prior to his marriage.[35]

However, the prince and his father were well aware that there was one considerable drawback to the marriage, and that was Joan's marital history. The prince had almost as much knowledge of his cousin's tangled marital history as Edward III, and realised it presented a considerable legal problem. Thomas Holand had served under him, while William Montague was one of the prince's childhood companions and a close personal friend as well as one of his most trusted military captains, with the prince giving him a gift of a helmet with a cower decorated in silver and a matching 'seinture al barber', also decorated in silver and gilded, in 1359.[36] Joan's widowed status in itself was no bar, but the irregularity of her original marriage to Thomas and the fact that William was still alive, with a potential legal claim to be her husband, was a serious complication. Neither the prince nor his father had any doubts about how William would react, and it is indeed intriguing that despite the history between Joan and William there is no evidence that this caused any long-term bad feeling between them or their families. In fact, in later life William was at hand to support and advise Joan, suggesting that they maintained a friendship over the years. But for Edward III and the prince the problem of the Montague entanglement was that this could conceivably, in time, threaten the legitimacy of any children Joan bore the prince, so it was imperative that this was resolved to ensure an undisputed succession. Somehow the prince and his father had to ensure that the legality of the marriage was watertight, and this meant obtaining the cooperation of the Pope. The usual dispensation would be required in any event, as the prince and Joan were related within the prohibited degrees of consanguinity, and the prince was also godfather to her eldest son and heir, Thomas. But although Joan was not a foreign princess there was no reason to suppose that the papacy would be any more accommodating in the matter of the prince's marriage than before. The relationship between the English Crown and the papacy had been strained by the war with France, and despite the Treaty of Brétigny there remained considerable friction, exacerbated by the presence in France of many disbanded soldiers, now banded together in armed companies. To make matters worse, in the spring of 1361 the Pope was personally threatened by one such band, led by an English renegade soldier.[37] Apart from the embarrassment this caused Edward III it was hardly helpful to have such an incident at this point in time, just when the king needed to ask the Pope for a considerable favour. Ensuring the prince's marriage was legally unassailable required more than a simple dispensation, and lengthy negotiations were out of the question as this would not fit into the timescale for the prince taking over Aquitaine. They needed to find a way of persuading the Pope that was quick and foolproof. Edward III was an astute man and it did not take him long to devise an ingenious and deceptively simple plan with his son.

Meticulously planned, their strategy to secure the Pope's consent bore a marked resemblance to one of their joint military campaigns. The first step was taken by the prince. The usual protocol was for the king to approach the pontiff with a request for the necessary dispensation. Instead the prince contacted the Pope direct individually, and by June and July 1361 he was in regular and continuous correspondence with the Pope, sending his squire Nicholas Bond back and forth to attend the pontiff in Rome and Avignon with his runner Picot couriering his letters, requesting politely and insistently that he be granted the requisite formal dispensation to enable him to marry Joan.[38] Neither the prince nor his father was concerned when there was no immediately favourable response, as for them this was simply preparing the ground for the next stage of their plan. The next step was audacious and risky. The prince secretly contracted to marry Joan. This was an extraordinary action to take, as by doing so he risked excommunication for himself and his bride. Not surprisingly, this secret contract of marriage was interpreted by Froissart as evidence that the prince had married Joan without his parents' knowledge or approval. But the clandestine union was a characteristically bold and deliberate manoeuvre executed with the sole intention of forcing the Pope's hand, and a vital part of the scheme. It seems quite likely that it was Edward III's idea. The king made the next move, probably in August, by presenting Innocent VI with a formal request concerning the prince's marriage. Edward III's petition was a masterpiece. First, the king requested a dispensation for his son's marriage on the grounds of his relationship to Joan; secondly, he asked the Pope to absolve the couple for having privately contracted to marry 'per verba praesenti', explaining disingenuously that the prince had intended subsequently obtaining the necessary dispensation (but without explaining why he had not waited to get it); and thirdly he asked the Pope to declare that any future offspring of the marriage was legitimate.[39] Presented with the marriage as a *fait accompli*, the Pope was cornered. He could hardly withhold his consent now, especially as he had been in correspondence with the prince about it for months without indicating that he would refuse. Innocent VI dared not risk causing offence to Edward III and his son, with the undesirable diplomatic and political consequences that would inevitably follow an open breach with the English Crown. The Pope knew he had been outwitted, and on 7 September replied, granting all the king's requests.[40]

Nevertheless the king and the prince must have been relieved and delighted with the speed of the Pope's reply. Innocent VI's authorisation for the prince's marriage was comprehensive and addressed each of Edward III's points separately. He dealt first with the simplest aspect, the relationship between the prince and Joan, by issuing a bull to Simon Islip, Archbishop of Canterbury, which provided the requisite dispensation.[41] The issue of the unauthorised marriage contract was resolved by instructing the archbishop to release the prince and Joan from the penalty of excommunication, subject to a suitable penance.[42] The king's last request was far and away the most significant and required the most detailed response. Innocent VI ordered a fresh investigation to be made into the circumstances of Joan's marriage to Thomas Holand, promising to formally ratify the decisions made by his two predecessors if this proved satisfactory. Archbishop Islip was instructed to conduct the examination and report back. This stage of the proceedings obviously had the potential for the greatest delay, but it is evident that pressure was brought to bear – and that the result was a foregone conclusion. By the time the archbishop submitted his report to the Pope on 18 October, confirming that he and the other bishops had re-examined the 1349 bull and were satisfied with its ecclesiastical legality, the archbishop had already solemnised the prince's marriage to Joan.[43] On 6 October Prince Edward and Joan were formally espoused, and the wedding itself took place four days later in the chapel at Windsor. Archbishop Simon Islip's extensive report to Innocent VI spelt out the formalities he had conducted on the Pope's behalf; he had pronounced the private contract for marriage null and void, released the couple from the penalties for excommunication, imposed a penance on them to found two chapels within a year and endow each with 20 marks a year, and finally he had solemnised their marriage.[44] Innocent VI concluded the matter by issuing his personal bull on 11 December 1361 confirming the validity of the prince's marriage to Joan.[45]

There is little doubt about the prince's relief, as his generosity in complying with the penance imposed by Archbishop Islip far exceeded the stipulated price. The prince chose to endow Canterbury Cathedral, for which he had a particular fondness. He had been on pilgrimage to Thomas à Becket's tomb on several occasions, notably in 1356 with his royal prisoner, John II, en route for London. Shortly after his wedding the prince paid for the construction of a chantry in the crypt to contain two altars, dedicated to the Holy Trinity and the Virgin Mary, with a priest at each, endowing the cathedral with the substantial and valuable manor of Vauxhall, comprising over thirty-one acres, with his father's formal consent being granted on 29 August 1362.[46] The Vauxhall revenue would more than cover the cost of maintaining the chapel, with income left to spare. At the prince's expense the Romanesque chapel in the crypt of the south-west transept was completely refurbished under the guidance of Prior Robert Hathbrand to a design agreed with the prince. The high standard of the work carried out, using the latest architectural style and creating the first major Perpendicular interior in a cathedral, included a ribbed, vaulted roof decorated with bosses on the intersections, and indicates that a highly skilled architect, possibly Henry Yevele, was used.[47] The remnants of the prince's generosity are still visible in the cathedral in the Huguenot chapel, used by the French Protestant congregation since the sixteenth century, although the masonry and decoration has gone and the pillars, bosses and roof are whitewashed. The bosses show the coats of arms of the prince and his father, and one features a woman's head, with her hair dressed in the style fashionable in the 1360s, held in a square-framed net close to her face. This may well be a representation of Joan but there is no evidence to suggest it was executed on the prince's orders and may well have been placed there some time after the initial work was completed. In fact, Joan is noticeably absent from the prince's gift, which is curious. In the charter document the prince requested prayers for his parents, his siblings and himself, without mentioning Joan, plainly implying that the gift, while fulfilling the penance, also expressed the relief and thanks of both the king and his son.[48] The lack of any reference to Joan herself was clearly deliberate, and this suggests the prince wanted this endowment to be very personal to him. The prince did not forget to reward his squire Nicholas Bond for his part in the affair. In October 1360 the prince had granted Nicholas the manors of Vauxhall and Kennington for life in return for a daily rental; in October 1362 the prince replaced this with an annuity of £76 6s 4d to come from Mere manor in Wiltshire and in May 1365 the prince granted Mere to Nicholas for life, free of rent.[49]

In spite of the elaborate care taken by all concerned, one important legal detail was overlooked. The dispensation regarding the prince's relationship with Joan only covered two of the three ecclesiastical prohibitions on their union. The prince's status as godfather to Joan's eldest son was a straightforward obstacle, but there were a confusing mix of blood relationship ties between them. Their obvious kinship came through Joan's father, Edmund, giving Joan and the prince a common grandfather in Edward I, but through her mother, Margaret, Joan could also trace ancestry to Eleanor of Castile, the prince's grandmother. It was probably this more distant relationship which escaped the notice of those preparing the dispensation. The king and the prince knew they could not afford to miss any legal nicety, and as soon as they realised Edward III swiftly applied to the Pope to rectify the omission. Unfortunately, by this time nearly a year had passed and Innocent VI had died. The king once again adopted a belt-and-braces approach, reiterating his original request, and in response the new pope, Urban V, issued his own bull on 6 December 1362, which not only supplied the missing part of the dispensation but also confirmed in full the terms of Innocent VI's bull.[50] Four different popes had now pronounced on the validity of Joan's marriage to Thomas Holand, and two had declared the prince's marriage to Joan lawful. This unanimity of papal opinion should have provided Edward III and the prince with the security they had sought.

Notwithstanding the apparent success of their plan, Edward III and the prince knew that there would always be a query over the legality of the prince's marriage. Archbishop Islip harboured his own private doubts, which he shared with the prince two days before the formal wedding ceremony, warning him of the risk of scandal because of Joan's marital history.[51] Edward III and the prince could only hope that the elaborate care they had taken to ensure that any legal loophole had been filled would be sufficient, and deter any potential challenge to the legitimacy of any children Joan bore the prince. Their concern to obtain the Pope's cooperation to resolve the legal complexities of the marriage proved well founded. Only three years later, in December 1364, the Pope denied Edward III's request for a dispensation to enable the prince's younger brother, Edmund of Langley, to marry Margaret of Flanders.[52] As this effectively prevented a diplomatic alliance which would favour England, the pontiff's refusal was a blatantly political act barely disguised by being worded as a general prohibition against any of Edward III's children marrying within the third and fourth degrees of consanguinity. Needless to say, the effect would have been to prevent the prince's marriage to Joan had it not already taken place. Then, in 1370, the Pope threatened to have Joan and the prince's son Richard (later to become King Richard II) declared illegitimate.[53] The importance of the documentation so painstakingly collected to prove the legality of the prince's marriage was deeply impressed on his heir. More than thirty years later, before he sailed to Ireland in November 1394, Richard II ordered his chancellor, the Archbishop of York, to take custody of a small chest which contained personal documents and to place them for safekeeping with the abbot and convent of Westminster. Richard considered these documents so important that he habitually kept them at his side in his own personal safe deposit box, and parted with them only on this sole sojourn abroad.[54] Apart from his will the majority of the documents, including eleven papal bulls, related to his parents' marriage, and collectively and comprehensively comprised written verification of the legality of Joan's marriage to Thomas Holand, the annulment of her marriage to William Montague, and the validity of her marriage to his father.[55] When Richard II was deposed in 1399, the chronicler Adam Usk commented that 'concerning whose birth many unsavoury things were commonly said, namely that he was not born of a father of the royal line, but of a mother given to slippery ways – to say nothing of many other things I have heard'.[56] Written many years after her death, Usk's remark confirms the effect Joan's marital past had on her reputation.

Prince Edward's wedding to his Jeanette on 10 October 1361 in the chapel at Windsor was the social event of the year. The chapel would have been packed. The service was conducted by Archbishop Islip in the presence of all the most prominent members of the nobility and the clergy.[57] Heading the guest list was the prince's own family – his parents Edward III and Queen Philippa, his sister Princess Isabella, his brothers John of Gaunt, Edmund of Langley and Thomas of Woodstock (Lionel and Princess Margaret were absent), his aunt Queen Joan of Scotland (Edward III's sister) – along with the bishops of Winchester, Salisbury, Lincoln and Worcester, the Abbot of Westminster and many more unnamed individuals.[58] Lady Blanche Wake would have been present, and probably Joan's sister-in-law Elizabeth, with her new husband Eustace d'Aubrichecourt. Among the guests also would have been Joan's erstwhile husband William Montague, Earl of Salisbury, and his countess, Elizabeth. The prince and his bride must have made a magnificently handsome couple, with Joan wearing a rich red dress with cloth of gold decorated with a variety of birds.[59] Joan's dress would have been in the prevailing fashionable style with a tightly fitting upper bodice and buttoned sleeves from which hung long decorative pieces, with a low waist and a flowing lower skirt. No list of gifts survives but no doubt these were plentiful, with presents of plate and jewellery for Joan. Eighteen months earlier, on John of Gaunt's wedding, the royal family had given gifts to his wife Blanche valued at £670 5s.[60]

The wedding of the heir to the throne was an occasion of national importance and surely warranted a fanfare of triumphal and celebratory events, particularly as it had been a difficult year in many respects for Edward III. In March, the king had lost one of his most valued family members when Henry, Duke of Lancaster, had died, and in September, just three weeks before the wedding, Princess Mary, who had so recently married John, Duke of Brittany, died aged seventeen.[61] Princess Margaret died very shortly after the wedding, and as she is not listed among the guests it seems probable that her illness prevented her from attending the festivities. The year had also been marked by a further outbreak of the plague and a hurricane which had devastated many areas, destroying houses and steeples on churches as well as trees.[62] The prince's marriage was an opportunity to put these catastrophes to one side. At the very least one might have expected a series of splendid tournaments and something special as a public celebration held in Joan's honour. The prince was as enthusiastic in his love of display as his father, and notably fond of lavish hospitality, most clearly in evidence when he escorted John II back from France after his victory at Poitiers in the celebrations held in London to mark the occasion. It is therefore surprising that nothing of this kind was arranged, in marked contrast to the two weeks of jousting held for John of Gaunt's wedding to Blanche of Lancaster in Reading in May 1359, including a special event to honour Blanche in London subsequently, or the Dunstable tournaments following Lionel's wedding to Elizabeth de Burgh in 1343. Nor is there any record that Edward III awarded an annuity to his new daughter-in-law as he had done for Blanche.[63] The prince even disguised the simple matter of giving his household staff new livery, waiting until 28 December and then giving orders that new liveries should be provided for New Year's Day (his livery was white and green, with green on the right), with hats adorned with gold ribbons and camaca for his knights and woollen cloth for his squires and yeomen.[64] A possible explanation is that the royal family were in mourning for Princess Mary, and that Princess Margaret was gravely ill. An added incentive for the relatively low-key approach to the prince's wedding may have been the king and prince's concern about Joan's marital history. Edward III was well aware that as Princess of Wales Joan might be regarded by her peers with some suspicion, and he was alert to the possibility that a weakness in his son's marriage might be exploited. As a consequence, the king wanted his son to be careful to ensure that their nuptials did not draw undue attention or invite criticism. A series of tournaments were indeed held, but because they did not take place until March and April 1362, several months after the prince's wedding, they were not specifically associated with it. Instead, after the ceremony, the prince and his bride retired to his palace at Kennington, and from there they moved on to his castle at Berkhamsted in Berkshire, where they were joined by Edward III and Queen Philippa for the Christmas festivities. Froissart was among those accompanying Queen Philippa. Joan was now referred to as the 'king's daughter', and she and the queen exchanged gifts, even clothes, with a touchingly intimate entry dated March 1362 recording Joan spending £6 13s 4d on mending a corset given to her by Philippa.[65]

The prince's circumspection regarding his wedding is apparent even in terms of his own personal expenditure. Notably generous in his gifts to others, and liberal in his spending on his own attire, it is hard to find evidence of any particular extravagance towards Joan. Like his father, Prince Edward believed that he should be visibly royal and dressed in fine clothes when not on campaign. Naturally he had decided views on how he wished his wife to appear, and even before their marriage took place he initiated changes in Joan's clothes, and that of her children, by providing them with apparel in a style he considered suitable. By midsummer 1361 he had ordered his tailor, Henry Daldrington, and a London embroiderer, Giles Davynell, to make new clothes for Joan and her daughters, as well as for himself, paying Daldrington 61/4*d* a day for each furrier and tailor.[66] The list of material to be used gives an indication of the taste: ells of long burnet, long scarlet, brown scarlet, blue and green longcloth, long tawny, long russet, blue azure, taffeta, canvas, furs of miniver, lamb, ermine, Venice ribbon, gold ribbon, gold cloth and cloth of ray.[67] Embroidery was used to decorate clothing, and outer garments were often trimmed with fur. Between April and November 1361 the prince spent over £3,000 on jewels, including nearly 9,000 pearls.[68] These were presumably for Joan and her daughters. Sleeves were usually buttoned on, with pearls often used as buttons, adding decoration to the garment, and many would have been used to adorn Joan's new clothes, possibly including her wedding dress.[69] These may seem exorbitant sums, but in fact they were relatively modest when judged by the prince's own standards. In 1353 he had purchased 779 pearls to adorn a single hood, and in 1355 he bought at least twenty-six rings, yet only four are listed for the year of his wedding.[70] It is also curious that there is no record of the prince giving any jewellery to Joan. Six months after the wedding, in March 1362, the prince spent £200 on a set of buttons for his wife, and a further £200 on two rubies, two brooches, and a ring with four diamonds, yet even if these were gifts for Joan they are hardly remarkable when compared to the richly jewelled gold brooches he had given his sisters Isabella and Joan in 1352, each set with three rubies, three emeralds, two diamonds and six pearls.[71] The restraint is even apparent in Joan's wedding dress, and it seems likely that the prince had a hand in the design of this. Red was a colour frequently worn by the royal family for public occasions of celebration, and cloth of gold (threads of gold woven on a web of silk) was a favourite splendid material. The decoration with embroidered birds is the only personal touch, an indication of Joan's own taste and a taste shared by Queen Philippa, whose dark-blue velvet churching suit for the birth of William in 1348 had similarly been embroidered with gold birds.[72] It was a sumptuous dress yet relatively modest compared, for example, to Philippa's churching outfit, which had used 400 large pearls, thirty-eight ounces of small pearls, thirteen pounds of gold plate, eleven pounds of gold thread, seven pounds of embroidery silks, 2,000 miniver bellies for the lining and sixty ermine skins, or Princess Mary's wedding dress, made from 'gold racamatiz of Lucca' covered by 'cloth of gold baldekyn d'outremer' with a long train and trimmed with 600 miniver furs given by the King of France.[73]

Although the evidence is clear that Joan was accepted and welcomed as a royal bride by the prince's family, the stigma that she was unsuitable, and disliked – by Queen Philippa at least – remains, and is repeated by many historians. This derives in part from the deliberate restraint exercised by Prince Edward and his father in the wedding arrangements, but also from the way in which the wedding was reported by the chroniclers. As befitted a marriage of such dynastic, social and political importance, all the chroniclers recorded it. Of these, only one, Higden, writing some years after the event, makes a subjective comment, stating that the marriage surprised many people.[74] As the prince had been expected to marry a foreign princess, this may have been true, but it is unremarkable given the secrecy with which the king and the prince went about the prince's affairs in the spring and summer of 1361. The proposal for his marriage was not disclosed until the Pope's cooperation was secured, and the facts surrounding Joan's early marriages were known to very few, while the plan for the prince to become ruler of Aquitaine was kept a closely guarded secret until it was publicly announced in July 1362. As Prince Edward was heir to the throne (indeed the *Anonimalle Chronicle* describes him as 'Edward de quarte'), when his marriage became public knowledge the chroniclers were in a dilemma, as they were aware that Joan had once been treated as married to William Montague, who was still alive in 1361, so they were naturally concerned to reassure their audience of the validity of the prince's marriage. In the main the chroniclers sought to stress Joan's royal ancestry, the *Anonimalle Chronicle* describing her as 'la feile le counte de Kente, sire Edmunde de Wodestoke, unkle al dit roy Dengleterre tiercz' (the daughter of Sir Edmund of Woodstock, Earl of Kent and uncle to Edward III).[75] John of Reading refers to Edmund and the circumstances of the papal dispensation needed for the marriage, with Walsingham and Knighton also referring to her father and to her separation from William Montague for the sake of Thomas Holand.[76] It is clear that none of the chroniclers fully understood Joan's marital history and in referring to her antecedents they meant to emphasise her eligibility. The only contemporary commentator not to dwell on her antecedents was Chandos Herald. Writing within ten years of the prince's death, the herald wrote that 'the gentle prince married ... a lady of great renown, who enkindled love in him, in that she was beauteous, charming and discreet'.[77]

Joan's life changed completely when she became the prince's wife. She now ranked as first lady in the land after her mother-in-law, Queen Philippa, and just as it was anticipated that the prince would succeed his father so Joan was expected to one day become queen. She was the first Princess of Wales. The title Prince of Wales had only been in existence for two generations, since Joan and the prince's shared grandfather, Edward I, had created his son Edward of Carnarvon Prince of Wales. Both Edward II and Edward III had married after they succeeded to the throne and thus there had not previously been a Princess of Wales. Joan was also Duchess of Cornwall and Countess of Chester, and retained her own title of Countess of Kent. Her enhanced status was reflected in a new coat of arms and seal denoting her as Princess of Wales, Duchess of Cornwall and countess of both Chester and Kent. There is only one known seal in existence, dating from 1380, and this shows a shield in half, with her father's arms on the right, emphasising her lineage and status as an heiress. Joan's arms can be seen impaled with those of the prince on the north side of Queen Philippa's tomb in Westminster Abbey.[78] A personal badge was created for her, probably under the guiding hands of the prince, of a white hart, sitting on the ground and tethered by a gold chain with a crown for a collar.[79] This badge was later used by her son, Richard II.

As soon as Joan agreed to marry the prince she, and all her affairs, were immediately subsumed within the prince's sphere of influence. Months before their wedding the prince took charge of Joan's household, making arrangements for several of Joan's retinue to join his service, including John Holand, Thomas' nephew, who became the prince's yeoman in May 1361, as did William Harpele, one of Joan's own clerks.[80] Joan already had her own household before she married the prince and it is likely that she retained many of her servants, acquiring additional staff she needed as a result of her newly enhanced status from among the prince's entourage, such as William Fulbourne, a clerk of the prince's who became Joan's chaplain and would remain in her service until her death. Having taken over Joan's personal income, after their marriage the prince arranged for his wife to have an annual allowance of 2,000 marks to cover her personal expenses and the cost of maintaining her daughters and her own household. This was initially paid to her in cash at regular intervals and delivered to her by the prince's servants, usually John Carleton and John Stene, the former becoming Joan's clerk.[81] Joan did not forget those staff who had given her and Thomas loyal and faithful service, and she ensured that the grants they had received during Thomas' lifetime were confirmed after she married the prince. These ranged from the £20 annuity for Thomas' falconer, John Sale, and his wife Hawise, to the 50 marks annuity given to Donald and Joan Heselrigg in Yorkshire.[82] Similarly the prince honoured the annuities granted to Thomas' comrades in arms Sir John Chandos, Sir Richard Pembridge (fellow Garter knights with Thomas) and Sir Henry Hay.[83] These gifts were unremarkable in size and there is no evidence that Joan was inclined to add to the grants after she became Princess of Wales. In view of the prince's own extravagant tendencies, it seems probable that the notable restraint exercised by Joan was her personal decision, rather than her being constrained by her husband. It certainly ensured that she did not invite criticism for undue generosity.

The transfer of management of Joan's estates was left until after the wedding. The prince naturally anticipated that these would be a valuable additional resource, and he was anxious to ensure that his wife's stewards understood this. By the end of October 1361 he had sent out orders to each steward to 'labour diligently about the said office and ... the speedy levying of moneys due to the prince' so that 'those parts may be ordered and governed to the best of his ability for the prince's honour and profit'.[84] On 24 October 1361 the prince appointed four of his trusted staff, John Carleton, Richard Stokes, William Spridlington and John Stene, to carry out a survey of his wife's estates and gave them authority to appoint new receivers and stewards.[85] John Carleton and Richard Stokes between them covered Joan's northern estates in Yorkshire, Nottinghamshire, Lincoln, Derbyshire, Leicestershire, Rutland, Northamptonshire and Huntingdonshire, while William Spridlington and John Stene took Norfolk, Suffolk, Cambridge, Essex, Hertfordshire, Kent and Sussex. The prince showed some sensitivity in handling his wife's affairs by being careful to ensure his staff spent time with Joan to discuss the arrangement of her estates, and carried out orders she had made during her widowhood to reward those who had served her and Thomas faithfully over the years. Her views were obviously valued, and the prince's staff clearly satisfied with the Holand stewards, as they confirmed the existing subdivision of Kent estates into six areas of responsibility, and kept each of Joan's stewards in post, merely imposing a new obligation to account to the prince's council in London. The prince's prime concern appears to have been to maximise his wife's income and assets and he was happy to achieve this by obtaining the cooperation of her local retainers. Having the Prince of Wales as their new lord may have given the Holand stewards increased self-esteem but they were not rewarded by a rise in pay, while the prince and his staff issued a continuous stream of orders prior to his departure for Aquitaine reminding them to collect the rent and to sell assets such as wardships and crops with as much profit as possible.[86]

After the Christmas break at Berkhamsted the newly-weds returned to London for the tournaments held at Smithfield in March and April 1362, possibly staying in the prince's apartments in Westminster. Joan continued to work on her clothing, and presumably on her daughters' wardrobe, spending £7 10s on a quantity of cloth while at Smithfield, and paying 66s 8d to the prince's tailor.[87] Subsequently they spent most of the summer at the prince's palace at Kennington. Berkhamsted and Kennington were only two of the prince's many residences, but they seem to have been the main ones used after his marriage. Before his marriage he had favoured his manor at Byfleet, used extensively throughout his childhood, but he rarely stayed there after his marriage, possibly for the simple practical reason that being smaller it was less easily able to accommodate the increased household. It is quite possible that before their wedding Joan had never visited either Berkhamsted Castle or Kennington Palace. She would quickly become familiar with both. Berkhamsted was originally a moated Norman castle, built by William the Conqueror's brother Robert, Count of Mortmain, and reverted to the Crown on the death of Edmund, Earl of Cornwall, in 1300. A year later Edward I gave the castle to his second wife, Joan's grandmother, Queen Margaret, and when she died in 1317 it passed to the prince's grandmother, Queen Isabella. Briefly owned by Edward III's brother, John of Eltham, the castle was given by the king to his eldest son with the remainder of the Cornwall estates in 1337.[88] As the prince grew to adulthood he discovered that the castle had been neglected by his predecessors, and gave his council instructions to put it back into good repair, ensuring that the castle was in sufficiently good condition to be used to house a royal prisoner (John II of France) in 1360.[89] Berkhamsted became one of the prince's favourite residences and he was frequently there for Christmas. In residence over Christmas 1361 with Joan and his parents, the prince found cause for concern, and further urgent repairs were ordered in January and February 1362.[90] Today the castle is a ruin, but enough of it remains to give an indication of what it would have been like in Joan's lifetime. The castle was never greatly expanded in size from its Norman origins, and, set on a gentle hill, surrounded by the remnants of its outer ramparts, it was one of the more modest royal residences. Despite the prince's fondness for Berkhamsted, Joan herself later favoured Wallingford Castle. Like Berkhamsted, Wallingford had also been the subject of much expenditure by the prince over the years, including the building of a new bakehouse, sixty feet long and twenty-eight feet wide, in 1358.[91] Planning his wedding, the prince made sure that Wallingford could also accommodate his new household, ensuring that the dean of the castle chapel increased his staff to six chaplains, six clerks and four choristers in July 1361.[92] Unfortunately today little of the castle remains, having been more or less demolished after a long siege during the English Civil War on the orders of Oliver Cromwell in 1652.

Kennington, just across the river from Westminster, was in contrast specifically styled as a palace. The prince acquired Kennington in 1337, the same year as Berkhamsted. The manor of Kennington and Vauxhall had been owned by Joan's cousin, Elizabeth de Burgh, and in 1337 Elizabeth agreed to exchange the manors for Ilketshall in Suffolk, nearer her other estates.[93] The main residence at Kennington, like the castle at Berkhamsted, was in considerable disrepair when acquired by Prince Edward, and was largely rebuilt by the prince between 1342 and 1362, transforming it into a comfortable palace. The prince employed more than one architect, and in 1358 he contracted the services of Henry Yevele, the master mason who also undertook work for the king.[94] Most of the old manor was replaced, with Yevele constructing a new hall approximately ninety feet long and fifty feet wide. He installed two new spiral staircases and three chimneys at the end of the hall, and a new house was constructed for the pastry cook.[95] The prince's crests liberally adorned the walls of the stairway and chimneys, and a finishing touch of two babewyns (ugly or demonic creatures) were carved into the two buttresses positioned on the porch leading into the hall.[96] Despite these extensive works, some of the chambers within the palace were still in need of attention when the prince married Joan, and shortly after their wedding in October 1361 the prince gave orders that the defects should be given attention as quickly as possible.[97] Kennington was intended to be their main home in the capital, and later became Richard II's childhood home.

Inevitably, Joan's marriage had an immense impact on the lives of her four Holand children. Her eldest, Thomas, was only ten or eleven at the time, and the youngest, Joan, was possibly no more than three years old. They gained a new father as well as a generous patron. From the beginning the prince treated them as his own and assumed responsibility for them, even prior to his marriage, ordering clothes for Maud and Joan and giving them each a fine psalter that had belonged to Sir Humphrey de Bohun, also giving one to Joan.[98] Thomas and John were soon described as his sons in the prince's accounts; Thomas joined his stepfather's retinue and was provided with equipment and a squire, John Pounfreit, a servant of his father's.[99] If the interests of her children had been uppermost in Joan's thoughts when she agreed to marry her cousin, she was rewarded by the immediate and tremendous interest he showed in them. The prince's concern for the Holand children was not solely altruistic. As his stepsons and daughters they acquired marriage potential and this was a factor which he and his father had obviously taken into account in their plans. Within a year of his own marriage the prince had arranged marriages for Thomas and Maud, and the baby of the family, Joan, was married within three years. Each made alliances which fostered relationships that were diplomatically important to the king, but they were also prestigious matches which Joan was unlikely to have been able to arrange had she remained a widow.

Shortly after his marriage the prince entered into discussions with the earls of Devon and Arundel with the suggestion that one of his stepchildren should marry one of their children. The earls were leading members of the nobility, wealthy and influential, and each was ambitious for their family. Both were well aware of Joan's marital history, having witnessed the Earl of Salisbury's grant of land to William and Joan in 1341.[100] Richard Fitzalan, Earl of Arundel, was a contemporary of Edward III, and owed the restoration of his title and lands to the king. His father had been executed during Edward II's reign, and his family, like Joan's, had lost everything. In 1331 Edward III had restored the young Fitzalan to his family estates, in the process depriving Joan's family of Arundel Castle. The earl had become a stalwart supporter of the king, although he remained careful to safeguard his own interests. In 1354 he had seriously considered an alliance with the Mortimer family, agreeing with Roger Mortimer that his daughter Alice would marry Edmund Mortimer, Roger's son and heir.[101] Tremendously rich, Arundel soon became known as a source to apply to for a loan, and the king and the prince were two of his most notable clients; the prince had yet to complete repayment of the £2,000 he had borrowed from Arundel in July 1359 on the security of a gold jewel-encrusted crown, let alone the further £1,000 borrowed in July 1362 to pay for equipment for himself and his men for the forthcoming trip to Aquitaine.[102] An alliance by marriage was in all their interests. Arundel had never completed the Mortimer match, and when approached by the prince, the earl had no hesitation in agreeing to his proposal for a match between Alice and Thomas Holand. Richard Arundel had served on the prince's council, and he clearly regarded a marriage for his daughter Alice with the prince's stepson as a considerable coup. Naturally Edward III granted his approval, and the prince applied for the necessary papal dispensation in September 1363 (Thomas and Alice were related in the third and fourth degrees).[103] The business was concluded by a formal indenture of agreement between the prince and the earl dated 4 June 1365, recording that the earl would pay the prince 4,000 marks, the first instalment due in July 1365, and in exchange the prince and Joan agreed to endow the young couple with three Yorkshire manors (Kirkby Moorside, Buttercrambe and Cropton), part of Joan's Wake inheritance.[104]

The prince was also discussing his stepdaughter Maud's future at the same time. By October 1362 the Earl of Devon had agreed that his grandson and heir, Hugh Courtenay, would marry Maud, and had promised that when the marriage took place Maud would be given an annuity of 200 marks and the manors of Sutton Courtenay in Berkshire and Waddesdon in Buckinghamshire.[105] The earl's two younger sons, Edward and William, confirmed the grant. In exchange the prince promised to pay the earl 1,000 marks in four instalments at six-monthly intervals. Again, papal dispensation was required and the prince applied for this at the same time as he did for Thomas, with the king confirming his permission shortly afterwards. By February 1365 the marriage had taken place, as the prince's register records the earl completing the grant of the manors to Maud.[106] The new Lady Courtenay can have been no older than her mother had been at the time of her marriage to Thomas Holand and she may well have remained with Joan until she was a little older, as it was generally appreciated that there were dangers for a young girl attendant on consummation at an early age. In the event Maud and Hugh had no children, and their marriage did not last long. Hugh died before February 1374, within ten years of their marriage, and after his death Maud returned to live with her mother.[107]

Joan's youngest daughter, her namesake Joan, made a prestigious marriage at an even younger age when she married Princess Mary's widower, John Montfort, Duke of Brittany, in 1365. Montfort was many years older than Joan Holand, and had extremely close ties to the English Crown, having been largely brought up at the English court. He owed his succession as duke to Edward III's support. Nevertheless Edward III had felt it prudent to secure the alliance with a personal tie, and in 1355 had concluded an agreement with John's mother about a marriage alliance between the families. Initially the proposal was for John's sister to marry one of the king's sons; then it was agreed that John would marry either Princess Margaret or Princess Mary. Princess Mary's death so shortly after her marriage had been a tragedy for all concerned; nevertheless Edward III had been swift to persuade John Montfort when he came of age in 1362 to enter into a formal alliance with England and to promise that he would not marry without the king's leave.[108] A new marriage to the prince's stepdaughter would once again provide the personal link. From Joan's perspective there must have been some comfort in the fact that she knew her new son-in-law well. As a child John Montfort had lived for some years in Queen Philippa's household, and ten years earlier, in 1355, he had spent nearly a year under Thomas Holand's protection in Brittany. In any event, as the new young duchess could only have been about seven or eight at the time of her marriage, there was no immediate separation of mother and daughter, as young Joan would remain with her mother until she was old enough to formally join her husband and consummate their marriage.

If Joan was motivated to marry the prince to secure a future for her children, then she was completely successful.

9

Princess of Aquitaine
1363–1371

Prudence teaches the princess or great lady how above all things in this base world she ought to love honour and a good reputation.

Christine de Pizan[1]

By virtue of her marriage Joan became the most important woman at court after Queen Philippa. Her position was unique, as there had never been a Princess of Wales before. As already noted, Edward II was the first Prince of Wales, and both he and his son had married after they became king. As the wife of the heir to the throne, Joan was expected to become queen when the prince became king, and her new position as his wife gave her considerable authority and influence. In addition, she would have substantial additional responsibilities and as queen in waiting would be expected to set an example. Now there was peace with France Joan might reasonably have expected that marriage to the prince would mean she would spend time at court and be able to receive guidance from her mother-in-law on how to conduct herself in her new position. Instead, nine months after their marriage, the prince was created Prince of Aquitaine, and they and their entourage set sail for Bordeaux to set up court. The prince would govern the duchy with Joan at his side. Joan was now both Princess of Wales and Princess of Aquitaine. With no predecessors, and so no precedent, in either role, what was expected of her and how would she cope?

On 19 July 1362, Edward III formally dubbed his son and heir Prince of Aquitaine at Westminster Abbey in a ceremony attended by all the most important members of the nobility and clergy, and the prince, clad in armour, knelt in homage to his father, undertaking to pay an ounce of gold annually in acknowledgement of his sovereignty.[2] It was intentionally a superlative propaganda exercise, with letters sent by the king to his subjects in Aquitaine to give them the news, publicly proclaiming throughout Europe Edward III's supremacy over the French king as acknowledged in the Treaty of Brétigny. The event was duly recorded in a formal charter, drawn up by the prince's clerk, John Carleton, setting out the terms on which the principality was granted to the prince. This charter can be seen in the National Archives. The main message is set out at the beginning of the charter:

Edward by the Grace of God, King of England, Lord of Ireland and of Aquitaine to our most dear eldest son Edward Prince of Wales, Greeting … Intending by a liberal Recompense to do Honour unto you who lately in the parts of Aquitaine and Gascoigne, while there the frequent storms of war raged, for our sakes did not refuse the Summer Dust, and the Labour of War, but under the Name and the title of Lieutenant have supported the Burthen of our Cares, and with your Presence supplied our Absence, out of the princely Prerogative we do convey and grant unto you by these Presents the principality of the under written Lands and Provinces of all Aquitaine and Gascoigne willingly and granting that of all and singular the said Places, Lands and Provinces in our Name, next and immediate under our Throne and Government you from henceforth the true Prince, and freely during your natural Life enjoy the Title, Appellation and Name of the Prince of Aquitaine …

The charter concludes,

Now to take away all Doubts and Contentions which may arise hereafter about this Matter, and to the end that the Affair may be more clear, we reserve to ourselves, and to our Majesty royal, expressly and by Tenor of these Presents, the direct Supremacy, and all the Sovereignty and resort of the whole principality of Aquitaine and Gascoigne. And for an evident Token and clear Demonstration that our said son shall hold, and ought to hold unto us of our said Majesty, and by liege Homage, the which he hath made unto us at present … he shall be obliged to pay unto us every Year at our Palace of Westminster, on the Feast of Easter one Ounce of Gold … in token and Recognition of our supreme Dominion. Given under our Great Seal at the Palace of Westminster 19 July 1362.[3]

This was a momentous occasion for both the king and his son. For Edward III, the prince's marriage and his appointment in Aquitaine completed with a satisfying resonance the desired order within the royal progeny. His heir was now settled, with a new kingdom of his own to govern and a wife, and it was confidently expected that in due course Joan would bear children, providing the hoped-for next generation. Comfortable that his heir was secure Edward III turned his attention to his younger sons, and using the occasion of his own fiftieth birthday on 13 November 1362 he created Lionel Duke of Clarence, John Duke of Lancaster and Edmund Earl of Cambridge. For the prince, now Prince of Aquitaine, a future beckoned away from his father's court. He had a newly created territory to rule, with the expectation that this would be his home until the time came for him to succeed his father. In 1362, with Edward III a hale and hearty fifty-year-old, this must have seemed a long way off.

When the prince and Joan arrived in Aquitaine, they would need to establish themselves with their own court. As Princess of Aquitaine, Joan would preside over what would in effect be a satellite royal court. Although there was no precedent for her position, she would be expected to behave as befitted a queen. Guidance for her role was limited. In terms of literary advice, the most notable text was Giles of Rome's *De regimine principum*, and Giles argued that queens should be noble, beautiful, virtuous, temperate, chaste and not given to idleness.[4] Few queens were able to live up to such exacting perfection. The prince's grandmother, Queen Isabella, had hardly conformed to this ideal when she took a lover and deposed her husband, although the Pope, rather than condemning her behaviour, went to great lengths to persuade Edward III and Philippa to be reconciled to the dowager queen, in order that 'her good name may remain intact'.[5] Chastity was of paramount importance. Isabella's sisters-in-law, Marguerite of Burgundy and Blanche of Hungary, were both imprisoned following allegations of adultery in 1314, with Froissart noting that Blanche 'kept but evil the sacrament of matrimony ... she was kept a long space in prison in the Castle Gaillard', after which unedifying episode Blanche's angry husband Charles (later Charles IV of France) put her aside to remarry.[6] Edward I's two queens provided more suitable role models, Margaret being Joan's own grandmother, but fortunately there was a living exemplar at hand in Queen Philippa. The difficulty for Joan was that as the first Princess of Wales there was no precedent for her role, and while she might look to her mother-in-law for guidance, their backgrounds were quite different. Philippa had been a princess in her own right when she married Edward III, and brought him prestige and a diplomatic alliance. Joan's own birth and wealth did not add to the prince's prestige, and there was the disadvantage of her marital history. Nevertheless, in terms of how she might conduct herself, she could look to Philippa's example. Although she had spent the last ten years away from the court, Joan was no stranger to its ways, and knew what would be expected of her. Before leaving England she had the opportunity to take her mother-in-law's advice. The queen had consistently throughout her marriage deferred to her husband and supported him in all ways, accompanying him on his travels whenever she could. This was a model that Joan would emulate.

In many respects the prince could hardly have chosen a woman better suited to be his wife. From the start of their marriage Joan took her lead from her husband. At thirty-one, Prince Edward was considerably older than either his father or his brothers had been when they married, and had a clear idea of his own distinction. He was used to commanding respect and obedience and from the beginning of their marriage had taken control of Joan's affairs. Having already been married to a man with a strong and dominating personality this would not have daunted Joan, but it would undoubtedly affect how she conducted herself as princess of both Wales and Aquitaine. At the time of their marriage the prince's career was at its peak. He was widely admired by his contemporaries, friends and enemies alike, and considered a model of chivalric virtue. Just as his father was being compared by contemporary chroniclers to Arthur, so, to many, did the prince resemble an Arthurian knightly hero. Marrying a popular and very public hero presented additional challenges, and brought with it the almost inevitable corollary that Joan would be expected to live up to her husband. The combination of Joan's beauty, her dubious marital history and her new status as Princess of Wales inevitably led chroniclers like Froissart to identify her as a flawed heroine of Guineverian proportions, a reputation which grew posthumously. It is hardly surprising that Joan would later be given the leading romantic role in various tales of doubtful substance, such as the founding of the Order of the Garter, and the tale of Edward III rescuing the beautiful and besieged Countess of Salisbury from Wark Castle. Yet Joan was not, and could not afford to be, simply an adornment at the prince's side. As his wife she would have her own responsibilities and duties, and she would need to exert her own authority while ensuring that she did not go against her husband's wishes. In Aquitaine Joan would play hostess to the local nobility as well as her husband's knights, and she would need to be diplomatic, tactful and patient, while retaining her dignity and good humour. Her marital history would be a crucial determinant in how she behaved. Apart from the fact that this had already caused the prince and his father to execute an elaborate plan to ensure papal cooperation, Joan's honour was at stake. Scandal must be avoided. Joan would hardly have needed reminding by her husband that she should not put her reputation at risk in any way.

Prince Edward had originally anticipated that they would leave for Aquitaine shortly after he was created Prince of Aquitaine. Preparations had been in hand for some months beforehand. There was a lot to do, not least in discussion with his father and with ministers on how his role in Aquitaine would relate to the English Crown. Every military campaign entailed months of preparation and planning, and the logistics for a permanent settlement in Aquitaine required similarly thorough if not more detailed thought and attention. The prince needed to consult his own council and ensure that his own estate affairs, and those of his wife, were in order before he left, and that they would continue to be run efficiently and competently while he was away. A secret cipher was devised for the prince to write himself using his two mottoes of 'Ich dene' and 'Houmont' and the ostrich feather, and a new seal made for him by his goldsmith John Hiltoft.[7] He made arrangements with his staff on how he would communicate with them from Aquitaine and how they would report to him. Decisions needed to be taken about who and what the prince took with him. Planning a lavish lifestyle, this included carefully securing the exclusive service of a goldsmith named Lyon and two embroiders, Hans Stowsburgh and Terri de Coloigne, promising them lodging and expenses in Bordeaux.[8] Joan made her own arrangements too, including having a litter made for her use in Aquitaine.[9] By July everything seemed to be in place. On 30 July the king granted his son the right to receive 60,000 crowns in gold due from John II's ransom, and on 29 August licence to make his will to ensure the payment of his debts, while throughout August and September ships were ordered to Plymouth to facilitate the prince's passage.[10] £1,000 was borrowed from the Earl of Arundel to help pay the immediate costs. At the end of August the prince and Joan left London and travelled to Cornwall, staying at Restormel Castle, and then journeyed on to Plymouth where they waited to embark. Restormel was a Norman castle which had fallen into some disrepair, and the prince had recently spent a considerable sum on bringing it back into a habitable state (today, little remains of the castle). However, a combination of poor weather conditions and insufficient ships prevented the prince's fleet from sailing as planned. Severe storms caused considerable damage throughout the country that winter, with entire houses being blown down, and at Kennington the roof of the chapel was virtually destroyed, requiring extensive repair.[11] The prince and Joan spent their second winter together at Restormel rather than in France as hoped.

Joan would naturally have been occupied with her husband's affairs, and with her children, during the months before their departure for Aquitaine, but she did not neglect her own affairs, remembering and rewarding friends and servants from her life with Thomas Holand, and ensuring that these were ratified by the prince. Throughout 1362 and 1363 grants and annuities were made and confirmed, particularly to estate workers and members of her household on Joan's Yorkshire and Derbyshire estates, especially Castle Donington, such as Reynold and Alice Lewes, granted a life interest in a property on the Donington estate, and Maud la Zouche, given 1*d* a day for her good service to Joan from Kirkby Moorside manor.[12] Old friends were remembered, like Sir Richard Pembridge, who was granted a life interest in the annual rental paid by the abbot of Stratford in Essex.[13] Joan might well have used her new position to assist some of these people in their career, but she was wise enough to do so in a very modest way. One recipient of her assistance was Robert Braybrooke, son of her parents' old friend Gerard Braybrooke. Gerard had acted as attorney for Joan's brother John, and then for Joan and Thomas prior to his death in 1355, and he had fought in the prince's division at Crécy. His older son Gerard had joined in the prince's entourage as a squire and would go to Aquitaine with them. Robert was the younger son, born in 1336 and destined for the Church. He went to

Oxford to read civil law and by 1359 had obtained a dispensation to become a priest, and after his father died was granted a rectory at Clifton in Bedfordshire while his older brothers, Gerard and Henry, both became squires to the prince.[14] Joan became friendly with Robert while she was married to Thomas Holand, and by the time she married the prince she had become very fond of him, describing him as her 'beloved kinsman' when she petitioned the Pope requesting a canonry at York for him in 1363.[15] Although this was an unexceptional promotion for an able young clergyman, it was an important step in his career. In view of the evident affection Joan had for him, and the close family ties, with his brothers being part of the prince's retinue, it is possible that Robert joined her household staff and accompanied her to Aquitaine, although there is no evidence to substantiate this. Despite the warmth of the attachment Joan had for Robert, her request did not display any special favouritism as she made similar applications for several other young men, including John Carleton and John Stene, formerly part of the prince's retinue, who became clerks to Joan immediately after her marriage and for whom she also requested canonries in September 1363.[16]

It was expected that Joan and Edward would take a sizeable entourage with them. Joan's daughters, Maud and Joan, would accompany them and they would need supervision and tutoring. Joan probably entrusted their care to her close friend Eleanor de la Warr, the wife of one of the prince's bannerets, Roger de la Warr, who was related to Joan by marriage. Roger was Thomas Holand's nephew, the son of his sister Margaret and John de la Warr. The de la Warr family seat was at Swineshead in Lincolnshire, and Roger's first wife Elizabeth came from a Lincolnshire family.[17] Roger was also distantly related to Joan through her mother's family; Joan's great aunt, Isabella Wake, married Thomas Grelley, and Thomas' sister Joan Grelley married Roger's grandfather, John de la Warr.[18] Roger had been knighted at La Hogue with the prince in 1346, fighting subsequently in the Crécy and Calais campaigns with Thomas, with his brother John, who was also one of Thomas' retinue, accompanying him to Brittany in 1354 and 1358.[19] Roger had also fought with the prince in the Poitiers campaign and in 1357 had become a banneret, receiving gifts from the prince of a helm for the jousts and a ventail in 1359.[20] Significantly, Roger had been one of the witnesses to the prince's wedding to Joan, indicating an attachment between the two men.[21] Eleanor was Roger's second wife, and as Blanche Wake's niece (her grandfather was Henry of Lancaster) the family connection was further strengthened.[22] It is not clear when she and Joan became friends but it seems likely that in 1349 when Joan officially became Lady Holand the close ties between their husbands drew them together. Roger was one of the few people who knew the full details of Joan's marital history, as he had also been a witness at William Montague's marriage to Elizabeth in 1349, after William's marriage to Joan was declared null and void.[23] Roger and Eleanor's second son was named Thomas, probably after Thomas Holand, while their daughter was named Joan; in all probability Thomas and Joan were their godparents. The entire de la Warr family sailed with Joan and the prince, with Roger and his eldest son John forming part of the prince's retinue, Thomas as Joan's clerk, and Eleanor and Joan among Joan's household. Eleanor endured the months of waiting in Cornwall with Joan, and in November 1362 the prince, probably at his wife's behest, ordered a tun of wine to be delivered to her as a gift.[24] In September 1363 Joan requested a dispensation for Thomas de la Warr to be ordained priest at the age of twenty, giving him a start in what became a successful ecclesiastical career.[25]

Another possible member of Joan's household was her sister-in-law Elizabeth, whose new husband Eustace d'Aubrichecourt had joined the prince's entourage. A hint of the continuing closeness between the sisters-in-law is indicated by Elizabeth's agreement to release her dower manor of Woking to Joan in June 1363 for £400.[26] The manor was a special place for them both, as it had been Joan's brother John's favourite residence, and where he had died. In 1364, Joan granted the manor to her son and heir Thomas on the occasion of his marriage to Alice. Joan would also be joined by the wives of many of her husband's retinue, some of whom she would become closer to than others. One new relationship forged in the summer and autumn of 1362 was with Elizabeth Luttrell, whose husband Andrew served the prince. Elizabeth was the daughter of the Earl of Devon, and the negotiations between Elizabeth's father and the prince for the marriage of Elizabeth's nephew, Hugh, to Joan's daughter Maud, fostered a growing relationship between Elizabeth and Joan. By September 1363 their friendship was of sufficient intimacy for Joan to request the Pope to permit Andrew and Elizabeth to have a portable altar and give them licence to choose their own confessors while making the same request for herself.[27] The family connection was strengthened when Andrew's relative, another Sir Andrew Luttrell, married Hawisia Despenser in the chapel of Blanche Wake's castle at Bourne in the autumn of 1363.[28]

Given the importance and potential power Joan now had as Princess of Wales, it is surprising that there is so little evidence of her exercising significant patronage between the time of her wedding and her return from Aquitaine in 1371. Although individual accounts for her household have not survived, had Joan shown any substantial and particular generosity towards an individual or a religious order or educational establishment this would be apparent from the official records, and would have been publicly recognised. It is evident that Joan took care to be restrained in her affairs, and chose not to copy her husband's lavish generosity. This did not mean that Joan had no interest in patronage. As is evident from the small ways in which she sought favours for her staff and gave gifts to her friends and rewards to her retainers, she had a close interest in their welfare, but favoured a modest approach towards promoting the individual and causes she held most dear. From the start of her marriage to the prince, it is apparent that Joan made the choice to be discreet in how she used her influence. Her discretion would be a quality which would stand her in good stead in the years to come.

By the end of May 1363 the prince and Joan, with her four children, were at last ready to depart for Aquitaine, and on 9 June they boarded their ship, the *Saint May Cog*, at Plymouth and set sail, landing at Lormont outside Bordeaux on 29 June.[29] They took a sizeable retinue with them, even the children having individual servants; Thomas Holand had his squire, John Pounfreit, and in August young John Holand had been given his own personal attendant in the prince's yeoman, John Hay (probably a son of his parents' old friend Sir Henry Hay).[30] Also accompanying them were sixty knights, including three bannerets (Roger de la Warr being one of these), among a retinue of 250 men-at-arms, with 320 archers.[31] Several wives of these knights formed part of Joan's household, including her friend Eleanor de la Warr, Lady Marion Louches, Joanna Peverel, and Anne Latimer, wife of Roger de la Warr's nephew Thomas Latimer. The entourage included most of the prince's closest companions, with senior members of the nobility such as Thomas Beauchamp, Earl of Warwick, and John, Lord Cobham, and trusted retainers like John Carleton.

This expedition was very different from the one Joan's father, Edmund, had undertaken to Gascony nearly forty years before. Edmund had served in Gascony as Edward II's royal lieutenant, based in Bordeaux, and was there for nearly twelve months before Joan was born, from the late summer of 1324 to the autumn of 1325. Joan knew that her father had not been happy in Bordeaux. Edmund had taken up residence in the city following his humiliating defeat in the Agenais by French forces which had invaded and overrun the duchy within five weeks of his appointment, and during his remaining service his authority had been consistently undermined by his half-brother's favourite, Hugh Despenser, who had secretly given orders to Edmund's deputies. These experiences had irretrievably soured Edmund's relationship with Edward II, and shortly after Edmund left Gascony he had joined Queen Isabella in Paris and returned to England with her invasion force in September 1326. Under Edward II English authority in Gascony had been fragile, and the duchy weak and divided. Much had changed since then. By 1360 Edward III's reputation was at its highest throughout Europe, and he was described by the chronicler le Bel as a 'second King Arthur', and by the *Chronique des quatre premiers Valois* as the 'wisest and shrewdest warrior in the world'.[32] The French king was a prisoner in England with his ransom set at the impossibly high level of 3 million écus (the French écu was worth 40*d*), equivalent to nearly ten times the annual revenues of the English Crown.[33] Under the Treaty of Brétigny Edward III had acquired nearly a third of the landmass of France, mainly in the south-west, of which the duchy of Gascony comprised only a part.[34] The borders of the new territory stretched from Poitiers in the north to Bayonne on the Atlantic coast and inland to Auch, Montauban, Rodez and Limoges.

Nevertheless, the prince knew that he had a difficult job ahead of him. The new state of Aquitaine inevitably evoked memories of the great Angevin empire. Two hundred years earlier, when Eleanor of Aquitaine had married Henry of Anjou, Aquitaine had been one of the wealthiest parts of Europe, and a rich cultural centre. Eleanor's Aquitaine was fabled for its society of troubadours and chivalric knights, brimming with literary and artistic talent at the court she inherited from her father at Poitiers. The new state of Aquitaine not only brought with it the Angevin association but also represented the English triumph in France, and Edward III and his closest advisers wanted the significance of this supremacy to be generally recognised. Hopes for the new Aquitaine were riding high in England. But unlike Eleanor's Aquitaine, the new Aquitaine was not a rich or prosperous land. It had been devastated by the war, and the prince was in part responsible for this. After the Treaty of Brétigny was signed, John II had sent a letter to all the regions of France which were to be handed over to English rule explaining why he had agreed to surrender them to Edward III. After his crushing defeat at Poitiers, held prisoner in England, John II had little choice other than to accept whatever terms he could agree with Edward III, but it is hard not to believe that he was genuine when he told his subjects that he wanted to put an end to the 'wars and the evils ... which have led to so much evil for the people'.[35] As the French king noted, 'many mortal battles have been fought, people slaughtered, churches pillaged, bodies destroyed and souls lost, maids and virgins deflowered, respectable wives and widows dishonoured, towns, manors and buildings burnt, and robberies, oppressions, and ambushes on the roads and highways committed. Justice has failed because of them, the Christian faith has chilled and commerce has perished, and so many other evils and horrible deeds have followed from these wars that cannot be said, numbered or written.'[36] The people living in the territories now newly incorporated into Aquitaine were all too bitterly aware of the truth of the king's words. The south-western areas of France had suffered catastrophically in two major campaigns, the first during Henry of Lancaster's six-month *chevauchée* in 1345, when the duke, landing at Bordeaux, had attacked Bergerac, then Périgueux, and after the defeat of the French army at Auberoche in October had marched south to conclude his campaign at La Réole in Gascony in March 1346, and more recently, from the prince's own *chevauchée* in 1355. As the *Anonimalle Chronicle* recorded, the prince had swept from Bordeaux to Bergerac devastating the counties of Périgueux, Limousin, the country of Gascony, the county of La Marche and all the county of the duchy of Berry, burning and destroying, and Sir John Wingfield, on the prince's staff, writing to the Bishop of Winchester describing the campaign, commented that 'it seems certain that since the war against the French king began, there has never been such destruction in a region as in this raid. For the countryside and towns which have been destroyed in this raid produced more revenue for the King of France in aid of his wars than half his kingdom.'[37] Now the people of these lands were to be ruled by the man who had so recently been responsible for the destruction of their countryside, their villages and towns. However glad they may have been to be told that peace had come at last, it seems unlikely that they would welcome the prince as their new ruler with open arms.

Not all of the region had suffered the horrific war damage caused by the *chevauchées*, but even those parts which had escaped were still feeling the effects of the bubonic plague epidemic (there had been another outbreak in 1362), and throughout the region there were significant economic difficulties. The main local trade in Gascony was wine, and the region was also a major market for English exports such as grain and wool, all badly affected by the war, with a growing armaments industry centred on Bordeaux. The town of Bordeaux also handled cloth, leather, tin and fish, all of which were sent to England. The peace, ironically, would ill suit the iron foundries and armourers. Economic problems were compounded by the breakdown in law and order, caused initially by the weakening of authority due to the war and exacerbated by the activities of the free companies of soldiers which terrorised many local populations after the withdrawal of the English army from France in May 1360. The campaigns waged by these brigand armies in many parts were almost as destructive as those conducted by Edward III and the prince, extracting money and goods while killing those who resisted.

As an artificial political creation the new Aquitaine had no obvious geographical or economic boundaries and lacked any element of cohesion, without political or cultural identity. There was no common government nor legal, financial or administrative system to bring unity. Edward III and his advisers were well aware of this but anticipated that the structure of the government of Gascony could be extended and adapted by the prince to enable him to weld his new domain together and impose an identity on it which would create a lasting union.[38] This was extremely optimistic. Gascony itself was fiercely independent and had been a thorn in the side for successive English kings, but at least the population historically owed allegiance to the English king. Adding to it new territories which had no such loyalties and would regard the prince's governance as that of an occupying power did not auger well for a stable future government. The prince would need the cooperation and active support of the local nobility, and this was a significant problem. In Gascony some of the nobility, such as the Albret family, had used the conflicting claims of the English and French kings to sovereignty of the area for their own vested interests, playing one off against another, and the prince's father, grandfather (Edward II) and great grandfather

(Edward I) had all struggled to keep the loyalty of the Gascon nobility. The nobility in the newly acquired territories had even less reason to feel dutiful towards the English crown; some, like the Count of Armagnac, had fought against the prince in 1355 and 1356 (Armagnac had been appointed lieutenant in Languedoc by John II in 1352), and many were used to their independence and had benefited from the weakness of the French king, enabling them to play the field and give their support where it most suited them. Although many of them had chosen to fight on the English side, they were neither committed nor steadfast in their loyalty. Their own self interest would always come first, and they deeply resented having a sovereign head of state foisted upon them, particularly one who would live among them. The counts of Perigord and Armagnac were not alone in their outspoken view that the king of France had no right to give their lands to England.[39] Edward III and the prince might also have remembered that even in the Angevin empire the local nobility had resented their overlord's authority. After Richard had been created Duke of Aquitaine in 1172 at the age of fifteen, formally invested by his father, Henry II, Richard had subsequently spent many years quelling unrest among his nobles and first displayed his considerable military abilities in imposing his authority in his own domain. Getting the local nobility on side would be key to the success of the prince's administration. To achieve this peaceably would require hosting and entertaining them, persuading them of the benefits of the new administration and the closer ties to the English crown, and in this, Joan, as his wife, would have an important role.

Although the task facing Joan and the prince in Aquitaine was daunting, they were well prepared. The prince had acted as Edward III's lieutenant in Gascony, and had been his father's deputy in England many times, albeit on his own home ground with strong support from his father's council and Parliament. In Aquitaine the prince would have far greater authority than any previous royal lieutenant, and he was secure in the knowledge he had his father's complete support. As a soldier he knew his own abilities and had confidence in the partnership he had forged with his men. Much of the groundwork had been accomplished by members of his staff prior to his arrival. The treaty terms included a timescale for the transition of all the ceded territories, and this process started in October 1360 as soon as the treaty had been signed. The first town to be transferred was La Rochelle. In July 1361, a year before the prince's investiture as Prince of Aquitaine, his trusted lieutenant Sir John Chandos had been sent to handle the annexation of the new territories. Although Chandos was about ten years older than the prince and had started his military career in Edward III's service, he had become a close personal friend. He fought with the prince at Crécy, and was one of his leading commanders in the 1355 campaign. As a knight and soldier he was widely respected (two chroniclers, Knighton and Walsingham, described him as one of the most famous knights of the age) and his reputation and tenacity were useful tools in securing the acquisition of the many castles and strongholds in the hands of individual commanders who were not surprisingly reluctant to give up their positions of power.[40] A mixture of local nobility and English captains, most owed nominal loyalty to the English crown, but they had become more interested in securing their own power in the area, exploiting and terrorising the surrounding countryside. Accompanying Chandos were several other able members of the prince's staff, including Sir Richard Stafford, Sir William Farley, Sir Nigel Loring, Sir Stephen Cosington, Thomas and William Felton and Adam Hoghton.[41] Their job was to take over the existing Gascon administrative network in preparation for the prince's arrival, and extend this throughout Aquitaine. In fact, the degree of cooperation which they received from the chief citizens in most areas of the new territories was considerable. There appears to have been general acceptance initially of the new change of allegiance and, other than a natural concern to ensure confirmation of privileges conferred by the French kings, the local nobility cooperated. This was partly due to self interest, as the new administration restored law and order and brought protection with it; by February 1362, when the transfer of the ceded territories had been completed, the influence of the free companies in those areas had virtually ceased.[42]

When the prince and Joan arrived at Bordeaux with their entourage on 29 June 1363 they were met by Sir John Chandos, and housed at the archbishop's palace. This was a welcome greeting for Joan, for Chandos, having been one of Thomas Holand's valued companions and awarded a £20 annuity from Joan's Chesterfield estate, was an old friend.[43] The prince and his father had given considerable thought to the way in which the prince would present himself to his new subjects. It is significant that despite the Angevin link, Edward III chose not to emulate Henry II in the ceremony of investiture for his son. Whereas in 1172 Henry II had held a formal enthronement for Richard at Poitiers, linking Richard directly to his forebears as dukes of Aquitaine, Edward III created his eldest son Prince of Aquitaine in Westminster, and a year was to pass before the prince arrived in the principality. The message for the populace was intentionally and unambiguously blunt. The Prince of Aquitaine might step in the footsteps of the dukes, but the title and the principality were both English creations, owing their existence to the king of England's triumphs in France. There was no pretence that the local populace had consented to the change. The first order of business therefore was for the prince to take homage from his new subjects, to reinforce the message that they recognised his authority and that they owed their allegiance to him. Within ten days of his arrival, on 9 July, the prince began to receive his Gascon vassals.[44] The first lord to pay homage was Arnaud Amanieu, Lord of Albret, and in a series of ceremonies held in the cathedral of St

Right: 1. Joan's grandfather, Edward I. A formidable king, he took great care to plan a generous financial provision for his youngest son, Joan's father Edmund of Woodstock, but died before he could complete the endowment.

Below: 2. Edward II was Joan's half-uncle. He was deposed by his wife, Queen Isabella, and her lover, Roger Mortimer, in 1327. Three years later Joan's father, Edmund, was tricked into believing Edward II was still alive, and executed for planning to rescue him from imprisonment in Corfe Castle.

3. Arundel Castle, Sussex. Joan lived here with her parents for the first eighteen months of her life and she was probably born here. The stone castle was originally built by one of William the Conqueror's relatives, Roger de Montgomery, in the eleventh century. It became the principal seat of the earls of Arundel. The second earl, Edmund Fitzalan, was executed by Roger Mortimer in 1326, and the castle was granted to Joan's father, Edmund, in 1327.

4. Arundel Castle, Sussex. This entrance was built in 1295 by Richard Fitzalan, 1st Earl of Arundel. Edmund, Earl of Kent (Joan's father), would have left the castle through this entrance on his last fateful journey to the parliament at Winchester in March 1330.

5. Queen Philippa took Joan and her brothers, Edmund and John, into her household six months after their father's execution in 1330. This effigy was commissioned by Philippa before her death.

6. This shows the king as he would have been in later life. Edward III was a young man of eighteen when Joan and her brothers came to live in his wife's household.

7. The Garter Book was commissioned by William Bruges, accredited as being the first Garter King of Arms, and was probably made between 1430 and 1440. The book has twenty-seven full-page miniatures showing the twenty-six Garter knights in their Garter stalls at St George's chapel, Windsor, each holding a panel with heraldic shields of their successors.

8. Otto Holand was Thomas Holand's younger brother and trusted lieutenant. John Chandos was one of Prince Edward's closest friends and a renowned and formidable fighter and commander. Both were founder members of the Order of the Garter.

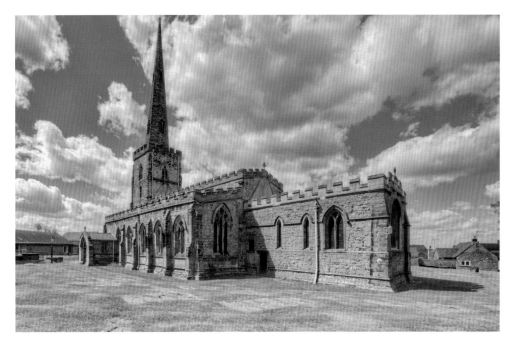

Above: 9. The church of St Edward, King and Martyr, Castle Donington, Leicestershire. Originally built in the thirteenth century, and extended in the fourteenth. Joan would have been familiar with this parish church.

Left: 10. The Bible Historiale of John the Good, King of France. This Bible was owned by King John II of France, captured at the Battle of Poitiers in 1356, and the book was subsequently purchased by William Montague, 2nd Earl of Salisbury, for his wife Elizabeth, for 100 marks.

Bottom: 11. The founding chapel of the Order of the Garter, Windsor Castle's St George's chapel contains a stall for each of the twenty-six knights of the Garter, and an annual service is held in the chapel on St George's day, 23 April. Joan and Prince Edward were married in the chapel in October 1361.

Top: 12. Windsor Castle, Berkshire. One of the many royal palaces Joan lived in as a child and where she would have stayed the night after her wedding to Prince Edward.

Above left: 13. Berkhamsted Castle, Hertfordshire. Originally a Norman castle, in 1337 Edward III granted Berkhamsted to Prince Edward as part of the duchy of Cornwall. It was the prince's favourite castle, and became Joan's first home with the prince after their wedding in October 1361. Prince Edward and Joan hosted Christmas here for Edward III and Queen Philippa in 1361.

Above right: 14. A reconstruction drawing of Berkhamsted Castle as it would have appeared in the twelfth century. Prince Edward paid for major renovation work to the castle before his marriage to Joan, and continued improvements to it afterwards.

Right: 15. The Bohun Psalter was made for either the 6th or 7th Earl of Hereford, both named Humphrey Bohun (d. 1361 and d. 1373, respectively). In 1362 Prince Edward purchased three psalters from the executors of the sixth earl, Humphrey de Bohun, and gave them to Joan and her two daughters, Maud and Joan Holand. The gifted psalters are likely to have been of similar quality to this psalter.

Below: 16. Detail of a historiated initial 'E'(dwardus) of Edward III, enthroned, giving a charter to the kneeling Prince Edward, at the beginning of a collection of documents relating to the principality of Aquitaine.

Top left: 17. Prince Edward's tomb in Canterbury Cathedral, Kent, to which Joan made annual pilgrimages after his death. The prince left careful instructions for its design. The tomb chest is decorated with six shields of peace and six of war, and above it, facing downwards towards his effigy, is a painting of the Holy Trinity, which the prince gave the cathedral in his lifetime. On the opposite side of the choir lies Henry IV, the prince's nephew and the man who deposed the prince's son Richard II.

Top right: 18. Hanging above the tomb are replicas of the prince's helmet, surcoat, shield, gauntlets and the scabbard of his sword. The originals are displayed in a glass cabinet.

Above: 19. The copper gilt effigy shows the Prince Edward as the consummate warrior. In the nineteenth century it was carefully blackened (presumably taking his posthumous appellation of the 'Black Prince' literally), and remained under layers of paint until it was uncovered in the early 1930s.

Top left: 20. Carved stone ceiling boss, reputedly representing Joan, in the chantry chapel beside the chapel of Our Lady Undercroft in Canterbury Cathedral. Prince Edward paid for the Chapel of Our Lady Undercroft to be redesigned, in fulfilment of the papal dispensation granted to enable him to marry Joan, and he left instructions in his will to be interred in the chapel. However, when he died, it was decided that his tomb should be placed in a more prominent position on the south side of the Trinity chapel. The chantry chapel is decorated with ceiling bosses; this carved stone boss is the largest human face and clearly represents Joan. Her hair is in a netted fret, a popular fashion at the time. However, there is no evidence that the prince ordered this and it is not known who carved it.

Top right: 21. St Albans Abbey kept a book listing their benefactors; Joan was obviously considered one of their more important ones as her image is pictured in the book. The abbot (from 1349 to 1396), Thomas de la Mare, was on friendly terms with Prince Edward, who, with his parents, Edward III and Queen Philippa, were also benefactors.

Right: 22. A statue of Edward III near the west door, on the outside of Canterbury Cathedral. He stands beside a statue of the prince.

23. Richard was Joan's youngest child, and heir to Prince Edward. He became king when he was ten. This portrait was probably commissioned by Richard shortly after Joan died, and shows him as a child king.

Within the miniature:

ilenie

A pelec estoit uilanie.
J. rmage qui felounie.

Above: 24. Detail of a miniature of Vilenie (villainy, abuse, baseness) offering the Lover (l'Amans) a potion. The book was owned by Sir Richard Stury, a cultured and literary man. He was one of the prince's knights and a friend to Joan, and was appointed as a household knight to Richard II.

Right: 25. Joan arranged Richard's marriage to Anne of Bohemia. Richard was very happy with the marriage, and was heartbroken when Anne died in 1394. They had no children.

26, 27, 28. Wallingford Castle, Oxfordshire. This was Joan's favourite residence after Prince Edward died, and where she retired to from Richard II's court. Joan died here on 8 August 1385. The castle was demolished on the orders of Oliver Cromwell, and these ruins are all that is left.

29. Wallingford Bridge, Oxfordshire. This bridge over the River Thames is beside the castle grounds. Joan travelled to Westminster by barge down the river.

30. St Andrews church, Wickhambreaux, Kent. Wickhambreaux was the only manor in Kent owned by Joan. It is probable that she visited and stayed at the manor on her annual pilgrimage to Prince Edward's tomb every June after he died. The manor no longer exists. The parish church of St Andrews dates from the fourteenth century, and Joan would have known it.

31. Joan's seal, attached to an indenture from 20 April 1380 made between Joan, Princess of Wales, and Richard de Walkington and others of the town of Beverley. The deed was signed at Missenden. This is the only surviving seal of Joan's. It is circular and two inches in diameter. Around the border edge are the words, in Latin, 'Joan, Princess of [obscured but probably Aquitaine], Wales, Duchess of Cornwall and Countess of Cheshire and Kent'. The round, ornamental inside panel surrounds a shield with France and England quarterly, a label of three points for Prince Edward, and a bordure for Edmund, Earl of Kent (her father). The letters around the shield are I, E and P.

32. The Princess Joan Psalter, so called because at the front of the book is John Somer's Kalendarium (an astronomical calendar). Somer dedicated his original treatise to Joan in 1380, and it was believed for a long time that this copy was presented to Joan. However, this copy was made some years after her death.

Above: 33. Image of the Trinity in the Princess Joan Psalter. Prince Edward had an especial connection with the Trinity, and died on the feast of the Trinity. (British Library)

Right: 34. The exquisite workmanship of the Princess Joan Psalter indicates that it would have been made for a patron of considerable wealth.

35. Wilton Diptych, interior panel. On the left, Richard II is kneeling and behind him are John the Baptist, St Edward (holding a ring) and St Edmund (with the arrow of his martyrdom). On Richard's cloak is his personal emblem of the white hart, with a gold crown around its neck and pearls decorating its antlers. On the right, the Virgin and Child. Probably painted around 1396–97, when Richard would have been twenty-eight or twenty-nine, the diptych shows Richard as a fresh-faced young boy.

36. Wilton Diptych, exterior panel. On the left-hand panel, Richard II's personal heraldic emblems. On the right-hand panel (which would be uppermost when the diptych is closed) is the white hart, Richard's personal emblem, which he adopted from Joan.

Andrews in Bordeaux, a succession of the greater nobles swore allegiance to the prince. In early August the prince left the city and travelled first to Bergerac, then on to Périgueux, Angoulême, Cognac, Saintes, Saint Jean d'Angely, La Rochelle and Poitiers, reaching Agen in time for Christmas, returning to Poitiers in February 1364.[45] At each stage the prince received the homages of the local nobility, dignitaries and municipal officers, the mayors, jurats, consuls of each town and city. This was a triumphal progress, deliberately impressing on the local nobility that the prince had come to stay, and reinforcing the message of English dominion with the physical act of swearing loyalty to him. Nevertheless, the prince and his administration were also careful to ensure that, as far as possible, charters of privilege for individual towns were confirmed or granted, in some cases with promises to pay for necessary work. The scale of the exercise was immense; it has been calculated that between 9 July 1363 and 4 April 1364 when the list closed the prince received over a thousand individual homages.[46]

Some of the nobility would have known the prince from earlier times while for others it would be their first encounter with their new lord. The prince was on show and would have wanted to look his best and make a good impression on his new subjects, so it is likely that his clothes and equipment, his retinue and all his accoutrements were the finest; a grandiose display of wealth and majesty designed to awe and impress. In many ways this was a similar progress to that made by the prince when he returned from his victory at Poitiers and entered London with his royal captive, greeted at every point along his route by crowds of well-wishers and rejoicing, but there was a crucial difference. The celebratory progress was also an opportunity to impress on the populace that the prince, their wealthy and powerful new lord, was here to stay. Joan's presence is not recorded throughout this period but as his wife, and the leading lady of the new Aquitanian court, she was a vital accompaniment, and it must be assumed that she was at her husband's side throughout the whole progress. This is substantiated by the only known mention of Joan during this period, in Poitiers in November 1363, when the Marshal of Brittany, Jean de Beaumanoir, is alleged to have responded to an unfavourable comment about his wife's clothing with a retort that Joan and her ladies favoured unsuitable garments, wearing furred gowns with slit coats and great fringes.[47] Given the prince's express intention of impressing his new subjects, and his own preference for luxurious clothing, he would have required his wife to be fashionably garbed (the more revealing style of clothing, tight-fitting with low-cut necklines and hair dressed with pearls and precious stones, was an existing fashion trend when they left England), and as a princess Joan was entitled to use the trimmed miniver fur reserved for royalty to decoratively adorn her clothing.[48] Certainly as the prince's wife she was expected to set an example and would also have dressed to impress; it would not be remarkable if her style of dressing had initiated a fashion trend among the local nobility. De Beaumanoir's offhand remark has been cited as evidence that Joan had a love of luxury but there is little to substantiate this, and it may simply have been French pique, as around this time Charles V of France and the Pope, Urban V, had issued laws forbidding what were deemed to be short suits and dissolute clothing.[49]

By April 1364 the prince had completed the business of making himself known to his new subjects and taking their oaths of allegiance. The six-month progress must have been exhausting, and Joan may well have felt relief when it came to an end. Initially returning to Angoulême, they seem to have divided their time mainly between the castle at Angoulême and the archbishop's palace at Bordeaux. The prince gave more attention to his family and domestic affairs, and finalised the marriages of two of his stepchildren. Joan's eldest son, Thomas, now aged fourteen, was married to Alice, daughter of the Earl of Arundel, and Maud, probably aged around ten, was married to the Earl of Devon's grandson, Hugh Courtenay. On her marriage Maud was granted the manors of Sutton Courtenay in Berkshire and Waddesdon in Buckinghamshire.[50] The prince would have been careful to ensure that his stepchildren were accompanied back to England by trusted members of his retinue, and it is possible that Thomas and Maud travelled back to England together. This was not the first time Joan had parted from her children, but it may have been more of a wrench this time, as there was no reason to anticipate that Thomas or Maud would live in her household again. However, Joan had known this day would come, and she would have been sensible, and no doubt pleased, with the considerable advantage her children were gaining through their stepfather's influence.

Although the administration of Aquitaine was largely delegated to the prince's appointees, the prince was closely involved and spent much of his time attending to the business of government. In England the king and his son had anticipated that setting up the new system of government would be achieved by extending the model used in Gascony, where royally appointed officials worked in conjunction with a council made up of the leading Gascon families. There are few surviving sources which provide any detail of the prince's administration in Aquitaine, but it seems clear that their original plan was implemented, and the court, council and Treasury continued to function from Bordeaux. The three principal royal Gascon offices of state were the seneschal, with overall responsibility, the constable of Bordeaux and the chancellor, and these offices were continued for Aquitaine, with Thomas Felton, John Chandos and John Harewell being appointed to these positions shortly after the treaty was signed.[51] The Gascon administrative structure was similarly retained and formed the basis for the new government, with a body of permanent officers appointed with responsibility to report directly to the prince. In the first few years it is evident that the government was a success, probably because the prince's centralised, vigorous and efficient council, balanced the interests of the local magnates against the prince's authority, and the resulting peace and order benefited the local population and stimulated trade, encouraged by the prince. Prosperity slowly began to return to the region.

As the intention was for Aquitaine to be self-financing, the natural recourse to raise money was through internal taxation. This proved considerably more difficult than the prince and his advisers had envisaged. Taxation was never likely to be popular, but whereas in England it had become an accepted and well-established practice and operated on a national scale, in France taxation was traditionally managed at a local level and with varying degrees of acceptance and success. Yet the prince's personal income, even supplemented by Joan's, could hardly support the costs of his administration in Aquitaine, and other than an initial grant to get him started his father had determined that there were to be no subsidies from England.[52] In Aquitaine the principal tax was the hearth tax, and the prince increased its rate shortly after his arrival. Inevitably this was not popular but initially the announcement was greeted with acceptance. However, when it became increasingly obvious that the tax would also be collected (due to the efficiency of the prince's administration) there were grumblings of discontent with a reluctance to pay that in some areas became outright refusal. Two leading members of the Gascon nobility, the Lord of Armagnac and the Count of Foix, simply refused to pay, and never agreed to do so throughout the prince's time in Aquitaine. Nevertheless, there was a sufficiently adequate response through direct taxation to ensure that more than a third of the prince's costs were met from these means.[53] Another obvious method for raising revenue was to control the issue of currency, or debase the value of the coinage. In 1364 the prince issued his own gold coinage, both sides of the coin having an image of the prince, with his arms, similar in design to coins which had earlier been produced by his father in Gascony. In 1365 a larger coin was produced, copying the style of the French coinage, and a few years later a smaller gold coin called a hardi. However, as each individual coin had a high intrinsic value, it appears that the new coinage was intended to advertise the prince's power and wealth and so an exercise in propaganda rather than a means of making money. The prince and his advisers do not seem to have resorted to debasing the value of the coins in order to raise revenue.[54]

Unifying Aquitaine in terms of government and finance required the active cooperation of the disparate groups of local nobility who had no previous history of working together and whose interests did not necessarily coincide. It would hardly be surprising if there had been opposition to the imposition of an English regime, and deep resentment of the victors. The natural ingredient to weld the collected nobility of the principality together was the prince himself, with Joan at his side.

Prince Edward was widely admired throughout Europe for his military feats and his chivalry, and the universal esteem in which he was held provided a considerable basis for unity. Similarly his closest companions in arms, like Sir John Chandos, were regarded with respect, and many of the local nobility had fought with or against them. Their shared military experiences formed a natural bond between them. Once the homage taking had been finalised, the prince based his court mainly at Bordeaux or Angoulême. In establishing his court, the prince deliberately set out to ensure this was a major source of patronage and thus a major instrument in his government. As the court was entirely based on the reputation and personality of the prince himself it was inevitably dominated by his own entourage, although the English influence was not necessarily resented. Joan, as his wife, was expected to preside over the court and complement her husband. She would set an example to the other ladies at their court, including those of the local nobility, and she would be an alternative source of patronage and a means of access to her husband.

The prince emulated his father in his style, and there are several contemporary references to the magnificence of the Aquitanian court. Froissart noted the splendidness of the court and its ostentation, while, according to the prince's biographer,

> ever he had at his table more than fourscore knights and full four times as many squires. There were held jousts and feasts in Angoulême and Bordeaux; there abode all nobleness, all joy and jollity, largesse, gentleness and honour, and all his subjects and all his men loved him right dearly, for he dealt liberally with them. Those who dwelt about him esteemed and loved him greatly, for largesse sustained him and nobleness governed him, and discretion, temperance and uprightness, reason, justice and moderation: one might rightly say that such a prince would not be found, were the whole world to be searched throughout its whole extent.[55]

Notwithstanding the hyperbole, this account gives an indication of the prince's popularity. It was a demonstrably royal style, with the prince emphasising his status and position; according to the *Anonimalle Chronicle* the prince required nobles to be on their knees when addressing him.[56] The combination of chivalry, display, luxury and entertainment made the court vibrant and attractive. The contemporary accounts indicate that the court successfully fulfilled its purpose, drawing in the local nobility, who were flattered by being recognised, while enhancing the dignity of the prince. However, it also gave the court a reputation for extravagance, and such a deliberately ostentatious display of wealth and power, with all its trappings, was inevitably expensive to maintain; it has been suggested that including the wages of his personal military retinue the cost was in the region of £10,000 a year.[57]

It is notable that the contemporary chroniclers, including Froissart, who spent some months at the Aquitanian court in 1366, barely mention Joan in their reflections on the prince's time in the principality. As Princess of Aquitaine, Joan was the presiding female at the Aquitanian court, and as such might have been expected to make some individual impression, yet she is rarely cited. The chroniclers credit the prince's flamboyance and style with setting the tone of the court, and not his wife. Had Joan established herself independently as an arbiter of fashion, or attracted a large literary entourage, or been extravagant in her patronage, there would surely have been reports. There is little doubt that Joan was faithful in following her husband's lead yet circumspect in everything she did. While the prince's energies were directed into the matter of government and creating a magnificent court, Joan was at his side but careful to complement and support him while never drawing attention to herself. In this, she emulated her mother-in-law, Queen Philippa. While Joan was discreet in exercising her influence, she nevertheless displayed competence as an intercessor, an expected and important part of her role. In one incident Joan responded to an appeal for help from the Count of Armagnac, after the prince had refused to use his influence. Armagnac owed a ransom sum to the Count of Foix which he could not afford to pay. When the prince declined, Armagnac turned to Joan, who is said to have approached Foix, and persuaded him to reduce the ransom by 60,000 francs. The prince later lent Armagnac money and persuaded others to make up the rest of the debt to free Armagnac.[58] Another recorded incident was in February 1366, when the Pope requested that Joan urge her husband to mediate between the kings of Castile and Aragon, and assist the Bishop of Chichester to foster peace between them.[58]

Settling to their new life after the homage taking progress ceased had an immediate effect on Joan, and in the summer of 1364 she conceived their first child. The prince must have been delighted, and he would have done everything he could to ensure his wife's health and happiness during her pregnancy. Although Joan had already given birth to four healthy children she too would have taken extra care, and it is probable that while the prince continued to travel throughout his new domain (he is known to have been in Périgueux in July and La Réole in November) Joan remained in the castle at Angoulême, attended by her women and a suitably sized retinue. Early in March 1365 Joan gave birth to a son, whom they named Edward in honour of the prince's father.[60] There can be no doubt about the prince's joy, as the occasion was marked with jubilant celebration, including a splendid tournament with forty knights attended by forty squires jousting in Joan's honour, marking the occasion of her churching on 27 April.[61] According to one contemporary account, 154 lords and 706 knights attended the festivities, which lasted for ten days, and the prince bore the cost of stabling 18,000 horses, and Joan is recorded as having a personal entourage of twenty-four knights and twenty-four ladies.[62]

Edward III's influence on his son is notable, as the account bears a striking similarity to earlier churchings of Queen Philippa, and the king's own fondness for lavish displays. The good news was taken to Edward III by one of the prince's yeomen, Sir John Delves, who received a handsome annuity of £40 from the delighted king, while the mayor and aldermen of London received a letter from Joan herself at the end of March, advising them of the news.[63] The baby prince's baptism in the cathedral of St Peter in Angoulême by the Bishop of Limoges was a grand affair, attended by numerous lords, including Peter, King of Cyprus, who stayed for a month (and during his visit endeavoured to persuade the assembled knights to join him on crusade; he was only partially successful, as the only one to take up his offer was the Earl of Warwick).[64]

Aside from the birth of Prince Edward, 1365 was also notable for the marriage of the prince's sister, Isabella, and that of Joan's youngest daughter. Princess Isabella was close to both the prince and Joan, being the nearest in age to the prince of his siblings, while Joan had spent several years with the princess when she had lived at court as a child. Isabella was now thirty-three, and still unmarried, a favourite with her parents and a major presence at court. Her choice of husband was somewhat unexpected. She had not only fallen for a relatively humble knight some years her junior in age, but for a Frenchman whose presence in England was due to his being one of the hostages for the fulfilment of the Treaty of Brétigny. On 27 July Isabella married Enguerrand de Coucy at Windsor, with her parents in attendance.[65] There is no indication that the king and queen disapproved of Isabella's unconventional choice, and in fact they celebrated the event in style, with Edward III paying £100 for minstrels to play at the wedding, and Philippa spending £1,273 6s 8d on jewels for the occasion.[66] Although the prince and Joan could not attend the wedding, their thoughts must have been with Isabella on such a momentous occasion. In November de Coucy returned to France, taking Isabella with him.[67] In April 1366 she gave birth to a daughter, Mary, and the following month, on 11 May, Edward III created de Coucy Earl of Bedford, and he was also shown specific favour by being made a knight of the Garter.[68] Isabella returned to England in 1367 and gave birth to her second daughter at Eltham, while in 1368 her husband resumed his military career in Italy.

Later in 1365 Joan's youngest daughter, Joan, married John Montfort, Duke of Brittany. This was a rather different match, re-establishing the close family tie between the dukedom and the English Crown, with Joan Holand stepping into Princess Mary's shoes as the new duchess. John Montfort had been living in the royal household and had travelled to Aquitaine with the prince in February 1363, as his claim to succeed his father as Duke of Brittany was still a matter of dispute with his rival claimant, Charles of Blois. After a truce between them signed at Poitiers in November 1363, in February 1364 Charles and John made submissions to the prince, in his capacity as Prince of Aquitaine, to resolve their dispute.[69] It was an awkward political scenario for the prince, as his father had supported Montfort all along while John remained a guest in the prince's household at the time. Perhaps wisely, the prince made no decision, but when John returned to Brittany to fight for his inheritance he was accompanied by Sir John Chandos. In September 1364 the matter was unequivocally resolved by the decisive military victory won at Auray by Montfort and Chandos, in which Charles of Blois was killed. John Montfort's marriage to the prince's stepdaughter a few months later cemented the already strong relationship between them. Although Montfort was now twenty-four, Joan Holand was no more than eight or nine years old and the couple would not be expected to live together as man and wife at this stage.[70] The new Duchess of Brittany remained under her mother's guidance for the time being. Joan had the satisfaction of her daughter making a prestigious marriage to a young man she knew well, while keeping her at her side. Maud and her husband Hugh were also part of her household by 1366, when the Pope granted her request for portable altars for Joan, Duchess of Brittany, and Sir Hugh and Lady Maud Courtenay.[71]

In the late spring of 1366 Joan conceived her second child by the prince. This was a naturally welcome and happy event and by now, after nearly three years in Aquitaine, everything seemed to be going well for them. The prince's administration in Aquitaine appeared to be well established, with his vibrant and thriving court at its hub. Joan's life in Aquitaine revolved around the prince and his concerns, and there must have been constant demands on her as his wife: entertaining the local nobility, managing their own entourage, as well as the more mundane administration of their household. Although Joan was a caring and fond mother, there is no evidence to suggest that she used her position to promote her children's interests. The marriages of Thomas, Maud and Joan were all at the prince's initiative, but none of them were granted land or income beyond that achieved by their marriages. The prince kept a watchful eye on his godson in England, and in October 1364 he appointed the fourteen-year-old Thomas escheator for the lordship of Denbigh, replacing one of his own men.[72] Although the prince took his responsibilities towards his stepchildren seriously this is the only evidence of special favour being shown to Thomas.

Joan now had little time for her Holand children, and it is likely it was around this time that Maud and Joan returned to England, with the appointment of John Delves and his wife Isabel as guardians to the young Duchess of Brittany in November 1367.[73] John Holand, now nearly fourteen, was close by, in his stepfather's retinue. Although there is very little evidence of Joan's activities at this time, she would have shared in some of the prince's leisure pursuits, such as music (the prince's fondness for music is evident from the expenditure on instruments and musicians noted in his household accounts[74]), but with her successive pregnancies it seems unlikely that she spent much time in more strenuous pastimes such as hunting.

Joan maintained a close personal interest in her English estates, even though these were being supervised by the prince's council on her behalf. Her close emotional attachment to Castle Donington is apparent in the order issued December 1363, just months after her arrival in Aquitaine, for her steward John Fouchier to investigate a report that the warden of the hospital was failing in his obligation to provide dwellings for a chaplain and six poor people at his own cost, and to communicate his findings to the council in London as soon as possible.[75] Similarly she intervened to assist Randolf Saleby, her former steward and attorney, who had worked faithfully for her for several years and whom she and Thomas Holand had rewarded with a lifetime interest in a shop and land at the nominal rent of a single rose, given every year. He retired from his position in March 1362, just a few months after Joan's marriage to the prince. By 1365 an annual rental of 20s was being demanded from him and he was described as being 60s (i.e. three years) in arrears. Joan became aware of his plight, and in November 1365 the bailiff at Greetham manor in Lincolnshire was ordered by the prince's council to suspend demands for the arrears until further order.[76] John and Christina Morel were evidently regarded highly by Joan as she used her personal seal to arrange for them to receive an annuity of 10 marks in May 1364 and was at pains to ensure they received the money, with subsequent orders issued in July and November. Similarly she remembered with affection the services of William, son of Reynold of Wallingford with a 5 mark annuity.[77] Nor did she forget her first husband, as in October 1364 she ensured that her reeve at Castle Donington was reimbursed for the 5 marks he paid the chaplain singing for Thomas' soul in the castle chapel.[78] Joan evidently ensured she was kept fully informed of estate affairs in England, and even the difficulties that her aunt, Lady Blanche Wake, was having in getting the drawbridge at Deeping manor repaired came to Joan's attention, with her steward at Torpel manor being ordered by the prince's council to supply Blanche with three suitable oaks for the purpose.[79] A more unusual intervention was a pardon granted at Joan's request in November 1366 for John Chamberlyn, presumably one of her retainers, who was accused of killing Richard Alcombury.[80]

Joan showed a considerable interest in several of the young clerks in her service. William Harpele was with her before her marriage to the prince, and his two brothers benefited from Joan's affection for William. In 1365 Laurence Harpele became her clerk and received a canonry and prebend (income) through her offices, while John Harpele had become squire to the prince by 1367.[81] Four applications by Joan to the Pope on behalf of a young man called William Croule have survived, starting in September 1363 with her request for him to be ordained priest while he was twenty. By 1365 he had become a constant member of her household and just a month after Prince Edward's birth, in May 1365, she asked for a benefice valued at 30 marks on his behalf, later that year asking for it to be increased by 15 marks. In 1366 she obtained the church of Paston in Northamptonshire for him (he would receive the benefice from Peterborough Abbey).[82] In 1365 and 1366 she asked for canonries, several with prebends, for more of her clerks: Thomas Yerd, Thomas Bullesden, John Ludham, Simon Lothebury and Hugh Bukunhull.[83] On 1 September 1365 an increased annuity of £10 was granted to Joan's yeoman of the wardrobe, Stephen, for his good service to her and the prince.[84] This was evidently a personal request by Joan as the annuity was to be funded from her Cottingham estate. While patronage was expected of a woman in Joan's position, and there is nothing unusual in these requests, it is notable that in each case she was giving these young men the crucial first step in their career, just as she had with Robert Braybrooke. These gestures show that she thought carefully about the effect of her intervention. The picture that emerges is one of interest and concern, with a thoughtful and considered approach to making rewards and requests on behalf of others. In this way Joan fulfilled her expected role, and provided quietly effective patronage while not drawing attention to herself, in contrast to her husband's more public and lavish generosity.

Without more detailed records it is only possible to make some reasonable suppositions about Joan's lifestyle at this time. Her time seems to have been divided between the archbishop's palace and abbey of St Andrews in Bordeaux and the castle at Angoulême, holding court in each, sitting alongside the prince on formal occasions. She may have accompanied the prince on some of his progresses through the duchy, but most of her time was spent in Bordeaux and Angoulême. Bordeaux was the administrative capital from where the prince's principal staff conducted their state business, a bustling city with an ever-changing population arriving and departing from its busy port. Although Bordeaux was the largest centre in the principality Joan appears to have spent more of her time in Angoulême, a smaller and less busy centre; certainly she did throughout the latter part of 1364, most of 1365 and the early part of 1366, often without the prince while he travelled to other centres. Presiding with the prince over their court occupied much of her time, as did playing hostess to the constant large number of guests while at the same time taking responsibility for supervising the upbringing of her children, as well as her household and staff. However, when the prince was away her lifestyle would have been considerably quieter. It was in every sense a royal existence, closely paralleling the lifestyle she had seen as a child and preparing her for the day when she would have to take Queen Philippa's place. The resemblance between Joan and her mother-in-law is in some ways striking, and it is easy to conclude that Joan consciously modelled her behaviour on Philippa's. It was also, presumably, a happy time for her, surrounded by her expanding family.

Then, in the autumn of 1366, Joan's Aquitanian idyll ended. After only six years of peace, the prince was once again going to war, although this time the campaign was in Spain, in response to a call for aid from an ally rather than as a result of a new English initiative in France. South of Aquitaine was a collection of smaller kingdoms including Navarre, Aragon, Granada and Castile, the last being the largest and richest as well as having a strong navy. When the war with France had started in 1340 both sides had made approaches to each of these kingdoms in the hope of securing their allegiance, with Castile the most potentially valuable. Castile initially was neutral, more concerned about the security of its own southern borders. In 1343 King Alfonso XI had called for assistance, receiving papal endorsement for his Crusade against the Moors. In the temporary lull in hostilities between France and England the Castilian king had attracted support from a large number of prestigious knights, including Edward III's close friend the Earl of Salisbury, his cousin Henry, then Earl of Derby, as well as knights seeking adventure and preferment, like Thomas Holand. In 1345 Alfonso had turned his back on his English friends and entered into an alliance with France, but by 1348 Edward III had persuaded the Castilian king to reconsider an alliance with England, and it was agreed that Alfonso's son Pedro would wed Princess Joan. When the princess died of the plague when embarking for Spain, Pedro had married the French princess Blanche of Bourbon instead, and succeeded his father two years later when Alfonso died in 1350. Notwithstanding the support given to France by the Castilians, most obviously when their navy fought Edward III in the sea battle at Winchelsea, diplomatic negotiations had continued. Just before the prince was granted Aquitaine in 1362, Pedro agreed to an Anglo-Castilian alliance, and the treaty was formally completed at St Paul's Cathedral on 22 June 1362.[85]

Pedro's change of heart was largely a matter of self-interest, as he had a rival for his throne in the shape of his illegitimate half-brother Henry of Trastámara. Henry had secured the backing of the kingdom of Aragon, and the support of the new King of France. John II, taken prisoner by the prince at Poitiers, had died in London in April 1364, and his death had signalled a change in French policy. Whereas John II had felt bound to honour the provisions of the Treaty of Brétigny, and to pay his ransom, his son and successor Charles V felt quite differently. Clever enough to appreciate that he needed to avoid open confrontation with Edward III, he made little effort to complete the outstanding ransom payments or treaty provisions, and it suited him well to encourage Pedro's rival. In the autumn of 1365 Henry of Trastámara invaded Castile with the aid of an army of mercenaries (including English captains, one being Eustace d'Aubrichecourt, who appears to have left the prince's service) raised under the auspices of the Aragonese king and led by the French generals Bernard du Guesclin and d'Audrehem, Marshal of France, with the tacit backing of France. Pedro immediately invoked the treaty, obliging

Edward III to provide troops at Pedro's expense to serve against his enemies.[86] He was disappointed in Edward III's initial response, which was simply to issue a proclamation forbidding English subjects to attack Castile, intended to deter English and Gascon subjects from joining Henry's mercenary army. In February the Pope wrote to Joan, asking her to urge the prince to mediate between the Castilian and Aragonese kings, and to help the Bishop of Chichester foster peace between them.[87] This is the first time the Pope is recorded asking for Joan's assistance, indicating that by this time her influence on her husband was universally recognised, as there is no evidence that he had already made a similar request directly to the prince, who had been one of the main promoters of Anglo-Castilian treaty. But whatever the Pope hoped Joan might be able to achieve, it was already too late. By March 1366 Henry of Trastámara's army had successfully taken most of Castile, and Henry had been crowned at Burgos while Pedro fled into exile. As Pedro's fortunes waned the debate in England changed in tone, as a pro-French King of Castile was not only undesirable for England but also posed a significant threat to Aquitaine. The prince was a party to the discussions, writing letters to his father and sending his chamberlain Sir Nigel Loring to England in the spring of 1366. Whatever their personal feelings about Pedro (and the prince had no great fondness for the Castilian king) he was at least an ally and so a more desirable proposition than Henry of Trastámara. They would have to assist Pedro, and it would be the prince who would play the lead role in providing that assistance. Edward III called Parliament at the beginning of May, and it was agreed that a small force would be sent, led by the prince's younger brother, John of Gaunt. In June orders were given for the requisitioning of shipping to use as transport. Meanwhile the prince began his own preparations, on 8 May ordering Sir Nigel Loring and his sixteen-year-old stepson Thomas Holand to bring a force of troops and sappers urgently to Gascony.[88]

At the end of July 1366 the prince travelled from Bordeaux and met with Pedro outside Bayonne at Capbreton, where agreement for assistance was reached in principle. The basic understanding was that the prince would raise and command an army which would invade Castile and restore Pedro to his throne. The inference from the tone of the contemporary commentators is that the English were not overly enthusiastic in responding to Pedro's request, and some historians have implied that it was the prince, anxious for another military campaign, who responded favourably to Pedro's pleas for help and persuaded his father to go along with it.[89] However, by the time the prince met Pedro at Capbreton the decision had already been taken in England that assistance should be given, and the prince was acting in response to instructions given by his father.[90] A formal agreement was signed at Libourne on 23 September covering the practical details of the operation. King Carlos of Navarre was a necessary party to the deal, as his kingdom controlled passes into Castile which the prince would need to use, and he was promised substantial payment and territorial concessions. The prince agreed to pay for his own army and to pay King Carlos on the understanding that Pedro would repay him when his kingdom was regained. Pedro also promised to give areas of coastal land in the north of Castile to the prince and to give him the titles of Lord of Biscay and Castro Urdiales.[91]

As soon as the agreement was signed the prince went to work to raise his army. It proved easy to obtain support, and he was joined enthusiastically by most of the Aquitanian nobility, and by men from the free companies in France, all of whom envisaged making their fortunes from the profits of a successful campaign. Nevertheless, the adventure promised in Spain was on a very different footing to the earlier campaigns in France. Despite the obligations imposed on England under the Anglo-Castilian treaty, and however much the language of the deal signed at Libourne dressed it up, the prince would in effect be acting as a mercenary, hired by one side in a civil war. Financial support from England was intended to be minimal, and the supporting force commanded by John of Gaunt modest in size. According to Froissart, some of the prince's closest advisors had strong reservations about the enterprise, although their scruples were a personal objection to Pedro himself on the grounds that he 'is now and has always been, a man of great pride, cruelty and wickedness', rather than the viability of the project.[92] From the outset the venture was risky in the extreme, with the financial basis being critically dependent not simply on the prince being successful but also on Castile being able to pay for the expenses of the major campaign. The only financial contribution Pedro was able to make at this stage was of his personal jewellery. Although the prince could rely on his own retinue, who formed the hub of the army, to cover most of their own expenses initially, huge sums of money were nonetheless needed to cover the initial expenses that would be incurred to pay for equipment and supplies, advance payments promised to the Gascon lords and the loan to Pedro to pay the King of Navarre. It has been calculated that the amount required, even before the army set out, was in the region of £100,000.[93] The sheer expense of the enterprise was daunting and the quantities of ready cash needed far exceeded anything the prince had to hand. The prince resorted to melting down his own household gold and silver and to minting additional coins, and Edward III was forced to contribute a substantial sum in gold, simply to finance the start of the campaign. There is some evidence that the prince tried to control the costs by restricting the size of the contingents provided by individual lords, but this was in itself a difficult issue. The Lord of Albret was probably not the only noble to refuse, angered by what he may have considered an unwarranted limit on his opportunity to make a fortune in plunder.[94] Nonetheless, Edward III and the prince confidently gambled that the prince would succeed, and that victory would ensure that the costs would be recovered, just as the diplomatic objective would be achieved.

The prince's army gathered during the autumn of 1366 in Dax, with the prince moving his court to Bordeaux to be nearer at hand, where he was joined by the Castilian king and his three daughters, Beatrice, Constance and Isabella. Joan and the prince stayed at the abbey of St Andrews. Pedro would naturally accompany the prince on campaign, while his daughters would remain, as surety for Pedro but treated as guests, in Joan's care.[95] John of Gaunt sailed from Plymouth early in December to join with Sir Robert Knolles in Brittany, having agreed to rendezvous with the prince at Dax where the main force was being assembled. Joan was in the last stage of her pregnancy by this time, and the prince was with her when their second son was born at the abbey of St Andrews in Bordeaux on 6 January 1367.[96] Among the women attending Joan at the birth was Lady Anne Stury, wife to Richard Stury, one of the prince's knights, and she brought the news of the birth to the prince.[97] The baby was christened Richard three days later in the cathedral by the archbishop, with their guests the kings of Majorca and Armenia acting as his godfathers. Froissart was among the many guests. Joan ensured that a wet nurse, Mundina Danos, was engaged for the baby along with a cradle rocker named Eliona de France; both were local women.[98]

According to Chandos Herald Joan was extremely unhappy at the prospect of her husband's departure:

[She] had right bitter grief at heart, and then she reproached the goddess of love who had brought her to such great majesty, for she had the most puissant prince in the world. Often she said, 'Alas what should I do, God, and love, if I were to lose the very flower of nobleness, the flower of loftiest grandeur, him who has no peer in the world in valour? Death! Thou wouldst be at hand. No have I neither heart nor blood nor vein, but every member fails me, when I call to mind his departure, for all the world says this, that never did any man adventure himself on so perilous an expedition. O very sweet and glorious Father, comfort me in your pity.' Then did the prince hearken to his gentle lady's words; he gave her right noble comfort, and said to her, 'Lady, let be your weeping, be not dismayed, for God has power to do all.' The noble prince gently comforts the lady, and then sweetly takes leave of her, saying lovingly, 'Lady, we shall meet again in such wise that we shall have joy, we and all our friends for my heart tells me so.' Very sweetly did they embrace and take farewell with kisses. Then might you see ladies weep and damsels lament, one bewailing her lover and another her husband. The princess sorrowed so much that being then big with child, she through grief delivered and brought forth a very fair son, the which was called Richard. Great rejoicings did all make, and the prince also was right glad at heart, and all say with one accord, Behold a right fair beginning.[99]

Chandos Herald wrote this in 1385, nearly twenty years later, and the account is clearly embroidered – there is, for example, no evidence that Richard was born prematurely or that Joan experienced any difficulty in the birth. In view of the outcome of the Spanish campaign it is hardly surprising that the herald depicted Joan being upset, as the prince's leaving her in January 1367 did indeed mark a real turning point in their relationship. At the time there was no real reason for Joan to feel apprehension. It was their first parting, but Joan had been a soldier's wife for many years and she would never have expected to keep the prince at her side throughout their married life.

The prince left Bordeaux shortly after Richard's christening and went south to Dax to join his army. He had succeeded in gathering an extremely large army, estimated variously at between 6,000 and 10,000 troops.[100] Most of his entourage were with him, many of whom had served with him in 1355 and had been with him at Poitiers – as well as the greater Aquitanian nobility led by Armagnac and d'Albret. This was a major enterprise, and the prince could anticipate being absent for many months. Naturally he needed to make provision for the governance of Aquitaine, and he gave his deputies his instructions for the action they were to take in his absence. It is perhaps surprising that the prince does not seem to have considered appointing his wife to be regent in his absence, but he had never envisaged Joan having a political role. Instead, Joan was to supervise what was left of their court. She watched as her husband left, taking with him her eldest son, Thomas Holand, supported by her friend Eleanor whose husband Roger de la Warr also accompanied him.[101] It is possible that she had been joined by her sister-in-law, Elizabeth, as Elizabeth's husband, Eustace d'Aubrichecourt, had just arrived to join the prince's entourage.[102] Prince Edward had not waited for his brother to arrive, and when John of Gaunt reached Aquitaine he first went to Bordeaux to pay his respects to his sister-in-law. Chandos Herald recalled that 'night and morning the noble Duke of Lancaster rode until he came right to Bordeaux, and found there the princess, mistress of all honour, who welcomed him sweetly and very graciously asked news of her country, how they fared in England. And the duke recounted all.'[103] It is unlikely that at this point the two knew each other very well. Joan was twelve years older than John, and it had been during Philippa's confinement giving birth to John that Joan had entered into her secret marriage to Thomas Holand. Being so much younger John would barely have seen his cousin as he was growing up, though he would no doubt have heard about her circumstances. John was the closest to the prince of his brothers, and had lived in the prince's household from March 1350 to May 1355 when he was an adolescent, but, by the time the prince married Joan, John was already married himself and occupied with his management of his own extensive affairs.[104] Joan had not attended John's wedding to Blanche of Lancaster, as she had been in France with Thomas

Holand.[105] When John arrived in Bordeaux it would have been natural for him to spend some time with Joan, bringing her up to date with news from England but also giving them a chance to get to know each other better. Seeing his new nephew Richard may have been poignant for John, as his wife was expecting their third child in a few months' time. The few days John spent with Joan in Bordeaux were the start of a strong and lasting friendship between them. While John stayed with Joan he would also have met his future wife Constance (of Castile) for the first time.

The prince was away from Joan for six months. The details of his campaign in Spain are described by Chandos Herald, who was almost certainly an eyewitness. Initially the prince had the task of getting his army assembled, and then across the Pyrenees into Navarre, relying on the cooperation of the King of Navarre, before continuing on into Castile. The army marched in three divisions, as was customary, with the prince commanding the centre, John of Gaunt and Sir John Chandos the vanguard, and the rearguard under the king of Majorca with most of the Gascon lords.[106] It was a bad winter and crossing the pass with such a large force was a difficult logistical undertaking, although one which the prince and his commanders were well equipped to deal with, with their considerable experience and strong working relationship. Fortunately the King of Navarre kept to his side of the bargain, enabling the army to traverse the pass without encountering resistance, and by February they had reached the capital of Navarre at Pamplona. As soon as news of the prince's invasion reached Henry of Trastámara he took counsel from his advisers and wrote to the prince while assembling his forces, and in mid-March the two armies converged outside Vittoria. The prince, assuming battle to be imminent, knighted several of his retinue (Chandos Herald suggests around 200 were knighted that day), starting with King Pedro of Castile (who had never been knighted) and including his stepson, Thomas Holand, his stepson-in-law, Hugh Courtenay (Maud's husband), Hugh's brothers Philip and Peter, and Nicholas Bond (the squire who had carried the prince's letters to and from the Pope when the prince was arranging his marriage to Joan).[107] However, although the prince drew up his army for battle, the following day the Spanish forces under Trastámara did not appear, and he was forced to withdraw. Du Guesclin and the other French commanders had advised Henry of Trastámara that he was more likely to be successful if he engaged in guerrilla warfare and avoided an open conflict, and following this advice the Spanish forces kept their distance, engaging only in occasional skirmishes. Despite the prince's efforts his enemy continued to elude him and by the beginning of April his army was short of food and other supplies; adding to their misery, the weather was wet, windy and cold. Frustrated but undaunted, the prince wrote to Henry of Trastámara, suggesting that if Henry gave up the throne the prince would act as mediator between him and Pedro. Henry had his own problems, as the loyalty of his Castilian forces was becoming increasingly uncertain, making the prospect of a head-to-head confrontation more attractive to him, in spite of the obvious risk. On 3 April the two sides finally met in battle on the banks of the River Nájera. According to Chandos Herald, Henry was confident that he would win; 'I am not in the least frightened that I shall not have the better of this battle.'[108] His optimism proved misplaced. The prince won a resounding victory, with very little loss of life among his men, while about half of Henry's army died, with over 5,000 bodies counted by the heralds after the battle, and large numbers were taken prisoner, including the two French commanders, Du Guesclin and Audrehem.[109] Henry himself escaped.

It is difficult to know what news, if any, Joan had of her husband's progress during this time. Certainly she would have been anxious, and not just for the prince; accompanying him were her eldest son, Thomas, her son-in-law Hugh Courtenay and many others she held dear. Two days after the battle the prince wrote to Joan. It is the only surviving letter of his to her, and although it was clearly intended by the prince for publication, he wrote in intimate and affectionate terms, giving the clearest indication of the very great love and trust he reposed in his wife. The original letter, in French, found in the National Archives in 1920, reads in translation,

My dearest and truest sweetheart and beloved companion, as to news, you will want to know that we were encamped in the fields near Navarrete on the second of April, and there we had news that the Bastard of Spain and all his army were encamped two leagues from us on the river at Najera. The next day, very early in the morning, we moved off towards him, and sent out our scouts to discover the Bastard's situation, who reported to us that he had taken up his position and prepared his troops in a good place and was waiting for us. So we put ourselves into battle order, and did so well by the will and grace of God that the Bastard and all his men were defeated, thanks be to our Lord, and between five and six thousand of those who fought us were killed, and there were plenty of prisoners, whose names we do not know at present, but among others are Don Sancho, the Bastard's brother, the Count of Denia, Betrand du Guesclin, the marshal d'Audrehem, Don Juan Ramirez, Johand de Neville, Craundon, Lebègue de Villaines, Senor Carrillo, the Master of Santiago, the Master of Saint John and various castellans whose names we do not know, up to two thousand noble prisoners; and as for the Bastard himself, we do not know at present if he was taken, dead, or escaped. And after the said battle we lodged that evening in the Bastard's lodgings, in his own tents, and we were more comfortable there than we have been for four or five days, and we stayed there all the next day. On the Monday, that is, the day when this is being written, we moved off and took the road towards

Burgos; and so we shall complete our journey successfully with God's help. You will be glad to know, dearest companion, that we, our brother Lancaster and all the nobles of our army are well, thank God, except only Sir John Ferrers, who did much fighting.[110]

This is not just the letter of a victorious commander, expecting his wife to pass on his comments verbatim, but the letter of a man who loves his wife, reassuring her of his safety, and that of her son, while knowing that she will appreciate the campaign details he includes. Joan had been a soldier's wife most of her life and she would have understood her husband's achievement. She did indeed do as her husband had hoped, and the prince's letter reached England before 30 April 1367. Edward III was delighted when the news reached him, expressing his pleasure by rewarding the Windsor herald who brought the message an annuity of 20 marks.[111]

Meanwhile in Spain, despite the prince's huge success, the disadvantages of his position quickly became clear. Almost immediately he was in conflict with Pedro over the fate of the prisoners, to whom the prince accorded the customary chivalry and planned ransom, as the Castilian king felt that those who had supported his half-brother were traitors and deserved to be executed. The divergence in their views had a practical as well as philosophical basis. It was an established, if unwritten, rule of warfare that knights were captured rather than killed and then ransomed, an expected reward for their victorious captors, and it had been written into the treaty signed at Libourne that all prisoners would belong to their captors. The largest ransom was that set for Alfonso, Count of Denia, captured by two English squires and bought by Edward III from the prince for £28,800, while Du Guesclin's ransom was agreed at £19,200.[112] The prince had the authority and was able to overrule Pedro, but this did not auger well for their future relationship. But in addition, the prince's job was now accomplished and he wanted to be paid for his services, while Pedro, barely back on the throne, needed to secure his position before he could contemplate raising the money he owed. Over the next few weeks the cost of the campaign, and the amount owed to the prince, was calculated. A figure of 272,000 gold florins was agreed (roughly £385,000, a sum equivalent to two-thirds of the ransom for John II), with formal deeds of obligation signed in a formal ceremony at Burgos on 2 May, stipulating that the first half of the money was to be paid within four months, after which time the prince and his army would leave Castile.[113] It soon became apparent that Pedro lacked the means to pay. It was simply too enormous a sum, dependent in the short term on prosperity and resources Castile lacked and in the long term on the newly restored Pedro's political longevity. Pedro left, promising to find the funds, and the prince and his army waited. As the days turned into months the summer heat brought with it a wave of epidemics of dysentery and enteric fever, and by June the prince himself was ill. By August it was obvious that there was no point in waiting any longer, and the prince ordered his army to leave Castile, returning to Aquitaine through Navarre and across the Pyrenees to Bayonne, disbanding his troops at the end of August.[114]

Joan had remained in Bordeaux while the prince was away, in the abbey of St Andrews, with Pedro's three daughters. It is not clear when they took their leave of Joan and returned to Spain to rejoin their father, and they may have waited until after the prince's return. In September the prince arrived back in Bordeaux, Chandos Herald recording that

> nobly was he received with crosses and processions, and all the monks came to meet him ... he dismounted at St Andrews. The princess came to meet him, bringing with her firstborn son Edward ... The gentle prince kissed his wife and son. They went to their lodging on foot, holding each other by the hand. There were such rejoicings at Bordeaux that everyone was glad of the return of the Prince and his companions, and everyone welcomed their friends. That night there was great joy throughout Aquitaine.[115]

The picture painted by the herald once again showed the very real affection between Joan and the prince, but the celebrations were muted in comparison to the tremendous rejoicing there had been in England after the Battle of Poitiers eleven years earlier. With his customary flourish and generosity the prince called all the Gascon nobility to his court and presented them with gifts, thanking them for their service.[116] He probably also arranged an escort for the three Spanish princesses to rejoin their father. Soon afterwards the prince and Joan left Bordeaux and returned to Angoulême. Joan's happiness at her husband's return was soon replaced by concern for his state of health, as the sickness from which he had suffered in Spain returned. The nature of the prince's malady has never been clearly identified, although it seems likely to have been dysentery, known as the bloody flux, or possibly recurring malaria.[117] Attacking him at irregular intervals, causing him great weakness, debilitation and fainting, at its worst the illness left him bedridden and unable to attend business or make decisions, while in between he would seem reasonably fit, but he never regained the strength and health he had earlier enjoyed. For a man who had enjoyed excellent health, and who had been on so many rigorous campaigns where he had spent all day in the saddle, these sudden, completely debilitating attacks must have been frustrating and humiliating.

The prince's problems then began in earnest. With Pedro unable to pay him, the prince's own finances were soon in crisis. He owed huge amounts of money. Every member of his army, from foot soldier and archer to knight, from his own retinue to the local nobility who had fought with him, looked to him for payment of their wages. He had used any spare money of his own in raising the army and starting the campaign, and now that it was over the ransoms from those who had been captured proved insufficient to cover the debts owing. The only payment he had received from Pedro was his personal jewellery, which when sold raised a sum of around £10,500.[118] Money had to be found from somewhere, and there was no suggestion that the English Treasury was about to come to the prince's aid. In January 1368 the prince summoned an assembly of the Aquitanian lords in Angoulême and proposed a further hearth tax of 10 sous a year for five years. Basking in the reflected glory of the prince's achievement at Nájera, the nobles voted for the tax, although they demanded in return a charter of rights.[119] Collection began peacefully enough; however, in itself the tax would be insufficient to cover all the outstanding commitments, and it was soon to provide a focus for discontent. The lack of surviving records makes it impossible to say whether the drain on resources forced the prince to use his own private income and that of his wife, though it seems likely that this is what happened, and it would certainly have been in character for Joan to have relinquished her own personal income to help her husband. But there was simply not enough. Crucially, in poor health and in financial difficulty, the prince could not sustain either his flamboyant and vibrant court or his earlier generosity towards the Gascon nobility which had set the tone of his rule prior to the Spanish campaign. His good relationship with the local nobility gradually disintegrated, and his reputation at home suffered. Even the usually supportive English chroniclers doubted the prince's behaviour, with the *Anonimalle Chronicle* recording that the prince was so proud he forced the local nobility to wait for hours on their knees before addressing him.[120] While this was patently absurd, the story indicated that there was a growing doubt about the prince and a suspicion that he was personally to blame for the situation. But Chandos Herald, writing with the benefit of hindsight (and no doubt through rose-tinted spectacles) had no doubt where the blame lay: 'As soon as it was known that the prince was ill and at death's door, his enemies decided to start the war again and began to negotiate with his enemies.'[121]

Charles V watched from Paris and took satisfaction in the realisation that the prince's position had been greatly weakened rather than strengthened by his Spanish war. The French king encouraged the growing dissatisfaction and discontent in Aquitaine, encouraging pro-French sentiments among local nobility. Gaston of Foix, who had never paid homage to the prince, and with whom the prince had had an uneasy relationship, became openly disloyal. The Gascon nobles, led by the d'Albrets, openly questioned the hearth tax. The prince owed the Count of Armagnac war wages of around £28,300 and had promised a pension of £1,000 a year to Arnaud Amanieu d'Albret, and now could not pay either.[122] By offering them both suitably large financial inducements, it proved easy for Charles V to persuade d'Albret and Armagnac to ally themselves with France and, on 4 May 1368, d'Albret married Charles V's sister-in-law, Marguerite. In June 1368, repudiating the allegiance he had sworn to the prince, the Count of Armagnac appealed to the French king against the imposition of the hearth tax; other Gascon nobles quickly followed suit. This was open rebellion. In direct contravention of the terms of the Treaty of Brétigny, Charles V ignored the prince's independent sovereignty and in November 1368 formally summoned the prince to appear before the parlement in Paris to answer for the tax.[123] The prince roused himself from his sickbed with a furious response, but he was unable to stem the growing mass of defections from his side. Personal tragedy compounded his woes; in May his brother Lionel died in Piedmont, and in September his sister-in-law Blanche of Lancaster died, just five months after giving birth to a son, Henry, at Bolingbroke Castle.[124] By December the disaffection among the Gascon nobility was so vociferous that the prince felt his honour was at stake, and he wrote to his father rejecting the complaints made about him. Worse was to follow. Any hope that Pedro might honour his agreement ended when Henry of Trastámara entered into an alliance with France and, aided once again by Du Guesclin (who had been ransomed by the prince), retook Castile from Pedro at the end of 1368, and killed Pedro himself in March 1369. The glowing Spanish victory had turned to ashes.

The catastrophic end to the Spanish campaign, and the incursions from Paris threatening the prince's sovereignty in Aquitaine, might not have mattered so much had it not been for the fact that the prince was too sick to respond effectively in a strong and decisive manner. Charles V sensed that his time had come, and in the spring of 1369 launched an invasion with the intention of taking part of Aquitaine. Nevertheless the French king was careful to rely principally on minor raids and to use diplomacy to attempt to win over the Gascon towns and cities, rather than risking a full confrontation with the prince which he knew he would probably lose. His policy was more successful than he could have anticipated, and there followed months of desultory fighting while successive towns and cities went over to the French. By March 1369 the French chancery listed over 900 cities, towns, fortresses and castles in Aquitaine allied to France.[125] The prince was summoned to appear before the parlement in Paris on 2 May to answer Charles V's summons about the hearth tax, and, as expected, did not attend. Diplomatic overtures from England failed, and at the beginning of June Edward III resumed the title of King of France. A resumption of war was inevitable. In England Edward III and his advisers determined on an expedition to northern France, and the advance force headed by John of Gaunt sailed to Calais at the end of July, with the king intending to join him later. This left the prince to defend Aquitaine on his own, although the king did send a small force to assist him led by the prince's younger brother, Edmund, Earl of Cambridge, and the Earl of

Pembroke. Never had the prince needed his abler captains more, but he lost several of his older companions in arms during the year; his friend Sir James Audley, whom he had left in charge of Aquitaine during the Nájera campaign, died that year, as did the earls of Suffolk and Warwick and Sir Bartholomew Burghersh.[126] To make matters worse, Queen Philippa died at Windsor Castle on 14 August after a short illness, and a mourning Edward III sent his army to northern France without him in September. When the news reached Aquitaine, it was a moment of great sadness for Joan and the prince, who had last seen Philippa six years earlier. For most of Joan's life the queen had acted as her foster mother, and more recently as her guide and mentor. The prince had always been very close to his mother, and her death was a real blow. The bond between the prince and his parents had not been weakened by the distance between them, and they had maintained regular contact, with tokens of affection in the form of gifts, such as the lion and leopard the prince had recently sent his father, but now his mother was dead, and the prince knew that his father too was in failing health, and had lost the drive and energy which had once characterised his behaviour.[127]

In November 1369 Charles V formally announced the confiscation of Aquitaine. So far the prince had taken no real part in the fighting himself, although he had moved to take up residence in Cognac, but now he knew that he faced a major campaign to secure his principality, and that he was probably on his own. The planned English campaign in northern France had petered out, with John of Gaunt returning to England in December, although intermittent fighting had continued. Then the prince's most trusted and brilliant captain, Sir John Chandos, was killed in a raid early in January 1370. Charles V had regained the services of du Guesclin, and early in 1370 the French army invaded Aquitaine in two separate offensives, with one apparently aimed at attacking the prince directly in Angoulême. In April Edward III agreed that once again John of Gaunt should go to his brother's aid, but only with a small force. In his absence Gaunt's three children, Henry, Philippa and Elizabeth, were looked after by Joan's aunt, Lady Blanche Wake. When John arrived in Aquitaine, with Edmund of Langley, they must have been shocked at their brother's condition. The prince could barely sit on a horse. Nevertheless he roused himself in August when he heard that the dukes of Berry and Bourbon had ridden through Limousin and occupied Limoges, persuading the bishop and the townsfolk to surrender to France. The bishop was godfather to the prince's eldest son, the young Prince Edward, and his surrender was seen as a personal betrayal as well as a direct rebellion against the prince. The prince assembled his army and left for Limoges early in September with the Earl of Pembroke and Sir Guichard d'Angle, plus his brothers as his captains, but he was a shadow of his former self. According to Froissart the prince was too incapacitated to sit on his horse, and had to be carried in a litter the sixty miles from Angoulême to Limoges. The prince is described as giving commands from his litter, but his perilous state of health makes it possible that he was only in nominal command.

Limoges refused to surrender to the prince. However, the prince's miners were able to breach one of the city walls and they entered the city on 19 September. This was to be the prince's last military engagement, and his last military success. But his reputation suffered from the critical reports of the conduct of the campaign. Froissart claimed that the prince was so angry that he ordered all the civilians, including the women and children, to be massacred, and the city itself was pillaged, robbed and burnt to the ground. The captured Bishop of Limoges was placed in Gaunt's custody, and after some negotiation was delivered to the Pope.[128] Froissart's account is not necessarily accurate. While it appears that the city was indeed comprehensively destroyed, it was an accepted practice at the time to do this in such situations to set an example and it is generally accepted that there is no evidence that civilians were killed. What happened was brutal, although not necessarily more so than in the previous *chevauchée* campaigns. But Froissart's opinion, whether justified or not, indicates that Limoges tarnished the prince's chivalric reputation. Although the success at Limoges to some extent restored the prince's authority, it did not result in any of the cities and towns which had allied themselves to France relinquishing their allegiance, and the prince knew that he had only achieved a temporary respite. In just a matter of months he had lost control of the principality and the loyalty of most of the Gascon nobility. It would be an uphill task to restore both, and the prince was in no fit state to do so.

Joan's whereabouts during the Limoges campaign are not clear. Only two contemporary writers mention her; Froissart suggests that she accompanied her husband part of the way and stayed at Cognac, where the prince joined her after the city was taken, while Chandos Herald indicates that Joan remained in Angoulême, and that the prince returned to her there.[129] This is more likely, as during the prince's absence their eldest son, Prince Edward, was taken ill at Angoulême. Joan's anguish must have been acute when the boy died after a short illness. Her grief was compounded when she had to break the news to the prince on his return, and found that her husband was in a considerably worse state of health than when he had left. The death of his eldest son was a bitter blow for the prince, and confirmed his belief that he needed to return to England. The unity and loyalty of Aquitaine depended on the person of the prince, and with his health destroyed the prince was simply unable to cope with the problems facing him. To add to his woes, according to Froissart, the Pope, incensed by the sack of Limoges, threatened to have the prince's younger son, Richard, declared illegitimate.[130] The prince hoped that once in England he would recover his health and that he would then be able to return with the energy he needed to maintain his authority in Aquitaine. The prince was by this time so ill, and so desperate to leave, that he decided on an immediate departure, and arranged for John of Gaunt to deputise for him for six months.[131] Joan, naturally, would accompany the prince back to England, as would most of their retinue, although it is possible that they decided it would be better for John Holand, now twenty-one, to start afresh and join Gaunt's retinue, instead of staying with his stepfather. The prince's helplessness was so acute that Joan probably had much to do with the planning and preparation for their departure from Aquitaine, liaising between her brother-in-law and the prince's staff. Sadly, the prince was so ill that their departure was made in haste, before Prince Edward was buried. It cannot have been easy for Joan to agree to leave before her son's funeral and it is indicative of the good relationship that she had established with John of Gaunt that she was happy to entrust him with the necessary arrangements. In January 1371 the prince and Joan, accompanied by Prince Richard and most of their retinue, sailed for England. Neither of them would ever return. Shortly after they left, John of Gaunt faithfully carried out his promise, and Prince Edward's funeral was held at the cathedral of St Andrews in Bordeaux.[132]

10

Return to England/
In Sickness and in Health
1371–1376

Alas what should I do, God, and love, if I were to lose the very flower of nobleness, the flower of loftiest grandeur, him who has no peer in the world in valour?

Chandos Herald

While there may have been some relief for Joan in leaving Aquitaine, she would have been grieving the death of her son, Edward, and there must surely have been a sense of anti-climax for her in their return. It was a sad day when her husband, 'the flower of all the chivalry of the world', returned an invalid, carried in a litter.[1] In addition, the reports that she and the prince would have received from England would not have been reassuring. With Edward III in failing health, there was clearly a need for a strong lead to be taken, and the prince was not fit enough to do this. His illness was severe, and it was possible he would not recover. Would he live to succeed his father? In accompanying the prince back to England and leaving her son Edward to be buried by his uncle, Joan had shown that she considered her first duty and loyalty was to her husband, but she also had their only surviving son, Richard, to consider, and his future to secure. Still mourning, and faced with uncertainties, Joan's role had become less clear-cut, and more challenging.

On their arrival back at Plymouth they were met by Sir Guy Brian, admiral of the fleet, on the king's behalf, but the prince needed some time to recover from the voyage, resting at Plympton priory before travelling on. They reached London on 19 April, where they were greeted by the king, the mayor and citizens of London and a band of minstrels, and then escorted to the Savoy, John of Gaunt's magnificent palace by the river in the Strand. The occasion was marked by a gift to the prince from the city of a new set of gold and silver plate to replace that melted down in Aquitaine.[2] This was nevertheless a muted celebration in contrast to previous triumphal returns. It must have been a shock for Edward III to see his son's condition at first hand, and a devastating blow when the weeks passed and there was no real sign of improvement in his health. Although they had not seen each other for more than seven years, father and son had always been close, and the affection between them would have made the prince's illness that much harder for the king to bear. It was also deeply worrying. Edward III was now fifty-nine, and finding it increasingly difficult to cope with his affairs. He was encountering political opposition at home, partly caused and certainly exacerbated by the renewed outbreak of war with France. Edward III had always expected that his eldest son would succeed him, and for years the prince had been his second in command. The king had assumed and anticipated that his son would be able to share the burden of government when he returned, and now it looked as if this might not happen. Edward III must have prayed fervently that his son would recover.

Equally, the evident deterioration in Edward III was a blow for the prince. The king had lost the fire which had characterised his earlier years; he was no longer the strong and commanding figure he had once been, and he had lost the ability to dictate affairs authoritatively. John of Gaunt had doubtless warned his brother what to expect, but facing the reality brought home to the prince how difficult matters had become, and he could see clearly for himself how much his father needed to depend on others. Since Philippa's death, Edward III had become more reclusive and less interested in affairs. He was increasingly dependent on his mistress, Alice Perrers, formerly one of the queen's bedchamber women, married to William of Windsor. Alice felt no need to be discreet and was keen to promote herself and those who supported her. Although the extent of her political influence is debatable, Alice undoubtedly used her position to advance herself and her friends. Increasingly, those who had connections to her – including her husband, and men like William Latimer, William Neville and Richard Lyons – became pre-eminent in politics. Initially, whatever distaste the prince might have felt for the way Alice Perrers flaunted herself, he evidently felt that it was a private matter for his father and not his concern. He was too loyal to remonstrate with his father in 1373 when Edward III gave his mistress Philippa's jewels and allowed her to wear these publicly as she presided over a tournament at Smithfield, although he might justifiably have pointed out to his father that it would have been more fitting for his own wife, as Princess of Wales and first in pre-eminence at court, to take precedence at the tournament, and for her to wear his mother's jewels.[3]

In the past Edward III had built up around him a strong and supportive group of like-minded nobles, men like Henry, Duke of Lancaster, who had shared the king's aims in France and provided the solid basis of collective will which had contributed so much to English success in France. Between 1340 and 1369 the war had become an enterprise shared by the nobility and the royal family, led by the king and by the prince, reliant on the enthusiasm with which so many of the nobility had embraced the cause, a camaraderie celebrated with the Order of the Garter. Now it was becoming progressively harder to sustain this successful partnership. The inevitable march of time meant that many of the king's closest friends, including Henry of Lancaster, had died, while others were now too old to effectively participate. There were few left of those who had played a major part in the previous campaigns, and the king was increasingly surrounded by a younger generation who did not necessarily share his outlook. Very few of the younger nobility showed enthusiasm for further expeditions to France, and even those who did, like the prince's youngest brother, Thomas of Woodstock, displayed little sign of the tremendous military ability which was so noticeable in the prince, or in some of the earlier captains. Even some of those who had participated and were close to the king, such as William Montague, Earl of Salisbury, were becoming less convinced that the way forward in France was to launch a fresh initiative. It was hardly surprising that John of Gaunt, the most able and active of the prince's surviving brothers, staunchly supportive of both his father and his eldest brother, had become the king's closest aide and support.

Before he left for Aquitaine the prince had only ever been involved on the periphery in domestic politics. He would also have been aware that there were many in England, including Gaunt, who assumed and expected he would take a central role in politics now he had returned. Despite the prince's poor health, he was still the heir to the throne and he was 'the hope of Englishmen'.[4] Yet initially the prince was determined to return to Aquitaine, even though he could now see for himself that his father was having difficulty handling affairs. His own poor health restricted his participation in politics, but, intent on his return, what energy he could muster was concentrated on pursuing the war in France, with the priority being raising the necessary funds and support to meet the expenses. In early May 1371 he roused himself to meet with a convocation of clergy from Canterbury, who had adjourned from St Paul's to John of Gaunt's Savoy Palace specifically to see him, in order to discuss their contribution to the expenses of the war.[5] He no doubt anticipated that he would be fit enough to take over from his brother at the end of June. Unfortunately it was not to be. Recovery proved elusive, and the prince remained largely bedridden, incapable of travelling far. His efforts were not enough to overcome the lack of general political will, and by July there was insufficient money to pay the troops still in Aquitaine. Gaunt evidently considered the position to be hopeless, and resigned his command on 21 July.[6] In August the prince was still so far from being well that he sent Joan in his place to attend the annual memorial service for his mother.[7] The prince was forced to put his plans for returning to Aquitaine on hold, and appointed Thomas Felton seneschal to caretake in his absence.

This was a difficult time for Joan. They had lost their eldest son, and they were still grieving his loss. Illness, frustration and disappointment would have made the prince a demanding consort, and Joan's priority was surely to ensure that her husband was settled comfortably and given the best care, in the hope that a respite from the problems in Aquitaine, and the possibility of fresh medical attention, would bring about a recovery. Yet domestic as well as national affairs continued to claim his attention, and although the prince could continue to rely on his council to oversee his and Joan's estates, it was inevitable that he would become involved, especially when his authority was challenged. In July 1371, for example, the prince was swift to obtain the Crown's permission to appoint commissioners to investigate several serious instances of assaults on his men, and theft of his property, including over 200 barrels of wine and many deer poached, from his estates in Cornwall and Dartmoor.[8] However, although the prince's retinue was substantial, his ill health meant that he could not hold court in the way he had been used to doing in Aquitaine. Having lost many of his closest friends, like Chandos and Audley, and old servants such as John Delves, the prince would have relied more heavily than before on his wife to assist him, and in particular in implementing his wishes in how their household should be conducted and making the necessary arrangements to travel between Berkhamsted, Kennington and Wallingford (the most conveniently situated and favoured of the prince's residences in and around London).

Yet there remained the hope that the prince would recover, and his undimmed popularity was a promise for the future. Joan had returned to find that she herself now enjoyed a very favourable reputation, her prestige having been enhanced by her time in Aquitaine. There was also the four-year-old Prince Richard to consider, and with the recent death of Prince Edward very much on their minds, and the new importance attached to Richard as the prince's heir, inevitably both parents would have been especially concerned for their young son's well-being, and Joan in particular watchful of her youngest child. Joan was able to rely for support on close family and friends, almost certainly including her daughter Maud Courtenay and her friend Eleanor. Hugh Courtenay is noted as one of the prince's entourage returning with them from Aquitaine, and he was called to parliament for the first time in January 1371.[9] Joan was doubtless glad to have her daughter by her side. Eleanor had lost her husband Roger de la Warr in 1370 while they were still in Aquitaine, and she had remained with Joan, while Roger's heir, John, was also a member of the prince's retinue.[10] Living in Joan's household brought Eleanor into daily contact with many of the prince's retinue and she did not remain a widow long. By 1372, probably shortly after their return from Aquitaine, Eleanor married Sir Lewis Clifford, one of the prince's knights. Clifford had entered the prince's service in 1360 as a yeoman, becoming a squire by 1364, and he was knighted by 1368, having fought in Spain with the prince.[11] He was valued by the prince, who rewarded him with a £40 annuity in 1364, and 100 marks in 1368 (a mark was worth 13*s* 4*d*).[12] Clifford's marriage to Eleanor brought him into closer contact with Joan and a personal friendship sprung up between them, strengthening the ties between Joan and Eleanor. It is also possible that Joan's sister-in-law, Elizabeth, spent considerable time with them, after Elizabeth's second husband, Eustace d'Aubrichecourt, died early in 1373. Joan would also have had the pleasure of being reunited with her eldest son Thomas on her return, also getting to know her daughter-in-law and meeting her grandchildren, visiting them at Woking manor.

By far the most important support for the prince and Joan came from John of Gaunt. As a child during the 1350s John of Gaunt had spent several years in his older brother's household, and throughout his formative years the prince had been at the height of his career. There can be little doubt that Gaunt admired and esteemed his older brother, while the prince had always shown a special affection towards him. Though their lives had taken different paths the bond between them had strengthened over the years. Amid all the troubles affecting them, John's steadfast loyalty to his father and brother was noticeable, and there is no indication that the prince later blamed Gaunt for the worsening situation in France or the growing unrest at home. The prince must have known how unlikely it was that his brother would be able to reverse the tide in Aquitaine after he himself had left. The continuing closeness between them, and the growing affection between Gaunt and Joan, is evidenced by the numerous gifts exchanged between them.[13] Gaunt's register notes the many gifts exchanged with the prince and those given by him to Joan, with presents to Joan's friend Eleanor and her daughter Maud Courtenay, including a pair of paternosters, an elaborately decorated drinking cup and a gift to Joan of a brooch in the shape of her personal emblem of the white hart. The presents given to Joan are invariably addressed affectionately by Gaunt to his 'very honoured and loved sister'. The prince's influence on his younger brother is striking. Gaunt came to share the same circle of friends, with Gaunt making gifts to several of those closest to his brother and sister-in-law: Lewis Clifford, Simon Burley, John Clanvowe and Philip la Vache. The prince was also indirectly responsible for his brother's second marriage. While in Aquitaine John of Gaunt had become acquainted with Pedro of Castile's eldest daughter and heir, Constance, and when he determined on marrying her, he received the prince's wholehearted support. In September 1371 Gaunt married Constance at Roquefort near Mont de Marson, and then returned to England to prepare for his bride's arrival.[14] When Constance arrived in England in February 1372 she was welcomed by the prince and Joan with the Mayor of London, with a procession through London to Savoy.[15] The prince and Joan gave Constance a wedding present of a golden brooch or pendant depicting St George decorated with sapphires, diamonds and pearls.[16] Similarly, when Edmund of Langley married Constance's sister, Isabella, in July 1372 the wedding was held at the prince's castle at Wallingford. Although both marriages fulfilled a diplomatic objective following Edward III's earlier policy of rapprochement with Castile, and had been arranged by Gaunt on his own initiative, it is unlikely that he did so without consulting the prince, who clearly approved and supported his brother's actions.

It was also in this period that John of Gaunt began his liaison with Katherine Swynford, governess to his children by Blanche of Lancaster, a passionate love affair which resulted in four children born between 1372 and 1379 (John in 1373, Henry in 1375, Thomas in 1377 and Joan in 1379).[17] Gaunt was much criticised for failing to keep his affair secret, but there is no indication that his family disapproved, and it is evident that the prince and Joan condoned his behaviour. Joan's own marital history may well have made her feel considerable sympathy for her brother-in-law, if not for his mistress. It seems likely that the name chosen by John and Katherine for their daughter, Joan, was in honour of Joan and she may even have been asked to act as godmother.[18]

In February 1372 the mayor and aldermen of London's gift to the prince arrived: a full set of plate including six large gilded pots, one spice plate, three gilded basins, six ewers, six basins of silver, twelve silver bottles, three dozen silver beakers, twenty silver chargers, ten dozen silver porringers (deep dishes), five dozen silver saltcellars, one gilded cup in the shape of an acorn, and a pair of ivory bottles. The prince had exhausted his energies and was too ill to receive it, and it was Joan who penned the letter of thanks. Describing herself as Princess of Aquitaine and Wales she wrote,

> Very dear and well beloved. We have fully heard of the great gifts that of your own free will for us you have ordained; for the which we do thank you with all our heart, letting you know for certain that if you shall have any matter to transact with us, as to the which we may reasonably avail you, we will well remember the same, and to the best of our power will do it with good heart ... Very dear and well beloved, may God have you in his keeping. Given under our signet at Berkhamsted, on the 23rd day of February.[19]

Although presumably written at the prince's instigation, the letter has a warmth and simplicity to it which was entirely Joan's, with no trace of hauteur or arrogance. By small acts like this Joan's reputation and popularity grew.

Notwithstanding Gaunt's withdrawal from Aquitaine, the prince and his father remained determined to re-establish English authority in the principality. In June 1372 a new expedition was dispatched, led by the Earl of Pembroke and the prince's friend Guichard d'Angle in the absence of the incapacitated prince. The venture was a fiasco, not even making it onto French soil, with the fleet annihilated by the Castilian navy of Henry of Trastámara at La Rochelle. Humiliatingly, Pembroke, d'Angle and several other nobles were taken prisoner; the Earl of Pembroke died and the others were later released on ransom. The failure left the way open for the inexorable march of the French king through Aquitaine, and successively the towns were lost, with Angoulême, then Poitiers, falling to the French. It was obvious to Edward III and the prince that they could not entrust the resumption of English dominance in France to anyone else, and in August 1372, having cemented an alliance with John Montfort, Duke of Brittany (the prince's stepson-in-law through his marriage to Joan Holand), they launched another expedition, under their personal command. Once again the prince made a superhuman effort to overcome his illness, hoping no doubt that once in the field he would be fit enough to direct the army, even if it had to be from a litter, as at Limoges. Accompanying Edward III and the prince were the prince's brothers, John of Gaunt and Edmund of Langley, and the earls of Warwick, Suffolk, Salisbury, March and Hereford; this was a major undertaking involving all of the military nobles and a huge number of troops. Hopes and expectations were high. The five-year-old Prince Richard was appointed guardian of the realm, and at least one chronicler recorded that aboard the king's flagship *Grâce de Dieu* at Sandwich the prince asked the nobles present to swear that they would make sure Richard succeeded to the throne if he and his father died. This was an unusual request and has been interpreted by some historians as evidence that the prince feared that in such an eventuality his brother Gaunt would force his own claims on the throne. But there is no evidence of any difficulty between the brothers and the prince's request is far more likely to reflect a continuing underlying nervousness about the legal validity of his marriage. Disastrously, poor weather prevented the fleet from landing in France and continued to do so. After two months at sea they were forced to return to England, and the army was disbanded in October. The frustration and disappointment of the commanders can only be imagined. Worse still, the sojourn at sea had considerably exacerbated the prince's ill health, and it became obvious that he was not well enough to lead a further operation. It was the prince's last attempt to engage in a military campaign.[20]

Reluctantly the prince, and everyone else, was forced to accept that he was unlikely to ever recover his health, which had obvious implications for Aquitaine. This was a hard truth for Edward III to swallow. In September 1372 the king made his heir guardian of the realm and in October summoned him to Parliament, 'as he loves the king and his honour and his own – as the king would not that business so difficult be treated or directed without the prince's advice and counsel'.[21] The king's affection for his son remained strong and his trust absolute, and it was therefore with a heavy heart that he was forced to accept the reality of his son's condition. On 5 November 1372 the prince, using Sir Guy Brian as his spokesman, confirmed to Parliament that he was formally relinquishing his title Prince of Aquitaine, and he surrendered the deeds of the principality to the king.[22] It was a sad end to all the hopes and expectations of just ten years earlier. Although the official reason cited for the prince stepping down was given as financial (specifically that the revenue recoverable from the principality was insufficient to meet the considerable expenses of maintaining the prince and his administration), no one was fooled. The prince had never been defeated in combat but he was no longer the man he had once been. Without the prince at the helm the Aquitanian experiment could not survive. His loyal and hard-working staff were only part of the package; managing the principality, retaining the loyalty of the local nobility and keeping the threat of French encroachment at bay had all depended on the prince being there in person. His illness had taken its toll, and he was simply too sick to return; there was no question that he would be able to sustain the style of government he had established, with his flamboyant court in Bordeaux and Angoulême. Conceding failure in Aquitaine was a huge and bitter blow, heralding a bleak future for the prince.

Christmas that year must have been a sombre time for Joan and their family. As it was now abundantly obvious that the prince would never regain his health, it also seemed probable that the prince might not outlive his father, and that if he did it was unlikely to be for very long. This inevitably changed the prince's attitude towards outside affairs. In many ways the prince simply gave up after the failure of the expedition. With his hopes dashed for a recovery of his health and a resumption of his place in Aquitaine, and no longer believing that he would succeed his father, he showed little interest in politics. His presence at court was muted, lacking the energy and flamboyance which had characterised Aquitaine. Nevertheless he remained the heir and was conscious of his responsibilities. Unable to cope with journeying frequently, he took up more or less permanent residence at Kennington, the palace having the advantage of being conveniently close to Westminster while keeping the prince and his family separate from the main centre of affairs. During the last three years of his life the prince rarely moved more than fifty miles from London. It must have been extremely difficult for a man who had been fit and active for so much of his life to accept that he would now always be an invalid, and frequently bedridden. His illness not only prevented him from actively participating in public life but from attending events and partaking in activities, like hunting and jousting, which he had so enjoyed and in which he had so excelled. Joan remained constantly at her husband's side, though she may well have found him a difficult and demanding companion. With the prince's continued physical dependency his relationship with his wife would inevitably have changed, and it is hard not to imagine that Joan was increasingly consulted and a party to decisions affecting them both. Inevitably the prince's thoughts turned inwards, as he contemplated his own death and what this might mean for his son. Increasingly the small figure of Prince Richard became the focus, as it was apparent that it was more likely that Richard, rather than his father, would succeed Edward III, and that when he did he would still be a minor. This, for the prince, increased the importance of his wife's role, and he doubtless spent much time discussing Richard's future with Joan.

Richard was six in January 1373, and it would have been around this time that arrangements were made for him to have a tutor. There does not seem to have been any discussion or intention that Richard should be given his own independent household or live separately from his parents, and it was probably the prince's wish as much as Joan's that he remained with them and accompanied his parents as they moved between Kennington and Berkhamsted. As Richard grew older he naturally needed a resident tutor to give him the education and skills considered necessary for one of his status, including riding and hunting, dancing and singing, and learning to read and write. Richard's first language was probably French, taught to him in his earliest days by his Aquitanian wet nurse and bed rocker, and probably also by his parents; later, when he was king, Joan wrote to her son in French. He also learned English and could read Latin. It seems unlikely that the prince chose his son's tutor without discussing it with his wife first. In fact, Richard seems to have had three tutors. One was Richard Abberbury, one of the prince's knights, who also acted as steward of his household. Another, Guichard d'Angle, an able Poitevin knight who had originally served the King of France, was captured at Poitiers and subsequently went on to serve the prince in Aquitaine and fought at Nájera, and with Gaunt in Aquitaine in 1371. He was made a knight of the Garter in 1372 and took part in the expedition to La Rochelle, where he was captured and spent the next two years as a prisoner in France. Simon Burley was Richard's last tutor, a long-standing member of the prince's retinue who served in Aquitaine (he fought at Nájera and Limoges, and was also at one stage a prisoner of the French) as well as in England.[23] Abberbury was probably Richard's first tutor and replaced by d'Angle on his return to England in 1374, who was in turn replaced by Simon Burley. Abberbury and Burley both became trusted and valued friends to Joan, and she would later appoint both to act as her executors in her will.

Richard's parents were anxious not to isolate their son, and ensured that, like his father and his grandfather, he grew up in the company of other boys of similar age, one of whom was his cousin, Henry of Bolingbroke, John of Gaunt's son, and another, Robert de Vere, son of Aubrey de Vere, one of the prince's knights and a member of his council. The presence of so many young boys would have enlivened the palace, and probably lifted the prince's spirits as he lay sick. Richard was also surrounded by his extended family; his half-brother John Holand was on the prince's staff, and his half-sister Lady Maud Courtenay spent much time staying with her mother, an arrangement that became permanent when Hugh died in 1374, leaving Maud a childless widow. When John Montfort was forced to return to England in April 1373 after Brittany was overrun by the French, his young wife, Joan, took the opportunity to stay with her mother and catch up with the family, remaining with them when John returned to France to join Gaunt a few months later.[24] The close ties between Richard and his half-siblings in later life indicate a happy and loving relationship with them that would have been established during his childhood.

In June 1373 the prince was sufficiently strong to preside at a council at Westminster debating a fresh papal demand to enforce papal taxation, and he was also able to consult with his own council, but such appearances were becoming increasingly rare.[25] With the prince incapacitated and his father in decline there was a vacuum in royal leadership; both turned naturally to John of Gaunt to handle Crown affairs and Gaunt was the obvious choice to lead a further expedition to France. In August 1373 Gaunt set off from Calais with 11,000 men, with hopes riding high.[26] A victory would restore national morale and improve England's prestige abroad. But although the *chevauchée* progressed from Calais to Bordeaux, the army suffered heavy losses through harassment and lack of provisions, and Gaunt was unable to bring the French army to battle. In England the expedition was considered a disaster. Gaunt returned in April 1374, with little to show for his nine months in France. This was not only a huge personal disappointment but a real setback in royal prestige, and bad luck for Gaunt. His father and brother had been so outstandingly successful that his own reputation suffered in comparison. Worse was to follow, as the atmosphere of goodwill and mutual support which had characterised Edward III's court in the 1360s dissolved. Cracks began to appear in the famously unified royal circle. Gaunt had fallen out with John Montfort, Joan's son-in-law, while in France, apparently incensed that Montfort had been unable to help with the payment of troops, with the result that Montfort withdrew and relations between the two remained difficult for some years. After the failed expedition Gaunt increasingly favoured negotiation with France and a dignified withdrawal of English interest, and he played a leading role in the peace negotiations promoted by the Pope later that year which ended inconclusively the following year, in June 1375, with agreement for a year's truce.[27]

After a lifetime devoted to the conflict the prince may not have viewed Gaunt's growing disenchantment with affairs in France with much sympathy, but he was powerless to do much about it. The prince manifestly lacked the strength, as did his father, to provide the leadership needed. While John of Gaunt was conducting the negotiations in Bruges royal leadership foundered. Edward III was a shadow of his former self, and seemed to be helpless in the hands of the officials who surrounded him, allowing more and more influence to his mistress, Alice Perrers. According to the *Chronicon Angliae* 'the English ... tolerated her for many years because they had great affection for the king and were afraid of offending him'.[28] The continued lack of success in the war with France inevitably led to discontent in Parliament, and resentment at the huge sums being expended on funding a war with so little apparent result. Inevitably opinion became divided between those who supported a continuation of the war and those who felt the time had come to reach a settlement. There was criticism of royal leadership and dissatisfaction with the conduct of affairs and a growing divide between those who supported the Crown and those who opposed royal policy. Many of those prominent in opposition were close friends of the prince, including William Wykeham, Bishop of Winchester, the earls of March and Salisbury, and John Harewell, who had been his chancellor in Aquitaine for six years, and it has been suggested that this indicates he shared their views, or that they reflected his opinion.[29] It is however unlikely that the prince at any time consciously opposed his father, although he may well have felt some distaste for the apparent influence permitted the king's mistress, but even if he had wished to, he was simply unable to intervene himself.

In contrast to Alice Perrers, Joan remained very much in the background. This is in some ways surprising, given the vacuum in royal leadership and the fact that Joan was the most senior woman in the royal circle. As the wife of the heir to the throne and the king's daughter-in-law she was in a singular position, and with the deterioration in Edward III, the prince's ill health and the growing certainty that her son would succeed his grandfather as a minor, it would have been natural if Joan had been accorded and taken a more distinctive role. Politically and socially the king and his family were naturally at the centre of affairs. However, it is notable that the prince did not encourage his wife to take a more prominent role. This is perhaps understandable in the political sphere. Traditionally women did not usually engage in politics, and as the prince was by upbringing and temperament used to relying on his male peers, the close relationship between him and his younger brother made Gaunt his obvious deputy. He may simply have felt that there was no need to involve Joan in the difficult maelstrom of domestic politics. But with Gaunt engaged elsewhere, and his own ill health, the prince might well have promoted his wife to represent their interests, trusting in her absolute loyalty and shared concern for their son. Joan herself might have taken advantage of the circumstances to take a more influential role. In fact, given the situation, it is evident that it was a deliberate decision by both the prince and Joan that she should not. The reason for this was almost certainly their concern to protect their son. Taking a leading role in political affairs would immediately attract criticism and unwelcome attention which might resurrect the whole matter of Joan's marital history, with the obvious danger that this could call into question their son's legitimacy, and threaten the succession. According to Froissart, the Pope had already threatened to declare Richard illegitimate after

Limoges.[30] Although Froissart is not always a reliable source this indicates that the legality and validity of the prince's marriage remained a matter of concern. Considering the care which had been taken by the prince with his father when his marriage to Joan had taken place, his guidance to his wife on her role, and the favourable esteem with which she was now held, it is unlikely that either of them would have wanted to risk her reputation at this stage by drawing critical attention to her.

At court, in terms of precedence, Joan as Princess of Wales was senior even to her childhood companion, Princess Isabella. With Edward III's decline court life by 1375 had become greatly subdued, and Joan made no attempt to change this, perhaps having no wish to do so bearing in mind her husband's precarious state of health and the king's deterioration. Whereas some women in her position might have taken advantage of the situation to pursue their own interests, Joan manifestly did not. Her Holand family, and her friends, remained very much in the background, while Joan conducted herself with quiet dignity, loyally supporting her husband and his family. She was naturally regarded as having influence with her husband and his father, and she was expected to adopt, and did assume, the role of intercessor, requesting pardons for individual servants and retainers such as Peter Bigg of Tokeby, Leicestershire, for the death of Robert Bailiff.[31] The Pope took advantage of this in May 1375, when he requested Joan to use her influence with the king and the prince to improve the position of his captive nephews by 'procuring' for them 'some consolation and relaxation'.[32] But her intercessory role remained strictly non-political. By behaving with modest restraint Joan consolidated her reputation and increased the respect with which she was regarded among the court circle. A poignant, though romanticised, picture of the family is represented in Ford Maddox Brown's painting exhibited at the Royal Academy in 1851, of the Prince's forty-fifth birthday, with Chaucer reading his works to the prince and the court.[33]

Political affairs reached a crisis in the parliament called in April 1376, known as the Good Parliament. The prince was carried from Kennington to Westminster so that he could attend its opening on 29 April by the chancellor, Sir John Knyvet, with his father, but he was too ill to remain, returning almost immediately to his apartments in the palace at Westminster. Similarly, Edward III retired, and with the tacit support and endorsement of his father and brother it was Gaunt, having returned from the Bruges conference at the end of January, who took the leading role in protecting the Crown's interests.[34] It was to be a poisoned chalice for Gaunt. Almost immediately the commons attacked Edward III's administration, expressing considerable discontent with the state of affairs, demanding that a council of senior churchmen and peers be appointed to advise the king; four bishops, four earls and four barons were duly suggested and accepted, including the earls of Arundel, March, Stafford and Suffolk, bishops Courtenay of London, Despenser of

Norwich and the prince's friends William Wykeham and John Harewell
of Bath and Wells. The knight elected to be their speaker by the
Commons, Sir Peter de la Mare, accused several of the king's servants of
corruption and mismanagement, naming the king's chamberlain, William
Lord Latimer, and the London merchant Richard Lyons, demanding their
arrest. It was not long before the Commons demanded the removal of
Alice Perrers as well. In the ensuing debate the Commons brought charges
of corrupt practices against several other royal servants and, disregarding
the king's request for funds, pursued their prosecution of these men. A
desperate Lyons tried to persuade the prince to help him, sending him
a barrel with £1,000 in gold inside, a bribe which the prince promptly
returned.[35] Although the Commons protested their loyalty to the king,
they made no secret of their dislike for Gaunt, and the clear personal
antipathy that developed between Gaunt and the speaker, Sir Peter de la
Mare, coloured the whole tone of the parliament. As Sir Peter de la Mare
was steward to Edmund Mortimer, Earl of March, who was married to
Lionel's daughter Philippa, it also threatened harmony in the royal circle.
Philippa was arguably senior to her uncle Gaunt in terms of the line of
succession to the throne because her father was his elder brother, but her
sex meant that her claim was not clear-cut. [36] It was an exceptional crisis,
with Parliament comprehensively indicting the royal government, and the
proceedings were, quite simply, a disaster for the Crown, with none of the
desired concessions in terms of raising finance to support royal policy. It
was also a personal disaster for Gaunt, as his handling of the crisis won
him few plaudits and merely exacerbated his growing unpopularity. It
heightened suspicion of his own ambitions, mainly because he was not
either the king or the heir, and his strong sense of family loyalty was
misread as evidence of his self-aggrandisement. It is possible that neither
Edward III nor the prince, faced with the mood of Parliament in the
spring of 1376, would have made a better job of it, but in the event it was
Gaunt's reputation which suffered.

Contemporary commentators were confused about the role played by
the prince, whom the *Chronicon Angliae* described as being 'the hope of
the Commons', while Walsingham went further, suggesting that the prince
played a leading political role in the parliament and was in conflict with
Gaunt.[37] Certainly, the prince's potential influence cannot be doubted, and
his position ensured that he had a close link to many in Parliament.[38] His
military successes had earned him an enviable reputation both abroad and
at home, ensuring him huge popularity, and like his father the prince had
deliberately courted and built up around him a strong and loyal group
of friends and allies. Many of these would have looked to the prince for
his guidance, but there is no evidence that the prince sought to direct his
friends to influence the proceedings of the Good Parliament, and historians
generally are dubious about the extent of his interest, let alone his
influence. The prince resembled his father in many ways, having a strong

sense of his royal status, with the will and ability to command, and it is probable that had he enjoyed better health the prince would have taken a far more prominent role in Parliament. Rather than being in disagreement with Gaunt, this would simply have resulted in the prince, rather than Gaunt, being the major royal representative. But the fact was that he was a very sick man, and far too ill to do more than lend a notional presence, leaving Gaunt on his own with the thankless task of placating Parliament.

Parliament was still sitting in June when news reached the Commons that the prince's condition had worsened, and that he was dying. Although the prince had been ill for so long, it was undoubtedly still a shock for those around him when they realised the end was near. The prince had planned carefully for his last days, doubtless helped by Joan. Foremost on his mind was the future of their son. He knew that Edward III would die while Richard was still a minor, and he remained concerned that his son's succession might be challenged. As he lay dying he did everything he could to ensure support for Richard, knowing that it would be difficult for anyone to refuse a deathbed request. Walsingham noted that the prince gave orders that the door of his room was to be shut to nobody, not even the lowliest groom, and distributed generous gifts to all his attendants.[39] According to Chandos Herald,

> he had the doors opened and all his men summoned who had been his servants and had willing served him. 'Lords, he said, 'by my faith, you have served me loyally; I cannot reward you properly myself, but God will do so in heaven' … he said in a loud voice, 'I commend my son to you, who is young and small, and ask you to serve him as you have served me' … then he called for his father, the king and his brother, the Duke of Lancaster; he commended his wife and son, whom he loved greatly, to them, and begged them to help them. They swore on the Bible to do so, and promised to comfort his children and uphold their rights: all the princes and barons did this.[40]

He asked the king to allow his debts to be paid without delay from his estate. The prince's last meeting with his father must have been particularly painful, each no doubt reflecting on their glorious past together. Richard was summoned to see his father as he lay dying, an ordeal for the young prince as the prince's last words, as recounted by the chroniclers, seem to have been restricted to commanding him to ensure that his servants received the gifts he had designated. It is hard to imagine that Joan was not present, and that the prince did not also bestow his blessing on his son. On 7 June the prince made his will, received the last rights from his friend the Bishop of Bangor, and, at three o'clock on 8 June, he died.[41] Dignified and noble to the end, the prince stage-managed his exit superbly, even, by an amazing coincidence, dying on the feast day he most treasured, that of the Holy Trinity.

The only sour note attached to the last days is Walsingham's account of Sir Richard Stury's visit to the prince. Stury had served with the prince, and was one of the king's chamber knights, and according to Walsingham had alarmed the king by suggesting that there were certain knights in the Commons who planned to depose him, in the same way as his father, Edward II, had been removed from the throne. When investigated the claim proved false and Stury was dismissed by Edward III from his council, only to be almost immediately reinstated by Gaunt. Walsingham records that Stury was admitted to the prince on his deathbed, to beg his forgiveness, and that the prince spurned him, requesting he leave his chamber and never trouble him further.[42] The account is not corroborated by any other source, which is surprising, considering the attention given to the prince's last days, and the veracity of the account is dubious, particularly in view of the fact that Stury was later to be one of the knights closest to Joan, a position he would hardly have won had there been animosity between him and the prince.

Once again, Joan was a widow. After the prince's long illness, she too had had plenty of time to prepare for his death, but she undoubtedly grieved for him. Chandos Herald wrote that at his death 'the lovely and noble princess felt such grief at heart that her heart was nigh breaking. There was such a clamour of sighing, weeping, crying and grieving that anyone alive would have felt pity at it.'[43] She was not the only one to lament his loss. The chroniclers make it clear that the prince's death was generally felt, with apparently sincere public mourning, even in France, where French writers penned eulogies and the king, Charles V, ordered Masses be said for him, attending a requiem Mass for him in Paris, accompanied by all the French nobility. The prince's renown in his lifetime and at his death was unsurpassed, his popularity having survived the years of illness and the defeat in Aquitaine. Eulogies were fulsome, many echoing the praise given by Thomas Brinton, Bishop of Rochester, preaching shortly after the prince's death, listing in his sermon the prince's many virtues and referring to his power, wisdom and goodness, and repeated by the chronicler John of Reading, who credited the prince with having followed wise council, never preferring secular affairs to divine office, for being honourable and having endowed the Church generously and kept his marriage vows. Many felt that their hopes for the future went with him. Walsingham, describing the prince as 'the comfort of all England', was quite clear that his death was militarily a disaster, stating that 'on his death the hopes of the English utterly perished; for while he was alive they feared no enemy invasion, while he was with them they feared no hostile encounter. Never, while he was with them, did they suffer the disgrace of a campaign that had been unsuccessful or abandoned. As is said of Alexander the Great, he attacked no nation which he did not defeat, and besieged no city which he did not capture.' For Walsingham, 'the good fortune of England, as if it had been inherent in his person, flourished in his health, languished in his sickness and expired in his death,' and he lamented, 'What great grief you cause his country, which believes that now he is gone it is bereft of a protector! … Rise up, O Lord, help and protect us for your name's sake!'[44]

The prince received an immense state funeral. His body lay in state in Westminster Hall from 8 June to 29 September, then on 30 September both houses of Parliament and the court escorted the hearse, drawn by twelve black horses, down to Canterbury, where the prince had requested he be buried. The funeral procession wound its way from Westminster past St Eleanor's Cross at Charing, along the Strand past the Savoy Palace, over London Bridge, through Southwark and Blackheath, then down into Kent, finally arriving through the west gate into Canterbury on 5 October. Through Canterbury the cortege was preceded by two warhorses, wearing the arms of war and peace, and was met at the chapel of Holy Cross by two knights dressed as the prince had requested in his will, one with a shield of war and the other with a shield of peace, both displaying the prince's silver ostrich feathers and motto, 'Ich dene'. The prince's coffin was then carried on to a bier in front of the high altar. In his will the prince had directed that he should be buried in the middle of the chapel of Our Lady Undercroft, in a marble tomb, ten feet away from the altar. He instructed that around the tomb there should be twelve escutcheons, six bearing his arms and the other six with ostrich feathers, and 'Houmont' was to be written on each escutcheon. He requested a frame around the tomb, with his image in relief of latten gilt, in armour, with folded arms and a meek facial expression, and with his leopard helm placed under the head.[45] As instructed, his tomb chest was decorated alternately with six shields of peace (three ostrich feathers on a black ground) and six of war (the quartered arms of England and France).[46] The prince was to be remembered in death, as he had been in life, as the consummate warrior.

The chapel of Our Lady Undercroft was the chapel which the prince had founded in accordance with the Pope's mandate giving him permission to marry Joan. It was a moving tribute to the love the prince felt for his wife that he wished to be interred in the chapel which commemorated their marriage. In the ceiling of the chantry chapel (now used by the French Walloon church) there can still be seen a carved stone boss of a woman's head, with her hair in a netted fret, which was a popular fashion at the time. It is the largest human face among the ceiling bosses, and clearly represents Joan, although it is not known when it was placed there. Although the prince's detailed instructions for his funeral and tomb were largely carried out, he was not buried in the chapel as he had requested, and his tomb was placed in a more prominent position behind the high altar on the south side of the Trinity chapel. The tomb itself was commissioned after his death, during his son's reign, and the design is usually attributed to Richard II. The location of the prince's tomb next to

Becket's shrine implies direct royal intervention, and it is similarly notable for being the only tomb of this period other than that of an anointed sovereign which is constructed of marble and bronze (the latter material used for the life-size effigy of the prince placed on top of the tomb), bearing strong similarities to the style of Edward III's tomb and effigy in Westminster Abbey.[47] It seems inconceivable that Joan was not consulted about her husband's memorial, and as the work was carried out in the early 1380s while Richard was still a child it is highly likely that Joan was closely involved in the design and planning for the tomb. The prince's tomb is well preserved and can be seen by any visitor to Canterbury Cathedral. Adorning the tomb are the prince's funeral achievements, his helm, crest, jupon, shield, a pair of gauntlets and the scabbard of his sword, while above his tomb, facing down towards his effigy, is a painting of the Holy Trinity; God the Father enthroned above the world, with the crucified Christ beneath him and the Holy Ghost in the form of a dove. The prince had given the cathedral the painting during his lifetime, intending that it should be placed over his tomb. The originals of these tomb adornments have deteriorated and faded badly, and those now on view are copies made in the 1950s, while the originals have been placed under glass elsewhere. Inscribed around the tomb is the epitaph chosen by the prince, a poem based on the *Clericalis Disciplina* written by Petrus Alphonus in the eleventh century. Translated into English it reads,

Thou, who silent passest by,
Where this corpse interr'd doth lie
Hear what to thee I now shall show,
Words that from Experience flow:
As thou art, once the world saw me;
As I am, so thou once shalt be.

I little could my death divine,
When Life's bright Lamp did sweetly shine;
Vast wealth did o'er my Coffers flow,
Which I as freely did bestow;
Great Store of Mansions I did hold,
Land, Wardrobes, Horses, Silver, Gold.
But now I am all bereft,
And deep in Ground alone am left:
My once admir'd Beauty's gone,
My flesh is wasted to the Bone.

A narrow House doth me contain,
All that I speak is true and plain;
And, if you should behold me here,
You'd hardly think (I justly fear)

That e'er the World to me, did bow,
I am so chang'd and alter'd now.

For God's sake, pray to Heaven's high King
To shade my Soul with Mercy's Wing,
All those that try on bended knee
To reconcile my God and me
God place them in his Paradise
Where neither Death can be, nor Vice.[48]

The prince had put considerable thought into his funeral and tomb, and the epitaph by which he wished to be remembered. While there is no reason to doubt the sincerity of the emotions expressed, it was also a propaganda exercise par excellence, drawing on his glory days and reminding the country of all that had been the best of him and the promise held in him, while the humility expressed in the epitaph suggested that any pride or arrogance had been humbled during the sufferings of his illness. His reputation, the manner of his passing, and his tomb memorial were the final legacies he left for his son.

The first part of the prince's will was wholly taken up with his directions for his funeral and interment, giving the cathedral gifts of clothing for use as vestments and altar cloths, his breviary and missal and a hall of ostrich plumes on black tapestry, and precious metal candlesticks, chalices and a tabernacle to adorn and serve in the chantry and fund the prayers that were to be offered up for him.[49] His second concern was to endow the monastic house he had founded at Ashridge, and his chapel of St Nicholas at Wallingford Castle; both were to receive similar items of clothing and altar ware, with Ashridge receiving a particularly precious table, described as being made of gold and silver and decorated with pearls, rubies, sapphires and emeralds, which contained precious relics including a relic of the Holy Cross. The prince made few personal bequests. Richard was his main beneficiary, receiving three costly beds identified by their hangings, including the blue gown embroidered with gold roses and ostrich plumes and matching bed given to the prince by Edward III, a bed with angels embroidered on the hangings and one of red silk with baudkin stripes (silk weft and gold warp), plus two sets of wall tapestries: his arras chamber hangings depicting Saladin, and worsted hangings embroidered with mermen of the sea. Joan was to receive silver vessels to the value of 700 marks (described as silver she had brought to the marriage), and the red worsted chamber hangings embroidered with eagles and griffons, with a border of swans with ladies' heads. The prince was careful to remember his illegitimate son, Sir Roger Clarendon (he too received a bed), his confessor Sir Robert Walsham and his servant Alan Cheyne. Otherwise he directed his executors to use the remainder of his goods to pay his funeral expenses and settle his debts, and distribute anything remaining between his servants according to their degrees and desserts. The prince had already very generously provided for his knights, squires and other retainers by granting them annuities, and he charged Richard with the duty of confirming these gifts.

Considering the great love which the prince was known to have for his wife and son, it is extraordinary that his last testament shows so little reflection of this. The terms with which he chose to describe them in his will are almost unnaturally restrained, with the simple designation of 'my son, Richard' and 'our consort the princess'. This is particularly surprising when in the same document the prince describes his brother Gaunt warmly as 'our very dear and well beloved brother of Spain, Duke of Lancaster'. The prince had thought long and hard about his will and the use of these terms was quite deliberate. In describing Joan as 'our consort the princess' rather than as his wife he was emphasising her status. Similarly, by referring to Richard with the plain designation 'my son', and to his illegitimate son as 'Sir Roger Clarendon' the prince was distinguishing clearly between them; Richard was his son and heir and there was no acknowledgement of his paternity of Roger. In emphasising the status and legitimacy of his wife and heir, it is clear that the prince's continuing overriding concern was to ensure the peaceful succession of their son, albeit at the expense of expressing affection. Nor did he appoint Joan as one of his executors, a quite deliberate omission which contrasts oddly with, for example, his brother Lionel's appointment of his wife Violanta in 1368, or his cousin Henry of Lancaster's appointment of his 'very dear sister Lady Wake' (Joan's aunt) in 1360.[50] But rather than implying a lack of trust in his wife, this omission suggests instead that just as he had not wanted her to take a public role in his name in political affairs, so he chose not to appoint her as one of his executors.

In contrast, the prince was all too aware of his brother's unpopularity and the ugly rumours that Gaunt had an eye for the throne. In appointing Gaunt his main executor and specifically describing him in warm terms, the prince was sending a clear message that he had absolute trust and faith in his brother. His remaining executors were longstanding friends and servants, men who he hoped would look after his wife's interests, and who would also serve his son: William Wykeham, Bishop of Winchester (a self-made man whose brilliance had found him high favour with Edward III that had remained after his forced resignation in 1371; according to Froissart, 'everything was done by him and nothing was done without him'[51]); John Harewell, Bishop of Bath and Wells; William Spridlington, Bishop of Asaph (who had been with the prince since 1348); Robert Walsham, his confessor; Hugh Segrave, his steward since 1372; Alan Stokes and John Fordham. The witnesses to his will were John, Bishop of Hereford, Lewis Clifford, Nicholas Bond, Nicholas Sarnesfield and his clerk William Walsham.[52]

The care and detail with which the prince set out his wishes makes it evident that he had spent considerable time considering his dispositions, and it is reasonable to assume that he had discussed them with his wife, so that she was well aware of his plans. They both knew that in material terms Joan would be well catered for after the prince died. Not only would she receive a third of all his estates for the rest of her lifetime, but she would also then become solely entitled to manage her own considerable property and income. The nobles chosen by the prince to handle his affairs were all well known to Joan and probably on good terms with her, as it is unlikely that he would have included any whom he did not feel had his wife's interests at heart, as well as those of his son, and she was of course especially close to her brother-in-law, John of Gaunt.

How would Joan have felt after the prince died? Grief was natural, and clearly evident. But was there also an element of relief? The prince had been ill for several years, and his demise expected for such a long time. In the last few months he probably bore very little resemblance to the energetic and charismatic leader and warrior she had married, on occasions he had probably been extremely demanding and difficult to live with, at times bitter and disappointed, and despite the note of humility expressed in the verse chosen for his tomb it is doubtful if he ever lost his imperiousness and habit of command. Joan was loyal and supportive throughout, but there must have been times when her patience was sorely tested. Nevertheless there was no hint of it in her outward demeanour. Joan respected the prince's wishes in death as she had in his lifetime, and, probably in accordance with his instructions, shortly after his death she gave her wedding dress to St George's chapel, Windsor.[53] As the founding chapel of the Order of the Garter the chapel held a special place in the affections of Edward III and his family, and had received many gifts of clothing from Edward III, Philippa and the prince himself, including a missal and gold cape. The sumptuous donated clothing was altered to provide vestments for the clergy serving in the chapel, and altar coverings, reflecting the peculiarly intimate and unique significance the Order of the Garter had for the royal family. The king had created his wife a Lady of the Order of the Garter prior to her death, and in 1376 he had also made his favourite daughter, Princess Isabella, a member. Edward III would certainly have wanted his son to be remembered in the chapel, and an obit was celebrated for the prince annually there after his death. Philippa was similarly remembered annually, as was Gaunt's father-in-law, Henry of Lancaster, and first wife, Blanche, and as Edward III would also later be remembered. Joan also faithfully kept her husband's memory every year, making annual pilgrimages to his tomb at Canterbury on the anniversary of his death.

11

Princess in Politics
1376–1377

... if the princess remains a widow while her eldest son is still young and under age, and by chance war and strife break out among the barons, for the sake of good government she must use her prudence and her knowledge to establish and maintain peace among them.

Christine de Pizan[1]

Now that the prince was dead Joan had one further task to fulfil for him, for the prince had entrusted to her the care of their son, Prince Richard. On his deathbed the prince had commended his wife and son to his father and brother. These were the four people he most loved in the world. He had always had a special relationship with his father, whom he sincerely admired and esteemed, and he had enjoyed an exceptionally fond fraternal bond with John of Gaunt, transcending the ten-year age gap between them, stronger than the affection he had for Lionel, closest to him in age, or Edmund or Thomas. John, in return, had worshipped his brother as a child and remained in awe of him in adulthood. The prince would naturally have expected and assumed that his father and brother would look after his family, but despite the great love and trust between them the prince still insisted that they swear on the Bible that they would do all they could to help them. He was acutely aware that, although his son was the acknowledged heir to the throne, Richard was still a minor, and his succession was by no means inevitable. Joan knew, as the prince had done, that her relationship with his father and brother would be crucial in the months to come.

Edward III's relationship with Joan was complicated by the past. While the prince was alive, the king honoured her as his beloved son's wife, and Joan always behaved with respect and deference towards her father-in-law. Would they behave the same way after the prince's death? Thirty years ago, the king's attitude towards Joan with the debacle over her Holand marriage had at best been ambiguous and at worst irresponsible; as her cousin and senior kinsman he had abandoned her and as her king he had abrogated his responsibilities. Edward III was conscious of his failure, and Joan's presence would always remind him of his shortcomings. Equally, Joan could never forget that the king had failed her when she had sorely needed his support. Once her marriage to Thomas Holand had been confirmed, their relationship had improved slowly, but it remained stiffly polite and formal, without warmth or affection. When the prince had told his father of his desire to marry Joan, Edward III's reaction had been immensely supportive, but this reflected his feelings for his son, and not for Joan. There is no evidence that the king ever developed a genuine fondness for his daughter-in-law, with references to Joan in official documents being carefully correct, addressing her with her titles or as the prince's wife, never in terms of affectionate endearment such as he used when addressing his son, or his daughter Princess Isabella. The king approved of his daughter-in-law's conduct as Princess of Wales, and as his son's wife he treated her with respect, but their relationship never progressed beyond this into one of real attachment. Appreciating this, the prince had done what he could on his deathbed to cement the ties between them.

It was a different matter with John of Gaunt; here the prince had no real qualms. An affection had developed between Joan and Gaunt on John's first visit to his brother and sister-in-law in Aquitaine at the start of the Nájera campaign, and their relationship had continued to grow in strength and warmth. By the time Joan returned to England with the prince in 1371 their friendship was noticeably sincere and loving. The genuine intimacy between them was quite independent of the prince's relationship with his younger brother, and in many respects resembled that of a brother and sister. This may indeed have been how each felt. For Joan, John may well have taken the place in her affections which her younger brother had once had and, poignantly, John had succeeded to Thomas Holand's garter stall in St George's chapel when he became a Garter knight. Her eldest son, Thomas Holand, joined Gaunt's retinue after Joan left Aquitaine, serving with Gaunt in France in 1373.[2] John, in turn, enjoyed a far closer attachment to his sister-in-law than he did with his own sisters, even his older sister, Princess Isabella. He gave regular gifts to Joan and to her family, expressing his evident affection in addressing them to her. In January 1372 the duke gave to 'our very honoured and loved sister' three 'leverers blankes surterragez' of gold, a 'pair of gold beads, a paternoster decorated with small pearls and precious gemstones'.[3] The following April the duke's register records a gift of a gold cup for Joan, while Gaunt also gave presents to those closest to her; her daughter Maud Courtenay received a pair of paternosters, as did Eleanor Clifford (formerly de la Warr).[4] Gifts between them were reciprocated, and Joan gave John a goblet with a cover embroidered with her personal insignia of a recumbent white hart.[5] In June 1374, probably while on a visit, John rewarded eight of Joan's minstrels and gave his 'very honoured lady and sister' a silver ewer and another cup.[6] The prince's deathbed injunction to his brother simply confirmed an existing and strong bond, and it was John and Joan's friendship that would be crucial in the months to come, as the king's health failed.

While the prince's body lay in state in Westminster Hall, Parliament continued to sit and family grief had to be restrained to allow proceedings to be concluded. The Commons were not deterred from continuing their attack on the Crown and its servants, and Gaunt, grieving for his brother and protective of his father and nephew, found himself completely unable to master the situation. He was forced to concede to their demands and agree to the impeachment of his father's servants and mistress. Alice Perrers was banished from court, Latimer was removed, and on 20 June, just two weeks after the prince's death, the royal steward John, Lord Neville, was dismissed. The other accused fared no better. The fact that Lord Neville was a retainer of Gaunt's, while Latimer was Neville's father-in-law, cannot have helped Gaunt's position. With barely any money voted for the Crown, the king's dire financial predicament remained, while Gaunt's unpopularity was confirmed and unsavoury rumours circulated about his ambitions. The chronicler Walsingham held Gaunt in particular contempt, convinced he wanted the throne for himself, and repeated virulent gossip and rumours current about the duke: that he had poisoned his first wife's sister in order to gain her inheritance (his first wife, Blanche, was joint heiress with her sister Maud to Henry of Lancaster; Maud died childless, leaving Blanche the sole heiress); that he was plotting with the French king, Charles V, to obtain a papal bull declaring Richard illegitimate; and that he planned to seize the throne himself when his father died. According to Walsingham, Gaunt tried to persuade the Commons to discuss the succession, and was so intent on removing opposition that he requested a law be passed to forbid a woman from inheriting the throne, which would obviate the claim of Lionel's daughter Philippa, who arguably held the most legitimate claim to the throne after the prince's son.[7] Although there was no evidence to support the allegations made against the duke, the Commons were sufficiently concerned about Gaunt's intentions that within three weeks of the prince's death they demanded Richard should be recognised as heir apparent.[8] Ironically, this was the one matter on which Gaunt was in complete agreement, despite the rumours. When Parliament concluded on 10 July, a feast was held to mark the occasion, attended by most of the court including Edmund of Langley and Thomas of Woodstock, but from which Gaunt was noticeably absent.[9] The Commons were triumphant in their exercise of will, leaving the prestige of the Crown in tatters. As the prince's cortege wound its way to Canterbury at the end of September, it was accompanied by many who had been in the now dissolved parliament, as well as the courtiers and the royal family. It cannot have been a companionable journey.

Underlying the rumours about Gaunt's designs on the throne was a renewed concern about the validity of the prince's marriage, which raised the question of Richard's legitimacy. It is impossible to determine who started the rumours or why they persisted so stubbornly, but there is no doubt that they were politically motivated. For decades the papacy had consistently used the Pope's power to grant dispensations facilitating marriages to influence one or other side in the Anglo-French conflict, and the Pope's alleged threat to declare Richard illegitimate after Limoges in 1370 was a clever ploy which served the purpose of weakening the English position at a time when the Pope was anxious to be seen as supportive to the French king. Similarly the rumour in 1376 that Gaunt was plotting with Charles V to secure a papal bull which declared Richard illegitimate not only increased Gaunt's unpopularity but undermined unity in the court circle. These rumours would have been in circulation throughout the court as well as in Parliament and there can be no doubt that they would have been reported to Joan. She, more than anyone, knew just how vulnerable her marriage was to an attack of this kind. William Montague was still alive, and it was, of course, perfectly possible for the Pope to overturn his predecessors' decisions and declare her marriage to the prince invalid, despite the effort that Edward III and the prince had made to ensure its validity. The prince himself had always been conscious of the threat, and his heartfelt plea to his father and brother on his deathbed to show favour to Richard reflected this, while demonstrating that he had absolute faith in their support for his son. But did anyone really intend to threaten it? William had never shown the slightest interest in doing so and on the contrary had remained on good terms with Joan and become a close ally of the prince. The charge laid at Gaunt's door was also groundless. Although he was ambitious, and had the most to gain by doing so, he was genuinely and completely loyal to his father and brother, as well as sincerely fond of his sister-in-law, and he fully supported Richard, actively promoting his nephew's interests after the prince died.

Nevertheless, Joan was deeply affected by the fear that Richard's position was dependent on the legitimacy of her marriage, and she knew that how she was perceived could attract or repel support for him. Her role was crucial, and her good reputation vital. It was therefore natural for her to seek to nurture that good reputation, and deflect attention away from her, and this entailed staying aloof from the political arena. There can be no doubt that Joan, as the widowed Princess of Wales and mother of the heir to the throne, had enormous potential influence in public affairs. In addition, as the prince's widow Joan was an exceptionally wealthy woman. She was now entitled to her own estates as Countess of Kent in her own right, and in addition she received one-third of his estates (in Chester, Cornwall and Wales, which between them brought in an annual income of around £8,600) as her dower, to enjoy for the rest of her life.

Wealth brought with it power. Yet the only area where her influence and concern was apparent was for Richard's personal safety and well-being. She wanted Richard to remain under her care, as she and the prince had discussed. In the months before his death, and on his deathbed, the prince had clearly indicated in his actions and his words that he wanted his wife and son to remain together. With Richard confirmed as Prince of Wales and heir to the throne it would have been appropriate for him to have had his own household, as his father and grandfather had done. Edward III could have chosen to appoint a guardian for the young prince, as had been done for Henry III, or placed Richard in the care of his uncle Gaunt. But the king, and Gaunt, had no intention of separating Joan from Richard. In October 1376, on Gaunt's information, the king and his council, with Gaunt acting for his father, made orders for Richard to be created Prince of Wales, and confirmed Joan in her own estates and dower rights.[10] The remainder of the prince's estates went to Richard, and the young prince now had ample funds to support his own household and had his own receiver, John Fordham, while his tutor, Simon Burley, became chamberlain of his household. There was no suggestion that Richard should be removed from his mother's household and given an independent establishment. His income was paid to Joan to recompense her for supporting him, and 'in consideration of her great charges on his behalf after his father's death, both before and after he was a prince'.[11] Within a few weeks of the prince's burial it was formally confirmed that Richard would remain with his mother, and Edward III paid £200 for his grandson's expenses to Joan's clerk William Fulbourne, the first of many such payments.[12] While it was unlikely that anyone would have disagreed with the king over such a sensitive issue, the fact that there does not appear to have been a single dissenting voice about the arrangement also reflects the universal esteem with which Joan was regarded.

Managing the prince's affairs took a considerable amount of time, and it was more than four years later when the last of the dower estates were confirmed to Joan. However, with a typically thoughtful and considered gesture, Joan requested that in the interim her son should receive her dower share of the income from the estates.[13] With her place at Richard's side confirmed, Joan was providing public affirmation of her concern that her son's interests should come before her own. In the meantime Joan and Richard remained living at Kennington. This was Joan's decision, determined to ensure that Richard's daily routine was maintained, and that few, if any, changes were made to their household. His education, under the tutelage of Simon Burley, continued with few interruptions, and the strong network of support within the household, including his half-brother, John Holand, and his half-sister, Maud Courtenay, as well as the company of other young nobles, including John of Gaunt's son Henry of Derby, who was the same age, and Robert de Vere, five years his elder, was retained. The Duchess of Brittany, Joan's younger daughter, was almost certainly part of the household also, as John Montfort remained an exile from his own country and did not return to Brittany until August 1379, while the duchess did not join her husband there until 1382.[14]

Gaunt returned from the prince's interment with resolve and determination to reverse the proceedings of the Good Parliament. A meeting of the great council was called which he chaired as royal lieutenant and the Good Parliament was declared invalid and its acts annulled. A new speaker, Sir Thomas Hungerford, Gaunt's steward and a member of his council, and who had also served the prince, was elected. Latimer was pardoned and resumed his seat, Sir Peter de la Mare was arrested and imprisoned, and Alice Perrers was allowed back to court. There was satisfaction for Gaunt in restoring Latimer, which Joan probably shared. Latimer had been one of the prince's retainers, he had taken part in Gaunt's expeditions, and had a family connection with Joan through Thomas Latimer, the son of Roger de la Warr's sister. When he had been impeached, his mainpernors (guarantors for his attendance) had been John Clanvowe, William Neville, Philip la Vache, John Montague and William Beauchamp.[15] Gaunt was personally enraged that his old friend William Wykeham, Bishop of Winchester, had been one of Latimer's principal prosecutors in the Good Parliament and, taking advantage of his initiative, ensured that Wykeham was banned from court and had his temporalities forfeited. His animosity towards Wykeham was intemperate and has never been fully explained; possibly Gaunt felt the bishop's move against Latimer was a personal betrayal. Whatever the cause, it was certainly unfortunate, as the bishop had also been a close friend of the prince's and was his principal executor after Gaunt. The two men needed to be able to work together. But for the time being Gaunt's wishes prevailed, and Wykeham was in disgrace and his temporalities were granted to Richard. All the proceedings were now being directed by Gaunt, who lost no time in restoring his family's solidarity and its prestige, making his own loyalties quite clear. Richard was created Prince of Wales, while Gaunt's youngest brother, Thomas of Woodstock, was made constable of England.

In January 1377 Parliament was called again, and Gaunt arranged for his nephew to preside over proceedings, hoping no doubt that the young prince's presence would encourage the Commons to unify in support of the Crown. His hopes were largely met as the Commons quickly responded by voting for the requested poll tax. There was no doubt of Richard's popularity. Just two days before Parliament convened, on 25 January, the City of London organised a tremendous entertainment for the young prince, arranging for a company of 130 mummers to ride out to Kennington from Newgate through Cheapside and across London Bridge. The event was well planned with the mummers dressed in various guises such as knights and squires and various clerical officials, and bearing a gift of loaded dice for the young prince. Joan and John of

Gaunt ensured a public display of royal unity by appearing with Richard when he received the revellers, together with his royal uncles Edmund of Langley and Thomas of Woodstock, and various other members of the aristocracy. Richard played dice with some of the mummers and won three gold objects, wine was provided and there was a party atmosphere, with dancing accompanied by minstrels.[16]

The proceedings of the parliament in January 1377 did not go as smoothly as Gaunt had hoped. The bishops in convocation refused to grant the requested poll tax until the Bishop of Winchester was reinstated. Gaunt's animosity towards Wykeham was unabated, and was no doubt exacerbated by the fact that the leader of the convocation was an old adversary, Bishop Courtenay, who had also played a prominent role in the Good Parliament. Gaunt refused to agree. A personal battle of wills developed between him and Bishop Courtenay. Courtenay's response was to summon Gaunt's protégé, the radical Oxford theologian and scholar John Wyclif, to appear before the convocation to answer charges regarding his teachings on the Church. Wyclif was an obvious and easy target. In sermons and treatises he advocated a devout and simple life, critical of what he saw as secular preoccupation among many of the clergy, and he had bravely preached against ecclesiastical abuses. He was also fiercely against the war with France, describing it as evil. Although his anti-papal and anti-clerical opinions were received with sympathy in some quarters, including that of Gaunt, his views were controversial and potentially heretical. Courtenay arranged for Wyclif to be summoned to appear before a bench of bishops on the charge of heresy. Gaunt realised that the attack was really directed at him rather than his protégé, and engaged several doctors of divinity to speak in Wyclif's defence, attending the inquiry in the lady chapel of St Paul's in person. However, his insistence on bringing an armed following with him did nothing to reduce the tension, and a bitter row broke out between him and Courtenay.

Wyclif's trial was well publicised, and inconclusive. When it broke up in confusion, there were rumours that Gaunt had either threatened or harmed the bishop. Angry mobs of Londoners took to the streets, looking for ways to attack Gaunt. The violence soon got out of hand, despite Courtenay's attempts to placate the rioters.[17] Gaunt's Savoy Palace was attacked, and anyone wearing his livery was in danger of being assaulted. Gaunt himself, with his companion Henry Percy, was having dinner at the house of Sir John d'Ypres, eating oysters, and as the mob advanced they were forced to flee for their lives. Gaunt chose to take to the water and row to Kennington, trusting that Joan would take them in, and that she would be able to protect him. Meanwhile the Londoners proclaimed Gaunt to be a traitor, and bills were posted suggesting he was the son of a butcher in Ghent and a changeling, not the real son of Edward III and Queen Philippa. With feelings running high, it was a difficult and dangerous situation. However, Joan had no hesitation in giving Gaunt and

Percy shelter, or in using her personal influence to defuse the situation. According to the chronicler Walsingham, 'the princess, after hearing what they had to say, consoled them with such words as she could for the time being, promising to settle the whole issue to their advantage, as in fact she did'.[18] She immediately sent three of her most trusted knights, Aubrey de Vere, Simon Burley and Lewis Clifford, to speak directly with the citizens of London, entreating with them that they make peace with the duke. Walsingham records that 'she asked the citizens to be reconciled to the duke on the grounds that she was pleading for this and loved them, and to bring such serious disturbances to an end because of the wider trouble that usually followed such civil strife'. Joan knew that the Londoners held her in high regard and she was right to appeal to them in her own name. For love of her they agreed, albeit grudgingly. According to Walsingham, they agreed, saying that 'with all respect that out of regard for her they would do whatever she commanded'.[19] The duke was not forgiven, and his behaviour not forgotten, but for the time being peace and harmony was restored.

This was Joan's first public foray into politics, and she risked her own reputation in coming to the aid of a man who was deeply unpopular, in doing so jeopardising her political neutrality. Yet she had shown no hesitation in doing so. Joan's reaction to the crisis, and her willingness to take independent action, indicates her confidence in her own ability. While her swift and immediate response showed the depth of her concern for Gaunt, and the close bond between them, it also showed that she was capable of handling a difficult and dangerous situation with considerable skill. Although she knew that the Londoners regarded her highly, she did not presume that they would automatically agree to her intervention. She was careful in her approach, exercising tact and discretion. Each of the three knights chosen was known for their association with the prince, and none were prominent in politics, so making them acceptable to the Londoners. They were also acceptable to Gaunt for the same reasons, while also being known and trusted by him; both Clifford and Burley had received gifts from him in the past.[20] They were also loyal to Joan and Richard, Clifford being married to her friend Eleanor, while Burley was Richard's tutor and de Vere one of the prince's old retainers. Joan instructed them to appeal to the Londoners in her name, relying on her personal influence. There was no mention of the king or of Prince Richard, and she made no command. Appealing to the Londoners on the basis of their regard for her was shrewd, allowing them to concede without losing face. By acting quickly and tactfully her sure touch defused an explosive situation. John of Gaunt had been right to have faith in his sister-in-law. Joan had shown that she was a natural conciliator, possessing sensitivity and judgement. While Gaunt stayed with her at Kennington, they had an opportunity to discuss what had happened, and Joan may have helped her brother-in-law to see that his dogged intransigence over Wykeham had been largely responsible for creating the crisis. In future, John showed great respect for Joan's judgement, and the strong bond between them was strengthened.

The winter of 1377 was cold and hard, and melting snow caused floods in Northumberland.[21] The king had spent Christmas at Havering-atte-Bower, and it is likely that he requested his heir's presence. Due to Edward III's deteriorating health and mental state the king was taking less interest in affairs and making fewer decisions. Joan, meanwhile, was increasingly seen as a force in politics. In February 1377 the lieutenant in Aquitaine, Thomas Felton (the prince's old servant), noted that Henry of Trastámara in Castile appeared to be building up shipping and troops with a view to invading England with the assistance of a claimant to the title Prince of Wales, one Owain Lawgoch.[22] A copy of Felton's communication to his deputies was sent to Joan from one of her dower Welsh provinces, warning her of the threat of invasion, advising her to take appropriate measures, clearly anticipating that she would act on the information and be able to take effective steps to counter it.[23] Joan may have received the letter at Kennington before she left the capital with Richard to spend time at Berkhamsted once the parliament had ended, and after conferring with her council the intelligence was passed directly to the king's council at Westminster. The threat was treated very seriously and on 15 March orders were issued to Gaunt and others to fortify their castles in Wales to defend against an invasion. The writer of the letter, in addressing the letter to Joan rather than sending it directly to the king or even to Parliament, evidently regarded the Princess of Wales as a trusted and authoritative figure, and someone who could be depended on to resolve a matter of national emergency.

Although Gaunt had earlier shown little enthusiasm for a renewed attack on France, he realised that the threat could not be ignored and he was at the forefront of the initiative to take active steps to ward off an invasion. A fresh expedition to France was proposed and on 23 April, St George's Day, Prince Richard and his cousin Henry of Bolingbroke (Gaunt's son) were knighted and admitted to the Order of the Garter, along with their uncle Thomas of Woodstock and other young nobles, in anticipation of their participation in the expedition. Ships were requisitioned, troops arrayed and contracts of service drawn up. The main expedition leaders were to be Prince Richard, Gaunt, Richard's brother-in-law the Duke of Brittany, his uncle Thomas of Woodstock, the Earl of Warwick, Lord William Latimer, Sir Guy Brian, Sir Michael de la Pole and two of the prince's knights, Sir Richard Stury and Sir Philip la Vache. Clearly the ten-year-old Prince of Wales was only expected to be leader in name only; Gaunt would be the principal captain. By June the preparations were well in hand with seventy ships in London, and the departure date imminent.[24] Then, on 21 June, Edward III died. This changed everything. The expedition's departure was immediately postponed, then delayed indefinitely, until eventually the whole affair was abandoned.

The king died at his palace at Sheen during the evening of 21 June 1377. According to Walsingham, Edward III was attended solely by a priest who spent some time persuading the old king to make his peace with God, having been abandoned at the end by his knights and esquires, and by his mistress Alice Perrers, who left his bedside after stripping the rings from his hands, having already received great wealth and vast numbers of possessions from the infatuated king.[25] If this account is correct, then it was a sad ending for a man who had been a hugely successful and popular king, and in direct contrast to the dignified and honourable death of his eldest son just eleven months beforehand. It seems inconceivable that his surviving children, John of Gaunt, Edmund of Langley, Thomas of Woodstock and Princess Isabella, would have abandoned their father in this way, and it is hard to imagine that Joan would have neglected her father-in-law, however difficult the personal relationship between them had been. Edward III had been in failing health for some time, and it may be that none of them realised quite how ill he had become, distracted by the preparations for the invasion of France. Indeed, Walsingham states that the king's death came 'almost unexpectedly' and that 'he was suddenly taken by surprise by the day of his death'.[26] Joan was with Richard at Kennington when the news was brought to them, within easy travelling distance of Sheen; had they appreciated the king was dying they would have made haste to be with him. However, in contrast to Walsingham, Froissart describes the king as being surrounded by his family, and certainly his three sons, John, Edmund and Thomas, were all present at Sheen the following day.[27]

Edward III had been king for fifty years, an extremely long time in an age where the average life expectancy was many years less than that. Most of the nobility, indeed most of the population, could not remember a time before Edward had been king. For most of his reign he had enjoyed huge popularity, and had successfully reconciled public opinion to his foreign policy. However, the glorious earlier days of his reign, the stunning victories he and his son had won in France, the spectacular celebratory tournaments and the enormous riches gained during the French campaigns were all becoming distant memories, while the last few years of his reign had been soured by successive crises, caused largely by the costly and unsuccessful French campaigns after 1369 which had achieved so little and tarnished the reputations of those participating (notably Gaunt) and by the increasingly tempestuous relationship between the Crown and Parliament. Economically, most of the population were still suffering from the combined effects of the Black Death, poor harvests and the taxes levied to pay for the war in France. Much was hoped for with a change of monarch, not least an end to the divisiveness and failure associated with those last years.

The king himself was determined that his grandson would succeed him and did his best to ensure a smooth transition. The prince and the king had always been conscious that despite every effort they made the validity of the prince's marriage would remain susceptible to challenge, and Richard's position was greatly weakened by the fact that it was certain he would be a minor when the king died. Edward III did his best to make a last attempt to circumvent any possibility of his grandson being supplanted as his heir. In preparation for his death he drew up his will, one of the witnesses being Sir Richard Stury, and in an entail specifically designated Richard as his successor.[28] He bolstered Joan's position, confirming his public approval of her by mentioning her first in his will, leaving 'the wife of our eldest son Edward' 1,000 marks, although he was not able to bring warmth to the gesture, and the tone is coldly formal, unlike his reference to 'our dear daughter Isabel for her support and that of her daughter 300 marks'.[29] Richard was still only a child of ten and his peaceful accession to the throne was by no means assured. He could easily be displaced by a powerful and ambitious adult, especially if there was insufficient support. As Edward III lay dying, many in Parliament feared that Richard might not become king and that Gaunt intended to seize the throne for himself. If Richard was not the rightful heir, then Gaunt, as the king's eldest surviving son, had a strong claim to be his successor. Gaunt was the richest and the most powerful noble in the land, and he was also, at thirty-seven, in the prime of life and supremely healthy. But Parliament's suspicion of Gaunt was misplaced, as the duke remained steadfastly loyal to his father and older brother, and did everything in his power to support his nephew and ensure a smooth succession. However, Parliament's distrust of Gaunt in demanding that Richard be created Prince of Wales after his father's death had the additional effect of affirming their recognition and acceptance of Richard's legitimacy, making a challenge to his position less likely. In the event, when Edward III died, no one came forward to challenge Richard's right to succeed his grandfather.

Gaunt's loyalty and determination to support his nephew was greatly facilitated by the fact that he enjoyed an affectionate and trusting relationship with Joan. As Richard was only ten when he became king, his mother's guidance and support behind the scenes was all important. The relationship between Joan and her brother-in-law was crucial, and they openly supported each other in working to further the interests of the prince's son. Joan's quiet influence was increasingly apparent as the months passed. When Edward III died the citizens of London sent a deputation to Kennington, conveying their respects and stressing their loyalty, requesting Richard's presence in London and asking him to resolve the quarrel between the city and the Duke of Lancaster. The following day, on 22 June, Thomas Latimer, Nicholas Bond, Simon Burley and Richard Abberbury, on Richard's behalf (though in practice almost certainly chosen by Joan), explained to London citizens that Gaunt had agreed to submit to the king's will and asking them to do likewise. According to Walsingham there then ensued over six hours of discussion as the citizens were alarmed by such a formula for peace and felt that Richard, as a boy, was too weak to protect them. Eventually they agreed, on the basis that Latimer, Bond, Burley and Abberbury gave personal pledges of assurance that if the Londoners submitted it would be to their advantage and 'not to their prejudice'.[30] Their success was reported back to Gaunt and the scene set for a public reconciliation. A second deputation of London citizens was then received by Richard, attended by his mother and by his uncles, in a display of family unity. Gaunt knelt before Richard and asked the young king to pardon the Londoners, and to be reconciled to them. The unexpected spectacle of the proud duke publicly abasing himself, described as a 'miracle' by Walsingham, followed by the duke kissing each and every one of the citizens in front of the king 'as a sign that peace was not feigned', was a piece of deliberate stage theatre which had the desired effect, and the citizens of London went home in peace.[31]

This was followed by a public reconciliation between Gaunt and Wykeham, with a full pardon and release of Peter de la Mare.[32] Publicly the credit for these conciliatory gestures was given to Richard, as Walsingham lauded:

> The young king, because of his own innate goodness, desiring that there be peace among his subjects everywhere, at the very beginning of his reign reunited the duke and the bishop of Winchester ... also whenever he discovered that a dispute had arisen anywhere in his kingdom he dealt with the case at issue himself, promising an outcome which would be advantageous and profitable to both parties. It was a happy beginning in a boy of so young an age, that he should be anxious about peace without anyone putting pressure upon him, and should know that peace was beneficial to his people without anyone telling him to do so.[33]

Walsingham's fulsome accolade makes no mention of Joan, but there can be little doubt of her guiding hand behind Richard. Hostile and acrimonious relationships were dangerous and could only damage the start of his reign. The pattern of personal intervention, of listening to both sides, of promising a solution which would be to both parties' advantage, were Joan's style, traits she used whenever she was involved. At every step she was behind Richard, counselling and advising him on handling each situation, helping him to restore harmony and peace. Her sure touch in conciliation was behind the reconciliation with Gaunt, her calming and reassuring presence facilitating his timely contrition, and it seems likely that it was Joan who suggested, and persuaded, Gaunt to adopt the humbling role in which he was cast.

All was now set for Richard's coronation.

12

The King's Mother
1377–1385

Many great things were hoped for in the time of this Richard's reign.

Adam Usk

Richard's succession was heralded with joy and his coronation was held on Thursday 16 July 1377, just three weeks after his grandfather's death and eleven days after Edward III's funeral was held at Westminster Abbey on 5 July.[1] Hopes and expectations of the young boy were high. Once Richard was safely crowned, what part would Joan play, and how would his accession change her position? Would she retire gracefully, or remain at the centre of affairs? Crucially, Richard was only ten years old, and his youth, and vulnerability, would be a decisive factor in her decisions. Although he would be surrounded by powerful people anxious to guide and influence him, he would need protection from those ambitious for their own interests. This included his father's family, in particular his uncles. What place would Richard's half-brothers and sisters have in the new regime, and would Joan encourage him to enhance their standing?

Richard had accompanied the old king's cortege as it made its solemn procession from Sheen to Westminster, stopping overnight at Wandsworth and Southwark.[2] Then it was his turn to be the centre of attention and, on the eve of the coronation, Richard slowly travelled from the Tower to Westminster through Cheapside, Fleet Street and down the Strand past the Savoy Palace. The city was decorated with gold and silver, with numerous bright silk banners above a series of newly constructed displays designed to entertain and amaze the crowds. The streets were thronged with well-wishers, with ample supplies of refreshments, provided in ingenious ways, with wine pouring out of the pipes of an aqueduct and from parts of the tower constructed in the market at Cheapside, and in such abundance that the wine lasted for over three hours. Preceding the procession were flute players, trumpeters, drummers and others musicians, all plying their instruments, proudly announcing the arrival of the young king. Trumpeters were posted by the Londoners above the aqueduct and at the tower, to blow their horns as the king arrived, maidens dressed in white blew gold petals and tossed imitation gold coins at the young king as he passed. Leading the procession were groups of loyal citizens, each wearing their own matching and differently coloured apparel, from Gascony as well as from the different London wards, followed by the nobility in order of seniority, earls, barons and knights, all attired in white, signifying innocence, in honour of Richard, making a blaze of colour and magnificence.[3] Each group had their own trumpeter. Henry Percy, the Marshal of England, and Gaunt as steward of England, rode great chargers, accompanied by men from their retinue, clearing a path for the king. Richard rode behind, splendidly attired in regal robes, with his tutor Simon Burley beside him, carrying his sword, while his father's squire, Nicholas Bond, held the horse's reins. The entire cavalcade took over three hours to process their way to Westminster. It was a day of revelry and joy, splendid, festive and clamorously noisy, all in honour of the small boy described by the chronicler Adam of Usk as 'fair among men as another Absalom'.[4]

Richard and Joan spent the night in Westminster Palace. Early on the following morning the Archbishop of Canterbury, Simon Sudbury, accompanied by the senior bishops, arrived to escort their young charge to the church of St Peter in the abbey itself for the coronation service. The way was led by the three great offices of state: the steward, marshal and constable – Gaunt, Percy and Thomas of Woodstock – all walking on foot, followed by the senior clergy and nobility. The service was conducted by Sudbury, and everyone of importance attended. William Montague, Joan's erstwhile husband, carried one of the ceremonial vestments. The coronation ceremony took place first, followed by a Mass. Once the service was concluded, and the newly crowned king acclaimed, a long state banquet followed. Richard was so exhausted he was carried back to the palace afterwards by Simon Burley, losing a shoe in the process. The whole affair went smoothly, watched over and controlled by Gaunt's benevolent, omnipotent presence. Gaunt had arranged and managed the proceedings entirely. No one could doubt his right to do so, and there was no one more suitable. Gaunt was the most senior nobleman and the king's eldest uncle; as Earl of Leicester he was the king's steward, as Duke of Lancaster he had the right to carry the king's principal sword and as Earl of Lincoln he was entitled to carve for the king at the coronation banquet. During the coronation itself he delegated the task of carrying the sword to his son Henry of Bolingbroke, and the Earl of Stafford cut Richard's meat and bread at the table at Westminster hall.[5] Eventually the long day ended, as Walsingham recorded: 'It was a day of joy and gladness ... the long awaited day of the renewal of peace and of the laws of the land, long exiled by the weakness of an aged king and the greed of his courtiers and servants.'[6]

For Joan, watching proudly as her youngest child swore his solemn oath and was proclaimed king, it was a day of great emotion, her joy mixed with sadness. Once she had anticipated that this day would belong to the prince, her husband; now it was their son who stood there, dressed in his coronation finery, barely old enough to understand the proceedings. Gaunt is rightly credited with the day's success, but there can be no doubt that he consulted and conferred with Joan at every opportunity and that her views would have been taken into account. It was an event for which both had planned over many months, working together in harmony, and considerable thought was given to all aspects of the event. Most of the preparations dealt with the practicalities of the event, as the actual ceremony itself was based on long-standing tradition. Nevertheless two small, seemingly innocuous changes were made affecting the coronation oath, and Joan's influence may well have been responsible for one of these. The coronation oath taken by Richard was essentially the same as that sworn by his grandfather, Edward III, and his great-grandfather Edward II; Richard swore to uphold the laws and customs of his ancestors, to protect the Church and the clergy, to do justice to all and to uphold the laws which the people chose. Traditionally the Archbishop of Canterbury presented the king to the congregation before the oath was taken, asking them to confirm their consent. In theory, at least, this format gave the assembly an opportunity to refuse, although it was extremely unlikely and had never happened. Richard took the oath first, and so was presented to the congregation as their king, with their positive response acting as an affirmation of his kingship. The effect of this change was to remove any elective element from the coronation while emphasising the legitimacy of his succession.[7] The long-standing concern regarding the legal validity of the prince's marriage to Joan probably explains the purpose behind this alteration, providing a powerful and incontrovertible barrier to anyone who might seek to challenge Richard's right of succession.[8] The other change was to the wording of one clause of the oath, inserting the words 'just and reasonably' to describe the laws chosen by the people. This clause was the most restrictive of the king's powers and had been added in 1307 when Edward II succeeded his father. The qualification would give the king a means to limit its effect on his powers. Gaunt was careful to ensure that a full record was kept of the coronation and its proceedings, and in his capacity as steward of England he delivered the record to chancery with his own hands.[9] The change made to the order of the oath was emphasised at the first parliament of the new reign when the Archbishop of Canterbury, in his opening speech on 13 October, stated that Richard was king 'not by election nor by any other way but by lawful right of inheritance'.

A new king and a new regime afforded the opportunity to create new members of the nobility, both to reward loyal and faithful friends and to bolster support for Richard. Four new earls were created just before the banquet held after the coronation ceremony, the greatest number to be so awarded since 1337, and again this was a staged and planned event. Though the titles were conferred by Richard he would have been prompted in their selection by those closest to him, almost certainly his uncle and his mother. His uncle Thomas of Woodstock was created Earl of Buckingham, Richard's first tutor Guichard d'Angle became Earl of Huntingdon, while Gaunt's friends and loyal supporters Henry Percy and Thomas Mowbray became respectively Earl of Northumberland and Nottingham. The elevation of d'Angle to a lifetime-only peerage was the most personal award, reflecting the regard with which he had been held by Richard's parents while he had served them as the boy's tutor, and was unlikely to be contentious as it was generally recognised as a just reward for his services to the young king. Joan's hand in his selection, supported by Gaunt, seems self-evident. Thomas of Woodstock was the only one of Edward III's sons who had not been granted an earldom in his father's lifetime. Both d'Angle and Thomas were also given an income of £1,000 a year to support their new status, a thoughtful addition as their newly created earldoms did not bring income and estates with them. Thomas was an ambitious and able young man, and while there was no reason to doubt his loyalty, with his nephew's accession it was natural and prudent to give him the status to which he was entitled by birth. Gaunt was anxious to promote family solidarity, and Joan had her father's experience to warn her of the dangers of overlooking royal relations. Henry Percy and Thomas Mowbray were wealthy and powerful northern barons who had proved their loyalty to the Crown during Edward III's last years, and their promotion was accepted with equanimity despite their connections with Gaunt and the latter's continuing unpopularity.

Richard was only ten years old. Clearly he was not old enough to direct his own household unassisted, let alone govern the country. The crown had passed to a minor only twice before; more than 150 years earlier in 1216 when King John died, leaving his nine-year-old son Henry to succeed him, and when Edward III had replaced his father in 1327 following Edward II's deposition. In 1216 the country had been in a state of civil war, which the death of King John halted but did not extinguish. There was a paramount need for a strong, authoritative figure to protect the royal interest, and this was provided by William Marshal, who became regent. The obvious candidate to be regent now was John of Gaunt, as the most powerful and richest noble, and the king's most senior uncle. But Gaunt was deeply unpopular, and he himself realised that any authority wielded by him in Richard's name would potentially harm the young king. Neither of his brothers would have been thought suitable candidates, as Edmund of Langley and Thomas of Woodstock lacked Gaunt's ability, gravitas and authority. Instead, the device to cover the day-to-day running of the country was the establishment of a council of twelve leading peers, with each rank represented: two earls, two barons, two prelates, two bannerets and four knights. This was similar to the council set up in 1327 to rule in the young Edward III's name after his father was removed from the throne.

What role could, or should, Joan take? Henry III's mother, the dowager queen Isabella of Angoulême, found she had no role in the new regime, and returned to France, leaving her son in the regent's care. This was not an option for Joan. In 1327, when Edward III had been crowned at the age of fourteen, it had been a theatrical and carefully stage-managed action to legitimise the removal of his father Edward II from the throne and to mask the seizure of power by his mother Isabella and her lover Roger Mortimer. Joan's situation was hardly comparable; nevertheless, after Richard's accession her position did subtly and irrevocably change. Although she had been one of the most important women at court for many years she was now the most senior and would remain so until her son married. In some respects there was no role model for her to follow as the king's mother. The precedents of Queen Isabella, and Henry III's mother, Isabella of Angoulême, were of limited value in guiding her. They had both been foreign princesses as well as queens, enjoying an independent authority and status Joan lacked. Yet Joan had advantages they did not have. The country was more stable and united in 1377 than it had been in either 1216 or 1327, and Joan was on extremely good terms with the strongest magnate in the land, John of Gaunt. Richard was very close to his mother and, aged ten, was rather younger than Edward III had been when he succeeded to the throne, and it is unlikely he would have resented her influence in the way Edward III had done with his mother. As the prince's wife she had gradually earned respect and affection, and she was genuinely universally well regarded by 1377. In addition, unlike her mother-in-law Queen Philippa and Edward III's mother Isabella, Joan was independently wealthy and had no need of income from the Crown to maintain a lifestyle commensurate with her status. Her position, greatly enhanced now that Richard was king, coupled with her wealth, gave her considerable potential to extend her influence. Queen Isabella had taken advantage of Edward III's minority to exercise power in the political arena as well as enhancing her own wealth, and rewarded her family and her friends. Arguably Joan could have done likewise. But Joan was a completely different personality and had absolutely no intention of repeating Isabella's example. In 1377 there were still some who remembered this time, and even those who had been born afterwards had heard and seen the consequences of Isabella's use of power, enriching herself and her lover, usurping the authority of the Crown for her own interests. As Joan knew, women were generally expected to play a passive role, and be of no political consequence. The idea that Joan might become regent for her son was never entertained, and it was certainly not one that she herself ever put forward.

As Richard had his powerful uncle to protect him, and a council to rule for him, Joan could have decided at this stage to retire from court. Now that Richard was king there could be no question of him continuing to live in his mother's household, or staying resident largely in Kennington as he had done in the months after his father's death. He was naturally expected to live in the royal palaces with his own household and retinue. Wallingford was Joan's favourite home and not too far from court, so that it would have been possible for her to visit easily whenever she wanted or was required to do so. Joan may well have considered it, and secured the appointment of Aubrey de Vere to be steward of the castle in October 1377.[10] But Richard was still very young and, despite the acclamation with which his accession had been greeted, and the support of his uncle Gaunt, his position was by no means secure. Joan did not yet feel that she wanted to leave him. Her overriding concern seems to have been to protect Richard and provide him with support. As the king's mother Joan had enormous influence, but she was so discreet in exercising it that it is hard to discern. Joan was clearly still wary of attracting attention in any way which might be detrimental to Richard and had no intention of becoming openly associated with the politics of the new regime. However, she was instrumental in enabling the appointment of many of those who would serve her son in his household. Inevitably there were many courtiers seeking positions close to the new king to further their own interests, and some who would see it as their right to do so by virtue of their rank. It was important for Joan that her son was surrounded by familiar, trusted retainers who would have his interests at heart rather than their own, and to a large extent she was able to ensure this. The emotional attachment between Richard and his tutor, Simon Burley, was strong, but now that Richard was king their time together would inevitably become more limited. On the day of his coronation Richard appointed Simon Burley master of falcons and keeper of the mews at Charing Cross, and in August he was made constable of Windsor Castle and given responsibility for looking after Kennington Palace.[11] In addition, Burley was appointed a chamber knight. These appointments were both a reward and ensured that Burley would have responsibilities which would keep him close to the king, even when he no longer needed as a tutor. The personal chamber of the king, where he slept, was guarded by chamber knights acting as bodyguards. They, and the chamber squires, would spend most of their time close to Richard. Although there is no direct evidence showing Joan was responsible for their appointment, there can be no doubt that she was behind it. Apart from Simon Burley, the other chamber knights appointed to serve Richard were mainly knights whom he had known from early childhood, who had served his father and retained a close bond with Joan: Richard's first tutor Richard Abberbury, Nicholas Bond, Lewis Clifford, Aubrey de Vere, William Beauchamp (married to Thomas Holand's sister-in-law, Joan, daughter of Richard, Earl of Arundel), William Neville, Baldwin Bereford, John Burley, Peter Courtenay, Nicholas Sarnesfield, as well as his half-brother John Holand, and John Holand's erstwhile guardian John Hay. In addition, nearly half of Richard's chamber squires (nine of nineteen) were also former servants of his father.[12] Richard Stury, another trusted knight and already a chamber knight under Edward III, continued in office.[13] Later William Neville and John Clanvowe, two other knights in the same circle, also became chamber knights.[14] All received allowances and fees as members of the household, and the chamber knights were granted annuities; Clanvowe and Neville each received 100 marks a year in May 1381.[15] Among the clerks entering Richard's service were several old servants of his father, such as William Packington (Joan's receiver), Reginald Hilton, Alan Stokes (the prince's receiver), John Fordham (the prince's secretary), and, significantly, Robert Braybrooke, who was appointed Richard's secretary on 20 August 1377.[16]

As the senior female member of the court Joan's own taste and preferences would undoubtedly have influenced the tone of the new court, but it is surprisingly difficult to ascertain these. This is in part due to the fact that there are no personal or financial records to indicate how Joan preferred to spend her time, and partly also to her success in adopting a discreet presence. However, it can hardly be a coincidence that many of the knights Joan chose to keep close to her were men with sophisticated literary taste. Simon Burley, Lewis Clifford, Richard Stury and Philip la Vache (later married to Lewis Clifford's daughter Elizabeth) were all enthusiastic book owners, of both serious-minded reading and courtly romances like *The Romance of the Rose*, while John Clanvowe wrote verse in English (his one surviving work is *The Book of Cupid*, originally thought to have been written by Chaucer[17]), and Sir John Montague (William Montague's cousin, who had been one of the prince's knights and continued in Richard's service, and became steward of the household in October 1381) wrote verses in French.[18] Some of them were close friends of Geoffrey Chaucer, whom Joan would have known well. As a young man Chaucer had held a position in the household of Elizabeth de Burgh (Prince Lionel's first wife), before joining the court as a squire, and he had gone to France on the ill-fated Rheims campaign in 1369, where he was captured. He was married to Philippa de Roet, whose sister Katherine Swynford had become governess to John of Gaunt's daughters, and then his mistress. Shortly after Richard's accession to the throne, in 1378, Chaucer had been appointed to be one of the confidential marriage commissioners negotiating the young king's marriage.[19] Although Chaucer was by this time a professional royal servant with considerable experience, he would hardly have achieved this appointment to a matter of such importance to Joan without her approval. Although there is no record of Joan having promoted or patronised Chaucer, or of his having dedicated any of his writings to her, it seems highly likely that Joan would have encouraged and welcomed his attendance at her young son's court, and enjoyed his work when he read them out to the assembled court.

Joan's religious views are not clear. The prince had been conventionally religious, patronising several religious foundations, most notably St Albans Abbey, but he had shown a marked devotion to the Trinity. There is no evidence that Joan shared the prince's interest in the Trinity. The only foundation that Joan is known to have supported is the Benedictine foundation at St Albans, but this does not give any indication of her individual taste, as the abbey enjoyed widespread support among the royal family, having been patronised by Edward III and Queen Philippa as well as the prince, and John of Gaunt was an equally generous patron, giving the monks numerous gifts and making frequent donations.[20] Joan's aunt Blanche Wake and her cousin Margaret, Countess of Norfolk, were also patrons.[21] The abbot, Thomas de la Mare, had been a personal friend of the prince, and was on similarly good terms with John of Gaunt. In supporting St Albans Joan was doing no more than was expected of her, and it is likely that she was also on good terms with de la Mare as she stayed at the abbey on several occasions after the prince's death. The abbey kept a careful list of its benefactors, the more important beautifully illustrated in the *Liber Benefactorum*, now in the British Library. This contains an image of Joan, indicating that they considered her one of their more important patrons, although this may have had more to do with her status as Princess of Wales than with the generosity she displayed towards them.

There is some evidence of a link between Joan and the Franciscan order, starting with the reinterment of Thomas Holand in the Franciscan church at Stamford (though she may simply have been carrying out his wishes), and in 1380 an astronomical calendar was composed by John Somer, a Franciscan, at the bidding of Thomas Kingsbury, provincial of the Franciscans, 'at the request of the most noble lady, Joan Princess of Wales'.[22] The calendar contained an algorism table, a table of dominical letters, feast days, a calendar of English saints, ruling planets, signs of the zodiac, a table of solar and lunar eclipses, and tables of conjunctions covering the period 1387 to 1462. The work in astrology was used in medical diagnosis and treatment and such works had become fashionably popular among the wealthy (John of Gaunt, for example, later commissioned a similar work).[23] The Franciscans had a greater interest in astrology than most of the other religious orders. Presumably Joan received the work, and perhaps she even commissioned Somer to cast her horoscope, or that of another member of the family, such as Richard, but there is no way of knowing whether she did so, or even if she appreciated the work, and gives little assistance in indicating Joan's own taste. Joan may simply have been continuing the favour towards the Franciscans exhibited by her grandmother Margaret and her mother-in-law Philippa. It is notable that Joan cannot be associated with the founding of any religious establishment, and that even her public support for St Albans cannot be considered unusual. Unlike her uncle, Thomas Wake, who founded an Augustinian priory at Haltemprice in Yorkshire and a Franciscan house at Ware in Hertfordshire, and her cousin Elizabeth de Burgh, who was famously generous towards several religious houses, as well as founding Clare College, Cambridge, there is no evidence that Joan was a major religious patron of any house.[24] Joan did not follow their example, though whether this was because she had no inclination to do so cannot be known.

It is possible that Joan had less conventional views, and there has been speculation that she had considerable sympathy for John Wyclif and the Lollard movement. John Wyclif was an Oxford theologian who was strongly critical of the Church and publicly preached against what he regarded as many corrupt practices, advocating a devout and simple life focussing on faith in Christ. His anti-papal and anti-clerical rhetoric appealed to many of the nobility, including John of Gaunt, and it was Bishop Courtenay's exposure of Wyclif's heretical views and attack on them which had sparked the feud between Gaunt and Courtenay in 1377. Joan's intervention on this occasion was obviously of assistance to Wyclif, but her motive appears to have been a desire to help her brother-in-law rather than an attempt to shield and protect the radical preacher. However, Gaunt was himself a sympathiser, and several of the knights close to Joan were adherents to Wyclif's ideas – John Clanvowe (who wrote a religious treatise known as *The Two Ways* which implicitly supports Wyclif's views), Lewis Clifford (who later became a member of Philippe de Mézières' Order of Passion and remained sympathetic to Wycliffite teaching throughout his life, repeating key sentiments in his will), Richard Stury, William Neville and Thomas Latimer. Although the evidence is inconclusive, it does seem likely that Joan was at least sympathetic. In a papal bull dated May 1377 the Pope issued instructions to the Archbishop of Canterbury and the Bishop of London to warn the king and his sons and specifically 'his beloved daughter in Christ, the noblewoman Joan, Princess of Aquitaine and Wales' about Wyclif's heresies, and in a separate bull he ordered Wyclif's arrest. Shortly afterwards Joan was writing privately to the Pope.[25] Although the subject matter of their correspondence is not known the timing is suggestive and quite possibly Joan was sending reassurance of her conformity. Certainly, if Joan shared any of Wyclif's views she was at pains to conceal this from being generally known. However, when Wyclif was brought for trial before the bishops, Lewis Clifford was sent as a messenger to request that they did not pronounce sentence against him, effectively asking the bishops stay their proceedings. Although Lewis Clifford was also one of Richard's household knights he was identified with Joan, and sending him with a message which contravened the Pope's direct instructions was risky. Her intervention, giving Wyclif royal protection, was decisive and secured his release. Once again Joan showed a willingness to take risks where she felt it was important to do so, in order to preserve harmony. It also showed her shrewd sense of judgment, as Walsingham noted that the Londoners were sympathetic to Wyclif on this occasion, and Gaunt at this time was still a supporter. It is possible that she did it out of personal conviction, but in this, as in so much else, Joan was extremely private. In terms of her own personal beliefs, all that can be stated for certain is that she generally behaved in the way expected of her in terms of piety and religious observance, without being identified as a major patroness of any individual foundation, other than the abbey of St Albans.

Family, and personal relationships, were what Joan cared about most and her interest in political affairs was limited to her strong maternal instinct to protect her son. In surrounding Richard with loyal and trusted men who had served his father Joan ensured there was a strong link between his household and the council who governed in his name, as again many of these had also served the prince. In the first three years of Richard's reign there were three councils, the first being replaced after three months with a second formed at the first parliament held in October 1377, this in turn was superseded by a third council appointed a year later in October 1378 during the parliament held at Gloucester that year. On each change some members were replaced, but the council consistently contained a significant number of former servants of the prince. The first council, appointed on 19 July 1377, included the earls of March and Arundel (Thomas Holand's father-in-law), Bishop Courtenay, the Bishop of Salisbury (a friend of Gaunt's), Sir Ralph Ferrers, Sir Roger Beauchamp, Sir John Knyvet and several knights associated with the prince: Hugh Segrave (who had been his steward and then became steward to Joan), William Latimer, John Lord Cobham, Richard Stafford and John Devereux.[26] Cobham, Stafford, Segrave and Knyvet were joined by William Wykeham, Bishop of Winchester; John Harewell, Bishop of Bath and Wells (both executors of the prince) and William Ufford and Aubrey de Vere (former members of the prince's council) in the council formed in October 1378.[27] All these men were loyal to the prince and it was natural that they would transfer their loyalty and dedication to his son. Many had also served and had connections with Gaunt.[28] This was unlikely to be a coincidence. The presence of so many of the prince's former servants on the council and their added connection to Gaunt could only be beneficial to Richard. It is even more difficult here to prove that Joan had any involvement, but it seems probable that she was consulted and made her views known, so influencing their selection as council members.

Joan's influence was not confined to the selection of trusted individuals to serve her son. She knew personally most of those influential in politics, and she had already shown that she could use her charm and tact to smooth working relationships. In this way, she was able to provide a steadying political influence without being directly involved.[29] This was particularly important with John of Gaunt. None of Richard's uncles were included on the councils. This was almost certainly a deliberate omission, and one endorsed, if not suggested, by Gaunt. He and his two brothers were given a quasi-supervisory role by being given authority to oversee cases involving maintenance of quarrels by any of the councillors.[30] Gaunt was well aware of his unpopularity and knew his presence could cause divisiveness. Despite the duke's obvious goodwill towards his nephew there remained those who found it difficult to believe in his sincerity, and unpleasant rumours continued to circulate about him, questioning the motives that lay behind his apparently quiescent and supportive role. Although Gaunt was ambitious and able, powerful and not averse to seizing power when he felt it was his due, he was first and foremost devoted and loyal to his father and older brother, and loved his nephew for their sake; he was also genuinely fond of his sister-in-law and his actions demonstrate that he had the interests of his nephew and his sister-in-law in mind. In 1327 the council had included the young king's uncles, Joan's father, Edmund of Woodstock and Thomas of Brotherton, but it had exercised little real authority, fatally weakened by the hold on power retained by Queen Isabella and her lover, neither of whom were on the council. This was not a situation Gaunt chose to emulate, although there were many who believed that Gaunt continued to control the government through his friends. Shortly after the coronation he withdrew from court and retired to his estate at Kenilworth; according to Walsingham, out of pique and because he feared he would be blamed if anything went wrong, after first approving the councillors chosen for the first council.[31] It is possible he felt that his presence was needed to deal with pressing government business on the Scottish border, where the Scots had used the opportunity of the change of regime to raid Roxburgh. This certainly provided an excuse for his absence, and at an Anglo-Scottish conference held in September he was asked to attend to help settle unresolved border grievances, but this is unlikely to have been the real reason. His self-imposed and immediate withdrawal from the court and the political arena so soon after the coronation was probably manufactured to enable the council to start its work unimpeded by his presence, and he would have discussed this with Joan. It was a further instance of his unequivocal loyalty to his nephew. Nevertheless, Gaunt's position at court had changed with his nephew's accession and, although his support was needed it was likely that he would have less influence in the new regime than he had had with his father. He could not necessarily guarantee his friends would continue to occupy influential positions. Henry Percy, for example, resigned his position as marshal just after the coronation, according to Walsingham because he did not want to be humiliated by being forcibly replaced. Joan's cousin, Margaret Brotherton, now Lady Segrave, was insisting that as her father, Thomas Brotherton, had been hereditary marshal she had the right to appoint a deputy to act for her. In fact, Margaret's claim was not upheld, and the Earl of Arundel's brother, Sir John Arundel, was appointed in Percy's stead. Gaunt also remained deeply unpopular, and his relationship with the City of London was fragile, while the public reconciliation with the Bishop of Winchester had yet to be tested.

Joan's conciliatory initiative to restore Gaunt's public reputation and standing was completed at the first parliament of Richard's reign, held in October 1377. Having returned from the north in time to attend, John of Gaunt was requested by the Commons to act as a liaison between them and the council. In an extraordinary act of theatre, Gaunt took this opportunity to publicly clear his name. Kneeling before his nephew he referred to rumours about his loyalty, saying that he was loyal and

> prayed him humbly that he would hear him a little on a weighty matter touching his own person. The commons had chosen him to be one of the lords to consult with them but nothing could be done until he had been excused of these things which had been evilly spoken of him. For, he said, albeit unworthy, he was a king's son and one of the greatest lords in the kingdom after the king: and what had been so evilly spoken of him could rightly be called plain treason … And if any man were so bold as to charge him with treason or other disloyalty or with anything prejudicial to the realm, he was ready to defend himself with this body as though he were the poorest bachelor in the land.[32]

His obviously sincere and moving oratory had the desired effect. Without exception all of the barons and prelates rose to their feet to reassure the duke and protested that none of them believed such rumours. Once again there is no evidence to indicate that Joan had a hand in this, but it is tempting to consider that Gaunt, already grateful to her for the beneficial effects of her mediatory efforts and willing to take her counsel, had taken her advice in adopting such a different approach. His humble, supplicatory stance bore little resemblance to the proud and angry man who had so riled the Good Parliament just two years earlier.

Joan discreetly helped Gaunt in other ways. She would have met his mistress Katherine Swynford in her capacity as governess to his two daughters by Blanche of Lancaster, Philippa and Elizabeth, probably shortly after her return from Aquitaine in 1371. Gaunt's affair with Katherine is generally considered to have started in the spring of 1372, shortly before his marriage to Constance of Castile, although it did not become public knowledge until 1375. In 1377 the couple's relationship was extremely strong and Joan would have come to know Katherine quite well, and have known how much Katherine meant to Gaunt. Joan knew Constance from their days in Aquitaine, but there is no evidence to suggest that the two women ever became close. In contrast there is some evidence to suggest that Joan and Katherine may have developed a friendship, and indeed Joan's own unusual marital history might well have made her more than usually sympathetic to Katherine's unusual position. On 20 July 1377 Richard II ratified a grant of Gringley and Wheatley to Katherine Swynford, on 21 July he nominated Katherine's niece Elizabeth Chaucer (eldest daughter of her sister Philippa Chaucer, married to Geoffrey Chaucer) to St Helen's Priory, Bishopsgate, and on 27 July nominated Margaret Swynford to Barking Abbey.[33] The exact identity of Margaret Swynford is a mystery but the timing of the favour shown to her is suggestive and it does seem probable that she had a connection, albeit unknown, to Katherine. Barking was one of the more prestigious convents and therefore a desirable destination, achievable by Margaret because of her aristocratic connections. Four years later, in 1381, Elizabeth Chaucer became a nun at Barking Abbey, with her admission expenses paid for by Gaunt as part of a larger gift to the abbey.[34] During the 1370s Katherine bore Gaunt four children – John, Henry, Thomas and Joan – all given the name Beaufort. Joan Beaufort is generally presumed to have been born in 1379, and it is possible that Gaunt had his sister-in-law in mind when choosing the name, and may even have asked Joan to act as godmother to his youngest child.[35] As a caring and loving mother herself, with her affection for Gaunt, it is easy to imagine that Joan may have grown fond of Gaunt's young Beaufort children, and that she and Richard spent time with them.

Richard's accession to the throne elevated his half-brothers Thomas and John Holand to the status of royal kinsmen, but despite this newly enhanced status neither of them was initially prominent in his affairs. This is perhaps surprising. Thomas was now twenty-seven years old. He had been knighted by his stepfather prior to the Battle of Nájera, and had been a member of his stepfather's retinue until his death. He had taken part in several campaigns, having served under the Earl of Hereford in 1371 and 1372, under John of Gaunt in Aquitaine in 1373, and then accompanied his brother-in-law John Montfort to Brittany in 1375, presumably competently as he became a knight of the Garter in 1376, but, with no record of an independent command, he does not appear to have inherited his father's notable military flair.[36] As Joan's heir he would one day become Earl of Kent and inherit all of her very considerable estates, which would make him one of the wealthiest and most powerful of the nobility. In 1377 he was a relatively obscure and modestly endowed young man, his only estates and income being the three manors granted to him on the occasion of his marriage in accordance with the marital agreement reached between his stepfather and his father-in-law, the Earl of Arundel, although his wife Alice had been left 5,000 marks by her father when he died in 1376. (Arundel was probably almost the richest man in England when he died, leaving £29,987 in gold and silver alone in Arundel Castle and total realisable assets of £72,245. He had been a notable moneylender to the Crown; Joan was among his debtors, owing him 1,000 marks when he died, having given him a single nouche as security).[37] With Richard's accession, it would have been a natural and obvious step for the young king to elevate his half-brother to the earldom of Kent, and for Joan to have handed over some of the many Kent estates to her heir. However, this would have put Thomas Holand on a par with Richard's uncles, in particular with Thomas of Woodstock. Joan, protective of Richard and sensitive of the prince's brothers, clearly felt that this would not be tactful, and she was careful to ensure this did not happen. Instead, in July 1377, Thomas was given an unremarkable official appointment as custodian of the royal forests south of Trent, replacing Sir John Foxley, a position with administrative and judicial duties which could be delegated (in November Baldwin Bereford was appointed his deputy and probably did the actual work) but which gave Thomas additional income.[38] He was not however made a justice of the peace, although some months later he was granted a gift of 100 marks, payable in three instalments between June and November 1378, followed by a further £200 annuity in April 1378.[39] It was not until 1380 that Thomas was created Earl of Kent, with the grants being supplemented by additional and substitute rents which, with his own income, were meant to ensure he had annual support in the region of £1,000.[40] Joan's influence was clear.

There is nothing to suggest that Thomas resented his mother's caution. He appears to have been consistently loyal and trustworthy, with a strong sense of family duty, and does not seem to have been a particularly ambitious young man. As the new reign started, he took his place at Richard's side as part of his entourage (he is known to have been at Sheen with Richard in November 1377), serving in a modest capacity. In the spring of 1378 he served in the fleet in the Channel during the projected French invasion, and with his brother accompanied Gaunt at the unsuccessful siege at St Malo, while in October he was appointed commissioner to treat with the Scots over more breaches of the peace. In time he and Alice would have nine children, all but one growing to adulthood and surviving him: his heir Thomas, Edmund, Eleanor, Joan, Margaret, another Eleanor, Elizabeth and Bridget.[41] The number of children suggests the marriage was a happy one, and the names chosen by Thomas include his father's and mother's names, his grandmother's (Margaret), his mother's best friend's (Eleanor), his aunt's (Elizabeth) and his maternal grandfather's (Edmund). It was natural and appropriate, and indeed dutiful, for Thomas to name his eldest son after his father, and his second son after his grandfather; he was, after all, succeeding to their inheritance, but the choice of Eleanor twice, and of Elizabeth, suggests further a fond relationship with his mother and her friend, and a respect for his aunt Elizabeth (who retained a dower interest in many of the Kent estates).

John Holand, twenty-five years old in 1377, was, in contrast to his older brother, completely reliant on royal patronage. He was the only one of Joan's four Holand children who was not yet married, and as a younger son he did not stand to inherit any of his mother's estates. The prince had taken his stepson under his wing, appointing John Hay his guardian, and ensured he would receive the education commensurate with his background. When the prince returned to England and withdrew from active affairs John had been placed with John of Gaunt, in his retinue. John had a very different personality to Thomas. His future career indicates that he was both ambitious and unscrupulous, with a propensity for getting into trouble, while possessing considerable charm and charisma. Joan clearly had a soft spot for this son, despite the wildness which must have been apparent as he was growing up. On Richard's accession, John was appointed one of his chamber knights, a prestigious position which brought little income with it. Perhaps Joan hoped that by keeping John close to her she would be able to keep an eye on her son, but the lifestyle did not suit John. Within a few months he returned to John of Gaunt's retinue and gained his first military experience, accompanying the duke on his abortive siege of St Malo in 1378. In March John received a modest gift from Richard of a £100 annuity, converted into a land grant nine months later when he was given the Berkshire manors of Ardington and Philberds Court at East Hanney, formerly owned by Alice Perrers.[42] This was followed by the award of a wardship valued at 250 marks and a life grant of some annuities in 1380. Joan was probably relieved that John was back under the watchful eye of her brother-in-law and hopeful that the experience he gained would stand him in good stead and curb his waywardness.

Joan remained close to her daughters. Neither of their marriages had quite turned out as hoped or expected. Joan had become John Montfort's wife when she was only eight or nine years old and had spent some years apart from her mother when she returned to England in 1366 or 1367. Despite Edward III's support, the Duke of Brittany had been unable to regain control of his dukedom, and he was forced to remain in exile in England from 1373 to 1379 with his young wife. After the prince's death he had been granted more property in Norfolk including Queen Isabella's estate at Castle Rising, Lynn, but the duke had no intention of retiring to the country to take up an English lifestyle.[43] Remaining at court, pressing for the support he needed to mount a campaign to restore him to his dukedom, he was happy for his wife to live with her mother. Naturally, Montfort was principally concerned to retain his dukedom, and did not want to remain dependant on the English Crown. At times he found it expedient to ally himself to the French, and on these occasions an English wife was a disadvantage. Their marriage may not have been a particularly happy one; certainly there were no children of the marriage, and the young Joan was apparently reluctant to join her husband in Brittany after his return in August 1379, and could not be persuaded to join him there until 1382.[44] Similarly, Maud had no children with her husband and, after Courtenay's death in 1374, rather than retire from court and live on her own estates (three manors had been settled on her at the time of her marriage), Maud preferred to live with her mother as part of her household. Neither of Richard's half-sisters received any special mark of favour from their little brother when he became king.

Richard's first Christmas as king was spent at Windsor, in the company of his mother and family, surrounded by the court. The first few months of the reign had not been without incident. On 24 June 1377, just three days after Edward III's death, the truce agreed with France at Bruges had ended, and the French had taken advantage of Edward III's death and his grandson's accession to invade England. Crossing the channel from Calais and Aquitaine, the French had attacked all along the south coast, burning Rye on 29 June then moving on to Rottingdean, Weymouth, Dartmouth, Plymouth, Southampton, Poole and occupying the Isle of Wight in August and September. Local defences proved powerless to prevent the invaders landing, although Walsingham scathingly remarked that the 'so-called impregnable' Isle of Wight would not have been captured 'had its defence been diligently maintained'.[45] The French had not come equipped to stay, and after burning, plundering and killing, they departed back to France, leaving the coastal towns devastated and counting their dead. This was a national humiliation and left many burning for revenge. But the safety of the realm was not at the forefront of the agenda of Richard's first parliament, which had assembled on 13 October and lasted till the end of November. Once John of Gaunt had been publicly reconciled the commons had plenty of demands, presenting a petition which included fourteen items taken almost verbatim from the Ordinances of 1311, and insisting that Alice Perrers be tried, pressing for her banishment.[46] Alice was duly condemned and all her possessions forfeited. Joan was not directly involved but she would have been kept abreast of affairs and may have influenced the choice of the knights deputed to check and make an inventory of the old king's jewellery and other personal belongings (as two of the knights were long-standing retainers Richard Abberbury and Nicholas Bond).[47]

Under the watchful eye of the Commons a new council was formed to govern on behalf of the king, their first task being to satisfy the Commons' requirements. Parliament made it clear that, as far as they were concerned, the king had sufficient resources to maintain the war with France without recourse to public funds. There was no enthusiasm for a renewed French campaign. However, towards the end of October news reached England of a large Spanish fleet at Sluys, and in response to the threat a fleet had been assembled under the overall command of the king's youngest uncle, Thomas of Woodstock, the newly appointed Duke of Buckingham, which set sail in early November. Unfortunately stormy weather scattered the fleet, and by December the project was abandoned and the by now mutinous troops disbanded.[48] It was a disappointing and dispiriting start for the new reign, with another expensive foreign expedition ending in failure.

Nevertheless Joan was probably not the only person who found the New Year, 1378, heralded a promising start. Richard was safely settled with his new household which included John Holand, while Joan was at hand with her own household, with her daughters and Eleanor

Clifford in attendance. Politically there seemed to be calm, with the council managing affairs and Gaunt reconciled with Parliament and the Londoners. Despite its grumbles, Parliament had voted sufficient grants to finance a new offensive in France under the overall command of Gaunt and the earls of Arundel and Salisbury. Hopes were high that England would re-establish its supremacy in France and avenge the raids on the south coast. Plans were drawn up and orders dispatched, and in April Arundel and Salisbury sailed as planned, with Gaunt scheduled to follow. Regarded with respect and affection, referred to as 'Madame la Meer', Joan settled into her role as the king's mother.[49] In April, at the annual Garter celebrations, there was a public display of family unity with eight female members of Richard's immediate family becoming Ladies of the Garter. This was a solely prestigious award as it carried no financial benefits. Only two women had previously been so honoured: Queen Philippa in 1358 and Princess Isabella in 1376. Now Joan, her daughters Maud, Lady Courtenay, and Joan, Duchess of Brittany, her sisters-in-law Constance, Duchess of Lancaster and Isabella, Countess of Cambridge (Edmund's wife), Gaunt's daughters Philippa and Elizabeth, and Princess Isabella's daughter Philippa were all honoured.[50] Special robes with hoods were made for them, matching in colour, quality and quantity of cloth and furs with those of the knights, with a garter for each embroidered with the motto of the order probably worn on the left arm, paid for by the Crown.[51] As Joan stood in St George's chapel at Windsor, dressed in her garter robes, her eyes on her son, this was a deeply emotional moment for her. Membership of the Garter had been of immense significance for the prince, and Thomas Holand, and their stalls were nearby, emblazoned with their arms. Now Joan too stood where they had done, joined to them in membership of this chivalric order. This was a family affair, as her oldest son Thomas had been made a member in 1376, at the same time as Princess Isabella. It would have been a proud and moving moment for Joan, on the eve of saying goodbye once more to many of her menfolk. When Gaunt finally departed in July, Thomas and John accompanied him, as did Lewis Clifford, William Neville, Richard Stury, Philip la Vache, John Clanvowe and William Beauchamp, all dear to her.[52] Watching the preparations, making her farewells to those leaving, Joan would have been reminded of earlier times with the prince, and perhaps she was relieved that Richard was far too young to take part in the expedition.

Then, in August, the political calm was broken. The murder of a squire who had taken sanctuary in Westminster Abbey to avoid arrest caused a national scandal. Two squires, Robert Hawley and John Shakell, who had been imprisoned in the Tower pending investigation of their claim for a reward for having taken a valuable prisoner, had escaped and fled to Westminster Abbey. They were pursued by the constable of the Tower, Alan Buxhill, and one of his men, a knight named Ralph Ferrers, was overzealous in his duty, wounding a sacristan and killing Hawley on the altar steps. This violation of sanctuary caused an outcry. Even though Gaunt was in France, many held him responsible and he was denounced as the instigator. The Bishop of London, William Courtenay, immediately excommunicated all those concerned, specifically excluding only Richard, Joan and Gaunt. Meanwhile the French campaign faltered and failed, and in September the returning soldiers were greeted without enthusiasm. Gaunt, his military reputation tarnished, found that he was held responsible for the disappointment of so many hopes. Immediately on the defensive, he launched his energies into the sanctuary affair and lost no time in furiously attacking Courtenay. For once, Joan's soothing and restraining influence was not in evidence, although, having deliberately distanced herself from the public political arena, the swift and immediate resumption of the old feud between her brother-in-law and the Bishop of London probably took her by surprise. When Parliament met in Gloucester the mood of the Commons was unsettled and unhappy, and the inevitable request for further subsidies for the Crown was received sourly and only granted grudgingly.

The grumblings of Parliament and the general dissatisfaction with the lack of progress in France did not affect Joan's growing sense of security in Richard's position. Her concern remained focussed on his personal welfare and she turned her attention towards his marriage. As Richard was barely twelve there was no great urgency, but Joan was very conscious of the importance of his marriage and she was determined that he should not follow his father's example. Richard's best friend, Robert de Vere, had married Princess Isabella's daughter Philippa the previous year. It was time, Joan felt, for a suitable bride to be found for Richard; this, for Joan, meant marriage to a foreign princess. Her own experience had reinforced rather than weakened the attractions of a traditional match. Under her influence a marriage council had been set up within a few months of Richard being crowned, its members comprised exclusively of people close to Joan and dominated by her. Potential matches were identified and considered. Initially, in January 1378, a French match had been discussed.[53] When this came to nothing, the possibilities of a Navarrese princess was considered. When this faltered, another foreign princess was soon identified, and negotiations began with the King of Bohemia for a match between his sister, Anne, and Richard. As ever, the choice of suitable foreign brides was restricted; nevertheless there was little, on the face of it, to recommend Anne, diplomatically or financially. With England's interests overseas firmly centred on France and the Spanish peninsula, Bohemia was not an obvious or particularly desirable ally, while the country's inability to supply Anne with a dowry was a considerable disadvantage. Joan does not seem to have regarded these as obstacles, although she was careful to enlist Gaunt's support, having the opportunity to discuss it with him at Christmas, which she and Richard spent as his guests at Kenilworth. Their relationship remained as close as ever. Gaunt's New Year gift to Joan of a covered gold cup and crucifix garnished with precious stones and pearls, and adorned with an image of the Blessed Virgin and St John, is revealing.[54] The implicit, if unconscious, identification of Joan with Mary and Gaunt with her protector, St John, is intriguing, suggesting that this, perhaps, is how Gaunt saw their relationship. By February Joan had returned to Kennington with the family, confident that she had the duke's support and, indeed, in June 1380 Gaunt played host to the King of Bohemia's envoy, continuing the discussions.[55] The king's marriage was naturally a matter of great importance and an affair in which all members of the nobility had an interest, but Joan's influence here was strong. Simon Burley was one of the principal negotiators and on 26 December 1380 Thomas Holand was appointed as one of the ambassadors to treat for his brother's marriage.[56]

Thomas and John Holand benefited from their mother's new confidence. By February 1380 Thomas was acting as Marshal of England, formally confirmed on the 13 March, and in May he was appointed justice of the peace for Surrey with his brother-in-law, the Earl of Arundel. When there was a renewed threat of invasion from France in June, he was placed in charge of defending Southampton with a garrison of 150 men at arms, seventy balisters and eighty archers, and a further eighty men were sent to joint them in July.[57] By the end of the year he was at last elevated to the earldom of Kent.[58] At the same time Joan granted him her interests in Kent: the manor of Wickhambreaux and £30 county annuity. A seal of Thomas' from 1380 shows his shield suspended from the neck of a white hind, incorporating his mother's personal insignia with the Holand arms.[59] John Holand similarly gained, receiving a life grant of Northwich town in Cheshire, the Hope and Hopedale lordships, rent from Overmarsh, Flintshire, and when Blanche Wake died in 1380 Joan granted John three Wake manors: Long Marton in Cumberland, Langton in Yorkshire and Stevington in Bedfordshire.[60] John also received public recognition from his young brother through official appointments; in September he was granted the Marensin lordship in the Landes region of Gascony and in March 1381 he was appointed justice for Cheshire for life, a strategically important post in view of the extensive Crown estates in the county, part of Richard's inheritance from his father.[61] This was a notable mark of approval, when in only August 1379 the most reward he had received had been a gift of clothing from his royal brother (eight long gowns and other garments).[62] Maud also gained from her mother's more relaxed attitude, and on 1 April 1380 Maud married Waleran, the Count of St Pol, at Windsor, the occasion notable for being celebrated with a great concourse of trumpeters and entertainers, in the presence of Richard and all of Maud's family, with most of the court in attendance.[63] Maud received a typically generous gift from John of Gaunt of a three-legged vessel, cup and ewer.[64] It was a year of marriages, with Gaunt's daughter Elizabeth being married to John Hastings, Earl of Pembroke, at Kenilworth on 24 June 1380, followed in October by the marriage of her brother, Henry of Bolingbroke, to Mary Bohun, at her mother's home at Rothford Hall in Essex.

As she became more convinced of the security of Richard's position as king, Joan felt able to turn her attention towards other areas, and she started to show a much greater personal interest in her own affairs. Loyal and long-serving retainers were high on Joan's list. Although the awards were made by Richard, there can be no doubt that Joan was using her influence to secure them. Her long-time clerk John Carleton had become sub-deacon at Lincoln Cathedral in April 1378 and canon at St Paul's in London in February 1379 while receiving an additional clerical appointment to the vicarage of Huyssh and Lamport, her chaplain John Yernmouth was given the church of Stoke Basset in Oxfordshire in August 1378, and in April 1379 Robert Braybrooke was nominated to Lichfield church.[65] William Harpele was granted a manor and other income in February 1381, and her squire Henry Norton received a life grant in April 1380 'in consideration of his services to her and to her daughter de Courtenay'.[66] In March 1378 Andrew and Elizabeth Luttrell were granted a lifetime annuity of £200 in recognition of their service to Joan and the prince during his lifetime, and when Andrew subsequently died Joan ensured this annuity was confirmed for Elizabeth.[67] Joan de la Warr, daughter of Joan's friend Eleanor, received a wardship in 1379.[68] William Beauchamp, her steward John Worthe and Adam Louches were all granted annuities in the spring of 1378; John Worthe was also granted a life interest in her Northweald manor, while Aubrey de Vere was given a life grant of the bailiwick of Rochford hundred in Essex in January 1380.[69] She committed the custody of Cardigan Castle to Lewis Clifford for life, and granted Richard Stury the post of constable and keeper of the castle and town of Aberystwyth in Wales for her lifetime, a position confirmed by Richard three weeks later.[70] Joan was almost certainly influential in ensuring rewards given by Richard to John Clanvowe, William Beauchamp, Richard Stury and Lewis Clifford around this time, small but significant grants in financial terms including those of wardship and marriage.[71]

Joan also showed a renewed interest in her estates, which she had previously been content to leave in the hands of her council. The only surviving copy of Joan's personal seal is attached to a document signed at Waghen on 20 April 1380 to record an exchange of rental at Miserden manor with Meaux Abbey.[72] A similar personal involvement is evident at this time in Joan's personal request for a series of commissions to investigate incidents on her estates held in Dartford, Cottingham, Essex, Deeping and Bourn, Chesterfield and Barnstable.[73] In May 1381 personal requests made by Joan in the interests of her uncle Thomas Wake's foundations at Bourne and Ware in Lincolnshire, on behalf of the prior

William Herbert, were granted, and a pardon issued to Adam Aldeby, the vicar of Stamford, for causing the death of John Bell.[74] The indication of Joan's new and detailed interest in personal affairs suggests that she was now considering her retirement from the court, and this is confirmed by the order for the construction of a new barge for her in May 1381, which would give her easy access downstream to Windsor, Kennington and Westminster from Wallingford.[75] In the same month Simon Burley became constable of Windsor Castle, an appointment which would have reassured Joan that he remained very close at hand for Richard (the favour shown to Burley included the gifts of manors at Windsor, Henley, West Hampstead and Charing Cross).[76]

It is easy to imagine that Joan would have been feeling generally well satisfied with affairs by the spring of 1381 and thinking that the time was right for her to retire from public life. She had clearly shown that she had little interest in taking a central role in public affairs and had taken great care to refrain from becoming too prominent. It is notable that she preferred to exercise her influence indirectly even as an intercessor where possible, with official requests for pardons to be given to individuals for capital offences made as frequently by members of her family (her daughter Maud, her sons Thomas and John and Robert Braybrooke) and her staff (such as her clerks William Fulbourne and William Harpele, her damsels Agnes Corby and Margery Lodewyk, and her knights John Worthe and William Neville) as by Joan in person.[77] Joan had no desire to maintain her public role. The last important aspect of Richard's life which she had wanted to oversee was his marriage, and now the final arrangements for this were in place. In April the conclusion of the marriage treaty was celebrated at a sumptuous banquet hosted at the Savoy by Gaunt for the envoy of the King of Bohemia.[78] This was a joyful occasion for Joan and very much a family affair. Her Holand children, now seemingly settled, were all in attendance. The choice of venue and host for the celebrations was natural, given Gaunt's position, but it was also a reflection of Joan's continuing close friendship with her brother-in-law, unaffected by his marriage to Constance of Castile or his affair with Katherine Swynford, evidenced by the regular visits between them and the many gifts exchanged (listed in the duke's register), including another gold drinking vessel and several books ('livres') given to Joan in March 1381, and further expensive gifts for Joan and her daughter the Duchess of Brittany in May 1382.[79] Having satisfactorily finalised his nephew's marriage arrangements, Gaunt then departed for Scotland, having been appointed to broker peace and agree a truce with the Scots. Joan meanwhile made preparations for her annual visit to Canterbury in June, to mark the anniversary of the prince's death. With Richard now fourteen, and his marriage imminent, Joan could feel that she had fulfilled the prince's expectations and done as much as she could for her son. She could not have realised or foreseen the danger which was so nearly upon them.

The popular armed rising which overwhelmed and paralysed the government for two weeks in June 1381 is usually described as the Peasants' Revolt, although this is a misnomer as it was hardly restricted to the peasant class. It appears to have been sparked by the arrival of royal officials into local areas to investigate and enforce the collection of a poll tax passed by the Northampton parliament in November 1380. The reasons for the uprising and its course and events continue to be debated by historians, but what is not in doubt is that it came at a time when the government was unpopular and weak. The conciliar government set up to rule for Richard had struggled to be an effective body, weakened at the outset by the lack of strong leadership, and the exclusion of the king's uncles. Unable to manage Parliament effectively and lacking clear direction, the councillors had resigned en masse at the beginning of 1380 and been replaced with a group of men headed by the Archbishop of Canterbury, Simon Sudbury. But the new councillors proved similarly unable to provide strong and decisive leadership. Worse still, there was no good news from abroad. Popular support for the war with France, weakened by successive failures, was probably at its lowest when the campaigning army which had set out in July 1380 returned from their *chevauchée* through France in April 1381 with little to show for their progress, having swallowed up the taxes raised in the Parliament of January 1380. The sad truth was that the spectacular victories of the prince and Edward III were becoming distant memories, and there was little sympathy for Thomas of Woodstock's bellicose enthusiasm and energy for a new campaign. Even John of Gaunt showed little interest. Fear of invasion from France now drove the war effort, rather than a belief in establishing and maintaining the English Crown's claim to the French throne. It was a disastrously expensive defensive policy which consumed and exhausted each successive round of taxation and had left the government in a state of financial crisis in the autumn of 1380. Sudbury's council, although horrified by the parlous state of the royal finances, had been overwhelmed by the responsibility for keeping Buckingham's army in France through the winter, and had managed to convince the Commons in the parliament held in November 1380 at Northampton of the need for further taxes to raise money. Parliament had grudgingly agreed to grant a further poll tax and in the wrangling between the various vested interests the resultant tax was passed on the basis it would be levied at a flat rate. Although this inevitably meant that it would fall hardest on the poorest, no one foresaw the extent to which the tax would be resented, or anticipated the resistance that would be encountered by those collecting the tax.

Despite the many reports of the events which took place in the first two weeks of June by the various chroniclers, it remains difficult to determine with accuracy the exact sequence of events.[80] It is generally considered that the rising started around the beginning of June with unrest in Essex and Kent which spread into London, sparked by the commissions of enquiry set up to investigate the widespread evasion of the latest poll tax. On 1 June the commission of enquiry set up at Brentwood in Essex erupted into violence with three jurors killed. In Kent the violence spread from the east coast at Gravesend through Dartford, Rochester, Maidstone and Canterbury and then up to London, led by Wat Tyler and John Ball. From the inception of the rising the targets for the rebels were government officials and representatives, rather than the king himself, but first on the list of their hated targets was John of Gaunt and very quickly their anger turned into demands for the executions of unpopular leading figures. The numbers of men joining in the rising rose rapidly and the *Anonimalle Chronicle* estimated that 50,000 men had taken to the roads by 2 June. Buildings of authority such as castles and prisons were targeted, along with the homes of those in authority; property was looted, burned and destroyed and many of those unfortunate enough to be caught by the rebels met a violent end.

The government was slow to react. It is evident that the first reports of unrest which came to the king did not give cause for concern. During the first week of June 1381 Joan left Richard at Windsor and made her way to Canterbury for her annual pilgrimage to the prince's tomb, accompanied by her daughter, Joan, and a handful of her women, probably including Eleanor Clifford. The cathedral at Canterbury was a major pilgrimage destination, as it housed the body of Thomas à Becket, and the route from London was well known, the road winding through Southwark, Deptford, Greenwich and down into Kent, to Canterbury via Sittingbourne. For Joan, this had become an annual private and personal pilgrimage to visit the prince's tomb on the anniversary of his death rather than to pray at the site of the saint's martyrdom. She would stay for a few days, arriving shortly before the 8 June, so that she could listen to services in commemoration of the prince throughout the day, returning a day or so later to London. Although Joan had recently given her manor at Wickhambreaux to Thomas, it seems likely that she stayed there on this occasion, and on previous annual visits, as it was only five miles east of Canterbury, in the valley of the Little Stour river.[81] Had Richard, or anyone else at court, realised the impending danger Joan would never have left Windsor for Canterbury. Joan appears to have left Canterbury after commemorating the prince's anniversary on 8 June without appreciating how near the rebels were to her. The *Anonimalle Chronicle* records that by Monday 10 June, just after Joan had set out on her return journey, about 4,000 rebels had gathered at Canterbury, entering the cathedral during Mass.[82] According to Froissart, as she was on the road travelling back to London to rejoin Richard and the court, she was overtaken and stopped by a large crowd: 'She was in great jeopardy to have been lost, for these people came to her carriage and dealt rudely with her, whereof the good lady was in great doubt lest they would have done some villainy to her or to her damosels. Howbeit, God kept her, and she came in one day from Canterbury to London, for she never durst tarry by the way.'[83]

Froissart is the only chronicler to record this encounter, and his account cannot be verified. However, other sources do corroborate the timing and the route of the rebels marching on London from Canterbury and the coincidence of Joan's return from her annual visit to Canterbury makes such an encounter at least possible. Froissart knew Joan personally, and it is not unreasonable to suggest that his account may have been drawn from a contemporary recollection. Joan would have been travelling in a carriage emblazoned with her arms, and although there were few in her party she would have had a small armed escort. To be stopped, and accosted in this way, was extremely unusual. The crowd would have realised Joan's identity from the insignia on her carriage, and although their behaviour towards her was familiar they appear to have held her in respect, as there was no suggestion that the personal safety of Joan or her companions was threatened. Exactly what the men said to Joan is unknown, but their demeanour and intention was apparently clear. It seems likely that they may have aired some of their grievances to Joan, and at least made it clear that they intended to see the king. It does not seem to have occurred to any of them that they could have taken the king's mother hostage, or that by accompanying her back to London they could have used her presence as a bargaining tool with her son. Joan's reaction, according to Froissart, was immediate; she returned to London as quickly as she could (in one day). This meant that she followed the rebels on the road to the capital, or possibly even overtook them; they, after all, were on foot, whereas she was in a carriage. This was not the action of a frightened woman; it was rather the instinct of a mother to protect her son. Knowing that this unruly mob was intent on accosting the king, Joan was desperate to reach him first; to warn him, and to ensure he was protected. Joan had no means of knowing what the situation was in London and whether this was an isolated group of discontented men or one of many. For all she knew no one in London was aware of the impending army of rebels advancing on the capital. She also knew that Richard was relatively unprotected, as many of the nobility were away, with Gaunt in Scotland and Edmund, Earl of Cambridge, on expedition abroad. It seems probable that Joan ordered one of her mounted escort to ride ahead of her back to the court to warn the king, and that she followed as quickly as she could. As she was uncomfortably jolted in her carriage as it swayed behind her straining horses, she would almost certainly have seen many more peasants and labourers marching along the road towards London, as the chroniclers testify that men poured into the capital from Kent over this period. Although estimates vary, by 12 June around 100,000 had gathered on the outskirts of London.[84]

When Joan arrived in London she made straight for the Tower of London, where she joined Richard; presumably she had received word from him while she was on the road that this was where he would be. Within days of Joan leaving Richard at Windsor news had reached the young king of the growing rebellion and that huge numbers of armed men were descending on the capital, having wreaked havoc and destruction en route. The reports of what was happening were alarming. All the chroniclers' accounts make it clear that Richard and his advisers had been taken completely by surprise. The immediate reaction was to make for the capital, and on 11 June Richard left Windsor and travelled by barge to the Tower.[85] Joan appears to have joined him the following day. By this time the king had learned that the rebels wanted to meet with him at Blackheath; possibly this message was delivered to the Tower by Sir John Newton, the keeper of Rochester Castle, who had been captured by the rebels on their progress through Kent. It is not clear how many people were with Richard in the Tower or what kind of armed escort the king had, as the chroniclers variously estimate between 150 and 600 fighting men.[86] Among those with Richard were his two half-brothers, Thomas and John Holand, his friend Robert de Vere, Earl of Oxford, William Montague, Earl of Salisbury, the earls of Warwick and Arundel, John of Gaunt's son Henry Bolingbroke, the chancellor Simon Sudbury and the treasurer Robert Hales.[87] One notable absentee was Simon Burley, as he had left England for Bohemia on 15 May to continue the negotiations with the Bohemian royalty for Richard's marriage.[88] Joan had remained on good terms with her erstwhile husband, William Montague, and she would have taken comfort from his presence, as he had been one of the prince's most able and reliable commanders in the prince's last campaigns. There were also a number of city men including the Mayor of London, William Walworth. The chroniclers do not mention the names of any women, but there were evidently a number of noblewomen and their servants in the Tower, in addition to those who had returned with Joan, which included her daughter Joan, Duchess of Brittany.

It is hard to imagine what the atmosphere must have been like within the Tower. Richard, at fourteen, was still very young and reliant on his older advisers. Conflicting intelligence probably made it difficult to assess exactly what was happening, and while the rebel numbers were not known and their intentions remained unclear it was impossible to know how far the unrest had spread or to appreciate the level of danger. Although there were soldiers in the Tower, it was evident that the rebels greatly outnumbered the royal party. The envoys sent on behalf of the king to the rebels had been told that they wanted to save the king but destroy the traitors. No one was in any doubt that the situation was serious; the dilemma was how best to deal with it. Disastrously, Richard's advisers could not agree among themselves and were unable to suggest a course of action. It must have made sense at this stage to at least find out what the rebels wanted. However, wary of becoming trapped, the decision was taken that Richard should travel to meet the rebels by barge from the Tower, so providing him with a modicum of safety and a means of escape should he need it. On Thursday 13 June Richard left the Tower, accompanied by his chancellor Simon Sudbury and treasurer Robert Hales, William Montague, the earls of Warwick and Oxford and a few other knights, probably including Thomas and John Holand. There were too many for one barge and it seems that perhaps as many as four barges made up the royal party. As they approached the rebels near Greenwich the vastness and noise of the crowd made the royal party nervous. Froissart credits William Montague with cautioning Richard against landing while the *Anonimalle Chronicle* suggests that although Richard wanted to agree to the rebels' demand for a personal meeting his chancellor and treasurer deterred him. Although the chroniclers' accounts vary about the exact demands which were presented to Richard, it is generally agreed that the rebels wanted those they held responsible for their woes to be punished, drastically – by death. The long list of 'traitors' included Richard's uncle John of Gaunt, his chancellor Simon Sudbury, his treasurer Sir Robert Hales and John Fordham, the keeper of the privy seal. There must have been consternation on the king's barge as the nature and implications of the demands became known. How could Richard agree to kill his own servants and members of his own family?

Whatever Richard's instincts may have been, it is hardly surprising in the circumstances that at this stage the safest course appeared to be to stall for time. Richard and the rest of his party returned to the Tower. Not satisfied by their meeting with the king, the rebels proceeded towards London. Access into London was denied to them at this point as the gates were closed. However, it is evident that no one among the king's party or among the City of London had thought to protect the capital, and gaining access to the capital proved alarmingly easy for the rebels, as the gates were opened for them, although it is not clear who took the decision to do so or why. At this point it seems that the orgy of violence and destruction really began. As they streamed through the streets their anger found expression in destroying many of the buildings owned by hated prominent figures, including the Archbishop of Canterbury's palace at Lambeth, the Temple, the house of the treasurer Sir Robert Hales, several in Fleet Street, opening the gates of the Marshalsea, Fleet and Newgate prisons, attacking Clerkenwell Palace, church and hospital. One of the more horrific acts was the murder of around 150 Flemings in the city area.[89] The most famous act of destruction was of Gaunt's Savoy Palace. The duke's possessions – his gold and silver ware, jewellery, clothes, furniture and tapestries – were hauled out, smashed, broken, burnt, thrown in the river, the lot worth probably in the region of £10,000, while all his papers and then the building itself was set on fire.[90] Anyone who was identified as being one of the rebels' targets, or any of servant of theirs unfortunate enough to be found, was killed.

That night Joan would have been able to see that many of London's buildings were burning, and would have been able to hear the cries of the crowds and their victims. The burning Savoy must have been an unbearably poignant and frightening sight, illustrating so vividly the depth of hatred felt towards Gaunt and the powerlessness of the Crown to protect even the king's uncle. The Tower, a formidable fortress which should have been a safe refuge, was quickly becoming a prison as the prospect of leaving was rapidly becoming unthinkable. It must have been absolutely terrifying. Having reached Richard after her own roadside experience, Joan's instinct had been to meet and talk to the rebels, never dreaming that they meant any harm to the king. These were humble peasants and labourers, who regarded the king with awe and respect. But her confidence in a peaceable approach must have been shaken to the core by the demands presented at Blackheath, and by the subsequent eruption of such unprecedented violence. It quickly became obvious that no one really knew what to do, and it was apparent that there were very few in the Tower who had the ability or confidence to deal with the situation. Joan could never have missed the prince and his supreme confidence and leadership skills more than at this moment of greatest danger for their son. The absence of her brother-in-law was a mixed blessing. Joan's close friendship with Gaunt may have blinded her to the extent of his unpopularity and the vitriolic hatred expressed by the rebels towards him may have taken her completely by surprise. If initially she regretted his absence, she would swiftly have appreciated that his presence would only have exacerbated the situation.

It was time for a decision to be made. Some way had to be found of dealing with the crisis. Naturally Richard relied on the advice of those with him. The *Anonimalle Chronicle* starkly recorded that he 'called all of the lords into a chamber of the Tower and demanded their counsel as to what he should do in this emergency; and none of them was able or willing to give his counsel'.[91] It had already been apparent earlier that there was no one individual who was sufficiently forceful to take the lead – not even Richard's uncle, Thomas of Woodstock, who was now with him (according to the *Anonimalle Chronicle*) – and Froissart indicates that there was a clear divergence of opinion between those like William Walworth, who advocated a tough response, mobilising the armed forces at the king's command to disperse the rebels, and those like William Montague, acutely aware of the royal party's weak military position, who preferred a cautious and conciliatory approach. While Joan is not mentioned as participating in these discussions, faced with the biggest crisis of his young life Richard would undoubtedly have been conscious of his mother's views. Joan's own instincts were conciliatory, and despite the escalating violence her own experience with the rebels may have led her to encourage her son to speak to them, confident that by doing so he may be able to dispel some of the anger and violence, reminding him of the respect and awe with which his father had been regarded. Guided and persuaded by those around him, including Joan, the decision was made by Richard, or for him, that he would meet the rebels and talk to them. On the following day, Friday 14 June, Richard left the Tower to meet the rebels again, this time at Mile End. A careful choice was made as to who would accompany him. As the young king's purpose in meeting the rebels was to talk to them, it was important that no one was present who might exacerbate the situation. This naturally precluded those who were top of their wanted list, so the chancellor and the treasurer were left behind, and it would have been equally unwise for John of Gaunt's son Henry of Bolingbroke to join the party. Richard was accompanied again by William Montague, and by both his half-brothers, Thomas and John Holand, his friend Robert de Vere, Earl of Oxford, his uncle Thomas of Woodstock, the Earl of Warwick, and, according to the *Anonimalle Chronicle*, by his mother, probably with a few of her ladies.[92] Although no other chronicler corroborates this, it does seem quite possible that Joan chose to accompany her son, at least initially. It is likely that she had been privy to the previous night's discussions and the decision to go with him was one which only she could have made, almost certainly hoping that her presence would have a calming effect, and so provide her son with additional protection. However, at some point on the way to Mile End Joan left Richard and returned to the Tower. As her return does not seem to have been prompted by any incident en route, it is likely that Joan's intention had been to accompany Richard for only part of the way, to ensure a safe start. According to Froissart Richard feared that the rebels might attack his half-brothers and so he made Thomas and John Holand also leave; they too returned to the Tower.[93] It is evident that no one dreamed the Tower would be attacked. Richard continued towards Mile End, probably nervously and in some trepidation, but confident that he left his mother and the others in the Tower in safety.

The timing of the attack on the Tower in relation to the meeting at Mile End is unclear, but it appears that as soon as the royal party had left the Tower and was safely en route a large crowd of rebels (Froissart estimates at least 400 in number) led by the main rebel leaders, Wat Tyler, Jack Straw and the radical preacher John Ball, broke into the Tower.[94] The chroniclers are clear that the rebels had deliberately waited for the king to depart and that they specifically and knowingly targeted the Tower, intent on gaining access and wreaking their version of justice on those they held responsible for their woes and whom they knew remained in the fortress. They were after the chancellor and the treasurer. This was an obvious oversight on the part of the royal advisers, and it seems extraordinary that the Tower guards were not better prepared, with Walsingham incredulous that no knight or squire challenged them as they streamed into the Tower. Once inside the rebels dragged Sudbury and Hales outside, taking them to Tower Hill where they were summarily beheaded. Both knew the fate that awaited them; the archbishop had earlier celebrated Mass for

Richard and was in the Tower chapel when he was taken. Two others were also beheaded: Friar William Appleton, physician to John of Gaunt, and John Legge, a serjeant-at-arms. The grisly trophy heads were stuck on poles and placed on display on Tower Bridge. Henry of Bolingbroke only escaped because he was hidden by a servant, John Ferrour.

Joan had a dramatic confrontation with the rebels. Walsingham recounts that they entered her bedchamber and invited her to kiss them, while according to Froissart 'also these gluttons entered into the princess' chamber and brake her bed, whereby she was so sore afraid that she swooned, and there she was taken up and borne to the waterside and put in a barge and covered, and so conveyed to a place called the Queens Wardrobe. And there she was all that day and night, like a woman half dead, till she was comforted with the king her son.'[95] The Queen's Wardrobe, the main financial office of the royal household, was a mile upstream on the City side of the Thames at Blackfriars. The shock of the attack on the Tower and the merciless executions of the archbishop and the others must have induced a state of extreme terror among those left in the royal party. They were in the hands of the rebels and could only fear the worst. Before Richard's departure the belief had been that the king and his party were the ones at risk and no one had envisaged that the Tower would fail to protect those left behind. Joan, face to face with the terrifying evidence of the rebels' capacity for extreme violence, would have been horrified and distraught at the thought of what might be happening to Richard. There was nothing she could do. It is hardly surprising if she collapsed, paralysed. As she waited, perhaps she was comforted by the thought that, once again, the rebels had neither threatened nor hurt her, or any of her ladies, and that their anger was directed at her son's ministers rather than at her son.

Meanwhile Richard had reached Mile End. Froissart records that the young king spoke to the assembled crowd of nearly 60,000, asking them what they wanted, and that when they replied that they wanted their freedom, Richard agreed to their demands and on the same day thirty royal clerks were ordered to draw up charters which gave the rebels their freedom from serfdom and pardoned them for any wrongdoing. The chroniclers generally concur that as soon as the charters were issued the rebels dispersed, returning to their homes. Conciliation had worked, but only to a limited extent. The crowd that Richard met at Mile End were only a part of the rebel forces, and he had still to deal with the ringleaders, Wat Tyler, Jack Straw and John Ball. Presumably word reached Richard of the attack on the Tower and of the fate of his ministers, and of Joan's relocation, for on leaving Mile End Richard and those in his party went directly to the Queen's Wardrobe. That night once again he and his now depleted advisers had to decide what to do. Although the policy of appeasement had worked at Mile End, would it work again in the light of the terrible events in the Tower? In the end there was little choice. It would be impossible to overcome the rebellion by the use of force in view of the numerical superiority of the rebels, their use of violence and the lack of royal troops. The only successful strategy so far had been to meet with the rebels and agree to their demands.

The following day, Saturday 15 June, after praying at the shrine of Saint Edward in Westminster Abbey, Richard set out once again to meet the rebels, this time at the site of a weekly horse market at Smithfield, with a retinue of about 200 knights including William Montague and the Mayor of London, William Walworth. The numbers of rebels had decreased (Froissart estimates 20,000), but the principal leaders were there and they were emboldened by their success. Wat Tyler was their spokesman, and he approached Richard, presenting a more extreme version of the demands which had been made to the king the day before. What happened next is disputed, but there appears to have been a scuffle between Wat Tyler and one of Richard's squires which was interrupted by William Walworth, who struck Wat Tyler down with his sword. As soon as the rebels realised that Tyler had been killed, their mood became ugly, and it was at this point that Richard bravely rode towards them, on his own, and addressed them directly to follow him. All the accounts concur that this was a spur-of-the-moment decision, taken by Richard on his own. It was a huge gamble, but it was spectacularly successful. As Joan had earlier thought, whatever the people's quarrel with the Crown and its government, they held their young king in respect and awe, they meant him no harm and they were ready to listen to him and to follow him to Clerkenwell fields away from the city, where Richard ordered them to go home, promising them that their demand for freedom from serfdom would be met.

It took time to persuade the huge crowds to disperse, and some were more receptive than others to following the king's command. However, this time the royal party had done its own planning, and swiftly on hand to envelope the rebels as they congregated at Clerkenwell were a number of armed forces, including one commanded by the experienced soldier Robert Knolles. Froissart credits Richard with the decision not to employ armed force to chase them out of the capital or to execute the leaders on the spot. Froissart also emphasises that Richard's first subsequent journey was to rejoin his mother, where she 'greatly rejoiced and said, "Ah! Fair son, what pain and great sorrow that I have suffered for you this day." Then the king answered and said, "Certainly, madam, I know it well; but now rejoice yourself and thank God for now it is time. I have this day recovered mine heritage and the realm of England, the which I had near lost."'[96] It was indeed the end of the uprising, and order was slowly restored. That same day Richard knighted several Londoners, including the mayor William Walworth, who had stood at his side during the confrontation with Tyler, and within hours Richard was countermanding the charters of liberties he had issued. On 18 June letters were sent to the sheriffs in each county requiring them to enforce the peace and take measures to restrain the rebels, while commissions granting military and judicial powers were issued to leading members of the nobility, including the Earl of Buckingham and Thomas Holand. The rebel leaders, including Jack Straw and John Ball, were caught, tried and executed. The heads of the archbishop and the chancellor and the others were taken down from Tower Bridge, and with a certain grim irony they were replaced by those of the rebels.

The duration of the rising had been barely more than two weeks, with the rebels having control of London for two full days, but it had been the most dramatic and dangerous threat to the Crown since Edward II was deposed, far exceeding the repeated fears of French invasion, and its consequences were politically and socially far-reaching. On a purely personal level, it changed Joan's attitude towards Richard. Hitherto she had been protective and intervened whenever she felt she needed to, and had relied on the support of her brother-in-law. The events of those two weeks in June showed her that Richard could take care of himself. It was notable that the revolt had been directed against government and royal officials and had not been against Richard or his family other than Gaunt. Despite the criticism and violence meted out to his ministers and Gaunt's property and retainers, none had been directed towards Richard himself. Richard had undoubtedly benefited from his parents' popularity and the esteem and affection with which his mother was regarded – Joan had, after all, encountered the rebels on two separate occasions and on neither occasion had there been any suggestion she might come to harm – but in addition Richard had shown that he was more than equal to defending himself. Surrounded by advisers who failed to agree among themselves and were unable to provide clear direction, with his powerful uncle Gaunt absent, Richard had shown he was his father's son with his display of leadership and bravery at Smithfield, and survived the crisis. Joan had been there to guide and support him but at the end of the day he had proved that he had the strength of character and maturity to deal with the situation. Proud of her son, Joan would have been reassured that Richard was well able to take care of himself.

The rebels who had poured into London had come from Kent and Essex and, inevitably, these counties received the most attention in the immediate aftermath. For two weeks after the dispersal of the rebels from London there was continued active resistance in Essex, quashed by forces commanded by Thomas of Woodstock and Sir Thomas Percy. Subsequently a commission headed by the new chief justice, Robert Tresilian, meted out severe punishment. Richard was in Chelmsford in Essex and then at Havering for much of this time, probably as a deliberate policy to make a show of royal force and restore his authority; according to Froissart he then moved to Kent. Richard entrusted the restoration of order in Kent to his older half-brother, Thomas, and on 17 June the

Earl of Kent was duly dispatched with a commission to enforce the peace and hear indictments in Maidstone and Rochester, reaching Canterbury by 8 July, generally re-establishing royal authority.[97] On 2 July all the charters granted by Richard were formally rescinded and cancelled. In the immediate aftermath of the revolt a newly constituted council was formed under the leadership of William Courtenay, Bishop of London, who became chancellor in August. In view of the chaos wreaked by the rebellion it was hardly surprising that the restoration of order brought in its wake repressive policies aimed at subjugating those who had dared to flout authority, but there were also those who realised that a more conciliatory long-term approach was needed. On 30 August Richard declared an end to all the arrests and executions. By the time Parliament was called in November at Westminster, the uprising and its repercussions were superficially well and truly over, though the focus of attention for all those attending was inevitably centred on the revolt and the response to it.

Joan's whereabouts in the weeks following the revolt are not known. There was no ostensible reason why she should have accompanied Richard as he travelled first to Essex, then to Kent, and then on to St Albans, where the abbey had survived remarkably unscathed from the local populace's fury due largely to the calm competence of the abbot, Thomas de la Mare. With admirable sangfroid de la Mare had talked to the local townsfolk, offering them bread and ale and agreeing to their demands, and so successfully stalled for time peaceably until order was restored. It would not have been surprising if Joan had chosen to retire to Kennington to recover from the harrowing and turbulent two weeks. Nevertheless it seems more likely that she chose to stay at Richard's side, as she had done throughout the revolt. Although Richard had handled himself well during the crisis it had still been a terrifying episode and there could be no assurance initially that his safety was secure. Having sent so many of the nobility, including his uncle Thomas of Woodstock and his half-brother Thomas, around the country with royal commissions to restore order, Richard had a depleted entourage. He may well have been comforted by his mother's presence, though if Joan was with her son, it is most unlikely that she would have witnessed the gruesome punishment meted out to John Ball on 15 July in St Albans where he was hanged, drawn and quartered in the king's presence. By August Richard and Joan were in London, attending the funeral of his old tutor Guichard d'Angle, Earl of Huntingdon, and Gaunt had returned from Scotland.[98] Joan's strong friendship with her brother-in-law was behind Richard's resilient defence of his unpopular uncle in July 1381 when Richard issued a writ denying defamatory reports against Gaunt 'whom the king declares to be most zealous in his cause'.[99] But despite Joan's affection for her brother-in-law the revolt showed her a different side to Gaunt. She had known for years that he was unpopular, but it can never have been more strikingly evident than in the venom and anger directed towards him by the rebels, symbolised by their burning of the Savoy palace. Far from providing Richard with protection, his very name and their close association had endangered the king. His own family had been imperilled. His wife, Duchess Constance, had fled to Pontefract Castle where the keeper refused to admit her, forcing her to continue on to Knaresborough Castle. Katherine Swynford vanished and on his return Gaunt publicly repented of his adultery with her. For the duration of the rebellion Gaunt had been in Scotland, initially agreeing and concluding his official business in negotiating a truce with the Scots. When news of the rebellion reached him he had left, intending to return south, but when the Earl of Northumberland refused to allow the duke to stay in his territory (presumably for fear of reprisals for harbouring such an unpopular noble), he was forced to seek protection back in Scotland and did not leave until summoned by his nephew, indicating it was safe for him to do so.

Joan must have been taken aback to find that Gaunt's main concern on his arrival back in London was his quarrel with Percy (the Earl of Northumberland). Furious and humiliated by his treatment, as soon as Gaunt presented himself to his nephew he complained about his treatment by Percy, and alleged that the earl had spread rumours that Gaunt was in league with the Scots. The argument between the two men continued all summer, and when the royal council convened at Berkhamsted in October Gaunt repeated his allegations. The problem had not been resolved by the time Parliament met in November, with Gaunt demanding an apology from Northumberland and insisting that his nephew force the earl to comply. The acrimonious dispute between the two men dominated the first few days of the parliament until, on the fifth day of the session, an accommodation was achieved through Richard's intervention, with Percy apologising to Gaunt on bended knee, and there was a public reconciliation with the two exchanging a kiss of peace. Although Joan had probably guided her son's mediatory efforts, even she must have been exasperated that her brother-in-law had not been able to resolve this personal quarrel privately. Yet again Gaunt's pride and obstinacy had brought a personal quarrel to the forefront of public affairs, creating a problem for his nephew without providing a solution. It is symptomatic of Joan's newfound respect for her son's abilities that on this occasion she chose not to intervene personally and instead relied on her son, with her support, to mediate. It must therefore have been demoralising for her to find that when Parliament turned its attention to the aftermath of the revolt, although Richard's revocation of the charters was supported, considerable criticism was levelled at the royal household and its conduct of affairs, many of them individuals whose appointment Joan had helped to secure. Parliament insisted on the appointment of a commission, headed by Gaunt and the Archbishop of Canterbury, to investigate and appoint 'good and worthy men' to be around the king. Even Joan may have found Gaunt's appointment, in the light of his recent behaviour, galling, and it is unlikely that this endeared him to his nephew.

Life slowly returned to normal for Joan. The impact of the events of those two weeks was obviously tremendous on all concerned but unfortunately there is little evidence to indicate how Joan was affected by it. In August she secured a royal commission, led by her brother-in-law Thomas of Woodstock, Earl of Buckingham, to investigate offences committed on her estates.[100] Other than some damage to her Essex properties her estates had been largely untouched by the rebels, possibly because the main areas of the disturbance – London, Kent, Essex, St Albans, Norfolk and Suffolk – were areas in which she had virtually no interests. However, the way in which Joan was treated by the rebels suggests that they regarded her with affection and esteem and it is therefore unlikely that they would have targeted her estates. Nevertheless, clearly, on a personal level, she cannot have been unaffected by what had happened. Throughout she had been with Richard and at the heart of it, she had encountered and been in danger from the rebels on more than one occasion in person, and she had heard and witnessed some of the most frightening and horrifying acts of violence. In July and August, in the immediate aftermath, as order was restored and individual ring leaders arrested and tried or held for trial, Joan could have had little if any direct involvement other than remaining with Richard and supporting the actions he took. It seems unlikely that Joan had any sympathy for the rebels or for the complaints they had made, and this is borne out by the fact that when a series of general pardons were issued to individual rebels after the trials and executions of the most notorious leaders in the November parliament there are few supplications made by Joan, and her intervention seems to have been restricted to men from her own estates.[101]

Joan must have been dismayed and disheartened by the inability of Richard's advisers to both protect their young king and deal with the crisis. Thomas and John had also been with their brother throughout, but there is no indication that either of them had played a prominent role. Perhaps Joan was disappointed that neither had shown their father's tough and aggressive leadership skills, although as their mother she must have known her sons' capabilities and realised neither had inherited their father's authoritative character. While her brother-in-law's absence during the revolt had been unavoidable, if she had placed any reliance on his capabilities to assist in restoring order in the aftermath with firmness and tact, she would hardly have found Gaunt's attitude and behaviour on his return reassuring. The only redeeming feature of the whole appalling experience was that Richard himself had shown exceptional bravery and leadership. Two years younger than his father had been at Crécy, his outstanding response to the revolt promised much for the future. He had truly shown himself to be a worthy heir to Edward III.

There are two outstanding pieces of art associated with Richard which are thought to give a good likeness of the king as he would have appeared at this time. The first is the full-length panel portrait of Richard which now hangs in Westminster Abbey, and the second is the personal altarpiece known as the Wilton Diptych, housed in the National Gallery. Both show Richard as the boy king, aged about fourteen. They indicate that Richard was an extremely good-looking boy, with delicate, fair features and reddish-gold hair. It is not known if he took after his father or his mother, but it is probable that he bore at least some resemblance to Joan. Little is known about these works, the identity of the person who commissioned and paid for them, the artist or the reason for their being made. Experts have however concluded that both were almost certainly painted in the 1390s, long after Joan had died, and therefore she would not have seen either work.[102] The consensus is that both were probably made on Richard's orders, although one of the many suggestions made about the Wilton Diptych is that it was commissioned by Maud Courtenay as a present for her brother and a memorial to Joan, with Edward of Angoulême as the Christ child handing over his inheritance to Richard.[103] Both works are striking images of kingship, although the Wilton Diptych is a more complicated piece, filled with hidden meaning. The Wilton Diptych is a portable altar containing a representation of Richard, attended by three saints (St Edmund, St Edward the Confessor and St John the Baptist) kneeling in front of the Virgin and Child, who are in turn backed by angels. Richard is depicted as a child of no more than fourteen or fifteen (there is no suggestion of a beard), his colouring and features bearing a marked resemblance to the portrait in Westminster Abbey. Richard is alone and there is no suggestion that he has a consort, making it improbable that the work was commissioned while he was married to Anne of Bohemia, as he would hardly have omitted all reference to her as queen. While there has never been any suggestion that the piece is directly related to Joan, there are nevertheless considerable coincidences and allusions within it which might indicate that, if indeed commissioned by Richard, his mother was never far from his thoughts. There is the prolific use of her personal emblem of the white hart, with the gold crown around its neck and the gold chain. Richard adopted the badge as his own but he rarely used it during his mother's lifetime, although white hart brooches were made and given as gifts by Joan herself (she gave one to John of Gaunt), and in 1379 Richard had included two such brooches among the jewels pledged to the City as security for a loan, later requested on loan for use at his marriage to Anne.[104] In the Wilton Diptych Richard's cloak is patterned with gold harts, with a white hart badge attached to his breast above his heart, its antlers adorned with pearls, while a smaller version, without the pearls, is also worn by all the angels. The beautiful, serene Virgin, holding the Christ child in her arms, conjures up the image of Joan herself, perhaps with Richard's older brother Edward in her arms. Is it just coincidence that St Edmund, the martyred king, bears the same name as Richard's maternal grandfather, murdered for his loyalty to Edward II, and that John the Baptist, Richard's patron saint, stands behind Richard presenting him to the Virgin, a reminder of the important support John of Gaunt played in his nephew's succession and the close friendship between John and Joan? Gaunt himself had given Joan a gift of a piece representing St John, the Virgin and Child. The banner held aloft by the angel resembles the flag of St George, with its direct association with the prince. The careful composition of the piece and its allegories continue to challenge interpretation, and it is surely not unreasonable to assume that Richard would himself have noted, if not intended, the allusions to his mother.

Following Sudbury's murder the see of Canterbury had fallen vacant, and shortly afterwards William Courtenay, Bishop of London, was appointed his successor. Although there is no direct evidence to indicate Joan's influence, it seems likely that she was at least partly responsible for the elevation in September of her kinsman, Robert Braybrooke, to the bishopric of London, a position Robert held until 1404. It was an appointment of great personal significance and joy for Joan, ensuring that Robert was now at hand to provide family support for Richard and Joan. Like Joan, Robert appears to have eschewed politics. Although he was appointed chancellor a year later, on 20 September 1382, unlike Sudbury and Courtenay Robert proved wary of becoming involved in politics, and his chancellorship was brief (he resigned 10 March 1383).[105] In contrast to Courtenay he was on good terms with John of Gaunt. Both men shared a deep affection for Joan. The destruction of the Savoy left Gaunt without a London home, and when Gaunt returned to London, he was given hospitality by Robert many times in his Fulham residence, and Joan may well have joined them on these occasions.[106] Thomas and John Holand were also duly rewarded for their part in the revolt. Even if neither had shown initiative or leadership during the crisis they had both been at their brother's side throughout and more than demonstrated their loyalty. In the immediate aftermath Richard entrusted his eldest half-brother Thomas with the task of dealing with the rebels in Kent, and in recognition of his service granted him an annuity of £100, while John was also enlisted in the peacemaking process by being appointed a justice of the peace in Cheshire.[107] A few months later, in the autumn, and no doubt after prior consultation with his mother, Richard granted Thomas his father's title of Earl of Kent, and Joan vested in him the Kent holdings which had accompanied the title when her father received it in 1321: the manor at Wickhambreaux and the annual county farm fees of £30.[108]

Of even more importance for Joan was the resumption of the arrangements for Richard's marriage, interrupted by the rebellion. The negotiations were finalised, with Thomas Holand being part of the team sent to meet King Wenceslaus, receiving £133 6s 8d in expenses for going to Flanders.[109] Anne left Bohemia in the autumn, travelling slowly across Europe, and in December 1381 Simon Burley, John Holand and John Montague, steward of the royal household, were entrusted with the delicate task of accompanying her to England.[110] On 18 December Anne crossed from Calais to Dover, moved on to Canterbury and from there to Leeds Castle in Kent where she stayed for Christmas. She arrived in London on 18 January and was married to Richard two days later in Westminster Abbey with Robert Braybrooke officiating. The honour of conducting the ceremony should arguably have gone to the Archbishop of Canterbury, William Courtenay, but he had not yet been officially designated in post. Robert Braybrooke had been involved in the marriage negotiations at an earlier stage, and now, as Bishop of London and a close family friend, he was an obvious choice. Joan's heart must have been full, watching her close friend and kinsman officiate at her son's wedding. On 22 January Anne was crowned in Westminster Abbey, this time with Archbishop Courtenay officiating.[111] This was followed by several days of celebrating, with a tournament and Parliament adjourned to allow its members to take part in the wedding festivities. Unfortunately the marriage was not popular and was greeted without enthusiasm, for the simple reason that Anne brought no dowry and no one could perceive any financial, and only limited diplomatic, benefit in the match.[112] This did not matter to Joan. Anne was granted a fixed annual dower of £4,500, exactly the same sum as had been awarded to Queen Isabella when she married Edward II in 1308.[113] Although there is no evidence to suggest that Joan was in any way involved in the financial arrangements of the marriage, she probably used her influence to encourage a suitable settlement for Anne, remembering the difficulties her own mother-in-law, Philippa, had suffered, when the parlous state of her finances had induced Edward III to take them over in 1363. At least one of Joan's trusted knights, Richard Abberbury, was attached to the new queen's household, Abberbury acting as an attorney for Anne within four months of the marriage and becoming her chamberlain.[114] It was quickly apparent that Richard adored his new wife. This, more than anything else, would have recommended Anne to Joan, and Joan must have felt truly satisfied with her work. Her son's throne was safe and he was now married, his future seemed secure. With the wedding and Anne's coronation safely accomplished, she could now safely retire.

Joan's decision to withdraw from court into retirement was entirely voluntary. There is no indication that Richard had any wish for his mother to retire, or that he encouraged her to do so, nor is there anything to indicate anyone else suggested it. Joan was now a hugely popular and well-respected figure, and held in considerable affection by those around her. However, she was now fifty-three, and although there is no indication that she suffered ill health she was nevertheless of an age when it would have been natural for her to want to lead a quieter life. The death of her childhood companion, Princess Isabella, on 5 October 1382, and her sister-in-law's burial in the church of Grey Friars in London, alongside Joan's grandmother Queen Margaret, was a reminder for Joan of her own mortality. But it is unlikely that this was what motivated Joan to withdraw from court. Joan's priority, always, was the interests of her own family. Her concern with Richard had primarily been to protect him, and with Richard having shown during the revolt that he was quite capable of looking after himself she now felt that he no longer needed her protection. She had never shown any inclination to dominate Richard or exercise overt control over him, and after the revolt Joan adopted an increasingly deferential attitude towards him, addressing him (she wrote in French) in correspondence as 'your humble mother' ('fils le roi supplies u humble mere').[115] This was partly her individual style, as she had always had a tendency towards reverence (in 1377, for example, she had appealed humbly as 'your daughter the princess' to the Bishop of St Davids); nevertheless it also reflected a change in attitude, from being the protective mother to taking a more subservient and humble role, and recognising his regal authority.[116] Richard's marriage was the determining factor. Marriage, and his mother's withdrawal from his side, marked Richard's emergence into adulthood and his new independence. In practical terms, Joan may also have felt, recalling her own experiences, that it would be easier for Richard to develop his relationship with Anne, and for Anne to settle in and establish her influence, without her presence.

The last mother of a reigning king to live in retirement had been Queen Isabella, fifty years earlier, forcibly retired by her son after Edward III had seized power in 1330 and made to live in relative seclusion in Castle Rising in Norfolk to ensure that she was kept away from the court and would be unable to have the influence and power she had once wielded. With Mortimer, Isabella had constrained, overruled and humiliated her son, usurping his authority in promoting the interests of her lover and herself, and the only way Edward III had been able to achieve his independence was by removing them from power. After Mortimer's execution, Isabella was an embarrassment and clearly could not remain at court. Nevertheless, despite her disgrace, Isabella had lived in luxurious comfort, maintained a cultured literary circle, continued to entertain on a generous scale and had been escorted regularly to attend court as her son's guest on occasions such as Christmas. Although their circumstances were quite different, the lifestyle Joan chose to adopt was not dissimilar to that enjoyed by Isabella. With her own circle of friends and family around her, Joan seems to have adopted a modest and retired lifestyle, albeit commensurate with her status, rarely attending court.

Wallingford Castle became her main residence. Although the castle was part of Richard's inheritance from his father, it formed part of Joan's dower, and so would remain hers for her lifetime. Built by the Norman Robert d'Oyley of Lisieux in the eleventh century, the castle had harboured Empress Matilda when she fled from Oxford in 1141 and was later owned by Henry III's younger brother Richard of Cornwall, so forming part of the Cornwall estates owned by Piers Gaveston, who held a magnificent tournament there in 1307, and after his death passed to Queen Isabella who used it as her headquarters when she returned to England in 1327. The castle was granted to the prince in 1335 when he became Duke of Cornwall. The castle estate included a meadow called Kingsmead, a fishery and two watermills. It had the advantage of being within easy reach of London, so that Joan could travel by barge to join Richard and the court should she wish to do so, but it was far enough away to give her some distancing from public life. There are unfortunately no records to indicate the identity of those who remained with her, but she would have had a sizeable household and this probably included her favourite knights and their wives. Among these were almost certainly her closest friend Eleanor Clifford, and Eleanor's husband Lewis Clifford. It is also possible that her daughters were frequent visitors. Since Maud's marriage to the Count of St Pol, it would have suited the count's ambitions to make the most of his royal relations, and Maud may have divided her time between attendance on Richard at court and visiting her mother at Wallingford. Similarly, Joan was very close to her younger daughter, Joan, whose marriage had not proved entirely successful. The absence of Joan's husband abroad for much of the time, fighting to re-establish himself in his homeland in Brittany, with the vacillations of the English Crown towards his cause and the duke's own ambivalence towards his ally, had left his duchess dependent on her family in England, and there were no children of the marriage. By 1382 the duke was sufficiently settled in Brittany to require his wife's presence, and however much Joan may have sympathised with the difficulties her daughter faced, she would have encouraged her daughter to rejoin her husband in Brittany. The young duchess would now have been about twenty-five, and had spent many months with her mother; with no idea when they might see each other again, tears were probably shed when they parted.

Joan would have continued to attend court for major occasions and seasonal festivities, including the annual Garter celebrations in April at Windsor. Possibly she was at the tournament held at Windsor in August 1382 and witnessed William Montague's tragic accident, when he killed his only son in a tilting match.[117] This devastating tragedy left William without a male heir, and Joan would have felt deeply saddened for her old friend's loss. But in the main she stayed in comfortable seclusion at Wallingford, taking a more energetic and personal interest in the running of her own estates than she had formerly. This was evidently something she relished, as she could have left matters in the hands of her council, or indeed have passed some of the responsibility on to her heir. Thomas Holand was now over thirty. Married and with a growing family, he had proved his loyalty to his half-brother and demonstrated his capability. Although he was now Earl of Kent, while his mother was alive he remained considerably under-endowed for a man of his rank, as he would not become entitled to his inheritance until Joan died. Joan was by no means the only wealthy dowager whose heir would have to wait for her death in order to inherit, but she could, had she wished, have passed more of her estates to Thomas during her lifetime. Considering her wealth, the sheer number and disparate geography of her estates, it is curious that she did not. There was even an obvious portion to pass on to Thomas. Joan's aunt, Blanche Wake, had died in July 1381, and Joan had then inherited Blanche's dower share of the Wake estates.[118] Having been managed separately for so many years, these estates would have been a uniquely distinct part of Thomas' inheritance for Joan to have handed over. However, despite the good relationship Joan appears to have enjoyed with Thomas, she does not seem to have considered doing so. Possibly Joan was still overly sensitive, and feared that if she did so this would enhance Thomas' status and might attract criticism, so potentially being damaging to Richard's interests. However, it is also possible that Joan found in retirement that she had more interest in managing her own affairs, and that she simply enjoyed doing so, showing she had inherited some of her mother's acumen for estate management, as indicated in her spirited insistence in November 1383 of a commission of inquiry to uphold the rights of her Warborough tenants (part of her Wallingford estate) to have the use of common land belonging to the Bishop of Lincoln, and her complaint that fishermen in Plymouth had been catching her fish for eight years and selling them without paying her dues.[119] Also, business affairs kept her in touch with friends, such as Michael de la Pole, who became her son's chancellor, and to whom she granted a licence to assign Maison Dieu in Myton, the Carthusian hospital at Kingston on Hull and tenement and land in Cottingham and Willerby in 1383.[120]

Joan would not have spent all her time on estate management. Many of her favourite knights who stayed close by her, including Lewis Clifford, John Clanvowe, Philip la Vache and Richard Stury, were enthusiastic book owners and notably cultured and erudite. Joan probably shared their tastes, and read and listened to their and other literary works at Wallingford.[121] Richard's own later highly developed aesthetic sense, love of literature, fashion, art and refinement is usually attributed to his tutors, but it is just as likely that he inherited some of his mother's tastes. Brought up to speak and write French fluently as well as English, by 1384 Richard is known to have owned dozens of books of French romances, ballads, songs and compositions.[122] All of this suggests that Joan herself shared these literary interests. Probably Joan entertained, having friends to stay, such as John of Gaunt, but unfortunately there is no evidence to confirm this. She may have numbered Geoffrey Chaucer among her house guests, as he was a good friend of several of her knights. Early in 1380 Chaucer was accused of rape, and was assisted in clearing his name by his friends. In May 1380

Cecily Champagne agreed to drop the action and the document recording this was witnessed by John Clanvowe and two other knights close to Joan, William Beauchamp and William Neville.[123] Chaucer's reputation survived this incident. Lewis Clifford may have been godfather to Chaucer's son Lewis, and later Chaucer addressed a poem to Clifford's son-in-law, Philip la Vache.[124] In view of his friendship with so many of her intimate circle it seems probable that the poet was invited to Wallingford. However, although Joan may have provided Chaucer with inspiration for his works, there is no evidence to indicate that she became his patron.[125]

Although Joan maintained a close and affectionate relationship with her brother-in-law, her faith in Gaunt's judgement had been shaken by his behaviour after his return from Scotland in the summer of 1381. More significantly, it is evident that this also irretrievably damaged his relationship with Richard. While Joan never doubted her brother-in-law's loyalty it became quickly apparent that Richard never really trusted his uncle again, and his suspicions of Gaunt's intentions were easily aroused. After the quarrel with Percy had been patched up at the beginning of 1382 there was little sign of open affection between uncle and nephew, and Richard was clearly wary of his uncle. At the Salisbury parliament held from 29 April to 27 May 1384, a Carmelite friar, John Latimer, gained an audience with the king and produced a document in which he detailed plots devised by John of Gaunt to seize the throne. The chroniclers' accounts of Richard's reaction vary, alternating between an extreme one of ordering his uncle's arrest, or even his death, restrained only by the lords who were present insisting on Gaunt's right to a trial, and Walsingham's account that Richard conferred with two clerks of his chapel and summoned the duke to discuss the document. Gaunt, strongly supported by Thomas of Woodstock, naturally denied the contents of the document and was vehement in protestations of his innocence. Richard accepted his uncle's assurances, no doubt mindful of his mother's frequent injunctions in Gaunt's support. At the duke's request, the friar was taken into custody and placed in John Holand's charge. According to Walsingham, that night Latimer was tortured to death.[126] Neither Richard nor Gaunt chose to censure either John Holand or his accomplice, Sir Henry Green. Hearing of this unsavoury incident can only have given Joan pain. Neither her brother-in-law, nor either of her sons, Richard and John, emerge from this incident with any credit. To add to her woes, in November 1384 her younger daughter, Joan, Duchess of Brittany, died. The cause of death is not known but it appears to have been sudden and unexpected. Joan had not seen her daughter since she had returned to Brittany two years earlier to join her husband, but they had an unusually close relationship as the duchess had been a part of her household for so many years. The young Joan's death was a tragedy, and a loss Joan must have felt keenly. Joan could at least be cheered by the progress her oldest son was making with his career, as on 20 November 1384 Thomas

Holand was granted the custody of the castle and town of Cherbourg, just as his father had been many years earlier.[127]

In February 1385, matters between Richard and his uncle Gaunt came to a head once more, and this time Joan resolved to intervene. Despite Joan's own fondness for her brother-in-law she was aware that her son could not bring himself to fully trust his powerful uncle, while Gaunt appeared to be incapable of showing the affection and concern towards his nephew which might have helped to restore that trust. It was perhaps fortunate that following the Latimer accusation an opportunity arose which required Gaunt's absence from court while putting his diplomatic skills to good use. At the end of May 1384 John of Gaunt and Thomas of Woodstock were appointed to conduct peace negotiations with the French Crown, and after three months of talks a truce was concluded in September, with Gaunt returning to London the following month, in October, in time to attend the parliament that was called in November and concluded in December. It is not clear what happened between Richard and Gaunt throughout this period but there appears to have been a major disagreement of some kind. In February 1385 rumours of a plot to kill Gaunt, with Richard's backing, alarmed the duke to such an extent that he retreated to Pontefract Castle in Yorkshire to gather support, and he then returned to London with a large armed following to confront Richard at Sheen. The chroniclers' record that, crossing the river, Gaunt spoke harshly and bitterly to Richard, and that the young king promised his uncle he would reform his ways. Gaunt then re-crossed the river and withdrew to his castle at Hertford.[128] This was extraordinary behaviour, and however justified Gaunt's outrage may have been, his show of power and aggression, forcing his nephew to apologise, and then failing to heal the breach by staying with him, can only have fuelled Richard's suspicions of his uncle. This angry, proud and powerful John of Gaunt showed none of the tact or conciliatory attitude which Joan had urged her brother-in-law to adopt in previous years.

Hearing about the row, Joan was shocked by the rift and reacted immediately. Leaving Wallingford she hastened first to Richard, reminding him of the need to keep on good terms with his uncles, especially Gaunt. The chroniclers' accounts vary slightly, one suggesting that she also criticised Richard for listening to flatterers, another that she pleaded with her son on her knees, and urged him to avoid quarrelling with his uncles and his nobles.[129] Then she travelled on to confront Gaunt (presumably still at Hertford) and persuaded him to come to London to meet Richard at Westminster, where, according to Walsingham, she pleaded with them humbly until she achieved her desire to restore peace and concord between them.[130] According to one source, Gaunt's anger was directed at several other nobles, including the Earl of Salisbury, the Earl of Oxford and the Earl of Nottingham, although no reason is given for this.[131] Joan's intervention achieved the desired effect and peace was restored between the king and his uncle. But despite her success Joan must have wondered how long the restored harmony would last, reflecting sadly that her brother-in-law and her son appeared to be unable to maintain a friendly relationship.

Walsingham, in recording Joan's conciliatory success, noted that she was 'not strong and used to luxury, and hardly able to move because she was so fat'.[132] He is the only chronicler to note that her health had deteriorated, and the description given suggests that she may have developed dropsy, which would cause swelling and weight gain. She was now fifty-eight, and may well have felt drained by her intercessory effort. However, Joan had recognised the urgency and significance of the situation, and had shown no hesitation in becoming involved. Perhaps only she could have intervened so successfully between her son and his uncle; certainly she had lost none of her old mediation skills. Returning to Wallingford it was perhaps a relief for Joan to throw herself back into her own affairs, and she showed both the energy and the desire to do so. In May 1385 she formally requested of Richard 'that it may please her son, of his especial grace, to grant to his mother that she may make Justices by her own commission to hold their Sessions from time to time at their leisure, and for the greater profit of the Princess; and that she may do all manner of things that belong to the office of justice in those parts within the precinct of all her dower, ... and issue all manner writs and commissions by her deputies under the seal of the princess in the same parts as entirely and fully as her son does'.[133] This was unusually forceful and vigorous for Joan and indicates a strong determination to be proactively involved in managing her own affairs. Possibly she realised that this would be her last opportunity to do so.

It is generally considered that the panegyric written about the prince by the herald of Sir John Chandos was composed during 1385. Several copies of the work survive, and it is elaborately and expensively decorated, indicating a wealthy patron arranging its publication.[134] John Chandos had been a close companion of the prince and had predeceased him by some years, while the prince himself had been dead for nine years. It may just be coincidence that the work was written during the last year of Joan's life, but it is possible that it was done at her behest, or that she was influential in encouraging its composition and accomplishment. The literary tribute to the prince is a chronicle of his life, written in French verse, primarily commemorating his feats of arms, though biographical details of his life are included. The poem describes the Battle of Crécy and the siege of Calais, gives details of the Poitiers campaign and an eyewitness account of the Nájera campaign, with an overview of the government in Aquitaine, and describes the prince's last years, listing his chief officers and a copy of the epitaph on his tomb. The composition is elaborately decorated with a frontispiece comprising a full-length miniature of the prince in gold and colours, one part of Trinity and second of the prince kneeling in adoration on a red cushion, clad in armour wearing leather jupon without sleeves, emblazoned with the arms of England and France, with sword and dagger, golden elbow, kneecaps and spurs, large silver ostrich feather and his motto, 'Ich dene'. The prince's victories and achievements are admired and celebrated, while the prince himself is described in terms which leave no doubt that the writer considered the prince to be the premier chivalric knight of his generation. The poem is a magnificent literary tribute, possibly intended for presentation to Richard, although the fact that more than one copy survives suggests it was intended for wide distribution. It had clear propaganda value for Richard as the prince's son. Joan is only mentioned in the poem eight times, although she is described in complimentary terms. In the words of Chandos Herald Joan was 'une dame de grant pris, Qe belle fuist, plesante et sage' (a lady of great worth, beautiful, pleasant and wise). It was also during 1385 that Richard commissioned a series of thirteen sculptures of the kings of England to adorn the Great Hall at Westminster, probably from Edward the Confessor to himself.[135] This was a grand project and clearly designed to be a display of royal lineage, with an emphasis on Richard's paternal ancestry. Richard may well have discussed it with his mother, and certainly she would have heartily endorsed it.

Early in June, meeting in Reading, the king's council agreed that, following the renewal of hostilities between Scotland and England after the arrival of a French force in Scotland, Richard should lead an expedition into Scotland. He would be accompanied by most of the leading nobility, including his uncle Gaunt. The duke was by this time back on good terms with his nephew, and with his peers. This was Richard's first military campaign and in honour of the momentous occasion, as was customary, there were noble promotions. The king created his uncles Edmund and Thomas dukes of York and Clarence respectively, and Michael de la Pole, the chancellor (and a friend of Gaunt's), Earl of Suffolk. Richard and Anne visited Joan at Wallingford before he left, the occasion recorded for posterity by a contemporary depiction of Chaucer (in a picture on the frontispiece of an original copy of his work Troilus and Criseyde) reading his works to the royal family at Wallingford.[136] Taking leave of his mother, Richard was mindful of earlier dangers and careful to leave her well attended, ordering a number of her favourite knights to 'assist continually about the person of the king's mother for her comfort and security wherever she shall abide within the realm, rendering other services so befitting the estate of so great a lady'. The men ordered to stay with Joan were her knights Lewis Clifford, Richard Stury, Philip la Vache, Thomas Latimer, her steward John Worthe, her clerks William Harpele, Lawrence Sebroke and Henry Norton, and Thomas Morwell, William Fitzrauf, Gilbert Wace, Garnius Arnaud and Richard Mewes.[137]

The royal army set out late in June and made its way slowly north. Accompanying Richard were Thomas and John Holand. Unfortunately the campaign got off to a disastrous start. John Holand, whose charismatic personality seems to have endeared him more to Richard than his older and steadier brother, had already shown a regrettable tendency towards thoughtless and uncontrolled violence. As the army neared York a quarrel broke out between John's retainers and those of Ralph Stafford, son of the Earl of Stafford and one of Queen Anne's household knights. One of John Holand's squires was killed, and Stafford's men fled to sanctuary at Beverley. Shortly afterwards, and it appears by chance, John Holand met Ralph Stafford near York. Unluckily it seems that neither were able to restrain themselves from making the quarrel personal, and in the ensuing fight, John killed Stafford. This was appalling behaviour for which there could be little excuse. Once news of Ralph Stafford's death reached Richard, the king had no choice but to react immediately. Richard ordered John's arrest and confiscated his property, swearing that John would have to face the full rigour of the law. According to the chroniclers, Richard was absolutely furious with his half-brother, as well he might be. John's intemperance, his failure to make any attempt to explain his actions or apologise for them, amounted to a personal affront, and the king was not going to leave this unchallenged. Thomas suffered indirectly for his brother's heinous crime, being replaced as earl marshal on 30 June by the Earl of Nottingham.[138] Yet, despite Richard's fury, he does not seem to have suggested that John should be tried for murder and executed for his crime. When the news reached Joan, she was aghast. Desperately afraid of the consequences for both her sons, she tried to intervene. The distances were too great for her to take to the road and talk to Richard in person, and she had to rely on messengers instead, sending them to beg Richard, according to Walsingham, 'not to reject so small a request of his mother, but to pity his brother, to pity his mother, and as a brother to show greater pity because he was his brother'. Her messengers included Lewis Clifford and reached the army before it left Carlisle.[139] Richard was too angry to listen and Lewis Clifford returned to Joan empty-handed. For once Joan was unable to deal with this crisis. She was too ill. Her health failed her, and she collapsed. According to Walsingham, 'it may be that because she was weighed down by too much grief she collapsed on her bed, and after four or five days she died'.[140] Conscious that she was dying, on 7 August Joan made her will, and she died the following day, on 8 August 1385.

Richard's reaction, when he heard of his mother's death, can only be imagined. The chroniclers were firmly of the view that the row had caused Joan's death, and that she had died of grief. More prosaically, Joan had probably been unwell for several months, and this fresh disaster had simply exacerbated her condition. Joan had experienced many difficult situations in her life, and she would surely have felt confident of her ability to manage this one if she had been fit enough to do so. At her bedside in her last hour, perhaps she was comforted by the presence of her daughter Maud and her good friend Eleanor. Although Joan died very quickly after her collapse, she was able to put her affairs in order and make her arrangements. She remained concerned with her children and their affairs to the last, as the provisions of her will showed. Her principal beneficiaries were her three sons, and if she had any doubts about John's future, she sought to dispel them by making equal provision for him in her will, a clear sign to Richard that she expected the king to find a way to forgive and rehabilitate his errant brother.

In her will, Joan committed her soul to God, the Virgin Mary and the saints, and specifically affirmed her adherence to the Catholic faith, 'fiden catholicam firmiter proficiendo'. This was a somewhat unusually adamant profession of faith, which might possibly reflect a greater piety than Joan had been willing to show publicly, but it could also have been intended to dispel any lingering doubts there might be about her having heretical Lollard sympathies, as Joan had always been concerned that any slur on her reputation might adversely affect Richard. Her 'dearest son' Richard was her principal beneficiary, and she left him her new red velvet bed embroidered with silver ostrich feathers and heads of leopards in gold with boughs and leaves issuing from their mouths, with all her belongings in her wardrobe in London ('meum de velvet rubrum novum operat' in broderieria cum pennies ostric' argent' et cum capit' leopardor, de auro' cum ramis et foliis argenteis procedentibus et utraquw parte quolibet ore ipso' cum appartu prout est in custodia garderobe mee London'). He was also to have the residue of her estate. She left Thomas a red camaca bed decorated in red and gold with a canopy quilt decorated with hatchments, and a quantity of rich furnishings.[141] John, also described as her 'dearest son', was similarly gifted a red camaca bed and canopy with luxurious coverings of silk curtains, tapestry and a scarlet fur cover. Joan only named her three sons as individual beneficiaries and it is evident that she intended them to understand from the gifts and her language that she was regarded them all with equal affection. Joan carefully stipulated that her executors should have a year to pay her debts, and discretion to make payments to her servants, according to their 'quality and merit', thus ensuring that her executors would have complete freedom to reward her retainers as they saw fit, probably in accordance with instructions she had already given. Joan made no other individual gifts; significantly, she does not mention either her beloved daughter Maud or her good friend Eleanor, nor did she make any gifts of alms, or to religious houses, or any other endowments. These omissions were clearly quite deliberate. By making her three sons the only named beneficiaries in her will Joan was sending them a message that she could not deliver in person, reminding them of their relationship, stressing the importance of family. She could, and probably did, make provision for Maud and Eleanor and any other family or friends by giving them gifts before her death or by separate instruction to her executors. Similarly, any patronage she chose to make was kept private, and if she made any deathbed provision she was careful to ensure it was sufficiently modest not to be noted. As she lay dying, Joan's first thoughts were for her family.

Joan appointed as executors to her will the following: her 'dear friend' and cousin Robert Braybrooke; William Wykeham, Bishop of Winchester; John Lord Cobham; William Beauchamp; William Neville; Simon Burley; Lewis Clifford; Richard Abberbury; John Clanvowe; Richard Stury; Philip la Vache (wrongly named 'John' Vache); her steward John Worthe; her 'dear' chaplains William Fulbourne (who had been with her since she married the prince in 1361) and John Yernmouth; her 'dear' squire William Harpele; and William Norton (this was probably meant to be Henry Norton).[142] The will was witnessed by the prior of Wallingford and John James, and it was proved on 9 December 1385. Joan's will was written in Latin; bearing in mind that it was written the day before she died, the choice of language was probably that of her clerk rather than Joan herself, as her own preference would more likely have been French, used by the prince and later John of Gaunt. Joan appointed sixteen executors in her will, a quite extraordinary number. No estate, however complex, would require the appointment of so many executors. The prince, in contrast, had named eight, while even Edward III had been content to appoint only ten. It is obvious that Joan had another motive for nominating so many people to be her executors, and as she had never sought attention for herself it is unlikely that she chose so many to signify her own importance. Therefore the reason had more to do with the individuals she named than with herself, and while it can only be speculative to suggest this, it seems likely that Joan was using the office of executor as a means of protecting, as well as rewarding, those closest to her. It is notable that, although all the knights appointed were loyal and close friends of long standing who had served first the prince and then Joan faithfully over many years, apart from Simon Burley and Richard Adderbury, the others – William Beauchamp, William Neville, Lewis Clifford, John Clanvowe, Richard Stury and Philip la Vache – were all Lollard sympathisers. Joan would have been aware that the Church was becoming more aggressive in its attack on the Lollard heresy, and appointing them as her executors may have been in part an attempt by her to ensure them future royal protection, relying on Richard respecting her wishes and preventing the prosecution of any of his mother's executors.

After her death, Joan's body was wrapped in waxed linen cloths and placed in a lead tomb at Wallingford to await Richard's return from Scotland. In September various members of Richard's household received cloth to use as liveries for mourning for Joan. These included Clanvowe, Clifford, Philip la Vache and Geoffrey Chaucer, the latter receiving three and a half ells of black cloth.[143] In her will Joan requested burial in the chapel at Stamford, next to the memorial to Thomas Holand; this was also where Blanche Wake was buried.[144] Joan left no instructions regarding her final journey, and there are no records detailing it. It would not have taken place until after Christmas 1385 as Joan was finally laid to rest in January 1386, in 'a sumptuous chapel recently built next to the choir', and

Richard ensured that his mother's burial place was kept in good repair.[145] Unfortunately the church in Stamford no longer exists and there is no trace of Joan's tomb. There is now no way of knowing what kind of tomb or memorial was erected for Joan, as there is no evidence from the royal accounts of any expenditure by Richard which might reveal this. The prince, Edward III and Philippa all had grand and imposing marble tombs with a life-size effigy of themselves made from bronze placed on top, and Richard arranged something similar for himself and Anne (though it was Henry V who ensured that Richard's wishes were carried out in respect of his own tomb). It seems unlikely that Joan would have wanted this kind of memorial for herself, especially as she had stipulated burial in the chapel at Stamford, which was a far humbler setting than Westminster Abbey and Canterbury Cathedral, and no doubt Richard followed his mother's wishes in providing her with a far less ostentatious monument.

Joan's request that she be buried at Stamford with Thomas Holand, rather than with the prince in Canterbury Cathedral, is intriguing. Having endowed two chantries at Canterbury when they were married, and stipulated in great detail his own burial in the cathedral, there can be little doubt that the prince anticipated that his wife would join him there, but it is clear from Joan's will that she did not want this. It is possible that even as she lay dying Joan was anxious not to draw attention to herself and wanted to be as unobtrusive in death as she had tried to be in life. The prince had not been buried as he stipulated, in the chapel of Our Lady Undercroft, and his tomb had been placed beside the altar in the main body of Canterbury Cathedral.[146] Had Joan been placed beside him she would have occupied a very public and prominent position in the cathedral, and her burial would inevitably have attracted considerable attention. Perhaps as she lay dying Joan felt concern that her death might renew the controversy over the legality of her marriage, with unforeseen consequences for Richard. But the other, and more probable, explanation is that Thomas Holand had been the great love of her life, and she wanted to be with him in death, and that this was in the end more important to her than any possible awkwardness this might cause Richard. It is touching, and to Richard's credit, that he respected his mother's wishes and had no hesitation in carrying out her instructions.

There is no way of knowing how Joan's Holand children felt when she died. As they all enjoyed a good relationship with their mother, there must have been a genuine sense of loss for all of them, and not just for Richard. Joan had been a stabilising influence in all their lives, and she had worked hard to keep them together as a family. Her Holand sons may well have had mixed feelings. Maybe John Holand was full of remorse, as he would have been aware how much distress his conduct had caused his mother. Perhaps for Thomas there was secret relief, as his mother's death at last released to him the huge Kent estates. They would both have been conscious of the influence their mother had exercised on Richard in restraining his inclination to advance them in his service, and now that bar had been removed; John in particular was ambitious. But she had died just as John was in disgrace and estranged from Richard. It would have been natural for him to feel some apprehension, as their mother had always been the one to heal any family rifts, and now she was not there to intercede on his behalf with Richard over the Stafford murder. John could not be sure that Richard would not impose a heavier punishment on him in addition to the forfeiture of his possessions, while Thomas too was conscious that he had fallen out of favour because of his brother's behaviour. Maud's grief was less complicated, as she did not gain materially from her mother's death; instead she lost the companionship of someone she had been very close to and with whom she had lived for most of her life.

Richard's grief cannot be gauged. When news of her death reached him, he was on campaign and hardly in a position to abandon everything and return to bury her. Perhaps her death did not come as a surprise, as he may well have been conscious of her poor health when he left her in June. Did he blame John for her death? Did he feel some responsibility for his own part in the quarrel which had caused her such distress? In withdrawing from the daily life of the court, Joan had removed herself from Richard's side as an everyday influence, and the distancing she had deliberately created would have helped Richard to miss her less than he might have done otherwise, while he also had his beloved Anne to comfort him. Nevertheless Richard was only eighteen when his mother died, and she had been at his side throughout his life, protecting, guiding, supporting and comforting him. Richard must have felt her loss keenly.

There are very few surviving reminders of Joan. The chapel at Stamford where she was buried no longer exists and there are no traces of her tomb. The only surviving contemporary picture of her is the stylised representation of her in the St Albans Abbey book of benefactors, while the boss in the ceiling in the chapel of Our Lady Undercroft at Canterbury Cathedral, if indeed it is intended to be Joan, is of insufficient detail and quality to be a good likeness. None of her possessions survive, nor any of the records made and kept for her. There is only one copy of her seal. The castles and palace she spent most time in and considered her homes, Castle Donington, Berkhamsted, Kennington and Wallingford, are either ruins or no longer visible at all. The most enduring image is the white hart emblem adopted by her son, Richard. Despite the emphasis which Joan had encouraged him to place on his paternal ancestry, he chose his mother's emblem of the chained and crowned white hart as his personal badge. Richard's use of the white hart is generally considered to have been formally publicly adopted at the Smithfield tournament held in 1390, five years after Joan's death, and it then became frequently used, appearing on buildings, the royal barge, banners, textiles and seals.[147] There can be little doubt that his adoption of Joan's emblem was Richard's way of honouring his mother.

15

Conclusion: Joan's Legacy

So absolute she seems
And in herself complete, so well to know
Her own, that what she wills to do or say
Seems wisest, virtuousest, discreetest, best.

Milton, *Paradise Lost*

Within a few years of Joan's death, commenting on the role of women in society, the writer Christine de Pizan described in detail the behaviour expected of a noblewoman in her book *The Treasure of the City of Ladies* or *The Book of the Three Virtues* (*Le Livre des Trois Vertus*).[1] Acknowledging that women were regarded as weak and irrational, subject to temptation, and expected to be obedient and quiet in public, Christine counselled noblewomen that as wives and mothers they should obey their husbands, run the household and bring up the children. But Christine also advised her readers that noblewomen should retain their independence and provide counsel to their husbands and children, and in their husband's absence they should take his place, and run the estates to safeguard the family's well-being and prestige. There was a balance to be struck between taking a subservient role to their husband and maintaining their own independence and integrity. Christine's advice for a princess was more circumspect: she should be loyal and true to her husband, incline her heart towards humility, 'behave respectably and speak softly, her conduct will be kindly and her expression gentle and pleasant ... she will be patient ... she will be an advocate and mediator between the prince her husband or her child if she is a widow and her people', distribute gifts with great discretion and prudence, and 'in neither word nor deed, appearance, ornaments nor bearing, conduct, social pomp or expression will there be anything for which she could be reproached or criticised' for 'above all things a princess should love honour and a good reputation'.[2] Christine could have been describing Joan, and it is tempting to speculate that Christine might have had her in mind when she was writing. The respect and affection in which Joan was held, and the popularity of her public persona, made her a role model for her contemporaries; as Princess of Wales she had become almost universally esteemed and admired for her quiet dignity, unfailing tact and discretion, her loyalty and devotion, and her gentle persuasiveness and conciliation skills.[3]

Joan also provided contemporaries with a different kind of role model, as her beauty and her circumstances made casting her in the role of romantic heroine irresistible for writers like Froissart, Jean le Bel and Chandos Herald. The love affair with Thomas Holand, his dispute with William Montague and the whirlwind courtship with the prince firmly established her allure, and her romantic credentials were only enhanced by the shadow cast over her by the dubious nature of the legality of her marriage to Holand. Like many of the heroines in the popular romances, such as Guinevere in the story of Arthur, Joan was flawed. The combined attributes of her beauty, royal blood and tangled marital history were an irresistible combination which they embellished to present Joan as an idealised and fascinating heroine. In an age of chivalry, with its emphasis on status and beauty, Joan embodied the perfect chivalric knight's consort, and it was hardly surprising that so many romantic stories cast Joan in the leading role. Froissart and Jean le Bel used Joan in their tales, as both one of the fair ladies for whom the chivalric knights at Valenciennes swore to wear an eyepatch until they had performed worthy deeds, and the young, beautiful and vulnerable Countess of Salisbury who defended Wark Castle until rescued by Edward III. Having firmly established Joan as a romantic heroine, subsequent writers were not slow to follow suit, and two centuries later Vergil seamlessly identified Joan as the inspiration for the founding of the Order of the Garter.

Such writings posthumously distanced and undermined the favourable reputation Joan had acquired during her lifetime. Joan was never the helpless beauty of the romantic stories she became associated with; she was both more complicated and more appealing, and had worked hard to acquire the universal approbation she enjoyed when she died. Joan's early life was a complex mix of great privilege with considerable hardship. Born into a wealthy and royal family, her early childhood was blighted by the execution of her father and her mother's subsequent obsession with the family estates. Adopted into the royal household and to a large extent abandoned by her mother, Joan was isolated and vulnerable, and seduced when she was barely into her teens by an attractive but unscrupulous young man. If she ever regretted her marriage to Thomas Holand she never showed it. This tough, ambitious career soldier was the great love of her life. In the ensuing nine years, as she grew into a young woman, she was bullied by her mother and uncle, forced into a bigamous marriage, incarcerated by her new husband and his family, abandoned by her foster parents and ostracised by society. Bravely defying her family and the pressures imposed on her, Joan showed tremendous strength of character and determination in her resolve to honour her marriage to Thomas Holand. She endured years of shameful treatment at the hands of the very people who should have been caring for her, becoming estranged from her immediate family. During that time her experience within the royal circle was in complete contrast to the chivalric ideal being fostered by Edward III, and she could only have been an embarrassment to him, reminding him of his failure to protect her and of his inadequacies with regard to the fate of her father. Joan's stubborn loyalty to Thomas was in the end the deciding factor in ensuring their marriage was finally recognised and she then willingly followed him to war-torn France, embracing her life as a soldier's wife and balancing her duties as his wife and the mother of his children. When her brother John died, the obligations and responsibilities of managing the vast Kent estates she inherited did not alter her determination to accompany her husband. When Thomas died, Joan had the freedom to live as she wanted for the first time in her life but she turned the focus of her love and concern to her family, and when her cousin proposed marriage she had no hesitation in accepting, knowing that the marriage would secure her children's futures.

Joan made the most spectacular marriage of her generation when she married the prince, and it has always been regarded as a love match which defied convention. Yet in many ways it was an extremely suitable match, particularly for the prince – a fortunate combination of personal choice and expediency. The most difficult and controversial aspect of their marriage was Joan's marital history, and they were both fully aware that her somewhat scandalous reputation could cause difficulties. The prince and his father took the steps they considered necessary to secure the legality of the match, but for Joan the consequences were more personal. The prince's love for Joan is well documented, but it has never been clear that she reciprocated his feelings to the same degree, and it is unlikely that she ever felt the same intensity of love that she had experienced with Thomas Holand. Marrying the prince meant becoming Princess of Wales, and this was both an opportunity and a burden for Joan. From the beginning of their marriage and up to her death Joan knew what was expected of her and she was at pains to both fulfil those expectations and to diminish the notoriety caused by her marital history. That she was right to do so is apparent from the gossip recounted by the chronicler Adam Usk in 1399, around the time of Richard's deposition ('... concerning whose birth [Richard's] many unsavoury things were commonly said, namely that he was not born of a father of the royal line, but of a mother given to slippery ways – to say nothing of many other things I have heard'), implying that her behaviour had been shameful, dishonourable, even outrageous.[4] If Henry of Bolingbroke had been able to prove Richard's illegitimacy in 1399, his claim to the throne would have been greatly strengthened. That Joan was successful is also clear, as she gained such approval and respect from her contemporaries that even the most ardent of Henry of Bolingbroke's supporters did not attempt to foster the slander to her reputation.

Joan's personality was a substantial contributory factor to her success as Princess of Wales. She was by nature gentle, warm and loving, a natural peacemaker with an innate ability to get on well with people and an inborn modesty and diffidence. During her marriages to Thomas Holand and the prince Joan was content to be dominated by and dictated to by her husbands, partly because this was a role which suited her personality but also because she loved them and knew and understood what was required of her. As the prince's wife she behaved as he expected, quietly and with dignity, choosing to exercise her tremendous influence with restraint. Uninterested in political power, she never considered using the considerable influence she had with Richard for her own purposes after the prince died, and continued to conduct herself as she felt was expected of her. Yet, as she had shown in her youth, Joan was also courageous and independently minded, and prepared to fight for what she considered important. She relied on her own judgement and risked her reputation to come to Gaunt's aid in February 1377, sheltering him from the wrathful London mob in the wake of the row with the Bishop of London and so ensuring her brother-in-law's survival, an act of tremendous political significance. She showed she had lost none of her personal bravery when she insisted on remaining at Richard's side during the Peasants' Revolt. But throughout Joan chose to use her influence judiciously and discreetly. Her great gift was her capacity for love and loyalty; in her personal life she attracted the lifelong devotion of friends and retainers, and made few, if any, enemies. With these attributes it is not surprising that she grew to be generally admired and loved.

Joan's most famous legacy was her son, Richard. Once it became clear that the prince would not live to succeed his father, Joan devoted herself to the future of their son, to the extent that she was prepared to suppress the interests of her older sons until Richard was secure on his throne. Much of her influence was beneficial. Her popularity and her good relationship with Gaunt eased Richard's peaceful succession; Gaunt's support for Richard's accession was crucial, and although his loyalty to his brother had never been in doubt there were many who feared he would not support the son and would make a bid for the throne himself. That Gaunt was so stalwart in his support of his nephew was in no small measure due to the affectionate and fond relationship he enjoyed with Joan, and their mutual trust and respect. Gaunt would never forget that his sister-in-law had been willing to risk her own safety and reputation in coming to his aid in February 1377. Once Richard became king his relationship with his powerful uncle was never an easy one, neither being comfortable with the other, and on several occasions their relationship fractured, with potentially serious political consequences; while she was alive, Joan's intervention was crucial in restoring accord between them. During the early years of Richard's kingship, his mother's conciliatory skills and her calm, authoritative and quiet tact helped achieve political harmony. She was a natural peacemaker with instinctive and natural warmth which enabled her to work quietly and effectively behind the scenes. Gentle and unassuming, Joan was generally respected as an influence for moderation and good sense.

Joan also forged strong friendships. Gaunt was not the only powerful magnate with whom she built a lasting friendship. Perhaps nowhere is her pleasant and gentle character better revealed than in the relationship she enjoyed with William Montague. Despite being married to him against her will and imprisoned by him, despite William's humiliation in having their marriage annulled, Joan and William remained on good terms throughout her life, forging a close bond that was never broken. Throughout her marriage to the prince William was welcomed as one of the prince's leading commanders, and maintained a regular presence among the prince's entourage, while after the prince's death William's loyalty and devotion to Richard was marked and he became one of the young king's most important supporters. There was never any doubt of William's allegiance. The families stayed close, with William's son (also called William) becoming brother-in-law to Joan's eldest son Thomas when he married Elizabeth, daughter of the Earl of Arundel. Joan's ability to maintain friendly relations with so many of the nobility was an undoubted factor in maintaining stability and accord among the conflicting interests.

Joan fostered family unity, maintaining close ties with her other brothers-in-law, Thomas of Woodstock and Edmund of Langley, while encouraging Richard's Holand brothers and sisters to stay close to their brother. Joan knew that undue favouritism could be deeply divisive and damaging to Richard as a young king, and she ensured that no special partiality was shown to any one individual, in particular that her Holand sons were not seen to benefit from their brother's status. Joan was remarkably successful in her management of her Holand sons, as both could reasonably have expected more preferential treatment from their brother after his accession, and might well have felt considerable resentment at their mother's restraint, but both were to be loyal to Richard throughout their lives. Joan also ensured that Richard was surrounded by loyal and devoted retainers, men who were also cultured, literary and erudite, like Simon Burley, Lewis Clifford, John Clanvowe, Sir John Montague, Richard Stury and Philip la Vache.[5] She provided a stable, unobtrusive, moderating and harmonious influence and her presence at Richard's side throughout his earliest years as king, giving him support and guidance – and during the Peasants' Revolt, when she encouraged in him the confidence and the resolve with which he faced the rebels – was invaluable. Joan was also, unusually, prepared to quietly remove herself from the centre of events when she felt the time was right, retiring to

Wallingford Castle once she was satisfied that Richard was safe and had a wife at his side, while remaining in readiness should he need her again.

However, Joan's influence may also have been detrimental to Richard, albeit unintentionally. Her genuine concern that her marital history could constitute a threat to Richard, coupled with the early death of Richard's older brother, Prince Edward, and the lingering death of the prince, almost certainly made her overprotective. Ensuring that her son was surrounded by men who had served his father was a means for her to provide him with support and protection, but it also meant that Richard was served by men who were predisposed to defer to him. In addition, these loyal knights acted as a constant reminder to Richard of his father, and he would have been very aware of the veneration and admiration in which his father was held. The prince, as the most renowned and respected chivalric knight and military commander of his generation, presented an almost impossible role model for the young Richard to follow. Richard's tutors, Abberbury, d'Angle and Burley, were all respected knights themselves, and had fought with the prince. Richard could hardly escape hearing almost daily plaudits about his father, although his own memories could only have been of a sick man. Joan's protective instinct was inherently contradictory. Although Richard was taught to ride, hunt, fight with a sword and joust there was always an underlying fear that he might be injured, perhaps fatally, so it is unlikely that Joan encouraged him to take risks or allowed his teachers to do so. He was too important. There is no record of Richard taking part in tournaments and he did not have the opportunity to take part in a campaign until he was eighteen, whereas his father and grandfather had both proved themselves in battle by this age. Similarly Joan would have influenced Richard in his attitude towards the war with France. Her views could hardly have been anything other than ambivalent. The war with France had given Thomas Holand and the prince the opportunity to display their military genius, and had brought them fame and glory (and fortune for Thomas Holand), but it had also brought untimely death for both of them. Joan would have wanted to protect her son from this. She was also a natural pacifist, both by instinct and by upbringing. Richard's marked disinclination towards continuing the war with France probably owed much to his mother's unconscious influence.

Joan was not only extremely protective towards Richard, but increasingly deferential, behaving quite differently towards him than to her other children. To some extent this was inevitable, given that he was heir to the throne and then king, but Richard's later exaggerated sense of his own importance probably had its origins in his mother's treatment of him. Conscious of her awkward marital past and the care Edward III and the prince had taken to ensure the validity of her marriage to the prince, Joan almost certainly overemphasised the importance of her son's royal lineage, while also passing on to him her own insecurity about it.

Ironically, her fears appear to have been groundless. There is no evidence that her marital history posed a real threat to Richard; it was never raised as an issue at his succession, and even when he was deposed in 1399 by Henry of Bolingbroke it was not used against him. By 1377 it should have been clear that the precautions taken by the prince and his father had been amply sufficient, and Joan should have been able to relax. But unfortunately it continued to be a concern for her and it is obvious that she made Richard overly aware of it. The many documents validating his mother's marriage to Thomas Holand, and her subsequent marriage to the prince, were considered so precious by Richard that he kept them in a safe box at his side at all times and it was only on his one military expedition abroad, when he went to Ireland in 1394, that he entrusted them to be kept for him elsewhere. Unlike his father and grandfather, as an adult Richard was obsessed with his lineage and royal status. The genesis for this, and for the insecurity which would later become so apparent in Richard, lay with his mother's own insecurity. Joan reinforced this by suppressing her own importance while emphasising Richard's, and this is most poignantly evidenced in the surviving letters she wrote to him, in which she addressed her son in humble, supplicatory tones.

Perhaps without realising it, Joan encouraged others to treat her son in a similarly reverential way, including his own brothers, who were kept so markedly dependent on their brother's favour. The change in the timing of his coronation oath, surrounding him with loyal and trusted men, smoothing over difficulties whenever she could, encouraged Richard to expect obedient homage on the basis of his birth. When even Gaunt, the most powerful noble in the land, adopted a humble stance in his presence, this simply reinforced and endorsed the extreme deference with which Richard was treated by those who sought to protect him. This was a far cry from the way his grandfather had been treated when he became king. Being treated with deference, even veneration, by older, experienced and respected noblemen of power and rank in his early years helped to create a distance between Richard and his peers that would later be hard to bridge. This was increased by the fact that Richard was able to exercise power and political influence during his minority. Joan actively encouraged him to do so by exercising her own influence in his name and ensuring that the credit for actions made under her guidance went to him, with appointments and rewards being made in his name. Protected and cosseted, encouraged to expect esteem and deference, enjoying power from his earliest days as king, Richard grew up in a deliberately rarefied atmosphere. He never enjoyed the comradely environment his father and grandfather experienced with their peers, and he was never given the opportunity to prove himself among them on an equal footing. Joan helped, unintentionally, to isolate her son, and this undoubtedly encouraged his dependence on those few peers with whom he was able to build a personal relationship. Joan failed to recognise the dangers inherent in his overreliance on individual friendships, and although she saw that Richard had inherited his father's tendency towards liberal generosity, she failed to instil in him any lasting caution. Richard did not inherit his mother's discretion, nor did he learn from her example, and without her guiding hand he was later to display partisanship and favour in excess, becoming disastrously reliant upon favourites such as Robert de Vere.

Later Richard was to be criticised for his insistence on a high degree of formality at court as well as absolute obeisance towards him as king.[6] In the early years of the reign Joan was the most important female figure at court and she could hardly avoid influencing its tone. The Aquitanian court she had presided over with the prince had been flamboyant, generous and extravagant, the affluence and largesse emulating the example set by Edward III. Inevitably this would be the model Joan would promote for her son, even if this was not her own choice. Similarly she would have encouraged her son to emulate his father in the attitude he adopted towards his subjects. The prince had attracted criticism in Aquitaine for being haughty and there were tales of his insistence on anyone approaching him adopting a bended knee. Joan's own style was in marked contrast, but the importance she attached to her son's royal heritage undoubtedly fostered in the young Richard any predisposition towards haughtiness he may have inherited from his father. Surrounded by his father's old servants, who could and did remind Richard of his father and the way he had lived, it was inevitable that Richard would emulate his father and grandfather's lavish generosity. However, a notable feature enjoyed by both the prince and Edward III was a strong rapport with the nobility, a result of their shared comradeship of arms and expressed in a common purpose in waging the war with France. Richard, succeeding to the throne as a child, and then presiding over a fading war effort and successive failures in France, was never able to develop this kind of relationship with the nobility. After his father's death Richard did not have anyone to provide him with strong and authoritative discipline, and he was surrounded by too many people who deferred to him, stressing his importance, while restricting his independence. Joan did her best to provide her son with support by surrounding him with close family and loyal retainers, but this could not replace the trust and respect her husband and his father had earned through their feats of arms. Reliance on formality, and ceremony, was no substitute for shared military experiences, and as time passed Richard's court became more formal and less flexible in style.

Richard was only eighteen when his mother died and there is nothing to suggest that he had any feelings other than love for her. He respected her wishes and ensured she was buried as she had directed, and although he does not seem to have visited the grave often or held annual commemorative services for her, he ensured her grave was maintained. As she had hoped and encouraged in him, he remained on good terms with all of those with whom she had been closest. John Holand was quickly reconciled to his half-brother through the good offices of John of Gaunt and was granted a full pardon in February 1386. His relationship with Richard never faltered again. It is extraordinary that Richard should forgive his half-brother for such an appalling and public crime, and that Gaunt should be the one to conciliate; their affection for Joan and grief at her death played a significant part in motivating their actions. Thomas was also restored to favour. Richard remained on good terms with his mother's knights, and it is notable that those who harboured Lollard sympathies – William Beauchamp, Richard Stury, John Clanvowe, Lewis Clifford and William Neville – later all escaped prosecution. Joan's death was a tragedy for Richard, as he lost his strongest supporter and his most ardent protector. It is notable that the two main portraits of Richard, the panel portrait hanging in Westminster Abbey and the Wilton Diptych, show Richard as the boy king, as he would have been during his mother's lifetime. If indeed he was the one responsible for their commission, perhaps the older Richard wanted to evoke memories of happier times.

For most of her life Joan occupied an unusually privileged position as one of an elite group of people surrounding the king, at the centre of political life, and as the prince's wife and Richard's mother she spent twenty-four years in a position of considerable influence. Blessed with beauty and a warm and affectionate nature, she was modest, unambitious and a natural peacemaker but she was also on occasions independent, strong-willed, brave and determined. She understood and accepted the society into which she was born, and she shaped her life within it. She fulfilled her responsibilities and duties in her different roles as wife, mother and landowner. As the first Princess of Wales Joan set a standard of behaviour for others to admire and emulate, earning the respect and affection of her contemporaries. Judging her by the standards of her time, Chandos Herald's description of Joan as 'beautiful, pleasant and wise' is a fitting epitaph.

Acknowledgements

Thanks to the team at Amberley, especially Nicola and Alex.

I would like to thank Professor Nigel Saul, of Royal Holloway, who kindly read the first draft of the book, for his encouragement, expertise and many helpful comments. Thanks to my family, in particular my husband Pete for his love and support, and my sons David and Richard for their enthusiasm, suggestions, and proofreading skills.

Notes

Full details of all works cited can be found in the bibliography. For books, the full title is given for the first reference, and thereafter short titles are used. The following abbreviations are used in the footnotes:

CChR *Calendar of Charter Rolls*
CCR *Calendar of Close Rolls*
CFR *Calendar of Fine Rolls*
CIPM *Calendar of Inquisitions Post Mortem*
CPR *Calendar of Patent Rolls*
RBP Register of the Black Prince
TNA The National Archives

Introduction

1. Jean Froissart, *Chronicles*, ed. S. Luce et al. (15 vols, Société de l'Histoire de France, Paris, 1869–1975), p. 304.
2. Joan was the daughter of the Earl of Kent. She is not referred to by any of the contemporary chroniclers as the Fair Maid of Kent; George Frederick Beltz, *Memorials of the Most Noble Order of the Garter* (London, 1861), p. 18. However the designation is now commonly used to describe her, e.g. Richard Barber, 'Joan, suo jure countess of Kent, and princess of Wales and of Aquitaine (called the Fair Maid of Kent) (*c.* 1328–1385)', *Oxford Dictionary of National Biography* (Oxford, 2004).
3. The Garter story first appears in Polydore Vergil, *Anglicae Historiae: Libri Vigintiseptum* (1570), p. 379. It was repeated by John Selden, *Titles of Honour* (London, 1672), 11, p. 658. Joan is first named as the countess by Camden at the end of the seventeenth century. This is discussed by Richard Barber, *Edward Prince of Wales and Aquitaine* (Woodbridge, 1978, reprinted 1998), pp. 85–87.
4. The first Prince of Wales was Edward I's son, Edward of Carnarvon, who became Edward II. He married Princess Isabella of France after he became king, so she became Queen Isabella and was never Princess of Wales. Edward III's eldest son Prince Edward is better known to historians as the Black Prince but this name was not used during his lifetime. The name was first used by John Leland in the mid-sixteenth century. The origin of the name is not known. Richard Barber, *Edward Prince of Wales and Aquitaine* (Woodbridge, 1978 reprinted 1998), p. 242. The contemporary designation of Prince Edward or the prince is used throughout this book.
5. Jean le Bel, *Chronique*, ed. J. Viard and E. Déprez (2 vols, Société de l'Histoire

de France, Paris, 1904–5), I, p. 124; James L. Gillespie, 'Ladies of the Fraternity of Saint George and of the Society of the Garter', *Albion*, 17 (1985), p. 259–278. Gillespie suggests Joan's beauty served as an inspiration for chivalry, citing this banquet as an example.

6. See works by Juliet Vale, *Edward III and Chivalry: Chivalric Society and its Context 1270–1350* (Woodbridge, 1982); Maurice Keen, *Chivalry* (London, 1984); Richard Barber, *The Knight and Chivalry* (Woodbridge, 1995); Nigel Saul, *For Honour and Fame Chivalry in England 1066–1500* (London, 2011).

7. David Green, *The Black Prince* (Stroud, 2001), pp. 19–36 discusses the prince's reputation.

8. *Life of the Black Prince by the Herald of Sir John Chandos*, ed. M. K. Pope and E. C. Lodge (Oxford, 1910), p. 48.

9. *Chronique des quatre premiers Valois (1327–1393)*, ed. S. Luce (Société de l'Histoire de France, Paris, 1862), p. 123.

10. *Life of the Black Prince*, p. 48.

11. Froissart, vi, p. 367, xvi, p. 142.

12. Walsingham, T., *Historia Anglicana*, ed. H. T. Riley (2 vols, Rolls series, 1863–64), i, p. 296; *Knighton's Chronicle 1337–1396*, ed. G. H. Martin (Oxford, 1995), p. 185; *Chronicon Anglie 1328–1388*, ed. E. M. Thompson (Rolls series, 1874), p. 50; *Chronica Johannis de Reading et Anonymi Cantuariasis 1346–1367*, ed. J. Tait (Manchester, 1914), pp. 212–213; Ranulf Higden, *Polychronicon, Ranulphi Higden Monachi Cestrensis*, ed. C. Babington and J. R. Lumby (9 vols, Rolls Series, London, 1865–86), viii, p. 360; J. Capgrave, *Chronicle of England*, ed. F. Hingeston (London, 1858), p. 221; *Chronicle of John Hardyng*, ed. H. Ellis (London, 1812), pp. 331–332.

13. Walsingham, *Anglicana*, i, p. 301; *Eulogium Historiarum sive Temporis*; ed. F. S. Hayden (3 vols, Rolls series, London, 1858–63), p. 236; *The St Albans Chronicle, 1, 1376–1394*; *The Chronica Maiora of Thomas Walsingham*, ed. J. Taylor, W. Childs and L. Watkiss (Oxford, 2003), pp. 92–93; *The Westminster Chronicle, 1381–1394*, ed. L. C. Hector and B. Harvey (Oxford, 1982), p. 114; *The Chronica Maiora of Thomas Walsingham*, pp. 424–425, 758–759.

14. Peck, *Annals of Stamford* (XII, 1727); F. Chambers, *The Fair Maid of Kent, An historical and biographical sketch* (Margate, 1877); M. le Colonel Babinet 'Jeanne de Kent princesse de Galles et d'Aquitaine', *Bulletin de la Societé des Antiquaries de l'Ouest*, 6 (1894), p. 438.

15. *The Complete Peerage*, ed. G. E. Cokayne., VII, pp. 153–154; *Dictionary of National Biography* (London, 1908), pp. 393–393. Richard Barber, Joan suo jure countess of Kent and princess of Wales and of Aquitaine (called the Fair Maid of Kent), *Oxford Dictionary of National Biography* (Oxford, 2004).

16. These include: W. M. Ormrod, *The Reign of Edward III* (Stroud, 2000) and *Edward III* (Yale, 2011); Ian Mortimer; *The Perfect King* (London, 2006); David Green, *The Black Prince* (Stroud, 2001); Nigel Saul, *Richard II* (New Haven and London, 1999); R. Barber, *Edward, Prince of Wales and Aquitaine* (Woodbridge, 1996); Anthony Steel, *Richard II* (Cambridge, 1941); Anthony Goodman, *John of Gaunt: The exercise of princely power in fourteenth century Europe* (1992). Works on Queen Isabella are Paul Doherty, *Isabella and the Strange Death of Edward II* (2003) and Alison Weir, *Isabella* (2005). John of Gaunt's third wife, Katherine Swynford, has also received attention: Jeanette Lucraft, *Katherine Swynford* (Stroud, 2006); Alison Weir, *Katherine Swynford* (London, 2007).

17. Margaret Galway, 'Joan of Kent and the Order of the Garter', *University of Birmingham Historical Journal*, 1 (1948), pp. 13–50. 'Chaucer's Sovereign Lady', *Modern Language Notes*, Vol. 33, No. 2 (1938), pp. 145–199.; 'Chaucer's Hopeless Love', *Modern Language Notes*, Vol. 60, No. 7 (1945), pp. 431–439. Her assertions were immediately disputed; Walter E. Weese, 'Alceste and Joan of Kent', *Modern Language Notes*, Vol. 63, No. 7 (1948), pp. 474–477.

18. Galway, 'Joan of Kent and the Order of the Garter', pp. 13–50. See also Antonia

Gransden, 'The alleged rape by Edward III of the countess of Salisbury', *English Historical Review*, 87 (1972), pp. 333–344. Gransden suggests this story and *The Vow of the Heron* were examples of war propaganda. She does not consider Joan as a candidate for the story.

19. Carolyn P. Collette, 'Joan of Kent and Noble Women's Roles in Chaucer's World', *The Chaucer Review*, Vol. 33, No. 4 (1999), pp. 350–359.

20. W. M. Ormrod, 'In Bed with Joan of Kent: The King's Mother and the Peasants' Revolt', *Medieval Women: Texts and Contexts in Late Medieval Britain: Essays for Felicity Riddy*, ed. J. Wogan-Browne, R. Voaden, A. Diamond, A. Hutchison, C. M. Meale, and L. Johnson (Turnhout, 2000).

21. See works by Juliet Vale, *Edward III and Chivalry: Chivalric Society and its Context 1270–1350* (Woodbridge, 1982); Maurice Keen, *Chivalry* (London, 1984); Richard Barber, *The Knight and Chivalry* (Woodbridge, 1995).

22. K. P. Wentersdorf, 'The Clandestine Marriages of the Fair Maid of Kent', *Journal of Medieval History*, 5 (1979), pp. 203–231. Throughout the book the spelling of Holand is as it appears in the contemporary accounts, rather than the later spelling of 'Holland'.

23. J. Chamberlayne, 'Joan of Kent's Tale: Adultery and Rape in the Age of Chivalry', *Medieval Life*, 5 (1996), pp. 1–12.

24. Mark Ormrod considers that the nickname 'Fair Maid of Kent' is partly sardonic and a reflection that Joan acquired a reputation for sensuality during her lifetime because of her marital history. W. Mark Ormrod, *Edward III* (New Haven and London, 2011), p. 418.

1 A Royal Inheritance 1301–1330

1. Edmund of Woodstock, Earl of Kent, and Margaret Wake were probably married in Paris in the late autumn of 1325. On 2 October 1325 Edmund was granted papal dispensation to marry Margaret and the marriage would have taken place shortly afterwards. *Calendar of Papal Registers, Papal Letters, 1305–1342* (London, 1902), p. 246. They returned to England in the entourage of Queen Isabella in September 1326. Their first child was probably born shortly before or after this. As births were not generally recorded it is impossible to know for certain whether Joan or Edmund was their first born, but it is likely, as has generally been assumed, that Edmund was their eldest child. There have been suggestions that Joan was born on 19 or 29 September 1328 (Alison Weir, *Britain's Royal Families: The Complete Genealogy* (London, 2002), p. 94 gives 29 September; http://en.wikipedia.org/wiki/joan_of_kent cites 19 September), but there is no evidence to support either date. It is probable that Joan was born early in 1328, making her twelve in the spring of 1340 when she entered into a clandestine marriage with Thomas Holand, which was later held in the papal court to be valid on the grounds of Joan's consent.

2. *Flores Historiarum*, ed. H. R. Luard, 3 vols (Rolls Series, London, 1890), iii, pp. 110, 304. Edmund was born on 5 August 1301 at Woodstock palace.

3. *Calendar of Patent Rolls 1327–1330* (London, 1900), p. 499.

4. *Calendar of Close Rolls 1323–1327* (London, 1900), p. 622.

5. *Calendar of Inquisitions Post Mortem* (London, 1900), ix, p. 455. James Byrne attested that the date of John's birth was Tuesday 7 April 1330. However, in 1330 Easter Sunday was on 8 April, so John was either born on Saturday 7 April or Tuesday 3 April.

6. Nicholas Orme, *Medieval Children* (London, 2003), pp. 27–35.

7. Edmund was born on 5 August 1301 at Woodstock palace.

8. Seymour Phillips, *Edward II* (London, 2010), p. 39.

9. An indenture detailing the preparations is described by Michael Prestwich, *Edward I* (2nd edition, New Haven and London, 1997), p. 131.

10. *CPR 1301–1307*, p. 7.

11. TNA E101/368/12, 4.
12. Her household expenditure was added to theirs. TNA E101/369/15.
13. Jean le Bel, *Chronique*, i, p. 101; Jean Froissart, *Chronicles*, ed. G. Routledge (London, 1891), p. 28.
14. Paul Doherty, *Isabella and the Strange Death of Edward II* (London, 2003), p. 11.
15. TNA E101/373/7, m. 4.
16. Phillips, *Edward II*, pp. 14–65, 96–101. Phillips suggests that Edward II may have seen Gaveston as the elder brother he never had.
17. *Vita Edwardi Secundi*, ed. N. Denholm-Young (London, 1957), p. 15.
18. *CPR 1301–1307*, pp. 460, 528; Clifford J. Rogers, *War Cruel and Sharp* (Woodbridge, 2000), p. xiii.
19. Michael Prestwich, *Edward I* (2nd Edition, New Haven and London, 1997), pp. 549–552.
20. *CPR 1301–1307*, p. 460. The charter is dated 31 August 1301.
21. *Vita Edwardi Secundi*, p. 15.
22. *Calendar of Charter Rolls 1300–1326* (London, 1916), pp. 202–203.
23. *CChR 1300–1326*, pp. 205–206.
24. J. S. Hamilton, *Piers Gaveston, Earl of Cornwall, 1307–1312, Politics and Patronage in the Reign of Edward II* (Wayne State University Press, 1988), pp. 100–101.
25. *CPR 1313–1317*, p. 360. The manors were Ashford (Derby) Kenton, Shebbear, Lifton, Chettiscombe, Braunton (Devon) Collingham (York) and tenements in Beesby and Waltham (Lincoln).
26. *CChR 1300–1326*, p. 304.
27. *CChR 1300–1326*, p. 304; T. Rymer, *Foedera, Conventiones, Litterae etc*, ed. G. Holmes (20 vols, London, 1704–35), I, p. 188.
28. *CPR 1317–1321*, pp. 139, 187, 269, 105.
29. *CChR 1300–1326*, p. 416.
30. *Vita Edwardi Secundi*, pp. 104–105.
31. *The Complete Peerage*, vii, pp. 142–143.
32. Phillips, *Edward II*, p. 385.
33. *The Complete Peerage*, xii, p. 295.
34. *The Complete Peerage*, xii, p. 297–302; *CIPM*, iii, pp. 448–450.
35. *The Complete Peerage*, xii, p. 302.
36. *Calendar of Close Rolls 1307–1313* (London, 1900), p. 70. Margaret appears to have named her own daughter after her mother.
37. *CPR 1307–1313*, pp. 196, 218–219, 224, 434.
38. Their younger brother seems to have died.
39. *CPR 1307–1313*, pp. 196, 218–219, 224, 434; G. E. C., xii, p. 302; *CCR 1307–1313*, p. 413.
40. *The Complete Peerage*, xii, p. 324; *CIPM*, vi, pp. 426–427.
41. *CPR 1317–1321*, pp. 581, 597; *Calendar of Fine Rolls 1319–1327* (London, 1900), pp. 62, 71.
42. TNA E101/378/11.
43. *Vita Edwardi Secundi*, p. 117; *The Anonimalle Chronicle, 1307–1334*, from Brotherton Collection MS29, ed. W. R. Childs and J. Taylor, Yorkshire Archaeological Society Record Series, 147 (1991), pp. 104–105.
44. *The Complete Peerage*, vii, p. 137.
45. *CFR 1319–1327*, p. 68; *CIPM*, vii, p. 222
46. The earldom of Cornwall remained vacant until 1336 when Edward III bestowed it on his own younger brother, John of Eltham.
47. *CPR 1317–1321*, p. 597; *CFR 1319–1327*, pp. 62, 68, 71; TNA E101/378/11; *Calendar of Memoranda Rolls Michaelmas 1326–Michaelmas 1327* (London, 1916), p. 42. In 1327 Edmund stated he had only received an annual income from Edward II of 2000 marks in fee, and 355 marks for life (given with the earldom) (*CChR 1327–1341*, p. 20; *CFR 1319–1327*, p. 68).

48. *Anonimalle 1307–1334*, pp. 106–107.
49. *Anonimalle 1307–1334*, pp. 106–109.
50. Phillips, *Edward II*, p. 417.
51. *The Complete Peerage*, vii, p. 142.
52. *The Complete Peerage*, vii, p. 142.
53. This is evidenced by the charter witness lists which show Edmund witnessing 11.4 per cent of charters in 1322, compared to 26.5 per cent in 1323. J. S. Hamilton, 'Charter Witness Lists for the Reign of Edward II', *The Fourteenth Century*, ed. N. Saul, pp. 13–16.
54. *The War of Saint Sardos 1323–1325 Gascon Correspondence and Diplomatic Documents*, ed. P. Chaplais (Camden, 3rd Series, 87, London, 1954), pp. viii–xii, 24–25.
55. *The War of Saint Sardos*, pp. 24–25.
56. *Foedera*, ii, I, p. 562.
57. *The War of Saint Sardos*, pp. 64, 104, 120, 126, 142, 217, 236. Despenser wrote directly to Edmund's officers. Chaplais suggests that all of these men owed their position to Despenser and had been sworn to secrecy by him.
58. Ibid, p. 143. In July 1324 Edward II had ordered Edmund to protect Caillou.
59. *The War of Saint Sardos*, p. 217.
60. *CCR 1323–1327*, p. 380.
61. *Anonimalle 1307–1334*, p. 119; *The War of Saint Sardos*, pp. 238, 240, 252, 271.
62. *Calendar of Papal Registers, Letters, 1305–1342*, p. 246. Dispensation was granted to Edmund on the grounds that he and Margaret were related within the third or fourth degree. Through Margaret's mother, she and Edmund shared a common ancestor, Eleanor of Castile.
63. *Vita Edwardi Secundi*, p. 141; *Foedera*, ii, p. 606.
64. *Vita Edwardi Secundi*, p. 142.
65. *The Complete Peerage*, xii, p. 302.
66. *CCR 1323–1327*, pp. 576–582.
67. Henry Eastry, prior of Christchurch Canterbury, wrote to Archbishop Reynolds on 16 April that he had seen a letter from Edmund assuring the king that he had not aligned himself with any foreign power and requesting permission to return to England. N. Fryde, *The Tyranny and Fall of Edward II 1321–1326* (Cambridge, 1996), p. 179.
68. *CCR 1323–1327*, p. 464.
69. Phillips, *Edward II*, p. 501.
70. *Flores*, iii, pp. 232–233 Edmund returned to England with Isabella.
71. *CPR 1324–1327*, p. 327; *CCR 1327–1327*, p. 650.
72. Phillips, *Edward II*, p. 509.
73. *Flores*, iii, p. 234; *Annales Paulini*, ed. W. Stubbs (Rolls Series, London, 1882), pp. 317–318.
74. *CPR 1330–1334*, p. 72 cites Edmund as his father's heir. His exact date of birth is not known.
75. *Calendar of Memoranda Rolls Michaelmas 1326–Michaelmas 1327* (London, 1916), p. 42.
76. *CPR 1327–1330*, p. 23.
77. *CChR 1327–1341*, pp. 2, 4, 5; *CCR 1323–1327*, p. 622; *CPR 1327–1330*, p. 97; *CMR Michaelmas 1326–Michaelmas 1327*, pp. 9, 10, 11.
78. Froissart, *Chronicles*, Luce, i, p. 87.
79. Edmund received grants in Surrey, Kent and Sussex, for example, where Isabella retained the castles of Rochester, Leeds, Guildford, Pevensey and the town of Sandwich herself. *CMR Michaelmas 1326–Michaelmas 1327*, p. 11.
80. Edward II's fate has been the subject of considerable conjecture, and the possibility that he did not die in September 1327 strongly asserted by some historians. Paul Doherty, *Isabella and the Strange Death of Edward II* (London, 2003); Ian Mortimer, *The Greatest Traitor* (London, 2003); *The Perfect King*

(London, 2006); 'The Death of Edward II in Berkeley Castle', *English Historical Review*, 120 (2005), pp. 1175–1214.

81. Doherty, *Isabella*, p. 149. Doherty cites TNA C53/114/7 stating that Edmund witnessed a charter there.

82. *Calendar of Plea and Memoranda Rolls of the City of London, 1324–1457*, ed. A. H. Thomas (London, 1926), p. 72.

83. *Annales Paulini*, p. 344; Holmes, 'The Rebellion of the Earl of Lancaster, 1328–1329', *Bulletin of Institute of Historical Research*, xxviii (1995), p. 85. Holmes cites 'Historia Roffensis' in Wharton, *Anglia Sacra* (London, 1691), I, p. 368.

84. *CPR 1327–1330*, p. 391.

85. *Adae Murimuth, Continuatio Chronicarum*, ed. E. M. Thompson (Rolls Series, London, 1889), p. 256; *The Brut, or The Chronicles of England*, ed. F. W. D. Brie (EETS, original series, cxxxvi, 1908), i, p. 263.

86. *Calendar of Papal Registers, Letters, 1305–1342*, p. 308. The papal letter places Edmund in Gascony in October 1329. The Pope gave Edmund and Margaret a dispensation releasing them from their pilgrimage vow in return for paying the costs of the journey to Santiago, and a penance imposed by their confessor.

87. *Murimuth*, pp. 256–257. Edmund's confession names several who offered support.

88. *CCR 1330–1333*, p. 132; *The Brut*, ii, pp. 265–267; *Rotuli Parliamentorum* (6 vols, London, 1767–1777), ii, p. 52.

89. *Murimuth*, pp. 256–257, contains a full transcript of the confession.

90. *Murimuth*, p. 257; *Chronicon Galfridi le Baker de Swynbroke*, ed. E. M. Thompson (Oxford, 1889), p. 43.

91. *The Brut*, ii, p. 265, suggests Edmund promised to reinstate Edward II.

92. *The Brut*, p. 266.

93. *Anonimalle 1307–1334*, pp. 142–143. The canonical hours of prayer covered the day starting with prime, with vespers in the early evening.

94. *Chronicon Galfridi le Baker de Swynbroke*, p. 43; *Anonimalle 1307–1334*, pp. 142–143.

95. Margaret Wake's mother was Roger Mortimer's aunt. *The Complete Peerage*. xii, p. 302.

96. *CFR 1337–1337*, p. 169.

97. *CFR 1327–1337*, p. 174.

98. *CPR 1327–1330*, pp. 502, 508.

99. *Calendar of Papal Registers, Letters, 1305–1342*, p. 499.

100. Fryde, *The Tyranny and Fall of Edward II*, p. 63.

101. On 4 April an order for the seizure of Thomas Wake's land and goods noted that he had 'secretly withdrawn from the realm'. *CFR 1327–1337*, p. 175.

102. *CPR 1327–1330*, p. 499.

103. *CPR 1327–1330*, p. 499; *CFR 1327–1337*, p. 166; *CCR 1330–1332*, p. 14.

104. *CCR 1330–1332*, p. 17.

105. *CCR 1330–1332*, p. 16.

106. Margaret and Roger's mothers were sisters.

107. *CPR 1327–1330*, pp. 506, 511, 520, 521.

108. *CChR 1327–1341*, p. 176.

109. *CIPM*, vii, pp. 222–235.

110. *CFR 1327–1337*, p. 175.

2 The Changing Fortunes of the Kent Family, 1330

1.   *CPR 1330–1334*, pp. 109, 110, 120, 193, 241. Several orders refer to the young Edmund, and subsequently to John, as being in the king's custody.

2.   Froissart, J, *Oeuvres*, ed. Kervyn de Lettenhove (Brussels, 26 vols, 1867–77), ii, p. 243.

3.   *CPR 1330–1334*, p. 36.

4. *CPR 1330–1334*, pp. 84, 106, 215.

5. *CCR 1330–1333*, pp. 158–159.

6. *CCR 1330–1334*, pp. 74–76.

7. *CPR 1330–1334*, pp. 20, 28; *CCR 1330–1332*, p. 77.

8. *CFR 1327–1337*, p. 207.

9. Juliet Vale, 'Philippa (1310–1369)', *Oxford Dictionary of National Biography* (Oxford, 2004).

10. T. F. Tout, *Chapters in the Administrative History of Medieval England* (6 vols, Manchester, 1936), v, p. 289.

11. *CFR 1327–1337*, p. 279. Margaret was granted wardship of manors during the minority of her son John, now cited as the heir.

12. *CPR 1330–1334*, p. 523, Tout, *Administrative History*, v, p. 315.

13. Tout, *Administrative History*, v, p. 315.

14. *CPR 1330–1334*, p. 178; *Early Lincoln Wills, 1280–1547*, ed. A. Gibbons (Lincoln, 1888), pp. 6–7.

15. *Calendar of Papal Registers, Papal Letters, 1305–1342*, p. 349.

16. Although Edmund's final burial place is generally considered to be Westminster abbey there is no evidence that the order was ever carried out. In February 2003 I consulted with Dr Tony Trowles, Librarian at Westminster Abbey, who confirmed that Edmund is listed in their records on the basis of the papal order but they have no corroborating evidence. The location of the burial place in the Abbey is unknown, nor is there a monument or chantry chapel. This is slightly unusual, even given the circumstances. It is possible that Edmund remains buried in Winchester. This might explain why Edmund's son and heir John chose to be buried at the Grey Friars church in Winchester although he had no known connection to it. *The Complete Peerage*, vii, p. 148.

17. *The Complete Peerage*, vii, p. 148.

18. *CFR 1327–1337*, p. 207.

19. *CIPM*, vii, pp. 222–235.

20. TNA SC1 38/77; *CCR 1330–1332*, p. 291.

21. *CCR 1330–1332*, p. 85.

22. Ibid, pp. 51–52, 189.

23. *CCR 1330–1332*, pp. 102, 189. Margaret continued to experience problems with her Comyn dower, as a year later David used the Earl of Pembroke's death in another attempt to obtain a greater share by petitioning the king for a new partition of the estates. *CIPM*, vii, p. 287.

24. *CFR 1327–1337*, p. 218; *CPR 1330–1334*, p. 72.

25. *CPR 1330–1334*, pp. 73, 178.

26. *CPR 1330–1334*, pp. 78, 96, 99, 100, 148, 164, 248.

27. *CCR 1330–1332*, p. 205.

28. *CCR 1330–1332*, pp. 291–292.

29. *CCR 1330–1332*, pp. 191, 208.

30. *CFR 1327–1337*, p. 218; *CCR 1330–1332*, p. 293.

31. *CPR 1330–1334*, p. 78.

32. *CChR 1327–1341*, pp. 2, 4, 5. Arundel Castle estate (Sussex) was valued at £600, and Keevil manor (Wilts) at £90.

33. *CFR 1327–1337*, pp. 246, 252.

34. *CPR 1330–1334*, p. 78.

35. *CPR 1330–1334*, p. 99.

36. Ibid, p. 164.

37. *CCR 1330–1332*, p. 351.

38. *CPR 1330–1334*, p. 174.

39. *CPR 1330–1334*, p. 516.

40. *CPR 1330–1334*, p. 41. Pulteney was knighted in 1337. He made a fortune through his draper business and evidently derived much satisfaction from his Kent estate with the building of his own stately home, Penshurst Place, which survives and was later home to Sir Philip Sidney.

41. *CFR 1327–1337*, pp. 246, 252, 277.
42. *CFR 1327–1337*, p. 279. The manors were Ollerton (Notts), Ryhall (Rutland), Miserden (Gloucs), Lifton, Shebbear and Chettiscombe (Devon), Bagshot and Tolworth (Surrey), and the town of Caistor (Lincs).
43. *CFR 1327–1337*, p. 279; *CPR 1330–1334*, p. 329.
44. *CPR 1330–1334*, p. 217.
45. *CPR 1330–1334*, p. 329.
46. *CCR 1333–1337*, pp. 65–66, 117.
47. *CCR 1333–1337*, p. 221.
48. *CPR 1330–1334*, pp. 11, 21, 79; Edward Bohun received Shebbear manor (Devon) and the fee farms paid by the abbeys of Ramsey (Huntingdon) and Stratford (Essex), and the town of Grimsby (Lincs). *CPR 1330–1334*, pp. 193, 217; William Bohun received the fee farm paid by Kirkstall abbey for Collingham (Yorks), town of Basingstoke (Hants). *CPR 1330–1334*, p. 114; Edmund Bacon received Beesby manor (Lincs). *CPR 1330–1334*, p. 113; William Montague received the manors of Queen Camel, Somerton, and Kingsbury (Somerset). *CPR 1330–1334*, pp. 115, 147–148; Thomas Bradeston obtained the manors of Lechlade, Siddington and Barnsley (Gloucs) and the fee farm of Gloucester.
49. *CPR 1330–1334*, pp. 221, 267. In November 1331 the king granted John Bures the rental from the manor of Iden (Sussex) in repayment of his debt, and similarly in February 1332, £50 rental from the abbey of Waltham Holy Cross (Essex) granted to Hugh Despenser.
50. *CPR 1338–1340*, p. 246, 465. On 2 May 1338 Shebbear manor (Devon) was granted to Roger Lameleye, then on 20 April 1340 to Peter Beauchamp.
51. *CCR 1330–1332*, p. 217.
52. *CPR 1327–1330*, p. 517; *CPR 1330–1334*, pp. 11, 79.
53. *CPR 1330–1334*, pp. 78, 96, 99.
54. *CCR 1330–1332*, p. 231; *CPR 1330–1334*, p. 148.
55. *CPR 1330–1334*, p. 20.
56. *CPR 1334–1338*, p. 100.
57. *CPR 1334–1338*, pp. 286, 295.
58. *CPR 1338–1340*, p. 27.
59. TNA SC1 38/86; *CPR 1338–1340*, p. 133.
60. *CCR 1339–1341*, pp. 140–141.
61. *CCR 1339–1341*, p. 280.
62. *CPR 1327–1330*, p. 246.
63. *CIPM*, vii, p. 227
64. *CPR 1327–1330*, p. 508.
65. Froissart, *Chronicles*, Routledge, p. 28.
66. *CPR 1330–1334*, pp. 34, 50, 96, 112, 247, 260, 280. In January 1331 he was unable to obtain seisin of two manors and collect the rental due to him from Dunwich (Suffolk) because they had been granted elsewhere, and the official records have several entries for 1331 confirming grants made previously by the earl.
67. *CPR 1330–1334*, pp. 523, 335.
68. *CPR 1334–1338*, pp. 426, 434.
69. *CCR 1307–1313*, p. 143.
70. *CPR 1330–1334*, p. 28.
71. *CPR 1330–1334*, p. 36.
72. *CPR 1330–1334*, pp. 133, 190.

3 Growing Up in the Royal Household, 1330–1338

1. Barber, *Edward Prince of Wales and Aquitaine*, p. 16.
2. Tout, *Administrative History*, v, p. 319. Wentersdorf, 'The Clandestine Marriages of the Fair Maid of Kent', p. 204, suggests that Montague and his wife were

Joan's governor and governess on the grounds that Montague was keeper of Woodstock Palace but this is unlikely. There is no evidence that the king appointed the Montagues to take on this role.

3. *CPR 1334–1338*, pp. 247, 559.
4. Barber, *Edward Prince of Wales and Aquitaine*, p. 21.
5. *CFR 1327–1337*, p. 215.
6. Galway, 'Joan of Kent and the Order of the Garter', pp. 13–50.
7. Beltz, *Order of the Garter*, p. 385.
8. A. E. Prince, 'A Letter of Edward the Black Prince Describing the Battle of Najera in 1367', *English Historical Review*, xli (1926), p. 418.
9. Orme, *Medieval Children*, p. 208.
10. Veronica Sekules, Women's Piety and Patronage, *The Age of Chivalry Art and Society in Late Medieval England*, ed. N. Saul (London, 1992). p. 123.
11. Sekules, 'Women's Piety and Patronage', p. 130
12. Edward and Philippa's religious practices are discussed by W. M. Ormrod, 'The Personal Religion of Edward III', *Speculum*, 64 (1989), pp. 849–911.
13. S. M. Newton, *Fashion in the Age of the Black Prince* (Woodbridge, 1980), p. 1. Newton comments on the distinct change in fashion at court around 1340.
14. Newton, *Fashion in the Age of the Black Prince*, p. 21; Nicholas Orme, *From Childhood to Chivalry, The Education of the English Kings and Aristocracy 1066–1530* (London, 1984), p. 32.
15. Orme, *From Childhood to Chivalry*, p. 49. Rolls and receipts from the privy wardrobe at the Tower for 1322–1341 illustrate the plenitude of royal books.
16. Vale, *Edward III and Chivalry*, p. 45.
17. Vale, 'Philippa', *ODNB*.
18. *History of the King's Works*, ed. R. A. Brown, H. M. Colvin and A. J. Taylor (3 vols, London, 1963), ii, pp. 1009–1017; *CCR 1333–1337*, pp. 243, 266.
19. Tout, *Administrative History*, v, p. 319.

4 A Clandestine Marriage, 1338–1340

1. *CPR 1330–1334*, p. 534.
2. Mortimer, *The Perfect King*, p. 149, describes the royal fleet's departure.
3. Tout, *Administrative History*, v, p. 322.
4. *CPR 1330–1334*, p. 224. In 1331 William Montague was charged with arranging a marriage for the baby Prince Edward with Philip VI's daughter, Joan.
5. Anthony Goodman, *John of Gaunt* (Essex, 1992), p. 28.
6. Jonathan Sumption, *Hundred Years War vol. i: Trial by Battle* (London 1990), p. 333, suggests Albret expended more than £9,000 towards the campaign in 1340 and brought with him the aid of several prominent and influential southern noblemen.
7. *Foedera*, v, ii, p. 177.
8. *Foedera*, v, p. 702.
9. Marc Morris describes Edward I as being reputedly broad browed, broad chested, blond haired and handsome and he was measured as six feet two inches in death, hence his nickname of 'Longshanks', and that his son, Edward of Carnarvon was considered tall and good looking. *A Great and Terrible King Edward I and the Forging of Britain* (London, 2008), pp. 22, 331. Dan Jones, *The Plantagenets: The Kings Who Made England* (London, 2012), pp. 440, 472, describes the striking looks of the Black Prince.
10. Evidence of the marriage comes from the papal letter dated May 1348 addressed to the Archbishop of Canterbury and the bishops of London and Norwich referring to Thomas Holand's petition referring to Joan 'to whom he was married upwards of eight years ago'. *Calendar of Papal Registers, Letters, 1342–1362*, p. 252.

11. Referred to in the brief of Pope Clement VI dated 5 May 1348 quoted in Appendix A in Wentersdorf, 'The Clandestine Marriages of the Fair Maid of Kent', pp. 205, 219–220.
12. TNA E30/67 Papal bull dated 13 November 1349.
13. *Calendar of Papal Registers, Letters, 1342–1362*, p. 252.
14. Froissart, *Oeuvres*, Lettenhove, iii, pp. 193–198, 313; TNA E101/391/9, f. 2 payment of war wages; *The Complete Peerage*, vii, p. 150.
15. W. M. Ormrod, 'Wake, Thomas, second Lord Wake (1298–1349), nobleman', *Dictionary of National Biography* (Oxford University press, 2004).
16. Jennifer Ward, *English Noblewomen in the Later Middle Ages* (London, 1992), p. 15; *CPR 1334–1338*, p. 298.
17. Wentersdorf, 'The Clandestine Marriages of the Fair Maid of Kent', p. 215.
18. Jean le Bel, *Chronique*, iii, p. 82; Froissart, *Chronicles*, Johnes, ii, p. 215; *Chronica monasterii de Melsa*, ed. E. A. Bond (3 vols, 1867), i. p. 100; *Life of the Black Prince by the Herald of Sir John Chandos*, p. 12.
19. Froissart, *Chronicles*, Johnes, ii, p. 316. Froissart describes him as 'un gentil chevalier … qui n'avoit qu'un oel'. He is described in identical terms by Jean le Bel, *Chronique*, ii, p. 82.
20. Jennifer Ward, *Women in England in the Middle Ages* (London, 2006), p. 19; Kim M. Phillips, *Medieval Maidens Young Women and Gender in England 1270–1540* (Manchester, 2003), p. 27. The complexities of the canonical law is discussed by J. H. Brundage, 'Concubinage and Marriage in Medieval Canon Law', *Journal of Medieval History*, I (1975).
21. The finding of the papal court that a de praesenti contract existed indicates that they were satified Joan had capacity to give consent, i.e. that she was twelve years old and not under the canonical age for consent.
22. J. R. Maddicott, 'Thomas of Lancaster and Sir Robert Holand: A study in noble patronage', *English Historical Review*, 311 (1971), p. 462. G. R. Holmes, *The Estates of the Higher Nobility in Fourteenth Century England* (Cambridge, 1957), p. 72.
23. Maddicott, 'Thomas of Lancaster and Sir Robert Holland', p. 467.
24. *Vita Edwardi Secundia*, p. 122.
25. Maddicott, 'Thomas of Lancaster and Sir Robert Holland', p. 468.
26. *The Brut*, p. 267; *CCR 1327–1330*, pp. 192, 286–287.
27. *CPR 1345–1348*, p. 87.
28. M. M. N. Stansfield, 'The Holland Family, Dukes of Exeter, Earls of Kent and Huntingdon, 1352–1475' (Corpus Christi College, Oxford, PhD. Thesis, 1987), p. 15.
29. *CPR 1327–1330*, p. 59.
30. *CPR 1327–1330*, pp. 467, 469; *CCR 1327–1330*, pp. 576, 587.
31. *The Chronicle of John Hardyng*, pp. 331–332 suggests Thomas Holand was William Montague's steward, but there is no contemporary evidence to support this.
32. *CPR 1345–1348*, p. 221. Warenne never divorced his wife but he obtained a royal licence to leave his estates to Isabella, which was revoked in 1346 on the application of the Earl of Arundel.
33. Froissart, *Oeuvres*, Lettenhove, ii, p. 398; *CPR 1338–1340*, p. 18.
34. Stansfield, 'The Holland Family', p. 18 citing TNA E36/203, 252, 267, 303 (printed as *The Wardrobe Book of William de Norwell 12 July 1338 to 27 May 1340*).
35. *CFR 1337–1347*, p. 119.
36. *CPR 1338–1340*, p. 409.
37. *CPR 1327–1330*, pp. 467, 469; *CCR 1327–1330*, pp. 573, 587. In December 1329 Maud, as Robert Holand's executrix, completed the surrender of the manor of Silkworth in Durham in exchange for an annuity of £26 to be paid to Thomas and his heirs.
38. *CCR 1337–1339*, p. 521.

39. Nigel Saul, *Knights and Esquires, The Gloucestershire Gentry in the Fourteenth Century* (Oxford, 1981), p. 10.

40. *Household Ordinances and Regulations* (Society of Antiquaries, 1790), pp. 3–10 lists the rates of wages in war and peace.

41. Keen, *Chivalry*, pp. 12–14, 154; Barber, *The Knight and Chivalry*, p. 138.

42. Sumption, *Hundred Years War, i: Trial by Battle*, p. 360 describes Edward III's grave financial difficulties at this time.

43. The warrants for travel are TNA Treaty Roll 15, m. 1 quoted by Wentersdorf, 'The Clandestine Marriages of the Fair Maid of Kent', p. 205.

5 A Bigamous Marriage, 1341–1349

1. Orme, *Medieval Children*, pp. 329–335.

2. *CCR 1339–1341*, p662; *CPR 1340–1343*, p. 145.

3. *CCR 1339–1341*, p. 662. The official entry is the acknowledgement of a debt for £3,000. A sum this size was almost certainly a dowry.

4. Joan's resistance to marrying William Montague was noted in the papal proceedings held in 1348/1349, when it was cited by her lawyer that she was forced into the marriage against her will. Wentersdorf,' The Clandestine Marriages of the Fair Maid of Kent'. The fact that she resisted the marriage suggests she told her family about her marriage to Thomas Holand.

5. *CPR 1340–1343*, p. 145.

6. *Montague Cartulary*, ff. 56–56v quoted by Holmes, *The Estates of the Higher Nobility*, p. 28.

7. *CCR 1323–1327*, p. 440; M. W. Warner, 'The Montague earls of Salisbury 1300–1428, A Study in Warfare, Politics and Political Culture' (University of London PhD thesis, 1991), p. 14.

8. R. Douch, 'The Career, Lands and Family of William Montague Earl of Salisbury 1301–1344', *Bulletin of Institute of Historical Research*, 24 (1951), p. 87; *CFR 1337–1347*, p. 111.

9. Holmes, *The Estates of the Higher Nobility*, p. 27; *CCR 1333–1337*, pp. 491–2; Warner, 'The Montague earls of Salisbury', p. 39.

10. *Foedera*, ii, I, p. 1117–1119; Ward, *English Noblewomen in the Later Middle Ages*, p. 21

11. Warner, 'The Montague earls of Salisbury', p. 40. Warner suggests the earl used pressure to obtain this union.

12. *CPR 1330–1334*, p. 402; *CCR 1333–1337*, p. 85.

13. Phillips, *Medieval Maidens*, p39.

14. Warner, 'The Montague earls of Salisbury', p. 20; Sumption, *The Hundred Years War, i: Trial by Battle*, p. 312. Sumption dates the earl's capture to 11 April 1340.

15. *CPR 1340–1343*, pp. 66, 73. The grant of the Earl of Moray to Montague is dated 25/26 October and confirmed in December.

16. CPR 1338–1340, p. 409.

17. *CCR 1333–1337*, pp. 491–491.

18. Holmes, *The Estates of the Higher Nobility*, pp. 42–43 suggests the usual sum was £1,000; *CCR 1333–1337*, pp. 491–492.

19. B. Wilkinson, 'The Protests of the earls of Arundel and Surrey in the crisis of 1341', *English Historical Review*, 46 (1931), p. 181.

20. Froissart, *Chronicles*, Johnes, i, p. 117.

21. *Foedera*, ii, p. ii 1195. The earl's movements at this time are not known for certain. Douch, 'The Career, Lands and Family of William Montague', p. 86 suggests the final arrangements for his release were not completed until mid-1342.

22. Stansfield, 'The Holland Family', p. 22 notes Otto drawing wages for the expedition. Throughout their military careers Otto and Thomas were generally

together, often with Otto as Thomas' lieutenant, so it likely that Thomas was with him. Thomas and Alan were paid war wages from 23 September 1342 to 15 February 1343.

23. Stansfield, 'The Holland Family', p. 22.
24. Warner, 'The Montague earls of Salisbury', p. 21.
25. Douch, 'The Career Lands and Family of William Montague Earl of Salisbury', p. 86; Warner, 'The Montague earls of Salisbury', p. 22.
26. TNA, C76/18, m. 13 3 attorneys appointed until Christmas; *CPR 1343–1345*, p. 15: in May John Holand and Henry Fitz Roger appointed.
27. Froissart, *Oeuvres*, Lettenhove, ii, p. 398.
28. *Foedera*, ii, p. ii, 1232, 1233.
29. Richard Barber, *Edward III and the Triumph of England: The Battle of Crécy and the Company of the Garter* (London, 2013), pp. 164–165, 170–171, 172–174.
30. *CFR 1337–1347*, p. 358. An escheator was appointed to take an inquisition of his lands at the end of January 1344.
31. *CPR 1345–1348*, p. 473.
32. This is a conclusion drawn by Mortimer in *The Perfect King*, p. 213.
33. *CPR 1345–1348*, p. 137.
34. *Foedera*, iii, i, pp. 30–31.
35. *Foedera*, iii, i, pp. 139, 330, 473.
36. *CIPM*, xii, p. 162.
37. Clifford J. Rogers, *War Cruel and Sharp English Strategy Under Edward III, 1327–1360* (Woodbridge, 2000), p. 221.
38. Sumption, *The Hundred Years War, i: Trial by Battle*, p. 497; Rogers, *War Cruel and Sharp*, p. 217 and based on Murimuth, p. 198.
39. *CPR 1345–1348*, p. 127.
40. The number of vessels is taken from Rogers, *War Cruel and Sharp*, p. 217.
41. Stansfield, 'The Holland Family', p. 24
42. *Murimuth*, p. 199.
43. Jean Le Bel, *Chronique*, ii, 77; Froissart, *Oeuvres*, Lettenhove, iv, p. 402.
44. W. Shaw, *Knights of England* (London, 1906), ii, p. 6. John is not listed but as he accompanied the king and was the same age as Prince Edward it is unlikely he was deliberately left out.
45. Sumption, *The Hundred Year War, i: Trial by Battle*, p. 503.
46. Barber, *Life and Campaigns of the Black Prince*, p. 17.
47. Froissart, *Chronicles*, Johnes, p. 155.
48. Barber, *Life and Campaigns of the Black Prince*, p. 18.
49. Jean Le Bel, *Chronique*, 2:83.
50. Barber, *Life and Campaigns of the Black Prince*, p. 35.
51. Le Bel and Froissart both state Calais was the ultimate destination. See Rogers, *War Cruel and Sharp*, p. 257–259.
52. Letter of Edward III to Sir Thomas Lucy dated 3 September, set out in Barber, *Life and Campaigns of the Black Prince*, pp. 21–23.
53. Rogers, *War Cruel and Sharp*, p. 273.
54. *CPR, 1345–1348*, pp. 337,538, 550, 551.
55. King David of Scotland was captured at Neville's Cross in 1346. In a secret ransom treaty of 1356 the ransom proposed was 90,000 marks (a mark was worth two-thirds of a pound, i.e. 13s 4d Rogers, *War Cruel and Sharp*, p. 337. After the Battle of Poitiers, the ransom set for King John was 4,000,000 écus, equal to £666,667 according to Rogers, *War Cruel and Sharp*, p. 389.
56. Sumption, *Hundred Years War, i: Trial by Battle*, p. 511.
57. McKisack, *The Fourteenth Century*, p. 247.
58. Ormrod, *The Reign of Edward III*, p. 116.
59. This cannot be confirmed definitively but it is a reasonable inference assuming that she had remained in the royal household as a companion for the princesses.
60. *CPR 1345–1348*, pp. 310–311.

61. *Calendar of Papal Registers, Letters, 1342–1362*, p. 235.
62. Stansfield, 'The Holland Family', p. 27; Wentersdorf, 'The Clandestine Marriages of the Fair Maid of Kent', p. 210.
63. Thomas' petition is not listed in the *Calendar of Papal Registers, Petitions, 1342–1419*. According to Wentersdorf there is no copy either in the Vatican's Secret Archives. Wentersdorf, 'The Clandestine Marriages of the Fair Maid of Kent', p. 229. However, the papal letter of May 1348 makes it clear Thomas had already petitioned.
64. The evidence for this comes from the Pope's brief dated May 1348 to the Archbishop of Canterbury and the bishops of Norwich and London which describes Joan as being in solitary confinement and under strong guard – 'solitariam et segretatam a consortio hominum sub forti et arta custodia'. Wentersdorf, 'The Clandestine Marriages of the Fair Maid of Kent', pp. 212, 220.
65. *CPR 1345–1348*, p. 431.
66. W. Shaw, *Knights of England* (London, 1906), i, p. i; *Register of Edward the Black Prince* (4 vols, London, 1930–33), iv, pp. 72–73.
67. Vergil, *Anglicae Historiae: Libri Vigintiseptem*, p. 379.
68. Wentersdorf, 'The Clandestine Marriages of the Fair Maid of Kent', p. 210, citing *Foedera*, iv, p. 25; *Calendar of Papal Registers, Petitions, 1342–1419*, pp. 24, 33; *Calendar Papal Registers, Papal Letters 1342–1362*, pp. 108, 177, 227, 344, 363, 425, 436, 470–1, 485.
69. Wentersdorf, 'The Clandestine Marriages of the Fair Maid of Kent', p. 210.
70. Brundage, 'Concubinage and Marriage in Medieval Canon Law', pp. 1–17.
71. *CPR 1348–1350*, pp. 212–213.
72. *Calendar of Papal Registers, Papal Letters, 1342–1362*, p. 252.
73. Beltz, *Memorials of the Most Noble Order of the Garter*, p. 385.
74. Wentersdorf, 'The Clandestine Marriages of the Fair Maid of Kent', p. 213.
75. The details of the proceedings have been taken from Wentersdorf, 'The Clandestine Marriages of the Fair Maid of Kent'.
76. TNA, E30/67.
77. *CCR 1349–1354*, pp. 30–31. Catherine had died by 12 May 1349.
78. *CIPM*, ix, p. 201.
79. *CFR 1347–1356*, pp. 116, 151, 154; Peter Fleming, 'Warr Family', *Oxford Dictionary of National Biography* (Oxford, 2004); *CPR 1348–1350*, pp. 327, 398. Margaret's arms of Or, 2 bars gulles and 3 torteaux in chief are still to be seen, impaled with those of Edmund, in a stained glass window in Chesterfield church in Derbyshire. The town of Chesterfield was held as part of the Kent estates.
80. Holmes, *The Estates of the Higher Nobility*, p. 26.
81. *CCR 1346–1349*, p. 315.
82. *The Complete Peerage*, vii, p. 149.
83. Clifford J. Rogers, *The Wars of Edward III, Sources and Interpretations* (Woodbridge, 1999), p. 63
84. Chamberlayne, 'Joan of Kent's Tale: Adultery and Rape in the Age of Chivalry', pp. 6–8.
85. *The Chronicle of Adam Usk 1377–1421*, ed. C. Given-Wilson (Oxford, 1997), p. 63.

6 Lady Holand: A Wife at Last, 1350–1352

1. Sumption, *Hundred Years War, i: Trial by Battle*, p. 592; Rogers, *Wars of Edward III*, p. xxii; England used the silver standard-£1 was equivalent to 1½ marks of silver, and a mark was 13*s* 4*d*. There were 20 shillings in a pound, and 12 pence in a shilling. The daily wage of a farm labourer was around 2 pence a day in the 1330s, and of a craftsman about 3/4d a day in the 1350s.

2. Saul, *Knights and Esquires*, p. 8–9.
3. Stansfield, 'The Holland Family', p. 26.
4. Ibid, p. 26.
5. *Foedera*, iii, pp. 191, 393.
6. Jonathan Sumption, *The Hundred Years War, vol. ii: Trial by Fire* (London, 1999), pp. 71–2.
7. William's wife also conceived very shortly after their marriage.
8. *CIPM*, vii, p. 552. When Thomas died in December 1360 his son Thomas is describe as being nine or ten years of age. There has been considerable speculation about the number of children Joan bore Thomas and various sources, including internet sites, continue to state that they had five children, the eldest of whom was a boy called Edmund who died. This appears to be based on the premise that Thomas and Joan would have called their eldest son after Joan's father, because they inherited his dignities. It is difficult to be accurate regarding the numbers of children as births and deaths were not recorded in a central register. However, there is no evidence to suggest that Joan bore a son called Edmund. As Joan's marriage to Thomas was not validated until November 1349 the earliest she could have borne their first child would have been August 1350, and even if Thomas was only nine in December 1360 it is unlikely that he was a second child. Until Joan's brother John died in December 1352 Thomas and Joan had no real anticipation that they would inherit the Kent earldom, and it would have been normal and natural for Thomas to name their eldest son after himself.
9. *Register of Edward the Black Prince* (4 vols, London, 1930–33), iv, p. 87.
10. Rogers, *The Wars of Edward III*, pp. 122, 133. Rogers notes that John is described among Henry of Lancaster's retinue in the King's Wardrobe records for 1346/1347 but suggests John did not join the royal host until the siege of Calais.
11. These figures are collated from using the incomplete figures given in the Inquisitions post mortem valuation taken at John's death in 1352 (*CIPM*, vii, pp. 41–57), the values cited in the dower valuation for his widow Elizabeth (*CCR 1349–1354*, pp. 530–1), and the valuations for the Kent estates from the original grants to Edmund.
12. *CFR 1347–1356*, p. 236; *CCR 1349–1354*, p. 578.
13. Warner, 'The Montague earls of Salisbury', p. 38. Joan Montague married William Ufford and died childless in 1362.
14. *CCR 1340–1354*, pp. 411–412, 459. In January 1352 Edward and Alice are cited assenting to a payment to Alice's mother, Mary, while in February 1352 an order was made to restore to Edward lands seized by the escheator in Norfolk and Suffolk on Alice's death.
15. Rowena Archer, 'The Estates and Finances of Margaret of Brotherton *c.* 1320–1399', *Bulletin of Institute of Historical Research*, LX (1987), p. 266.
16. *Calendar of Papal Registers, Papal Letters, 1342–1362*, pp. 381, 391.
17. Archer, 'The Estates and Finances of Margaret of Brotherton', p. 266; *CPR 1354–1358*, p. 325; Ward, *English Noblewomen in the Later Middle Ages*, pp. 30–31.
18. Archer, 'The Estates and Finances of Margaret of Brotherton', pp. 266–267.
19. *Foedera*, v, p. 702.
20. TNA, C76/30 m3.
21. Colvin, *History of the Kings Works, I*, p. 424; Sumption, *The Hundred Years War, i: Trial by Battle*, p. 583.
22. Allmand, *Hundred Years War*, p. 97.
23. *CPR 1350–1354*, p. 231.
24. John Holand's date of birth is unknown. Joan bore Thomas four children, and all that is known for certain are the dates Thomas and John died. Thomas was clearly the elder of the two boys as he inherited the earldom. I think it is reasonable to suggest that Thomas and Joan named their second son John after Joan's brother,

and requested he stand as godfather to the child. John Holand would therefore have been born before the death of Joan's brother in December 1352.

25. *CPR 1350–1354*, p. 312.
26. *CPR 1350–1354*, p. 383; *CIPM*, vii, p. 41.
27. *The Complete Peerage*, vii, pp. 1480150; College of Arms MS Staff. C. 10/160.6. John's arms can still be seen in Lichfield Cathedral; per pale gules, three lions passant guardant a bordure argent with the Juliers arms of Or a lion rampant sable. It is not clear what connection John had to the Cathedral and why his arms are there.
28. *The Complete Peerage*, vii, pp. 150–154.
29. J. Nichols, *Collection of the Wills of the Kings and Queens of England* (London, 1780), p. 212; Lambeth Register Arundel, p. 2, ff. 154v, 155r.
30. There were thirty-eight counties in England at this time. Ormrod, *Edward III*, p. 161.
31. *CIPM, vii*, pp. 41–57.
32. A total of thirty advowsons and 124 knight's fees in all.
33. *CCR 1349–1354*, pp. 530–531, 552–554, 594. The annual income per county was: Surrey £80, Hampshire £314 15s, Devon £114 13s 4d, Somerset £294, Gloucestershire £187 6s 8d, Sussex £4 16s 8d; the knight's fees and advowsons are valued separately and indicate an annual income from these of £1,000. Altogether these come to nearly £1,800 a year.
34. *CCR 1349–1354*, p. 578; *CPR 1338–1340*, p. 133; *CCR 1346–1349*, p. 417; *CPR 1350–1354*, p. 86–91, 435. James Beaufort was presented to Keggeworth Church in the Lincoln diocese (in the king's gift) in 1353.
35. *CCR 1349–1354*, pp. 530–531, 594; *CFR 1347–1356*, pp. 356–357.
36. *CCR 1349–1354*, pp. 585, 588.
37. *CCR 1350–1354*, p. 77.
38. *The Complete Peerage*, vii, p. 150. The summons came in July 1353.
39. Catalogue of Seals, HMSO, 1978, pp. 398–399; de Gray Birch, iii, p. 386.
40. The castle has not survived, as it was demolished in the eighteenth century and the stones were used to build a house in Donington Park, which was pulled down in its turn in 1793 by the Marquis of Hastings and rebuilt as Donington Hall. The only trace of the medieval castle now is a slight depression where the moat once stood and a few stones in the wall of a private garden. The park is now the site of the Donington Park racing circuit. The church at Castle Donington, originally built in the thirteenth century, survives, though in its present condition, after various alterations and more recent restoration, there is no trace of any connection to Joan.
41. Rev. R Lethbridge Farmer, Notes on two Churches visited by the Archaeological Society 1914; Castle Donington Church, *Derbyshire Archaeological and Natural History Society*; pp. 1–10.
42. *CPR, 1348–1350*, p. 274.
43. *CIPM*, vi, p. 233.
44. *CIPM*, vii, p. 43.
45. *CIPM*, xv, p. 182.
46. For a more detailed analysis of the machinery of a large noble household see Saul, *Knights and Esquires*, C. Given-Wilson, *The English Nobility in the Late Middle Ages* (London and New York, 1996); C. M. Woolgar, *The Great Household in Late Medieval England* (London, 1999); Holmes, *Estates of the Higher Nobility*.
47. Stansfield, 'The Holland Family', covers the history of the Holland family from 1353 to 1475 and comments on the absence of family and estate papers. In 2005 I searched the manorial documents register at the National Archives and could find no entries for any of Joan's estates contemporaneous with her lifetime. On Joan's death the estate records would have been passed to her eldest son Thomas Holand. The vicissitudes of time and fortune meant that the direct male family line died out within a hundred years of Joan's death, and the estates were split up, the records similarly split no doubt.

48. *CIPM*, xv, p. 181, Blanche died on 3 July 1380; *CIPM*, xix, p. 306, Elizabeth died on 6 June 1411.
49. *CIPM*, vii, p. 43.
50. *CPR 1350–1354*, p. 383. *CPR 1350–1354*, p. 435, Beaufort was presented to a church in the diocese of Lincoln in 1353; *CPR 1350–1354*, p. 497, Aspale is described as the king's yeoman; *CPR 1350–1354*, pp. 92, 482, Loxley appointed JP in Surrey.
51. *CCR 1349–1354*, p. 578.
52. *CPR 1350–1354*, pp. 86–91. *CPR 1327–1330*, p. 268, in 1328 Gerard and Henry received pardons for actions committed on Edmund's behalf. L. H. Butler, 'Robert Braybrooke, Bishop of London (1381–1404) and his kinsmen' (University of Oxford D. Phil. thesis, 1952), p. ii.
53. *CPR 1327–1330*, p. 159; *CFR 1327–1337*, p. 72; *CPR 1327–1330*, p. 385; *CPR 1334–1338*, p. 295; *CCR 1346–1349*, p. 417; *CPR 1350–1354*, pp. 27, 28, 84, 88.
54. *Foedera*, iii, p. 78.
55. *CPR 1348–1350*, p. 309.
56. *CPR 1350–1354*, pp. 46, 52–55, 172, 306.
57. *CPR 1348–1350*, pp. 184, 412.
58. *CPR 1350–1354*, pp. 231, 455, 482, 487, 498, 518.
59. Holmes, *Estates of the Higher Nobility*, pp. 22–23.
60. *CCR 1354–1360*, pp. 204, 208; *CCR 1360–1364*, p. 5.
61. Holmes, *Estates of the Higher Nobility*, p. 58; Margaret Wade Labarge, *Women in Medieval Life* (London, 2001), p. 89–90.
62. Labarge, *Women in Medieval Life*, p. 90.
63. *CPR 1354–1358*, p. 27; G. R. Davis, *Medieval Cartularies of Great Britain* (London, 1958); *Victoria History of the County of Lincolnshire* (London, 1906), Vol. 2, p. 315.
64. *CChR 1341–1417*, p. 133.
65. TNA, C143/321/3; *CPR 1354–1358*, p. 411; *CIPM*, x, pp. 447–448.
66. *CIPM*, x, pp. 447–448.
67. *CPR 1358–1361*, p. 480.

7 A Soldier's Wife, 1352–1360

1. *Foedera*, iii, i, p. 274; Stansfield, 'The Holland Family', p. 35.
2. TNA, E403/371, mm. 7, 16 lists payments of £100 and 100 marks for Thomas' service in Brittany.
3. Sumption, *The Hundred Years War, ii Trial by Fire*, p. 98; describes the improvements to Calais' defences achieved by October 1352, although he does not mention Thomas.
4. TNA, C76/32, m. 7, 8; Stansfield, 'The Holland Family', pp. 35, 280.
5. *CPR 1354–1358*, p. 15.
6. Froissart, *Oeuvres*, Lettenhove, ii, p. 398.
7. *CPR 1350–1354*, pp. 103, 188,; *CPR 1348–1350*, pp. 184, 412; *CPR 1345–1348*, p. 139.
8. *CPR 1345–1348*, pp. 112, 169, 324; *RBP*, iii, p. 368; *CPR 1350–1354*, p. 43; *CPR 1334–1338*, p. 163.
9. *CPR 1350–1354*, p. 480.
10. TNA, C76/32 m. 7.
11. TNA, SC7/22/16.
12. Sumption, *The Hundred Years War, ii: Trial by Fire*, pp. 134–135, describes the campaigning.
13. TNA, C76/32, m. 4.
14. *CPR 1354–1358*, p. 27.
15. John Aberth, *Criminal Churchmen in the Age of Edward III, The Case of Bishop Thomas de Lisle* (Pennsylvania, 1996), pp. 119–138.

16. *Testamenta Vetusta*, ed. N. H. Nichols (2 vols, London, 1826), i, pp. 64–66.
17. *The Complete Peerage*, VII p. 154, *CCR 1385–1389*, p. 13.
18. TNA, E101/93/8.
19. *CPR 1354–1358*, p. 26
20. Sumption, *The Hundred Years War, ii: Trial by Fire*, pp. 272–3, 421, 544, 459.
21. TNA, C76/32, m. 3; C76/33, m. 7, 14; *Foedera*, i, p. 307.
22. TNA, C76/33, m. 7.
23. Rogers, *The Wars of Edward III, Sources and Interpretations*, p. 148.
24. Rogers, *War, Cruel and Sharp*, p. 295.
25. TNA C76/33, m. 6, *Foedera*, v, pp. 826–827; M. Jones, 'Edward III's Captains in Brittany', *England in the Fourteenth Century Proceedings of the Harlaxton Symposium*, ed. W. Ormrod (Woodbridge, 1986), p. 118.
26. Barber, *Life and Campaigns of the Black Prince*, p. 52.
27. *Foedera*, iii, i, p. 312; TNA, C76/33, m. 6.
28. *CFR 1327–1337*, p. 328.
29. *CFR 1356–1358*, p. 7; *CPR 1354–1358*, p. 411.
30. *The Anonimalle Chronicle 1333–1381*, ed. V. H. Galbraith (Manchester, 1927), pp. 35–39.
31. Sumption, *The Hundred Years War, ii: Trial by Fire*, p. 274.
32. *CFR 1356–1368*, p. 43.
33. TNA, C76/35, m. 5.
34. *Foedera*, v, pp. 871–2, *Foedera*, vi, p. 72
35. Stansfield, 'The Holland family', p. 42.
36. *Foedera*, iii, i, p. 408; Stansfield, 'The Holland family', p. 42.
37. *Foedera*, iii, i. p. 409.
38. The dates of birth of Thomas and Joan's four children are not known. The Inquisitions Post Mortem taken at Thomas' death in 1360 describes the young Thomas as his heir and aged ten, making him the eldest, and born sometime in 1350. On the assumption that Thomas and Joan appointed her brother godfather to their younger son, John would have been born before his uncle's death in December 1352. This would make Maud and Joan younger, and probably born in 1353/4 and 1355/6 but this can only be speculative.
39. Stansfield, 'The Holland family', p. 43.
40. TNA C76/38, mm, 6, 7, 15; *Foedera*, vi, p. 142.
41. Sumption, *The Hundred Years War, ii: Trial by Fire*, p. 421–422.
42. *CPR 1354–1358*, pp. 15, 162, *RBP*, iii, pp. 218–219; TNA, C76/36 m7, m. 8; C76/38 m15.
43. The campaign is detailed in Sumption, *The Hundred Years War, ii: Trial by Fire*, pp. 424–445.
44. Sumption, *The Hundred Years War, ii: Trial by Fire*, p. 445.
45. Sumption, *The Hundred Years War, ii: Trial by Fire*, pp. 446–447.
46. *The Complete Peerage*, vii, p. 152.
47. *The Complete Peerage*, vii, pp. 149–150.
48. Shaw, *Knights of England*, ii, p. 1. The records for the Garter record a Sanchet d'Aubrichecourt as a founder member. Mark Ormrod in *Edward III*, p302, suggests that this is Eustace, as there are no other records of a Sanchet d'Aubrichecourt.
49. Sumption, *The Hundred Years War, ii: Trial by Fire*, p. 432.
50. *CPR 1358–1361*, p. 456.
51. TNA C76/40, m. 4; E403/402, m. 1; Stansfield, 'The Holland Family', p. 44.
52. *Foedera*, iii, I, pp. 510, 522.
53. In February 1360 official records (*CCR 1360–1364*, p. 5), still refer to Sir Thomas and Lady Holand, and it is not until October 1360 that Thomas is recorded as Earl of Kent (TNA, C76/43, m. 3).
54. *CPR 1358–1361*, p. 480.
55. *Chronique des quatre premiers Valois 1327–1303*, p. 123.

56. TNA C76/43, p. 3; *Foedera*, vi, p. 298; *Chronique des quatre premiers Valois*, p. 123; Stansfield, 'The Holland Family', p. 44.
57. *RBP*, iv, p. 536.

8 A Royal Bride, 1361–1363

1. *CCR 1360–1364*, pp. 175–176.
2. British Library MS. Cotton Nero D vi, f. 31.
3. Margaret Sharp, The Administrative Chancery of the Black Prince before 1362, *Essays in Medieval History presented to T. F. Tout*, ed. A. G. Little and F. M. Powicke (Manchester, 1925), p. 327; Tout, *Administrative History*, v, p. 372. Tout notes that the Prince's intelligence was commented on in 1352.
4. *The Itinerary of John Leland in or about the Years 1535–1543*, ed. L. T. Smith (London, 1909), iv, p. 38. See Barber, *Edward Prince of Wales and Aquitaine*, pp. 242–243.
5. Barber, *Edward Prince of Wales and Aquitaine*, p. 68. Barber points out that there is no actual evidence to link the prince's use of the feather to the king of Bohemia.
6. Loosely translated to mean 'houmont', high spirits, and 'ich dene', I serve.
7. Froissart, *Chroniques*, Lettenhove, v, pp. 63–64; *Chronicon Galfridi le Baker*, pp. 53–54.
8. *Chronique des quatre premiers Valois*, p. 123.
9. *Life of the Black Prince by the herald of Sir John Chandos*, p. 135.
10. Roger was remembered by the prince in his will, his mother was Edith de Willesford, a member of Queen Philippa's household. Beltz, *Order of the Garter*, p. 17.
11. *CPR 1330–1334*, p. 224; *Foedera*, ii, p. 1140; *Foedera*, iii, i, p. 35, in October 1340 Edward III asked for papal dispensation for the prince's marriage to the Duke of Brabant's daughter, repeating the request in April 1345. *RBP*, i, p. 76, in May 1347 Sir Robert Stratton was negotiating the prince's marriage with Leonora of Portugal.
12. Ward, *English Noblewomen in the Later Middle Ages*, p. 20.
13. In December 1344, for example, the Pope stated that he would not grant the dispensation for the Prince to marry the Duke of Brabant's daughter in the hope that this would promote a match between Brabant and either France or the Duke of Normandy instead. *Calendar of Papal Registers, Papal Letters, 1342–1362*, p. 14. The Pope's tactic seems to have worked as in 1347 Louis, son of the Count of Flanders, married Margaret of Brabant.
14. *Calendar of Papal Registers, Papal Letters, 1342–1362*, p. 14.
15. It has generally been presumed by historians that this was Edward III's method of providing his sons with land and income. See the discussion by Ormrod, *The Reign of Edward III*, pp. 110–111; McFarlane, *The Nobility of Later Medieval England*, p. 156; M. Prestwich, *The Three Edwards, War and State in England, 1272–1377* (2nd ed, London, 2003), p. 251.
16. *Foedera*, ii, ii, p. 1159.
17. *Foedera*, iii, i, p. 181.
18. *Foedera*, iii, pp. 1, 218.
19. *Foedera*, ii, ii, 1168.
20. *Chronique des quatre premiers Valois*, p. 123.
21. *Chronique des quatre premiers Valois*, pp. 123–125.
22. Beltz, *Memorials of Most Noble Order of the Garter*, p. 385; *Life of the Black Prince by the herald of Sir John Chandos*, p. 141.
23. The prince wrote to Joan in 1367 after the Battle of Nájera addressing his letter to her 'trescher et tressentier coer, biene ame compaigne'. TNA, SC1/42/33 translated by A. E. Prince, 'A Letter of Edward the Black Prince Describing the battle of Nájera in 1367', *English Historical Review*, xli (1926).

24. Green, *The Black Prince*, p. 83, it 'was not the match his father wanted'; Barber, *Edward, Prince of Wales and Aquitaine*, p. 172, the 'choice was in many ways remarkable'; J. Harvey, *Black Prince and his Age* (New Jersey, 1976), p. 102, Queen Philippa 'opposed it'; McKisack, *The Fourteenth Century*, p. 266, the 'marriage a disappointment'; N. Saul, *Richard II* (New Haven and London, 1999), p. 11, the marriage was 'arranged without prior approval of the king'; H. Cole, *The Black Prince* (London, 1976), pp. 138–139, 141, says it was a 'surprising choice', 'unlikely and scarcely acceptable' and that Edward III was 'outraged' and 'exiled the couple'; J. Laynesmith, *The Last Medieval Queens* (Oxford, 2004), pp. 36–38 suggests that the prince rejected the royal tradition of marrying for the good of the realm by marrying Joan. Frances Underhill, *For Her Good Estate: The Life of Elizabeth de Burgh* (Basingstoke, 1999), pp. 110–112. Elizabeth died a month before Thomas Holand.
25. Froissart, *Oeuvres*, Lettenhove, i, p. 367.
26. See discussion by Barber, *Edward Prince of Wales and Aquitaine*, p. 171; Green, *The Black Prince*, p. 85.
27. Sumption, *The Hundred Years War ii: Trial by Fire*, p. 35; Barber, *Edward Prince of Wales and Aquitaine*, p. 177.
28. Estimates of the prince's income are based on *CIPM*, xv, pp. 67–77; Tout, *Administrative History*, v, p. 363 calculates the prince received around £3,000 from North Wales, £1,700 from South Wales, £2,350 from Cornwall and £1,300 from Cheshire and comments that these were not extraordinary sums.
29. Tout, *Administrative History*, v, p. 364, suggested that by 1359 the prince was showing an 'incapacity to make ends meet and inability to attempt adjustment of expenditure to income'.
30. *RBP*, iii, p. 60.
31. *RBP*, ii, pp. 103, 106, 141, 147, 150, 154, 158.
32. *RBP*, iv, pp. 301–302.
33. *Anonimalle 1333–1381*, p. 49.
34. Joan's wealth has been consistently underrated by historians as an attraction adding to her suitability as a royal bride. Prestwich, *The Three Edwards*, p. 247, goes so far as to claim that Joan was 'not a notably wealthy woman'. Although Tout, *Administrative History*, v, p. 243 remarks that 'her inheritance was by no means to be despised' and Barber, *Edward, Prince of Wales and Aquitaine*, p. 174 comments that 'she did bring considerable income', neither recognise the very considerable benefits Joan's wealth brought to the prince, while Green, *The Black Prince*, p. 83 does not mention her inheritance at all.
35. D. Green, 'Politics and Service with Edward the Black Prince', *The Age of Edward III*, ed. j. S. Bothwell (York, 2001), p. 57.
36. *RBP*, iv, p. 323.
37. This is discussed by Sumption, *The Hundred Years War ii: Trial by Fire*, pp. 466–473.
38. *RBP*, iv, pp. 401, 405, 427.
39. TNA, SC7/22/15.
40. Ibid.
41. Ibid.
42. TNA, E30/180; *Foedera*, iii, ii, p. 626.
43. Lambeth Palace Library, Register of Archbishop Islip, fol. 180v–181v: TNA, E30/180.
44. TNA, E30/180; *Foedera*, iii, ii, p. 626.
45. TNA, SC7/22/17; *Foedera*, iii, ii, p. 626.
46. TNA, E40/1400; Canterbury Cathedral, DCC/Carta Antique F49 (the deed of foundation of the chantry); Cathedral Guide, Jonathon Keates and Angelo Hornak.
47. F. Woodman, *The Architectural History of Canterbury Cathedral* (London, 1981), p. 148.
48. TNA, E40/1400.

49. *RBP*, iv, pp. 360, 472, 551.
50. *Calendar of Papal Registers, Papal Letters, 1362–1401*, p. 29.
51. British Library, Harl. MSS.6148: note dated 8 October 1361 from Simon Islip, Archbishop of Canterbury to the prince (quoted in *Testamenta Vetusta*, i, p. 14.
52. TNA, SC7/22/1.
53. S. Armitage-Smith, *John of Gaunt* (London, 1964), p. 142.
54. A. K. McHardy, 'Richard II: a personal portrait', *The Reign of Richard II*, ed. G. Dodd (Stroud, 2000), p. 11, 12, 155.
55. Westminster Abbey Muniments, no. 9584. This is the receipt of the list of the contents of the chest, and refers to the 'instrumentum processus et sentencie' between Thomas Holand and the Earl of Salisbury, the execution of that process by papal bull from Pope Clement VI, an instrument of execution under the seal of the bishop and Pope Clement VI's bull ordering Joan be set at liberty to appoint a proctor in the case between Thomas Holand and William Montague. The National Archives hold Clement VI's bull dated 13 November 1349 (TNA, E30/67); Innocent VI's bull dated 2 August 1353 (TNA, SC7/22/16); Innocent VI's bull dated 6 October 1361 (TNA, SC7/22/15).
56. *Chronicle of Adam Usk 1377–1381*, ed. and translated by C. Given-Wilson (Oxford, 1997), p. 11.
57. TNA, E30/180; *Foed*, III, ii, p. 626.
58. Prince Lionel and Princess Margaret are not individually mentioned, the latter may have been too ill to attend.
59. *Inventories of St George's Chapel Windsor 1348–1416*, ed. M. F. Bond (Windsor, 1947), p. 41.
    The entry describes 'one red vestment of cloth of gold powdered with various birds, in which the lady Princess was espoused'. After Joan donated her dress to the chapel it had been altered into a clerical vestment.
60. A. Goodman, *John of Gaunt* (Harlow, 1992), p. 35.
61. Goodman, *John of Gaunt*, p. 42, states Mary died before 13 September 1361.
62. Higden, *Polychronicon*, viii, p. 524.
63. Goodman, *John of Gaunt*, p. 35.
64. *RBP*, iv, p. 409.
65. *CPR 1361–1364*, p. 126; Vale, 'Philippa (1310?–1369)', *ODNB*; *RBP*, iv, p. 476.
66. *RBP*, iv, pp. 463, 476.
67. *RBP*, iv, p. 463.
68. *RBP*, iv, pp. 402–403. The prince paid Martin Parde £1447, and John de la Mare and his companions £1,883 6s 8d.
69. Newton, *Fashion in the Age of the Black Prince*, p. 3.
70. Newton, *Fashion in the Age of the Black Prince*, pp. 3–4, 21; *RBP*, iv, pp. 88, 141–142.
71. *RBP*, iv, pp. 69, 427–428.
72. Newton, *Fashion in the Age of the Black Prince*, p. 34.
73. Newton, *Fashion in the Age of the Black Prince*, pp. 34, 61.
74. Higden, *Polychronicon*, viii, p. 360.
75. *Anonimalle 1333–1381*, p. 49.
76. *Chronica Johannis de Reading*, pp. 212–213; Walsingham, *Historia Anglicana*, 1, p. 296; *Knighton*, ii, p. 116.
77. *Life of the Black Prince by the Herald of Sir John Chandos*, p. 141.
78. *The Complete Peerage*, vii, p. 153; Sandford, *Royal Genealogies*, p. 215.
79. The choice of a chained white hart is intriguing, a wild and unusual animal held captive by royalty.
80. *RBP*, iv, pp. 389, 392, 456.
81. *RBP*, iv, pp. 427–428.
82. *RBP*, iv, pp. 424–425, 482.
83. *RBP*, iv, pp. 442, 450, 537; *CCR 1360–1364*, p. 372.
84. *RBP*, iv, pp. 397, 399.

85. *RBP*, iv, pp. 397–398.
86. *RBP*, iv, pp. 444, 447, 450, 517; *CCR 1360–1364*, p. 215.
87. *RBP*, iv, p. 475.
88. *History of the King's Works*, ed. R. Allen Brown, H. M. Colvin, A. J. Taylor (2 vols, London, 1963), ii, pp. 562.
89. *RBP*, iv, pp. 243–244, 256, 265, 342, 400, 411–12; *CCR 1360–1364*, p. 11; *CPR 1358–1361*, p. 341.
90. *RBP*, iv, pp. 411, 421.
91. *RBP*, iv, p. 42, 65, 250, 363.
92. *CPR 1361–1364*, p. 35.
93. Ward, *English Noblewomen in the Later Middle Ages*.
94. *History of the King's Works*, ii, pp. 967–968.
95. *RBP*, iv, p. 476, 250, 283/4, 400; Barber, *Edward, Prince of Wales and Aquitaine*, pp. 174–175.
96. *RBP*, iv, p. 247.
97. *RBP*, iv, p. 400.
98. *RBP*, iv, pp. 476
99. *RBP*, iv, pp. 461, 467, 476, 558.
100. Holmes, *The Estates of the Higher Nobility*, p. 28.
101. *CCR 1354–1360*, p. 93.
102. *RBP*, iv, pp. 302, 381, 449.
103. *Calendar of Papal Registers, Petitions, I, 1342–1419*, p. 453.
104. *RBP*, iii, pp. 480–481; *CPR 1361–1364*, p. 480, in April 1364 Edward III granted Joan and the prince permission to grant the manors to Thomas and Alice.
105. *RBP*, ii, p. 194.
106. *RBP*, iv, p. 545.
107. *CCR 1374–1377*, p. 52.
108. *Calendar of Papal Registers, Letters, 1342–1362*, pp. 614–615; *Foedera*, iii, ii, pp. 662–3.

9 Princess of Aquitaine, 1363–1371

1. Christine de Pizan, *The Treasure of the City of Ladies*, translated by Sarah Lawson (London, 2003); p. 28.
2. *Foedera*, iii, ii, pp. 667–668.
3. TNA E30/1105; Barbara Emerson, *The Black Prince* (London, 1976), pp. 165–166.
4. Giles of Rome, *The Governance of Kings and Princes: John Trevisa's Translation of De Regimine Principum of Aegidius Romanus*, ed. D. C. Fowler, C. F. Briggs and P. G. Remley (London, 1977), pp. 186–208.
5. *Calendar of Papal Registers, Papal Letters, 1305–1342*, pp. 500–501.
6. Froissart, *Chronicles*, Johnes, i, p. 6.
7. Tout, *Administrative History*, v, pp. 371, 428; Barber, *Edward, Prince of Wales and Aquitaine*, p. 178.
8. *RBP*, iv, p. 467.
9. *RBP*, iv, p. 500.
10. *Foedera*, iii, ii, pp. 671, 675, 676.
11. *RBP*, iv, p. 426.
12. *RBP*, iv, pp. 424–425, 442–443, 452–453, 456, 460, 482.
13. *CPR 1361–1364*, p. 258.
14. Butler, 'Robert Braybrooke, Bishop of London (1381–1404), and his Kinsmen', p. iii.
15. *Calendar of Papal Registers, Petitions, 1342–1419* (London, 1896), p. 397.
16. *Calendar of Papal Registers, Petitions, 1342–1419*, p. 456.
17. *The Complete Peerage*, iv, pp. 139–151.

18. Butler, 'Robert Braybrooke, Bishop of London (1381–1404), and his Kinsmen', p. 33.
19. TNA, C76/32, m8.
20. *RBP*, iv, p. 55, *RBP*, iv, pp. 208, 323.
21. *Foedera*, iii, ii, p. 626–627; TNA, E30/180.
22. *The Complete Peerage*, iv, pp. 139–151.
23. *Testamenta Vetusta*, i, p. 14.
24. *RBP*, iv, p. 480.
25. *RBP*, iv, p. 456.
26. *CIPM*, xix, p. 307, *RBP*, iv, p. 500; *CCR 1364–1368*, p. 4.
27. *Calendar of Papal Registers, Petitions, 1342–1419*, p. 456. Andrew Luttrell was a distant relation of Geoffrey Luttrell, famous for the Luttrell psalter.
28. Janet Backhouse, *The Luttrell Psalter* (London, 1989), p. 32.
29. Barber, *Edward, Prince of Wales and Aquitaine*, p. 179; TNA E61/76, m. 4.
30. *RBP*, iv, pp. 478, 467.
31. *Foedera*, iii, ii, pp. 666, 671, 720; Green, *The Black Prince*, p. 145.
32. Jean le Bel, *Chronique*, i, I118; *Chroniques des quatre premiers Valois*, p. 114.
33. Rogers, *The Wars of Edward III*, p. xiii, xxii.
34. Green, *The Black Prince*, p. 140.
35. Rogers, *The Wars of Edward III*, p. 183.
36. Ibid.
37. *Anonimalle 1333–1381*, pp. 35–39; Barber, *Life and Campaigns of the Black Prince*, p. 52.
38. Green, *The Black Prince*, pp. 140–141.
39. Green, *The Black Prince*, p. 140.
40. Chris Given-Wilson, *Chronicles, The Writing of History in Medieval England* (London, 2004), p. 110.
41. Green, *The Black Prince*, pp. 141–142.
42. Sumption, *Hundred Years War ii: Trial by Fire*, p. 473–475.
43. *RBP*, iv, p. 537.
44. *Chronica Johannis de Reading 1346–1367*, p. 370.
45. Barber, *Edward, Prince of Wales and Aquitaine*, pp. 179–180.
46. Barber, *Edward, Prince of Wales and Aquitaine*, p. 180.
47. Barber, *Edward, Prince of Wales and Aquitaine*, p. 184.
48. Newton, *Fashion in the Age of the Black Prince*, p. 40.
49. Newton, *Fashion in the Age of the Black Prince*, p. 61.
50. *RBP*, iv, p. 545. Maud was married by February 1365.
51. Barber, *Edward, Prince of Wales and Aquitaine*, p. 181; Green, *The Black Prince*, p. 142.
52. Barber, *Edward, Prince of Wales and Aquitaine*, p. 177.
53. Sumption, *Hundred Years War ii: Trial by Fire*, p. 543, calculates 36 per cent raised by direct taxation.
54. Barber, *Edward, Prince of Wales and Aquitaine*, p. 185.
55. Froissart, *Chroniques*, Luce, vii, p. 66; *The Life of the Black Prince by the Herald of Sir John Chandos*, p. 141.
56. *Anonimalle 1333–1381*, p. 56.
57. Sumption, *Hundred Years War ii: Trial by Fire*, p. 542.
58. Hubert Cole, *The Black Prince* (London, 1976), p. 155.
59. *Calendar of Papal Registers, Letters, 1362–1404*, p. 21.
60. *Chronicon Angliae 1328–1388*, ed. E. Maude Thompson (London, 1874), p. 56; There is some doubt about the date of Edward's birth. *Eulogium Historiarum* ed. F. Haydon (London, 1963) p. 236, cites 27 January as date of birth. However, the March date is more likely bearing in mind the date of Joan's own letter and the celebrations in April.
61. Froissart, *Chroniques*, Routledge, p. 81.
62. Antonia Gransden, 'A Fourteenth Century Chronicle from Grey Friars at Lynn', *English Historical Review, Vol. LXXII* (1957).

63. *CPR 1364–1367*, p. 180.
64. Cole, *The Black Prince*, p. 159.
65. *Chronicon Angliae*, p. 58.
66. Devon, *Issue Rolls*, Vol. 39, p. 188, 41, 44, p. xliii; James L. Gillespie, 'Isabella, countess of Bedford (1332–1379), *Oxford Dictionary of National Biography* (Oxford University Press, 2004.).
67. *Foedera*, iii, p. 778.
68. James L. Gillespie, 'Isabella, countess of Bedford (1332–1379), *Oxford Dictionary of National Biography* (Oxford, 2004).
69. Barber, *Edward, Prince of Wales and Aquitaine*, p. 184.
70. John de Montfort came of age in June 1362.
71. *Calendar of Papal Registers, Letters, 1362–1404*, p. 54.
72. *RBP*, iii, pp. 471–2.
73. *CPR 1367–1370*, pp. 27, 305; *CPR 1370–1374*, p. 16. John Delves was appointed in November 1367, his wife Isabel in September 1369 and Godfrey Fojambe in November 1370. They were all the prince's retainers; John Delves was the prince's yeoman.
74. Green, *The Black Prince*, p. 149.
75. *RBP*, iv, p. 520.
76. *RBP*, iv, p. 563.
77. *RBP*, iv, pp. 529, 533, 540, 549.
78. *RBP*, iv, p. 536.
79. *RBP*, iv, pp. 507, 525.
80. *CPR, 1364–1367*, p. 328.
81. *Calendar of Papal Registers, Petitions, 1342–1419*, p. 508; *CPR 1367–1370*, p. 58.
82. *Calendar of Papal Registers, Petitions, 1342–1419*, p. 456; *RBP*, iv, pp. 505, 509, 521.
83. *RBP*, iv, pp. 521, 525, 527, 537.
84. *RBP*, iv, p. 561.
85. TNA E30/191.
86. Sumption, *The Hundred Years War ii: Trial by Fire*, p. 481.
87. *Calendar of Papal Registers, Papal Letters, 1362–1404*, p. 21.
88. Sumption, *The Hundred Years War ii: Trial by Fire*, p. 344.
89. Green, *The Black Prince*, p. 157.
90. Barber, *Edward, Prince of Wales and Aquitaine*, pp. 188–189.
91. Tout, *Administrative History*, v, p. 408.
92. Froissart, *Oeuvres*, Lettenhove, vii, p. 96.
93. Sumption, *The Hundred Years War ii: Trial by Fire*, p. 545 estimates £35,400 and £42,500 for the Gascon lords.
94. Sumption, *The Hundred Years War ii: Trial by Fire*, p. 546.
95. *Foedera*, iii, ii, p. 800.
96. Saul, *Richard II*, p. 12.
97. Green, *The Black Prince*, pp. 221–129.
98. *CPR, 1377–1381*, pp. 120, 609; *CPR 1391–1396*, p. 505.
99. *Life of the Black Prince by the Herald of Sir John Chandos*, pp. 152–153.
100. Green, *The Black Prince*, p. 160, suggests between 6,000–8,500; Sumption, *The Hundred Years War ii: Trial by Fire*, p. 546, 8–10,000, Barber, Edward, *Prince of Wales and Aquitaine*, p. 194, puts the figure as low as 6,000.
101. Barber, *Life and Campaigns on the Black Prince*, pp. 114, 117.
102. *CPR 1367–1370*, p. 12. Eustace d'Aubrichecourt appointed attorneys for a year in October 1367 in order to join the prince in Gascony.
103. *Life of the Black Prince by the Herald of Sir John Chandos*, p. 153.
104. Goodman, *John of Gaunt*, p. 31.
105. TNA, E101/393/10.
106. Barber, *Edward, Prince of Wales and Aquitaine*, p. 196.
107. *The Complete Peerage*, p. 325; *Life of the Black Prince by the Herald of Sir John Chandos*, p. 157.

108. Barber, *Life and Campaigns of the Black Prince*, p. 123.
109. Sumption, *The Hundred Years War ii: Trial by Fire*, pp. 554–556.
110. TNA SC1/42/34; translation taken from A. E. Prince, A Letter of Edward the Black Prince describing the battle of Nájera 1367, *EHR* (xli, 1926), p. 415.
111. *CPR, 1364–1367*, p. 408.
112. Sumption, *The Hundred Years War ii: Trial by Fire*, p. 556.
113. Sumption, *The Hundred Years War ii: Trial by Fire*, p. 556.
114. Barber, *Life and Campaigns of the Black Prince*, p. 205.
115. *Life of the Black Prince by the Herald of Sir John Chandos*, p. 167; Barber, *Life and Campaigns of the Black Prince*, pp. 133–134.
116. Barber, *Life and Campaigns of the Black Prince*, p. 134.
117. Barber, *Edward Prince of Wales and Aquitaine*, p. 214; Green, *The Black Prince*, p. 169.
118. Sumption, *The Hundred Years War ii: Trial by Fire*, p. 545.
119. Barber, *Edward Prince of Wales and Aquitaine*, p. 210; Green, *The Black Prince*, p. 180.
120. Barber, *Edward Prince of Wales and Aquitaine*, p. 217.
121. Barber, *Life and Campaigns of the Black Prince*, p. 134.
122. Green, *The Black Prince*, p. 181.
123. Green, *The Black Prince*, p. 181; Barber, *Life and Campaigns of the Black Prince*, pp. 1208–220.
124. *Testamenta Vetusta*, i, pp. 70–71.
125. Barber, *Edward Prince of Wales and Aquitaine*, p. 221.
126. Barber, *Edward Prince of Wales and Aquitaine*, p. 221–225; Green, *The Black Prince*, pp. 181–190.
127. Devon, *Issue Roll*, 39 Edward III, p. 184.
128. Details of the Limoges campaign are taken from secondary sources: Barber Barber, *Edward Prince of Wales and Aquitaine*, p. 221–226; Green, *The Black Prince*, pp. 191–192.
129. Barber, *Life and Campaigns of the Black Prince*, p. 138.
130. Froissart, *Oeuvres*, Lettenhove, viii, p. 460.
131. Goodman, *John of Gaunt*, p. 48; Gaunt acted as the prince's lieutenant until 24 June 1371.
132. Froissart, *Oeuvres*, Lettenhove, viii, pp. 60–61.

10 Return to England/In Sickness and in Health, 1371–1376

1. Froissart, *Chronicles*, Luce, vii, p. 53
2. Barber, *Edward Prince of Wales and Aquitaine*, p. 227.
3. *CPR, 1370–1374*, pp. 331, 347; Ormrod, *Edward III*, pp. 534–537.
4. *Chronicon Angliae*, p. 91.
5. Barber, *Edward Prince of Wales and Aquitaine*, p. 227.
6. Goodman, *John of Gaunt*, p. 48.
7. Barber, *Edward Prince of Wales and Aquitaine*, p. 228.
8. *CPR, 1370–1374*, pp. 170–3.
9. *The Complete Peerage*, p. 325.
10. *CFR, 1369–1377*, p. 99.
11. Peter Fleming, 'Clifford, Sir Lewis (c. 1330–1404)', *Oxford Dictionary of National Biography* (Oxford, 2004).
12. *RBP*, ii, pp. 208, 210.
13. *John of Gaunt's Register, 1371–1375*, ed. S. Armitage-Smith (Camden Society, 3rd Series, 20), pp. 96, 112–13, 191–3, 278. Gifts listed to the prince on 23 November 1372, 24 December 1372, 13 April 1373, 8 January 1375 and to Joan and Eleanor and Maud Courtenay in January 1372 and April 1373.

14. Goodman, *John of Gaunt*, p. 48.

15. *Anonimalle 1333–1381*, p. 69.

16. *John of Gaunt's Register, 1371–1375*.

17. Jeannette Lucraft, *Katherine Swynford: The History of a Medieval Mistress* (Stroud, 2006), p. 23.

18. Joan was a Plantagenet family name and John had an older sister Princess Joan, but the princess died in 1348 when John was only eight, and by the time his own daughter was born, he was extremely close to his sister-in-law.

19. H. T. Riley, *Memorials of London and London Life* (1868), p. 362; Emerson, *The Black Prince*, p. 245.

20. Emerson, *The Black Prince*, p. 248; Barber, *Edward Prince of Wales and Aquitaine*, p. 228; Barber, *Life and Campaigns of the Black Prince*, p. 138; Ormrod, *Edward III*, pp. 512–514; Goodman, *John of Gaunt*. p. 52.

21. *CCR 1369–1374*, pp. 403, 404, 406, 463, 467.

22. Barber, *Edward Prince of Wales and Aquitaine*, p. 229.

23. TNA, E101/400/4, m. 20; Saul, *Richard II*, pp. 13–17; Green, *The Black Prince*; p. 213. Some historians have speculated that Simon was nephew to Walter Burley, who tutored the prince as a boy.

24. Michael Jones, 'John de Montfort', *Oxford Dictionary of National Biography* (Oxford, 2004).

25. Saul, *Richard II*, p. 13.

26. Goodman, *John of Gaunt*, p. 232.

27. Goodman, *John of Gaunt*, p. 53; Jonathan Sumption, *The Hundred Years War, vol. iii: Divided Houses* (London, 2012), pp. 187–202.

28. *Chronicon Angliae*, p. 96.

29. Tout, *Administrative History*, v, pp. 398–399.

30. Froissart, *Oeuvres*, Lettenhove, viii, p. 460.

31. *CPR 1370–1374*, p. 331.

32. *Calendar of Papal Letters, IV, 1361–1404*, p. 146.

33. www.royalacademy.org.uk/exhibitions/making history/the-arts. Antiquaries-and the Gothic Revival. Maddox Brown based his subject matter on antiquarian sources, taking his composition from a medieval miniature which no longer survives, and basing the royal figures on their tomb effigies.

34. Goodman, *John of Gaunt*, p. 54.

35. *Anonimalle 1333–1381*, p. 92.

36. Goodman, *John of Gaunt*, p. 56.

37. *Chronicon Angliae*, pp. 91–92.

38. Green, *The Black Prince*, pp. 63–65.

39. *The St Albans Chronicle, 1, 1376–1394, The Chronica Maiora of Thomas Walsingham*, ed. J. Taylor, W. R. Childs and L. Watkiss (Oxford, 2003), p. 35.

40. Barber, *Life and Campaigns of the Black Prince*, p. 139.

41. *Chronicon Angliae*, p. 89.

42. *The St Albans Chronicle, I, 1376–1394*, p. 37.

43. *Life of the Black Prince by the Herald of Sir John Chandos*, p. 170.

44. *Anonimalle 1333–1381*, p. 92; Walsingham, *Historia Anglicana*, I, p. 321. A. Collins, *Life and Glorious Actions of Edward, Prince of Wales* (1740), p. 304; *The Chronica Maiora of Thomas Walsingham*, pp. 37–39.

45. *Collection of the Wills of the Kings and Queens of England*, ed. J. Nichols (2 vols, London, 1780, reprod. 1969), p. 67.

46. Juliet and Malcolm Vale, 'Knightly Codes and Piety', in *Age of Chivalry, Art and Society in Late Medieval England* ed. N. Saul (London, 1992), p. 27.

47. Paul Binski, *Westminster Abbey and the Plantagenets, Kingship and the Representation of Power 1200–1400* (London, 1995), pp. 111, 119, 197.

48. Collins, *The Life and Glorious Actions of Edward Prince of Wales*, pp. 301–2.

49. *Collection of the Wills of the Kings and Queens of England*, p. 67.

50. *Testamenta Vetusta*, i, pp. 64–66, 70–71.

51. Tout, *Administrative History*, iii, p. 239.

52. Tout, *Administrative History*, iii, pp. 397–398.
53. *The Inventories of St George's Chapel, Windsor Castle, 1348–1667*, ed. M. F. Bond (Windsor, 1937), pp. 40–41. In 1384 inventory of St George's chapel lists vestments made from Joan's wedding dress.

11 Princess in Politics, 1376–1377

1. Christine de Pizan, *The Treasure of the City of Ladies*, translated by Sarah Lawson (London, 1985 revised 2003), p. 58.
2. *John of Gaunt's Register 1372–1376*, ii, p. 50.
3. *John of Gaunt's Register 1372–1376*, ii, p. 22.
4. *John of Gaunt's Register 1372–1376*, ii, p. 191.
5. *John of Gaunt's Register 1372–1376*, ii, pp. 193–194. Gaunt gave this to his father in May 1373 'un cerf blank gisant deinz une corone sur le covercle q'estoit done nous par ma tres chere dame la princesse'.
6. *John of Gaunt's Register 1372–1376*, ii, pp. 193–194, 224–225.
7. *The Chronica Maiora of Thomas Walsingham*, p. 39; Froissart, *Oeuvres*, Lettenhove, viii, p. 460; McKisack, *The Fourteenth Century*, p. 393.
8. *Rot. Parl*, ii. 330.
9. Goodman, *John of Gaunt*, p. 57.
10. *CPR 1374–1377*, pp. 374–377.
11. *CCR 1374–1377*, pp. 403, 405, 406, 408, 409, 420–422; *CPR 1377–1381*, p. 180.
12. F. Devon, *Issue Roll Thomas of Brantingham 44 Ed III* (London, 1835), p. 51.
13. *CPR 1374–1377*, pp. 376–377.
14. Jones, 'John de Montfort', *ODNB*.
15. K. B. McFarlane, *Lancastrian Kings and Lollard Knights* (Oxford, 1973), pp. 164–166.
16. *Anonimalle 1333–1381*, pp. 102–3.
17. *The Chronica Maiora of Thomas Walsingham*, pp. 90–91.
18. *The Chronica Maiora of Thomas Walsingham*, pp. 90–91.
19. *The Chronica Maiora of Thomas Walsingham*, pp. 92–93.
20. *John of Gaunt's Register 1372–1376*, ii, pp. 191, 193–194.
21. *The Chronica Maiora of Thomas Walsingham*, p. 65.
22. Goodman, *John of Gaunt*, p. 62.
23. *Anglo Norman Letters and Petitions*, ed. M. D. Legge (Oxford, 1941), pp. 162–166.
24. Goodman, *John of Gaunt*, pp. 63–64.
25. *The Chronica Maiora of Thomas Walsingham*, p. 119.
26. *The Chronica Maiora of Thomas Walsingham*, p. 119.
27. Ormrod, *Edward III*, p. 577.
28. Green, *The Black Prince*, p. 67; M. Bennett, 'Edward III's Entail and the Succession to the Crown, 1376–1471', *English Historical Review*, 113 (1998), pp. 580–607.
29. *Testamenta Vetusta*, ii, pp. 10–12.
30. *The Chronica Maiora of Thomas Walsingham*, pp. 126–127.
31. *The Chronica Maiora of Thomas Walsingham*, p. 131.
32. *Chronicon Angliae*, pp. 148–150.
33. *The Chronica Maiora of Thomas Walsingham*, p. 131.

12 The King's Mother, 1377–1385

1. *Anonimalle 1333–1381*, p. 106.
2. Saul, *Richard II*, pp. 22–23.
3. Saul, *Richard II*, pp. 24–25 gives an account of the coronation procession and ceremony.

4. *Chronica Maiora of Thomas Walsingham*, p. 139 describes the procession.
5. *Anonimalle 1333–1381*, p. 114; Goodman, *John of Gaunt*, pp. 70–71.
6. *Chronicon Angliae*, p. 155.
7. Discussed by Saul, *Richard II*, pp. 25–27.
8. When Richard was deposed in 1399 it is notable that Henry of Bolingbroke did not argue that Richard was not the legitimate heir.
9. *CCR 1377–1381*, pp. 1–5.
10. *CPR 1377–1381*, p. 60.
11. *CPR 1377–1381*, pp 21, 78.
12. Green, 'Politics and Service with Edward the Black Prince' *The Age of Edward III* ed. J. S. Bothwell, York Medieval Press 201) p. 67, C. Given-Wilson, *The Royal Household and the King's Affinity: Service, Politics and Finance in England 1360–1413* (New Haven and London, 1986), pp. 161–2.
13. McFarlane, *Lancastrian Kings and Lollard Knights*, p. 164.
14. McFarlane, *Lancastrian Kings and Lollard Knights*, p. 164; *CPR 1381–1385*, p. 54
15. McFarlane, *Lancastrian Kings and Lollard Knights*, p. 185; *CPR 1381–1385*, p. 8; *CCR 1377–1381*, p. 452.
16. Tout, *Administrative History*, vi, pp. 57, 329.
17. Nigel Saul, 'Sir John Clanvowe (c1341–1391)', *Oxford Dictionary of National Biography* (Oxford, 2004).
18. Scattergood, V. J., 'Literary Culture at the Court of Richard II', *English Court Culture in the Later Middle Ages*, ed. V. J. Scattergood and J. W. Sherborne (London, 1983), p. 23; McFarlane, *Lancastrian Kings and Lollard Knights*, pp. 166–167, 185; *CPR 1381–1385*, pp. 97, 560.
19. Margaret Galway, 'Chaucer's Hopeless Love', *Modern Languages Notes*, LX, November 1945, Number 7, p. 438; Anthony Burgess, *The Riverside Chaucer* (Oxford, 1988), p. xiii.
20. Goodman, *John of Gaunt*, p. 261.
21. British Library, Cotton Nero D VII folio 7v: St Albans Book of Benefactors.
22. British Library, Royal MSS 2B. viii. This copy, bound within a Psalter with an Office for the dead, was written around 1462, although it was formerly believed to have been a presentation copy. See Linne R. Mooney, 'John Somer Franciscan friar and astronomer' *Oxford Dictionary of National Biography* (Oxford, 2004).
23. H. Carey, *Courting Disaster: Astrology at the English Court and University in the Later Middle Ages* (London, 1992), pp. 22, 80.
24. *CPR 1307–1313*, pp, 563, *CPR 1327–1330*, pp. 87, 178, 251, *CPR 1330–1334*, pp. 41, 67, 84, 151, 260; F. A. Underhill, F. A., *For Her Good Estate: The Life of Elizabeth de Burgh* (London, 1999).
25. *The Chronica Maiora of Thomas Walsingham*, p. 181; *CCR 1377–1381*, p. 527.
26. Tout, *Administrative History*, vi, p. 327.
27. Saul, *Richard II*, pp. 29–30.
28. There has been a suggestion that Joan attempted to secure her influence by bringing into office dependants of prince as a counterpoise to the influence of Gaunt (N. B. Lewis 'The Continual Council in the Early Years of Richard II, 1377–1380', *English Historical Review* 41 (1926), 246–251, p. 249). There is ample evidence that Joan had absolute faith in Gaunt, so this seems unlikely.
29. As noted, for example, by Saul, *Richard II*, p. 11.
30. Goodman, *John of Gaunt*, p. 72
31. *The Chronica Maiora of Thomas Walsingham*, p. 157.
32. McKisack, *The Fourteenth Century 1307–1399*, p. 401; *Rot Parl*, iii, p. 5.
33. *CPR 1377–1381*, p. 7.
34. Jeannette Lucraft, *Katherine Swynford: The History of a Medieval Mistress* (Stroud, 2006), pp. 20–21.
35. Lucraft, *Katherine Swynford*, pp. 23–37 discusses the Beaufort children.
36. *The Complete Peerage*, VII, p. 154.; Stansfield, 'The Holland Family', pp. 52–3.
37. C. Given-Wilson, 'Wealth and Credit, Public and Private, the earls of Arundel 1306–1397', *English Historical Review*, vol. CVI, 1991, pp. 1–22.

38. Stansfield, 'The Holland Family', pp. 55, 60.
39. In July 1377 there was a general appointment of JPs throughout the country. Thomas and John Holand are not listed.
40. Stansfield, 'The Holland Family', p. 55. In fact, it seems that due to difficulties in collecting the rent Thomas received rather less than this.
41. Stansfield, 'The Holland Family', p. 310; M. M. N. Stansfield, 'Holland, Thomas, fifth Earl of Kent (1350–1397)', *Oxford Dictionary of National Biography* (Oxford, 2004).
42. *CPR 1377–1381*, p. 141; Stansfield, 'The Holland Family', pp. 69, 71.
43. David Green, *The Battle of Poitiers 1356* (Stroud, 2002), p. 17.
44. Michael Jones, 'John de Montfort', *ODNB*.
45. *The Chronica Maiora of Thomas Walsingham*, p. 161.
46. McKisack, *The Fourteenth Century*, p. 403; *Rot Parl* iii 15.
47. *CPR 1377–1380*, pp. 121–2.
48. Saul, *Richard II*, pp. 30–34.
49. Bodley, Ms Eng, hist. C. 775 indenture of 13 May 1378 recording delivery by William Sleford of plate charged to him under Edward III to John Bacon, keeper of jewels and plate of R11. Her arms are engraved on plate used for food and drink and records refer to her as 'Madame la Meer'. I am indebted to Jenny Stratford of Royal Holloway for this reference.
50. E. Fellowes, *The Knights of the Garter* (London), pp. 102–104. Evidence of membership comes from the account of Alan Stokes, keeper of the Great Wardrobe, for expenditure in connection with the celebration of the Garter feast in 1379. TNA E101/400/12. This list includes Mary duchess of Brittany, which is clearly a mistake by the scribe as Joan's daughter Joan became duchess of Brittany in 1365, some time after the death of her predecessor, Princess Mary, who was John Montfort's first wife.
51. James L. Gillespie, 'Ladies of the Fraternity of Saint George and of the Society of the Garter', *Albion* 17 (1985), p. 263.
52. TNA E403–466 lists payments to military commanders April 1378. John Holand was not a commander but he is mentioned by Froissart at the siege of St Malo (Froissart, *Oeuvres*, Lettenhove, ix, 68).
53. *Foedera*, iv, p. 28.
54. *John of Gaunt's Register 1379–1383*, p. 327.
55. *CChR*, p. 263; Stansfield, 'The Holland Family', p. 56; Goodman, *John of Gaunt*, p. 75. In February 1380 Joan made a grant of special grace to mayor and citizens of Canterbury while at Kennington, her son Thomas Holand also made grant from Kennington the same month.
56. *The Complete Peerage*, vii, p. 154.
57. Stansfield, 'The Holland Family', p. 57.
58. *CPR 1377–1381*, p. 488.
59. Stephen Friar and John Ferguson, *Basic Heraldry* (London, 1993), p. 84.
60. The earlier grants were confirmed in October 1381. Stansfield, 'The Holland Family', pp. 63, 70.
61. Stansfield, 'The Holland Family', pp. 70, 71.
62. Stansfield, 'The Holland Family', p. 70.
63. Froissart, 1969, vol. 9, pp. 131–2, 182.
64. *John of Gaunt's Register 1379–1383*, pp. 112, 181, 231.
65. *CPR 1377–1381*, pp. 168, 272, 275, 329, 330; *CPR 1381–1385*, pp. 20.
66. *CPR 1377–1381*, pp. 463, 595, 616/676?
67. *CPR 1377–1381*, p. 170; *CPR 1381–1385*, pp. 15, 20.
68. *CPR 1377–1381*, p. 385.
69. *CPR 1377–1381*, pp. 156, 170, 564; *CIPM*, xvi, pp. 110–111.
70. McFarlane, *Lancastrian Kings and Lollard Knights*, pp. 185, 189; *CPR 1377–1381*, pp. 185, 453.
71. McFarlane, *Lancastrian Kings and Lollard Knights*, pp. 188–190.
72. BL, Add. Ch 27703.

73. *CPR 1377–1381*, pp. 92–3, 357; *CPR 1381–1385*, pp. 78, 201, 424; *CCR 1381–1385*, p. 634.
74. *CPR 1381–1385*, pp. 4, 13, 20.
75. *CPR 1381–1385*, p. 18.
76. *CPR 1377–1381*, p. 626.
77. *CPR 1377–1381*, pp. 267, 282, 293, 322, 334, 376, 382, 391, 392, 393, 440, 460, 483, 506, 529, 543, 546, 590, 626.
78. Goodman, *John of Gaunt*, p. 78.
79. *John of Gaunt's Register 1379–1383*, pp. 112, 181, 231.
80. I have relied on Alistair Dunn, *The Great Rising of 1381: The Peasants' Revolt and England's Failed Revolution* (Stroud, 2002) for the sequence of events in the Peasants' Revolt.
81. The manor at Wickhambreaux no longer exists but it is still possible to see the church of St Andrew's, which Joan would have known. A new church was built in the fourteenth century on the site of the original Norman church (which itself replaced the previous Saxon church). However, there are no arms or other regalia in the church which relate to Joan or her family.
82. *Anonimalle 1333–1381*, p. 137; Dunn, *The Great Rising of 1381*, p. 77.
83. Quote cited from *The Chronicles of Jean Froissart* in Lord Berners Translation, selected, edited and introduced by Gillian and William Anderson (London, 1963), p. 162; Froissart, *Oeuvres*, vol. ix, p. 391.
84. *The Chronica Maiora of Thomas Walsingham* p. 415, *Anonimalle 1333–1381* p. 139.
85. Saul, *Richard II*, p. 63.
86. *Anonimalle 1333–1381*, p. 600; *The Chronica Maiora of Thomas Walsingham* pp. 150–180.
87. Froissart, *Oeuvres*, vol. ix, p. 397; *Anonimalle 1333–1381* pp. 139–150.
88. A. Tuck, *Richard II and the English Nobility* (London, 1973), pp. 52–53.
89. *The Chronica Maiora of Thomas Walsingham*, p. 431; *Anonimalle 1333–1381* pp. 145–146; *Westminster Chronicle*, pp. 6–8.
90. Dunn, *The Great Rising of 1381*, p. 87, referring to a pre-1381 inventory of possessions.
91. *Anonimalle 1333–1381*, p. 143.
92. *Anonimalle 1333–1381*.
93. *The Chronicles of Jean Froissart* in Lord Berners' Translation, Selected, Edited and Introduced by Gillian and William Anderson (London, 1963), p. 169.
94. *The Chronicles of Jean Froissart*, p. 168.
95. *The Chronica Maiora of Thomas Walsingham*, p. 425; *The Chronicles of Jean Froissart*, p. 169.
96. *The Chronicles of Jean Froissart*, p. 174.
97. Stansfield, 'The Holland Family', p. 58.
98. *The Chronicles of Jean Froissart*, p. 178. *Testamenta Vetusta*, i, p. 109; d'Angle's executors were William Beauchamp, William Neville, Lewis Clifford and John Clanvowe.
99. *CPR 1381–1385*, p. 25.
100. Anthony Goodman, *The Loyal Conspiracy* (London, 1971), p. 170; *CPR 1381–1385*, pp. 71, 78–79.
101. She intervened on behalf of Thomas Sampson, a prominent Suffolk rebel, in 1383. *CPR 1383–1385*, pp. 226, 229, 268, 319, 332, 441, 448.
102. M. Clarke, 'The Wilton Diptych', *Fourteenth Century Studies* (Oxford, reproduced 1968), pp. 273–292, concludes the Wilton Diptych was painted no earlier than 1395; Binski, *Westminster Abbey and the Plantagenets, Kingship and the Representation of Power 1200–1400*, p. 203.
103. Green, *The Black Prince*, p. 218 notes the suggestion that it was commissioned by Maud Courtenay. Dillian Gordon, *Making and Meaning: The Wilton Diptych* (London, 1993), p. 59 suggests it is unlikely the diptych was commissioned by anyone other than Richard II himself for his personal use.

104. Gordon, *Making and Meaning: The Wilton Diptych*, p. 49.
105. Tout, *Administrative History*, vi, p. 17.
106. Goodman, *John of Gaunt*, p. 284.
107. Calendar of Ancient Deeds, i, p. 166; Stansfield, 'The Holland Family', p. 70.
108. TNA E403/481, m. 12; C136/92/11; *CPR 1381–1385*, p. 98.
109. TNA E403/481, m. 12; C136/92/11; *CPR 1381–1385*, p. 98.
110. *CCR 1381–1385*, p. 77.
111. Saul, *Richard II*, pp. 89–90.
112. Saul, *Richard II*, p. 90.
113. Tout, *Administrative History*, v, p. 280. The sum was never paid to Anne.
114. *CCR 1381–1385*, p. 54; Tout, *Administrative History*, v, p. 261.
115. TNA SC8/269/13410; SC8/249/12447.
116. TNA SC8/180/9000; SC8/180/117678.
117. *Testamenta Vetusta*, i, p. 145.
118. *CIPM*, xv, pp. 181–183.
119. CMisc Inq Vol. IV 1377–1388 pp. 145, 148. The commission found in favour of the bishop of Lincoln.
120. BL, Eg. Ch 2130.
121. Scattergood, *English Court Culture in the Later Middle Ages*, p. 23.
122. Richard F Green, *King Richard II's Books Revisited*, The Library 5th Service, 31 (1976), pp. 238–239.
123. *CCR 1377–1381*, p. 374.
124. Peter Fleming, 'Sir Lewis Clifford (1330–1404)', *Oxford Dictionary of National Biography* (Oxford, 2004).
125. Margaret Galway, Chaucer's Sovereign Lady, Modern Languages Review Notes, xxx III April 1938, pp. 145–199. Galway argues that Joan was Chaucer's inspiration for Queen Alceste in *The Legend of Good Women*, and that Chaucer harboured a secret love for Joan. Galway also suggests that Joan asked Chaucer to write *The Legend of Good Women*.
126. *The Chronica Maiora of Thomas Walsingham*, pp. 723–727; Goodman, *John of Gaunt*, p. 100.
127. *The Complete Peerage*, vii, p. 154.
128. Goodman, *John of Gaunt*, pp. 102–3.
129. *Chronicon Angliae*, p. 364; *The Westminster Chronicle 1381–1394*, ed. L. C. Hector and R. Harvey (Oxford, 1982), pp. 114–115; *Chronicon Adae de Usk, 1377–1421*, ed. E. M. Thompson (London, 1904, pp. 143–144.
130. *The Chronica Maiora of Thomas Walsingham*, pp. 751; *The Westminster Chronicle 1381–1394*, p. 114.
131. Ranulph Higden, *Polychronicon Ranulphi Higden, Monachi Castrensis*, ed. C. Babington and J. R. Lumby (9 vols, Rolls Series, London, 1865–86), ix, pp. 57–58.
132. *The Chronica Maiora of Thomas Walsingham*, p. 751.
133. *Calendar of Ancient Petitions relating to Wales*, ed. W. Rees, Board of Celtic Studies, History and Law Series, 2 (Cardiff, 1935), p. 415. (249) No 12447.
134. There is an original MSS in the University of London library, and a second MSS in Worcester College, Oxford.
135. Binski, *Westminster Abbey and the Plantagenets, Kingship and the Representation of Power 1200–1400*, p. 202.
136. MS.61, Corpus Christi College, Cambridge, Frontipiece to Troilus and Criseyde. Ford Maddox Brown.
137. *CCR 1381–1385*, p. 553.
138. Stansfield, 'The Holland Family', p. 61.
139. Froissart, *Oeuvres*, Lettenhove, xi, p. 271.
140. *Chronicon Angliae*, p. 365; *The Chronica Maiora of Thomas Walsingham*, p. 759.
141. *Collection of the Wills of the Kings and Queens of England*, pp. 78–81. The list included three silk curtains or hangings, a pallet bed covered in fine material,

probably silk, two supports, and two camaca cushions, with an embroidered quilt: 'unuum lectum de cama pallata in camaca rub' et radiate de auro cum appartu, videlicet, cum dorfsor'ciel integro, uno quilt quolibet operat' in broderia de v hachements in compass, 111 curtins (curtains or hangings) de Tarteren (another rich silk fabric) rub' verberat 1 transversiam de syndone, 1 etc.' Camaca was a fine material, possibly silk.

142. This is almost certainly another mistake made by the scribe, and that Joan intended appointing Henry, rather than William, Norton. William Norton is described as a yeoman of the prince's and then of Richard II (*CPR 1377–1381*, pp. 207, 278, 335) whereas Henry Norton, described as Joan's esquire, received a grant for life from Joan in April 1380 'in consideration of his services to her and to her daughter de Courtenay' and Henry was ordered by Richard II to be one of those guarding Joan when the royal army went to Scotland in June 1385 (*CPR 1377–1381*, p. 463; *CPR 1381–1385*, p. 553).

143. Chaucer Life Records, ed. Martin M. Crow and Clair C. Olson (Oxford, 1966), 103F.

144. *The Chronica Maiora of Thomas Walsingham*, p. 759.

145. *Foedera*, vii, 527.

146. On the opposite side of the altar to the prince, directly parallel, lies Henry IV and his wife Joan of Navarre. One wonders how the prince might have felt about being juxtaposed with his son's usurper.

147. Gordon, *Making & Meaning: The Wilton Diptych*, p. 49.

Conclusion: Joan's Legacy

1. Christine de Pizan, *The Treasure of the City of Ladies*, translated by Sarah Lawson (London, 2003); pp. 21, 29, 32, 39, 40, 41, 54.

2. Christine de Pizan, *The Treasure of the City of Ladies*, pp. 19–21.

3. It is similarly tempting to speculate on her influence on Chaucer, for example, in his depiction of his perfect heroine Prudence, in *The Melibee*.

4. *Chronicle of Adam Usk 1377–1421*, p. 63.

5. Scattergood, *English Court Culture in the Later Middle Ages*, p. 23.

6. Saul, *Richard II*, p. 16.

Bibliography

Manuscript Sources

London: National Archives
C76 Treaty Rolls.
E30 Exchequer: Diplomatic Documents.
E36 Wardrobe Books.
E40 Ancient Deeds Series A.
E101 Exchequer: Various Wardrobe and Household Accounts.
E403 Exchequer: Issue Rolls.
SC1 Special Collection Ancient Correspondence.
SC7 Special Collection Papal Bulls.

London, British Library
Cotton Nero D VII folio 7v: St Albans Book of Benefactors.
MSS Harley 6148: Note from Archbirshop Islip to Prince Edward dated 8 October 1361.
Royal MSS 2B viii: 1380 Psalter with office of the dead.

London, Lambeth Palace Library
Reg. Islip, 1: Register of Archbishop Islip.

Canterbury Cathedral Archives
DCC/Carta Antique F49.

Printed Sources

Adae Murimuth, Continuatio Chronicarum, ed. E. M. Thompson (Rolls Series, London, 1889).
Anglo-Norman Letters and Petitions, ed. M. D. Legge (Anglo-Norman Text Society, iii, 1941).
Annales Paulini, ed. W. Stubbs (Rolls Series, London, 1882).
The Anonimalle Chronicle 1307–1334, from Brotherton Collection MS29, ed. W. R. Childs and J. Taylor, Yorkshire Archaelogical Society Record Series, 147 (1991).
The Anonimalle Chronicle 1333–1381, ed. V. H Galbraith (Manchester, 1927).
The Brut, or *The Chronicles of England*, ed. F. W. D. Brie (EETS, original series, cxxxvi, 1908).
Calendar of Ancient Petitions relating to Wales, ed. W. Rees, Board of Celtic Studies, History and Law Series, 28 (Cardiff, 1935).

Calendar of Charter Rolls 1300–1341 (London, 1916).

Calendar of Close Rolls 1323–1385 (London, 1900).

Calendar of Fine Rolls 1319–1391 (London, 1900).

Calendar of Inquisitions Miscellaneous 1307–1347 (London, 1900).

Calendar of Inquisitions Post Mortem, volumes 3, 6, 8, 9, 10, 12 (London, 1900).

Calendar of Memoranda Rolls 1326–1327 (London, 1916).

Calendar of Papal Registers, Papal Letters, 1305–1342 (London, 1902).

Calendar of Papal Registers, Papal Letters, 1342–1362 (London, 1902).

Calendar of Papal Registers, Papal Letters, 1362–1404 (London, 1902).

Calendar of Papal Registers, Petitions, 1342–1419 (London, 1902).

Calendar of Patent Rolls, 1301–1389 (21 vols, London, 1900).

Calendar of Plea and Memoranda Rolls of the City of London, 1324–1457, ed. A. H. Thomas, i (London, 1926).

Capgrave, J., *Chronicle of England*, ed. F. Hingeston (London, 1858).

Christine de Pizan, *The Treasure of the City of Ladies*, tr. with intro, by S. Lawson (New York, 1985).

Chronica Johannis de Reading et Anonymi Cantauriasis 1346–1367, ed. J. Tait (Mancester, 1914).

Chronica Monasterii de Melsa, ed. E. A. Bond (3 vols, 1867).

Chronica Monasterii St Albani Johannis deTtrokelowe, ed. H. T. Riley (London, 1866).

Chronicle of John Hardyng, ed. H. Ellis (London, 1812).

Chronicle of Adam Usk 1377–1421, ed. C. Given-Wilson (Oxford, 1997).

Chronicon Anglie 1328–1388, ed. E. M. Thompson (Rolls Series, 1874).

Chronicon Galfridi le Baker de Swynbroke, ed. E. M. Thompson (Oxford, 1889).

Chronicon Henrici Knighton, ed. J. R. Lumby (Rolls Series, London, 1889).

Chronique des quatre premiers Valois, 1327–1393, ed. S. Luce (Société de l'Histoire de France, Paris, 1862).

Collection of the Wills of the Kings and Queens of England, ed. J. Nichols (2 vols, London, 1780, reprod. 1969).

Early Lincoln Wills, 1280–1547, ed. A. Gibbons (Lincoln, 1888).

Eulogium Historiarum sive Temporis, ed. F. S. Hayden (3 vols, Rolls Series, London, 185801863).

Flores Historiarum, ed. H. R. Luard, 3 vols (Rolls Series, 1890).

Froissart, J., *Chronicles*, ed. T. Johnes (2 vols, London, 1862).

Froissart, J., *Oeuvres*, ed. Kervyn de Lettenhove (Brussels, 26 vols, 1867–77).

Froissart, J., *Chronicles*, ed. S. Luce et al. (15 vols, SHF, Paris, 1869–1975).

Giles of Rome, *The Governance of Kings and Princes: John Trevisa's Translation of De Regimine Principum of Aegidius Romanus*, ed. D. C. Fowler, C. F. Briggs and P. G. Remley (London, 1977).

Household Ordinances and Regulations (Society of Antiquaries, 1790).

The Inventories of St George's Chapel, Windsor Castle, 1348–1667, ed. M. F. Bond (Windsor, 1937).

Issues of the Exchequer, Henry III–Henry VI, ed. F. Devon (London, 1847).

Jean le Bel, *Chronique de Jean le Bel*, ed. J. Viard and E. Deprez (2 vols, Société de l'Histoire de France, Paris, 1904–5).

John of Gaunt's Register, 1372–1376, ed. S. Armitage Smith (2 vols, Camden Society, 3rd Series, xx–xxi, 1911).

John of Gaunt's Register, 1379–1383, ed. E. C. Lodge and R. Somerville (2 vols, Camden Society, 3rd Series, lvi–lvii, 1937).

Knighton's Chronicle 1337–1396, ed. G. H. Martin (Oxford, 1995).

Letters of Edward, Prince of Wales, 1304–1305, ed. H. Johnstone (Cambridge, 1931).

Life of the Black Prince by the Herald of Sir John Chandos, ed. M. K. Pope and E. C. Lodge (Oxford, 1910).

Nichols, J., *Collection of the Wills of the Kings and Queens of England* (London, 1780).

Ranulph Higden, *Polychronicon Ranulphi Higden Monachi Cestrensis*, ed. C. Babington and J. R. Lumby (9 vols, Rolls Series, London, 1865–86).

Register of Edward the Black Prince (4 vols, London, 1930–33).

Rotuli Parliamentorum (6 vols, London, 1767–77).

Rymer, T. *Foedera, Conventiones, Litterae etc.* ed. G. Holmes (20 vols, London, 1704–35).

The Chronicles of Jean Froissart in Lord Berners' Translation, Selected, Edited and Introduced by Gillian and William Anderson (London, 1963).

The St Albans Chronicle, 1, 1376–1394; The Chronica Maiora of Thomas Walsingham, ed. J. Taylor, W. Childs, and L. Watkiss (Oxford, 2003).

Testamenta Vetusta, ed. N. H. Nichols (2 vols, London, 1826).

Vita Edwardi Secundi, ed. N. Denholm Young (London, 1957).

The War of Saint Sardos, 1323–1325 Gascon Correspondence and Diplomatic Documents, ed. P. Chaplais (Camden, 3rd Series, London, 1964).

Walsingham, T., *Historia Anglicana*, ed. H. T. Riley (2 vols, Rolls Series, 1863–4).

The Westminster Chronicle, 1381–1394, ed. L. C. Hector and B. Harvey (Oxford, 1982).

Secondary Sources

Aberth, J., *Criminal Churchmen in the Age of Edward III, The Case of the Bishop of Thomas de Lisle* (Pennsylvania, 1996).

Allmand, Christopher, *The Hundred Years War* (Cambridge, 1989).

Alexander, J. J. G., 'Painting and MSS Illumination', *English Court Culture in the Later Middle Ages*, ed. V. J. Scattergood and J. W. Sherborne (London, 1983).

Archer, R., 'The Estates and Finances of Margaret of Brotherton, *c.* 1320–1399'; *Bulletin of Institute of Historical Research*, 60 (1987).

Archer, R., 'Piety in Question: Noblewomen and Religion in the Later Middle Ages'; *Women and Religion in Medieval England*, ed. D. Wood (Oxford, 2003).

Armitage-Smith, S., *John of Gaunt* (London, 1964).

Babinet, M. le Colonel, 'Jeanne de Kent princess de Galles et d'Aquitaine'; *Bulletin de la Societé des Antiquaries de l'Ouest*, 6 (1984).

Barber, R., *Edward, Prince of Wales and Aquitaine* (London and New York, 1978).

Barber, R., *Edward III and the Triumph of England: The Battle of Crécy and the Company of the Garter* (London, 2013).

Barber, R., 'Joan, suo jure countess of Kent, and princess of Wales and of Aquitaine (called the Fair Maid of Kent) (*c.* 1328–1385)'; *Oxford Dictionary of National Biography* (Oxford, 2004).

Barber, R., *The Knight and Chivalry* (Woodbridge, 1995).

Barber, R., *Life and Campaigns of the Black Prince* (Woodbridge, 1986).

Beltz, G., *Memorials of the Most Noble Order of the Garter* (London, 1961).

Bennett, M., 'Edward III's Entail and the Succession to the Crown, 1376–1471', *English Historical Review*, 113 (1998).

Binski, Paul, *Westminster Abbey and the Plantagenets, Kingship and the Representation of Power 1200–1400* (London, 1995).

Brundage, James A., 'Concubinage and Marriage in Medieval Canon Law', *Journal of Medieval History*, 1 (1975).

Burgess, Anthony, *The Riverside Chaucer* (Oxford, 1988).

Carey, H., *Courting Disaster: Astrology at the English Court and University in the Later Middle Ages* (London, 1992).

Chamberlayne, J., 'Joan of Kent's Tale: Adultery and Rape in the Age of Chivalry', *Medieval Life*, 5 (1996).

The Complete Peerage, ed. G. E. Cokayne et al (2 vols in 13, London 1910–57).

Chambers, F., *The Fair Maid of Kent, An historical and biographical sketch* (Margate, 1877).

Clarke, M., 'The Wilton Diptych', *Fourteenth Century Studies* (Oxford, reproduced 1968).

Cole, H., *The Black Prince* (London, 1976).

Collins, A., *Life and Glorious Actions of Edward, Prince of Wales* (1740).

Collette, C., 'Joan of Kent and Noblewomen's Roles in Chaucer's World', *The Chaucer Review*, 33 (1999).

Coss, P., *The Lady in Medieval England, 1000–1500* (Stroud, 1998).

Crawford, A., 'The Piety of Late Medieval Queens' in C. M. Barron and C. Harper-Bill, eds, *The Church in Pre-Reformation Society* (1985).

Davis, G. R., *Medieval Cartularies of Great Britain* (London, 1958).

The Dictionary of National Biography, ed. S. Lee (London, 1908).

Delachenal, R., *Histoire de Charles V* (5 vols, Paris, 1909–31).

Doherty, Paul, *Isabella and the Strange Death of Edward II* (London, 2003).

Douch, R., 'The Career Lands and Family of William Montague Earl of Salisbury 1301–1344', *Bulletin of Institute of Historical Research*, 24 (1951).

Dunn, Alastair, *The Great Rising of 1381* (Stroud, 2002).

Dunning, R., 'Luttrell family (per. c. 1200–1428)', *Oxford Dictionary of National Biography* (Oxford, 2004).

Emden, A. B., *A Biographical Register of the University of Oxford to A. D. 1500* (3 vols, Oxford, 1957–59).

Emerson, B., *The Black Prince* (London, 1976).

Facinger, M., 'A Study of Medieval Queenship: Capetian France 987–1237', *Studies in Medieval and Renaissance History*, 5 (1986).

Fellowes, E., *Knights of the Garter* (London).

Fleming, Peter, 'Clifford, Sir Lewis (c. 1330–1404)', *Oxford Dictionary of National Biography* (Oxford, 2004).

Friar, Stephen and Ferguson, John, *Basic Heraldry* (London, 1993).

Fryde, N., *The Tyranny and Fall of Edward II 1321–1326* (Cambridge, 1979).

Galway, M., 'Joan of Kent and the Order of the Garter', *University of Birmingham Historical Journal*, 1 (1947–48).

Galway, M., 'Chaucer's Hopeless Love', *Modern Language Notes*, 60 (1945).

Galway, M., 'Chaucer's Sovereign Lady', Modern Language Notes, 33 (1938).

Gee, L. L., *Women, Art and Patronage from Henry III to Edward III 1216–1377* (Woodbridge, 2002).

Gillespie, James L., 'Ladies of the Fraternity of Saint George and the Society of the Garter', *Albion* 17 (1985).

Gillespie, James L. 'Isabella, countess of Bedford (1332–1379)', *Oxford Dictionary of National Biography* (Oxford, 2004).

Given-Wilson, Chris, *Chronicles The Writing of History in Medieval England* (London, 2004).

Given-Wilson, C., *The English Nobility in the late Middle Ages* (London and New York, 1996).

Given-Wilson, C., *The Royal Household and the King's Affinity: Service, Politics and Finance in England 1360–1413* (New Haven and London, 1986).

Given-Wilson, C., 'Wealth and Credit, Public and Private: The Earls of Arundel 1306–1397', *English Historical Review*, 106 (1991).

Goodman, A., *John of Gaunt* (Harlow, 1992).

Gordon, Dillian, *Making & Meaning: The Wilton Diptych* (London, 1993).

Gransden, A., 'The Alleged Rape by Edward III of the Countess of Salisbury', *English Historical Review*, 87 (1972).

Gransden, A., 'A Fourteenth Century Chronicle from Grey Friars at Lynn', *English Historical Review*, lxxii (1957).

Green, D. S., *The Battle of Poitiers 1356* (Stroud, 2002).

Green, D. S., *The Black Prince* (Stroud, 2001).

Green, D. S., 'Politics and Service with Edward the Black Prince', *The Age of Edward III*, ed. J. S. Bothwell (York, 2001).

Green, Richard F., *King Richard II's Books Revisited*, The Library 5th Service, 31 (1976).

Green, M. A. E., *Lives of the Princesses of England from the Norman Conquest* (6 vols, London, 1849–1851).

Hamilton, J. S., 'Charter Witness Lists for the Reign of Edward II', *The Fourteenth Century*, ed. N. Saul.

Hamilton, J. S., *Piers Gaveston, Earl of Cornwall, 1307–1312, Politics and Patronage in the Reign of Edward II* (Wayne State University Press, 1988).

Harvey, J., *The Black Prince and His Age* (New Jersey, 1976).

History of the King's Works, ed. R. A. Brown, H. M. Colvin and A. J. Taylor (3 vols, London, 1963).

Holmes, G. A., *The Estates of the Higher Nobility in Fourteenth Century England* (Cambridge, 1957).

Holmes, G. H., 'The Rebellion of the Earl of Lancaster, 1328–1329', *Bulletin of Institute of Historical Research*, xxviii (1995).

Huneycutt, L., 'Images of Queenship in the High Middle Ages', *Haskins Society Journal*, 1 (1989).

Johnstone, H., *Edward of Carnarvon* (Manchester, 1946).

Jones, Michael, 'John de Montfort', Oxford Dictionary of National Biography (Oxford, 2004).

Jones, M., 'Edward III's Captains in Brittany', *England in the Fourteenth Century Proceedings of the Harlaxton Symposium*, ed. W. Ormrod (Woodbridge, 1986).

Keen, M., *Chivalry* (London, 1984).

Knowles, D., and Neville Hadcock, R., *Medieval Religious Houses in England and Wales* (London, 1971).

Labarge, M. W., *Women in Medieval Life* (Bath, 2001).

Laynesmith, J. L., *The Last Medieval Queens* (Oxford, 2004).

Lawne, Penny, 'Edmund of Woodstock, Earl of Kent (1301–1330): A Study of Personal Loyalty', *Fourteenth Century England VI*, edited by Chris Given-Wilson (Woodbridge, 2010).

Lewis, N. B., 'The Continual Council in the Early Years of Richard II, 1377–1380', *English Historical Review*, xli (1926).

Leyser, H., *Medieval Women* (London, 1995).

Lewis, N. B., 'The Continual Council in the Early Years of Richard II, 1377–1380', *English Historical Review* 41 (1926).

Lucraft, J., *Katherine Swynford The History of a Medieval Mistress* (Stroud, 2006).

Maddicott, J. R., *Thomas of Lancaster 1307–1322* (Oxford, 1970).

Maddicott, J. R., 'Thomas of Lancaster and Sir Robert Holland: A Study in Patronage', *English Historical Review*, 311 (1971).

Mate, M., Women in Medieval English Society (Cambridge, 1999).

Maurer, H., *Margaret of Anjou: Queenship and Power in Late Medieval England* (Woodbridge, 2003).

McFarlane, K. B., *Lancastrian Kings and Lollard Knights* (Oxford, 1972).

McFarlane, K. B., *The Nobility of Later Medieval England* (Oxford, 1973).

McHardy, A. H., 'Richard II: a personal portrait' in *The Reign of Richard II*, ed. G. Dodd (Stroud, 2000).

McKisack, M., *The Fourteenth Century 1307–1399* (Oxford, 1959).

Mooney, Linne R., 'John Somer Franciscan friar and astronomer' *Oxford Dictionary of National Biography* (Oxford, 2004).

Morris, Marc, *A Great and Terrible King, Edward I and the Forging of Britain* (London, 2008).

Mortimer, Ian, *The Greatest Traitor: The Life of Sir Roger Mortimer 1st Earl of March Ruler of England 1327–1330* (London, 2003).

Mortimer, Ian, *The Perfect King, The Life of Edward III Father of the English Nation* (London, 2006).

Newton, S. M., *Fashion in the Age of the Black Prince* (Woodbridge, 1980).

Norton, Elizabeth, *She Wolves: The Notorious Queens of England* (Stroud, 2009).

Okerlund, A., *Elizabeth Wydville* (Stroud, 2005).

Orme, Nicholas, *From Childhood to Chivalry, The Education of the English Kings and Aristocracy 1066–1530* (London, 1984).

Orme, Nicholas, *Medieval Childhood* (London, 2003).

Ormrod, W. M., 'In Bed with Joan of Kent: The King's Mother and the Peasants' Revolt', *Medieval Women: Texts and Contexts in Late Medieval Britain: Essays for Felicity Riddy*, ed. J. Wogan-Browne, R. Voaden, A. Diamond, A. Hutchison, C. M. Meale and L. Johnson (Turnhout, 2000).

Ormrod, W. M., 'Edward III and his Family', *Journal of British Studies*, 26 (1987).

Ormrod, W. M., *Edward III* (New Haven and London, 2011).

Ormrod, W. M., 'The Personal Religion of Edward III', *Speculum*, 64 (1989).

Ormrod, W. M., *The Reign of Edward III* (Stroud, 2000).

Ormrod, W. M., *Political Life in Medieval England 1300–1450* (London, 1995).

Ormrod, W. M., 'Wake, Thomas, second Lord Wake (1298–1349), nobleman', *Dictionary of National Biography* (Oxford University press, 2004).

Packe, M., *Edward III* (London, 1983).

Parsons, J. C., *Eleanor of Castile: Queen and Society in Thirteenth Century England* (Basingstoke, 1994).

Payling, S., 'The Politics of Family: Late Medieval Marriage Contracts', *The McFarlane Legacy, Studies in Late Medieval Politics and Society*, ed. R. H. Britnell and A. J. Pollard (Stroud, 1995).

Peck, *Annals of Stamford*.

Phillips, Kim, M, *Medieval Maidens Young Women and Gender in England 1270–1540* (Manchester, 2003).

Prestwich, M., *Edward I* (New Haven and London, 1997).

Prestwich, M., *The Three Edwards, War and State in England, 1272–1377* (London, 2003).

Prestwich, M., 'The Unreliability of Royal Household Knights in the early Fourteenth Century', in *Fourteenth Century England 11*, ed. C. Given Wilson (Woodbridge, 2002).

Prince, A. E., 'A Letter of Edward the Black Prince Describing the Battle of Najersa in 1367', *English Historical Review*, xli (1926).

Reitemeier, R., 'Born to be a Tyrant? The Childhood and Education of Richard II' in *Fourteenth Century England*, 11, ed. C. Given-Wilson (Woodbridge, 2002).

Riley, H. T. *Memorials of London and London Life* (1868).

Robert, A. K. B., *St George's Chapel Windsor Castle 1348–1416* (Windsor, 1947).

Rogers, Clifford J., *The Wars of Edward III, Sources and Interpretations* (Woodbridge, 1999).

Rogers, Clifford J., *War Cruel and Sharp English Stragey Under Edward III, 1327–1360* (Woodbridge, 2000).

Saul, Nigel, *Death, Art and Memory in Medieval England: The Cobham Family and their Monuments 1300–1500* (Oxford, 2001).

Saul, Nigel, 'The Despensers and the Downfall of Edward II', *English Historical Review*, xcix (1984).

Saul, Nigel, *For Honour and Fame Chivalry in England 1066–1500* (London, 2011),

Saul, Nigel, *Knights and Esquires: The Gloucestershire Gentry in the Fourteenth Century* (Oxford, 1981).

Saul, Nigel, *Richard II* (New Haven and London, 1999).

Saul, Nigel, 'Sir John Clanvowe (*c.* 1341–1391)', *Oxford Dictionary of National Biography* (Oxford, 2004).

Scattergood, V. J., 'Literary Culture at the Court of Richard II' in *English Court Culture in the Later Middle Ages*, ed. V. J. Scattergood and J. W. Sherborne (London, 1983).

Selden, John, *Titles of Honour* (London, 1672).

Seymour Phillips, *Edward II* (New Haven, 2010).

Sharp, Margaret, The Administrative Chancery of the Black Prince before 1362, *Essays in Medieval History presented to T. F. Tout*, ed. A. G. Little and F. M. Powicke (Manchester, 1925).

Shaw, W., *Knights of England* (2 vols, London, 1906).

Stansfield, M. M. N., 'Holland, Thomas, fifth Earl of Kent (1350–1397)', *Oxford Dictionary of National Biography* (Oxford, 2004)

Steel, Anthony, *Richard II* (Cambridge, 1941).

Strickland, Agnes, *The Lives of the Queens of England.*

Strohm, P., *Hochon's Arrow* (Princeton, 1992).

Sumption, Jonathan, *The Hundred Years War, vol. i: Trial by Battle* (London, 1990).

Sumption, Jonathan, *The Hundred Years War, vol. ii: Trial by Fire* (London 1999).

Sumption, Jonathan, *The Hundred Years War, vol. iii: Divided Houses* (London, 2012).

Tout, T. F., *Chapters in the Administrative History of Medieval England* (6 vols, Manchester, 1920–33).

Tout, T. F., *The Place of the Reign of Edward II in English History* (Manchester, 1936).

Tuck, A., *Richard II and the English Nobility* (London, 1973).

Underhill, F., *For Her Good Estate: The Life of Elizabeth de Burgh* (London, 1999).

Underwood, M. G., 'Politics and Piety in the Household of Lady Margaret Beaufort', *Journal of Ecclesiastical History*, 38 (1987).

Vale, Juliet, *Edward III and Chivalry: Chivalric Society and its Context 1270–1350* (Woodbridge, 1982).

Vale, Juliet and Malcolm, 'Knightly Codes and Piety', *Age of Chivalry, Art and Society in Late Medieval England*, ed. N. Saul (London, 1992).

Vale, Juliet, 'Philippa (1310–1369)', *Oxford Dictionary of National Biography* (Oxford, 2004).

Vergil, Polydore, *Anglicae Historiae: Libri Vigintiseptum* (1570)

Victoria History of the County of Lincolnshire (London, 1906).

Ward, Jennifer, *English Noblewomen in the Later Middle Ages* (London, 1992).

Ward, Jennifer, *Women in England in the Middle Ages* (London, 2006).

Waugh, S., 'Edmund, first Earl of Kent (1301–1330), *Oxford Dictionary of National Biography* (Oxford, 2004).

Waugh, S., 'Thomas Brotherton, first Earl of Norfolk (1300–1338), magnate', *Oxford Dictionary of National Biography* (Oxford, 2004).

Weese, W., 'Alceste and Joan of Kent', *Modern Language Notes*, 63 (1948).

Wentersdorf, K. P., 'The Clandestine Marriages of the Fair Maid of Kent', *Journal of Medieval History*, 5 (1979), 203–31.

Whiting, B. J., 'The Vows of the Heron', *Journal of Medieval Studies*, 20 (1945), 261–278.

Wilkinson, B., 'The Protests of the earls of Arundel and Surrey in Crisis of 1341', *English Historical Review*, 46 (1931).

Wilkinson, L., 'Pawn and Political Player: Observations on the Life of a Thirteenth Century Countess', *Institute of Historical Research*, 73 (2000).

Woodman, F., *The Architectural History of Canterbury Cathedral* (London, 1981).

Woolgar, C. M., *The Great Household in Late Medieval England* (London, 1999).

Unpublished Theses

Butler, L. N., 'Robert Braybrooke, Bishop of London 1381–1404) and his kinsmen' (University of Oxford D. Phil. thesis, 1952).

Lawne, P. J., 'Joan of Kent, daughter of Edmund of Woodstock: Royal Kinship and Marriage in the Fourteenth Century' (University of London PhD thesis, 2006).

Stansfield, M. M. N., 'The Holland Family, Dukes of Exeter, Earls of Kent and Huntingdon, 1352–1475' (University of Oxford D. Phil thesis, 1987).

Warner, M. W., 'The Montague Earls of Salisbury, c. 1300–1428: A Study in Warfare, Politics and Political Culture' (University of London PhD thesis, 1991).

List of Illustrations

1. Joan's grandfather, Edward I. A formidable king, he took great care to plan a generous financial provision for his youngest son, Joan's father Edmund of Woodstock, but died before he could complete the endowment. (Courtesy of Jonathan Reeve, JRb18p2)

2. Edward II was Joan's half-uncle. He was deposed by his wife, Queen Isabella, and her lover, Roger Mortimer, in 1327. Three years later Joan's father, Edmund, was tricked into believing Edward II was still alive, and executed for planning to rescue him from imprisonment in Corfe Castle. (David Satwell via Elizabeth Norton)

3. Joan lived here with her parents for the first eighteen months of her life and she was probably born here. The stone castle was originally built by one of William the Conqueror's relatives, Roger de Montgomery, in the eleventh century. It became the principal seat of the earls of Arundel. The second earl, Edmund Fitzalan, was executed by Roger Mortimer in 1326, and the castle was granted to Joan's father, Edmund, in 1327. (Arundel Castle Trustees Ltd, www.arundelcastle.org)

4. This entrance was built in 1295 by Richard Fitzalan, 1st Earl of Arundel. Edmund, Earl of Kent (Joan's father), would have left the castle through this entrance on his last fateful journey to the parliament at Winchester in March 1330. (Peter Lawne, by kind permission of Arundel Trustees Ltd, www.arundelcastle.org)

5. Queen Philippa took Joan and her brothers, Edmund and John, into her household six months after their father's execution in 1330. This effigy was commissioned by Philippa before her death. (© Dean and Chapter of Westminster)

6. This shows the king as he would have been in later life. Edward III was a young man of eighteen when Joan and her brothers came to live in his wife's household. (Ripon Cathedral)

7. The Garter Book was commissioned by William Bruges, accredited as being the first Garter King of Arms, and was probably made between 1430 and 1440. The book has twenty-seven full-page miniatures showing the twenty-six Garter knights in their Garter stalls at St George's chapel, Windsor, each holding a panel with heraldic shields of their successors. (British Library)

8. Otto Holand was Thomas Holand's younger brother and trusted lieutenant. John Chandos was one of Prince Edward's closest friends and a renowned and formidable fighter and commander. Both were founder members of the Order of the Garter. (British Library)

9. The church of St Edward, King and Martyr, Castle Donington, Leicestershire. Originally built in the thirteenth century, and extended in the fourteenth. Joan would have been familiar with this parish church. (LeicesterPhoto Ltd)

10. The Bible Historiale of John the Good, King of France. This Bible was owned by King John II of France, captured at the Battle of Poitiers in 1356, and the book was subsequently purchased by William Montague, 2nd Earl of Salisbury, for his wife Elizabeth, for 100 marks. (British Library)

11. The founding chapel of the Order of the Garter, Windsor Castle's St George's chapel contains a stall for each of the twenty-six knights of the Garter, and an annual service is held in the chapel on St George's day, 23 April. Joan and Prince Edward were married in the chapel in October 1361. (Royal Collections Trust/ © Her Majesty Queen Elizabeth II 2014)

12. Windsor Castle, Berkshire. One of the many royal palaces Joan lived in as a child and where she would have stayed the night after her wedding to Prince Edward. (Royal Collections Trust/ © Her Majesty Queen Elizabeth II 2014)

13. Originally a Norman castle, in 1337 Edward III granted Berkhamsted to Prince Edward as part of the duchy of Cornwall. It was the prince's favourite castle, and became Joan's first home with the prince after their wedding in October 1361. Prince Edward and Joan hosted Christmas here for Edward III and Queen Philippa in 1361. (© Skyscan Balloon Photography)

14. A reconstruction drawing of Berkhamsted Castle as it would have appeared in the twelfth century. Prince Edward paid for major renovation work to the castle before his marriage to Joan, and continued improvements to it afterwards. (© English Heritage)

15. The Bohun Psalter was made for either the 6th or 7th Earl of Hereford, both named Humphrey Bohun (d. 1361 and d. 1373, respectively). In 1362 Prince Edward purchased three psalters from the executors of the sixth earl, Humphrey de Bohun, and gave them to Joan and her two daughters, Maud and Joan Holand. The gifted psalters are likely to have been of similar quality to this psalter. (British Library)

16. Detail of a historiated initial 'E'(dwardus) of Edward III, enthroned, giving a charter to the kneeling Prince Edward, at the beginning of a collection of documents relating to the principality of Aquitaine. (British Library)

17. Prince Edward's tomb in Canterbury Cathedral, Kent, to which Joan made annual pilgrimages after his death. The prince left careful instructions for its design. The tomb chest is decorated with six shields of peace and six of war, and above it, facing downwards towards his effigy, is a painting of the Holy Trinity, which the prince gave the cathedral in his lifetime. On the opposite side of the choir lies Henry IV, the prince's nephew and the man who deposed the prince's son Richard II. (Reproduced with permission from Canterbury Cathedral Archives)

18. Hanging above the tomb are replicas of the prince's helmet, surcoat, shield, gauntlets and the scabbard of his sword. The originals are displayed in a glass cabinet. (Reproduced with permission from Canterbury Cathedral Archives)

19. The copper gilt effigy shows the Prince Edward as the consummate warrior. In the nineteenth century it was carefully blackened (presumably taking his posthumous appellation of the 'Black Prince' literally), and remained under layers of paint until it was uncovered in the early 1930s. (Peter Lawne, taken by kind permission of the Dean and Chapter of Canterbury Cathedral)

20. Carved stone ceiling boss, reputedly representing Joan, in the chantry chapel beside the chapel of Our Lady Undercroft in Canterbury Cathedral. Prince Edward paid for the Chapel of Our Lady Undercroft to be redesigned, in fulfilment of the papal dispensation granted to enable him to marry Joan, and he left instructions in his will to be interred in the chapel. However, when he died, it was decided that his tomb should be placed in a more prominent position on the south side of the Trinity chapel. The chantry chapel is decorated with ceiling bosses; this carved stone boss is the largest human face and clearly represents Joan. Her hair is in a netted fret, a popular fashion at the time. However, there is no evidence that the prince ordered this and it is not known who carved it. (Peter Lawne, taken by kind permission of the Dean and Chapter of Canterbury Cathedral and the Trustees of the French Walloon Church)

21. St Albans Abbey kept a book listing their benefactors; Joan was obviously considered one of their more important ones as her image is pictured in the book. The abbot (from 1349 to 1396), Thomas de la Mare, was on friendly terms with Prince Edward, who, with his parents, Edward III and Queen Philippa, were also benefactors. (© The British Library Board. All rights reserved. Cotton Nero DVII f.7v.)

22. A statue of Edward III near the west door, on the outside of Canterbury Cathedral. He stands beside a statue of the prince. (Peter Lawne, taken by kind permission of the Dean and Chapter of Canterbury Cathedral)

23. Richard was Joan's youngest child, and heir to Prince Edward. He became king when he was ten. This portrait was probably commissioned by Richard shortly after Joan died, and shows him as a child king. (© Dean and Chapter of Westminster)

24. Detail of a miniature of Vileŋie (villainy, abuse, baseness) offering the Lover (l'Amans) a potion. The book was owned by Sir Richard Stury, a cultured and literary man. He was one of the prince's knights and a friend to Joan, and was appointed as a household knight to Richard II. (British Library)

25. Joan arranged Richard's marriage to Anne of Bohemia. Richard was very happy with the marriage, and was heartbroken when Anne died in 1394. They had no children. (Jonathan Reeve JR2152b97plate22 13501400)

26, 27, 28. Wallingford Castle, Oxfordshire. This was Joan's favourite residence after Prince Edward died, and where she retired to from Richard II's court. Joan died here on 8 August 1385. The castle was demolished on the orders of Oliver Cromwell, and these ruins are all that is left. (Peter Lawne, taken by kind permission of South Oxfordshire District Council and the Earth Trust)

29. Wallingford Bridge, Oxfordshire. This bridge over the River Thames is beside the castle grounds. Joan travelled to Westminster by barge down the river. (Peter Lawne, taken by kind permission of Wallingford Town Council)

30. St Andrews church, Wickhambreaux, Kent. Wickhambreaux was the only manor in Kent owned by Joan. It is probable that she visited and stayed at the manor on her annual pilgrimage to Prince Edward's tomb every June after he died. The manor no longer exists. The parish church of St Andrews dates from the fourteenth century, and Joan would have known it. (Peter Lawne, taken by kind permission of the parish priest of St Andrews, Wickhambreaux)

31. Joan's seal, attached to an indenture from 20 April 1380 made between Joan, Princess of Wales, and Richard de Walkington and others of the town of Beverley. The deed was signed at Missenden. This is the only surviving seal of Joan's. It is circular and two inches in diameter. Around the border edge are the words, in Latin, 'Joan, Princess of [obscured but probably Aquitaine], Wales, Duchess of Cornwall and Countess of Cheshire and Kent'. The round, ornamental inside panel surrounds a shield with France and England quarterly, a label of three points for Prince Edward, and a bordure for Edmund, Earl of Kent (her father). The letters around the shield are I, E and P. (© The British Library Board. All rights reserved. Add. Ch. 27703.)

32. The Princess Joan Psalter, so called because at the front of the book is John Somer's Kalendarium (an astronomical calendar). Somer dedicated his original treatise to Joan in 1380, and it was believed for a long time that this copy was presented to Joan. However, this copy was made some years after her death. (British Library)

33. Image of the Trinity in the Princess Joan Psalter. Prince Edward had an especial connection with the Trinity, and died on the feast of the Trinity. (British Library)

34. The exquisite workmanship of the Princess Joan Psalter indicates that it would have been made for a patron of considerable wealth. (British Library)

35. Wilton Diptych, interior panel. On the left, Richard II is kneeling and behind him are John the Baptist, St Edward (holding a ring) and St Edmund (with the arrow of his martyrdom). On Richard's cloak is his personal emblem of the white hart, with a gold crown around its neck and pearls decorating its antlers. On the right, the Virgin and Child. Probably painted around 1396–97, when Richard would have been twenty-eight or twenty-nine, the diptych shows Richard as a fresh-faced young boy. (National Gallery)

36. Wilton Diptych, exterior panel. On the left-hand panel, Richard II's personal heraldic emblems. On the right-hand panel (which would be uppermost when the diptych is closed) is the white hart, Richard's personal emblem, which he adopted from Joan. (National Gallery)

Index